D0433739

The Chatto Book of DISSENT

BY THE SAME AUTHORS

David Widgery
The Left in Britain 1956–68
Sex 'n' Race 'n' Rock 'n' Roll
Some Lives!

Michael Rosen (for adults)
Did I Hear You Write?
Culture Shock (ed.)
Goodies and Daddies
Rude Rhymes (ed.)

The Chatto Book of DISSENT

Edited, with an Introduction, by
MICHAEL ROSEN *and* DAVID WIDGERY

Chatto & Windus
LONDON

Published in 1991 by
Chatto & Windus Ltd
20 Vauxhall Bridge Road
London SW1V 2SA

A CIP record for this book is available
from the British Library

ISBN 0 7011 3754 1

Typography by Humphrey Stone
Photoset by Rowland Phototypesetting Ltd
Bury St Edmunds, Suffolk
Printed in Great Britain by Mackays of Chatham plc
Chatham, Kent

Contents

For Geraldine, Joe, Naomi, Eddie, Laura, Isaac – M. R.
For Juliet, Jesse, and Annie – D. W.

Introduction

Disagreement is universal. In trivial or fundamental ways, people proceed through life disagreeing. A *Chatto Book of Disagreement* might include Othello's views on Desdemona's fidelity, Churchill's analysis of Chamberlain's foreign policy or John McEnroe's opinion of his line judges. And we might agree or disagree with the disagreements. This collection however focuses on a level of intellectual friction which is more fundamental because it questions the given rules of those who govern society.

All literate societies have been controlled by an elite whose power is derived in turn from the ownership of people, land and livestock, buildings and machinery, or the distillate, money. The possession of this power generates dualities: hunger and plenty, terror and force, silence and speech, toil and leisure, restriction and freedom. It also creates a constant voice of objection – sometimes tentative, sometimes confident, sometimes hopeful, sometimes grim. The voice is at times unhappy, silly, brave or absurd . . . but however it appears, it expresses an insubordination. At its least it says: there is a ruling elite, but no, I'm not a member of it. At its most it says: not only am I not a member but what a ridiculous/wasteful/vicious/unfair way to run the show. This we take to be dissent.

It follows from this that we have excluded a massive and sophisticated discussion which for thousands of years has filled palaces, parliaments and the pages of the press – a debate within the elite on how best to rule. No place is found here for the voices, admittedly often in disagreement with the elite, that advocate, say, monarchy or army rule and superior methods of exploitation or domination. Similarly, the years are full of loud objections to fellow humans on the basis of their genes. These too are excluded. We have not shown much sympathy to conservative dissenters or accepted the claim of, say, anti-semites like Hilaire Belloc to be in some way at odds with the establishment since they beckon so clearly backwards and are so frequently used by the powers that be for their own ends. Dissent sets itself against the established powerbrokers, whether the Catholic Church of the 16th century, the late Victorian Empire or modern Stalinism. Dissent which can be so easily utilised by the Establishment is no dissent at all.

We have tended also to exclude that marvellous form of dissent which consists of dreaming, of yearning for an imaginary way of life. The if-only tendency ranges from peasant visions of jellies jumping up and saying 'Eat me' to *The Big Rock Candy Mountain* (where the lemonade springs, and the bluebird sings) through to John Lennon's *Imagine*. Someone else will need another book as big as this to do *The Chatto Book of Utopias*.

Given these parameters, on what basis did we select? We have chosen little-known passages by some well known writers like Strindberg or Dickens which show them as more heretical than is widely known; one of our objections to conventional bibliographic texts is their tendency to trivialise or omit the political radicalism of distinguished writers. We have emphasised the dissent of those at the bottom who often, when their testimony has been recorded or recalled, made the sharpest and most telling criticism.

We have also included acts of dissent: strikes, demonstrations, shows of defiance even if sometimes they are described by observers who are themselves hostile or only moderately sympathetic. And we have taken the opportunity to seek out the original texts in famous acts of dissent: the first theorists of materialism, or Galileo's defiance of the papal court. Often referred to, they are seldom read in the original where the intensity of the act of reasoning and the scale of the impertinence is best savoured.

Many forms of dissent were for long periods subject to severe legal and religious punishment and we have included chap books, sermons, posters, unstamped press, pamphlets, popular songs, manifestos, shanties, underground press, leaflets and so on. An editorial prejudice against fame led to rejections at the final fence. Thus, Swift's *Modest Proposal*, Luther King's *I had a dream* and Wilfred Owen's *Dulce et Decorum est* are all important texts but Owen lost out on grounds of being too familiar.

We were particularly keen to seek out the visions of rebellious and recalcitrant sans-culottes, the unknown footsoldiers of progress. They rarely have the chance to join the more privileged dissenters within the institutions of the elite – Byron on the frame breakers in the House of Lords is very fine but we wanted to find the songs of the frame breakers themselves too. Dissenting is often a lonely business and dissenters have often lacked the solidarity provided by the organised political groupings. Look, for example at Menocchio voicing his homegrown relativism at the Inquisition in Italy in 1599, inventing his theory from his own experience and being punished by death. Or the defiant speech of the Irish rebel made in the shadow of the gallows.

We were also enthusiasts for rhetoric. In their anger, anguish, fear or pride, dissenters have often treated language with an attack we find attractive and inspiring. The pungency and directness of the writing of the English Civil War or the Abolitionists contrasts vividly with the dishwater prose which characterises the discourse of contemporary politics. But inevitably we have occasionally been thrown back on reportage of a more secondary nature. In part, this is where a report of rebellion has itself been a way of proudly preserving the memory of boldness (see Louis Riel by Joaquin Miller p. 280) but other times this has been where the account is of historical importance, eg. Appian on Spartacus. We have tried to avoid Anglo-centrism, but inevitably, partly because of the availability of material, and partly in anticipation of its readership, England dominates as a source.

The fact that many of these dissenting visions are only glimpses reveals a history of prioritisation. The French sociologist Henri Lefebvre in *Everyday Life in the Modern World* notes that there exists a metalanguage, whereby the scribes, clerks, bureaucrats and hacks interpose themselves between primary acts of expression and in their place produce summaries, commentaries and analyses. Anyone attempting to compile a book such as this finds the voice of the metalinguists deafening. We learnt to be grateful for those chroniclers, court transcribers, witnesses and biographers who transcribed the voice of defiance itself, not their gloss of it.

It is clear, that for a long time there has been an awareness of alternative traditions in radical literature. Robert Southey (in his radical days) wrote *Wat Tyler*, and the anthology *Songs of Freedom*, edited by H. S. Salt (1895), includes Cowper, Allingham and Burns. And it is interesting to note that in 1905 in a pub in Cornwall, and again in Hampshire a year later, men and women were recorded singing a lament for Robert Parker, (one of the leaders of the mutiny at the Nore in 1797), that had in its original form been circulated as a broadside on the streets of London at the time of Parker's execution. Who passed on this ballad for a hundred years, and why? This bestowing of value has been largely invisible to the eyes of critics.

Can patterns in the tradition of dissent be discerned? Is there a common rhetoric of dissent? It is tempting to suggest that there is: sarcasm and parody figure large and, in terms of tone, indignation, mockery, plaintiveness and triumph seem to predominate. Humour is vital. There is a strong emphasis on first hand experience, on witness: the progress of Abolition, to take only one example, depended on 'freedom suits' and petitions and on the accounts such as that of Mary Prince (p. 268), written by black people themselves. However, we also need to remind ourselves that this book is a selection, and common qualities in the pieces may merely reflect the tastes of the anthologists.

We need to remind ourselves constantly of the courage and sacrifice upon which our present freedoms rest. We need to be reminded of the ingenuity with which dissenters have disseminated their messages and in particular the force that satire and wit can have against even the most powerful potentate. And the symbolism of dissent itself has enormous power. Consider Spartacus. The rising of the gladiators was in protest against a slave system as cruel and casual as the 18th century African trade. But what Plutarch sought to laugh off as a 'commotion of fencers' inflicted a series of military and strategic defeats on the Roman war machine including their worst defeat since the battle of Cannae against Hannibal. The first impulsive act of refusal grew till over 40,000 men were under Spartacus's discipline. And their eventual defeat at the hands of Crasso was followed by an appalling terror with over 6,000 crucified along the Appian Way in an attempt to obliterate the memory of the uprising. Yet, despite the fact that many historians found this holocaust justified, the name of Spartacus survived as a symbol of resistance. It was evoked by Voltaire who called the Servile War 'perhaps the only just war in history', was adopted by the German ex-Jesuit Adam Weishaupt in the French Revolution and again by the international socialists of the German Left led by Rosa Luxemburg and Karl Liebknecht in their stand against war in 1919. The story of Spartacus has inspired three 20th century novels, a famous film which played some part in the revival of the left in Hollywood. The only other successful slave rising, that of Toussaint L'Ouverture in Haiti in the late 18th century, was exterminated with no less brutality. Toussaint himself died in a fortress in the Jura mountains after months of brutal treatment and a French general wrote to Napoleon advocating 'exterminating all the blacks in the mountains, women as well as men, except for children under twelve. Wipe out half the population of the lowlands and do not leave in the colony any single black who has worn an epaulette.' Yet the Toussaint legend was revived by the Trinidadian historian and revolutionary, C. L. R. James, and the book he wrote about it, *The Black Jacobins*, served as an inspiration to a new generation of black dissidents and inspired *Quemada*, one of Marlon Brando's best films.

Brecht's play, *The Life of Galileo* derives its power from his attempt to re-understand the principles of the Italian astronomer's stand in the context of a capitalist world defined by the rise of Hitler, the discovery of atomic weapons and the anti-communist inquisition in America. Graham Greene adopted the form of Zola's *J'Accuse* to expose the corruption of the Mayor of Nice. The publishers of the first important transcripts in protest against the American War in Vietnam again chose the slogan 'We Accuse' to entitle their dissent. Despite the authorities' attempts to expunge resistance from the records, it has a habit of persisting. Richard tried to wipe out systematically the name of Wat Tyler, but six centuries later, his name was brandished by supporters of another 'Peasants' Revolt', this time successful, against the Poll Tax.

Dissent is not an end in itself. Non-conformity alone can quickly become outmoded, obsessional and even reactionary. Dissent needs to be sharpened on the grindstone of a larger politics, and linked to systematic action, if it is to be brought to political fruition. But politics without dissent has a corpse in its mouth and the Left, often surprisingly conformist in its attitudes, needs to recognise the importance of a much wider notion of subversion. We hope that readers will find much that is subtle, inspiring, admirable and actionable within these pages.

We hope that readers will also be moved to ask quite how far we have all progressed. At the end of the 20th century, some of us fondly imagine ourselves as emancipated from superstition simply because we shop in supermarkets, have electronic TV channel changers and a wide choice of newspapers all saying more or less the same thing. In fact, religion, often of an extremely irrational kind, is spreading as fast as radio waves, thanks often to philandering puritans. Our main sources of information are controlled by a handful of multimillionaires ('we have a free press because it is owned by free millionaires'); people who have nothing to sell but their ability to work are still served up a diet of bread and circuses to keep them poor but ignorant, while the middle class imagines itself intellectually independent because it reads a newspaper of that name. We are thus in urgent need not just of the voice of Tom Paine but of Pelagius, the first British heretic. We still worship the car and pay extravagant homage to the military-industrial machine while putting on red noses once a year in an attempt to stop famine. We accept as unquestioned the right of various unelected policemen, civil servants and financiers to govern the fine details of our personal life. Yet we noisily boast about our democracy because every five years we can fill in an election ballot, making as many as ten crosses in our political lifetime.

What would Milton have made of Sizewell B, Zola of the Birmingham Six, or Russell of the road to Basra? The values of the bourgeois revolution may have been applied inconsistently but they were sharply held. Many late 20th century intellectuals seem to have recoiled so far from Stalinism as to have jettisoned politics altogether. And the amoral middle ground of get-what-you-can-and-the-devil-take-the-hindmost mentality makes choices about ideas not so much difficult as irrelevant. We live in a world where we are told forcibly that alternatives to the present order are not feasible, that to believe otherwise is suspect, and that the wise know best. As Winstanley put it: 'the actors for freedom are oppressed by the talkers and the verbal professors of freedom'.

There is still more to political life than there seems. People have not lost the ability to say No, or, I disbelieve, or, That's wrong, or simply to laugh in the face of pomp and tyranny. We hope this book will inspire them to do so with yet more fervour.

One

RISE LIKE LIONS AFTER SLUMBER

The Admonitions of a Prophet

Behold. A thing has been done, which never happened before. It has now come to this, that the King has been taken away by Poor Men.

Behold. The land is full of confederates. The Wretched now rob the Mighty of their goods.

Behold. Ladies lie on cushions and magistrates in the storehouse. He that had no wall on which to sleep now sleeps upon a bed.

Behold. The rich man sleeps thirsty. He that once begged him for dregs now possesses strong beer.

Behold. They that possessed clothes are now in rags. He that wove not for himself now possesses fine linen.

Behold. He that had no shade has shade now. They that had shade are now in the full blast of the storm.

Behold. He that had no knowledge of harp-playing now possesses a harp. He to whom never a man sang, now praises the goddess of music.

Behold. She that had no box now possesses a coffer. She that looked at her face in the water now possesses a mirror . . .

Anon., Ancient Egypt

The Spartacus Uprising

116. At the same time Spartacus, a Thracian by birth, who had once served as a soldier with the Romans, but had since been a prisoner and sold for a gladiator, and was in the gladiatorial training-school at Capua, persuaded about seventy of his comrades to strike for their own freedom rather than for the amusement of spectators. They overcame the guards and ran away. They armed themselves with clubs and daggers that they took from people on the roads and took refuge on Mount Vesuvius. There many fugitive slaves and even some freemen from the fields joined Spartacus, and he plundered the neighboring country, having for subordinate officers two gladiators named Œnomaus and Crixus. As he divided the plunder impartially he soon had plenty of men. Varinius Glaber was first sent against him and afterward Publius Valerius, not with regular armies, but with forces picked up in haste and at random, for the Romans did not consider this a war as yet, but a raid, something like an outbreak of robbery. When they attacked Spartacus they were beaten. Spartacus even captured the horse of Varinius; so narrowly did a Roman prætor escape being captured by a gladiator. After this still greater numbers flocked to Spartacus

till his army numbered 70,000 men. For these he manufactured weapons and collected apparatus.

From The Histories by Appian, *c.* 160 AD describing 71 BCE

Diabolical Dances

The fact is recorded by Cedranus, one of the Byzantine historians, who flourished about the year 1050, in the following words: 'Theophylact introduced the practice which prevails even to this day, of scandalizing God, and the memory of his saints, on the most splendid and popular festivals, by indecent and ridiculous songs, and enormous shoutings, even in the midst of those sacred hymns, which we ought to offer to the divine grace with compunction of heart, for the salvation of our souls. But he, having collected a company of base fellows, and placing over them one Euthyonius, surnamed Casnes, whom he also appointed the superintendent of his church, admitted into the sacred service diabolical dances, exclamations of ribaldry, and ballads borrowed from the streets and brothels.'

Warton, quoted in *Ancient Mysteries Described* by William Hone, 1823

'Now That I'm Young'

Now that I'm young
  I want my fun,
I can't serve God
  being a nun.

Now that I'm young
  and come of age,
why be a nun
  in a convent caged?
I can't serve God
  being a nun!

Now that I'm young
  I want my fun,
I can't serve God
  being a nun.

Anon., medieval Spain

'Robin Hood and the Bishop of Hereford'

Some they will talk of bold Robin Hood,
And some of barons bold,
But I'll tell you how he servd the Bishop of Hereford,
When he robbd him of his gold.

As it befel in merry Barnsdale,
And under the green-wood tree,
The Bishop of Hereford was to come by,
With all his company.

'Come, kill a venson,' said bold Robin Hood,
'Come, kill me a good fat deer;
The Bishop of Hereford is to dine with me today,
And he shall pay well for his cheer.

'We'll kill a fat venson,' said bold Robin Hood,
'And dress it by the highway-side;
And we will watch the Bishop narrowly,
Lest some other way he should ride.'

Robin Hood dressed himself in shepherd's attire,
With six of his men also;
And, when the Bishop of Hereford came by,
They about the fire did go.

'O what is the matter?' then said the Bishop,
'Or for whom do you make this a-do?
Or why do you kill the king's venson,
When your company is so few?'

'We are shepherds,' said bold Robin Hood,
'And we keep sheep all the year,
And we are disposed to be merry this day,
And to kill of the king's fat deer.'

'You are brave fellows!' said the Bishop,
'And the king of your doings shall know;
Therefore make haste and come along with me,
For before the king you shall go.'

'O pardon, O pardon,' said bold Robin Hood,
'O pardon, I thee pray!
For it becomes not your lordship's coat
To take so many lives away.'

'No pardon, no pardon,' says the Bishop,
'No pardon I thee owe;
Therefore make haste, and come along with me,
For before the king you shall go.'

Then Robin set his back against a tree,
And his foot against a thorn,
And from underneath his shepherd's coat
He pulld out a bugle-horn.

He put the little end to his mouth,
And a loud blast did he blow,
Till threescore and ten of bold Robin's men
Came running all on a row;

All making obeysance to bold Robin Hood;
'Twas a comely sight for to see:
'What is the matter, master,' said Little John,
'That you blow so hastily?'

'O here is the Bishop of Hereford,
And no pardon we shall have:'
'Cut off his head, master,' said Little John,
'And throw him into his grave.'

'O pardon, O pardon,' said the Bishop,
'O pardon, I thee pray!
For if I had known it had been you,
I'd have gone some other way.'

'No pardon, no pardon,' said Robin Hood,
'No pardon I thee owe;
Therefore make haste and come along with me,
For to merry Barnsdale you shall go.'

Then Robin he took the Bishop by the hand,
And led him to merry Barnsdale;
He made him to stay and sup with him that night,
And to drink wine, beer, and ale.

'Call in the reckoning,' said the Bishop,
'For methinks it grows wondrous high:'
'Lend me your purse, Bishop,' said Little John,
'And I'll tell you bye and bye.'

Then Little John took the bishop's cloak,
And spread it upon the ground,
And out of the bishop's portmantua
He told three hundred pound.

'Here's money enough, master,' said Little John,
'And a comely sight 't is to see;
It makes me in charity with the Bishop,
Tho he heartily loveth not me.'

Robin Hood took the Bishop by the hand,
And he caused the music to play,
And he made the Bishop to dance in his boots,
And glad he could so get away.

Anon., 1495

'A Songe in Praise of Musique'

Sweete musique mournes and hath donne longe –
these fortie yeares and almost five –
God knowes it hath the greater wronge
by *puritanes* that are alive,
Whose hautie, proude, disdainfull myndes
Much fault agaynst poore musique findes.

Yet haue they nothinge to replye
within godes bookes that they canne finde
Against sweete musique's harmonye,
but their owne proude, disdainfull myndes:
They are soe holie, fyne, and pure,
Noe melodie they canne endure.

They doe abhorre, as devilles doe all,
the pleasant noyse of musique's sounde,
Although kinge *David* and st. *Paule*
did much commend that art profound;
Of sence thereof they have noe smell,
Noe more then hath the develles in hell.

From an anonymous poem, 1604, written almost forty-five years after Queen Elizabeth I had banned the payment of choristers in 1559

The Liberty to Know

I deny not, but that it is of greatest concernment in the Church and Commonwealth, to have a vigilant eye how books demean themselves as well as men; and thereafter to confine, imprison, and do sharpest justice on them as malefactors. For books are not absolutely dead things, but do contain a potency of life in them to be as active as that soul was whose progeny they are; nay, they do preserve as in a vial the purest efficacy and extraction of that living intellect that bred them. I know they are as lively, and as vigorously productive, as those fabulous dragon's teeth; and being sown up and down, may chance to spring up armed men. And yet, on the other hand, unless wariness be used, as good almost kill a man as kill a good book. Who kills a man kills a reasonable creature, God's image; but he who destroys a good book, kills reason itself, kills the image of God, as it were in the eye. Many a man lives a burden to the earth; but a good book is the precious life-blood of a master spirit, embalmed and treasured up on purpose to a life beyond life. 'Tis true, no age can restore a life, whereof perhaps there is no great loss; and revolutions of ages do not oft recover the loss of a rejected truth, for the want of which whole nations fare the worse.

We should be wary therefore what persecutions we raise against the living labours of public men, how we spill that seasoned life of man, preserved and stored up in books; since we see a kind of homicide may be thus committed, sometimes a martyrdom, and if it extend to the whole impression, a kind of massacre; whereof the execution ends not in the slaying of an elemental life, but strikes at that ethereal and fifth essence, the breath of reason itself, slays an immortality rather than a life. But lest I should be condemned of introducing licence, while I oppose licensing, I refuse not the pains to be so much historical, as will serve to show what hath been done by ancient and famous commonwealths against this disorder, till the very time that this project of licensing crept out of the inquisition, was catched up by our prelates, and hath caught some of our presbyters . . .

If we think to regulate printing, thereby to rectify manners, we must regulate all recreations and pastimes, all that is delightful to man. No music must be heard, no song be set or sung, but what is grave and Doric. There must be licensing dancers, that no gesture, motion, or deportment be taught our youth but what by their allowance shall be thought honest; for such Plato was provided of; it will ask more than the work of twenty licensers to examine all the lutes, the violins, and the guitars in every house; they must not be suffered to prattle as they do, but must be licensed what they may say. And who shall silence all the airs and madrigals that whisper softness in chambers? The windows also, and the balconies must be thought on; there are shrewd books, with dangerous frontispieces, set to sale; who shall prohibit them, shall twenty licensers? The villages also must have their visitors to inquire what lectures the bagpipe and the rebeck reads, even to the ballatry and the gamut of every municipal fiddler, for these are the countryman's Arcadias, and his Monte Mayors.

Next, what more national corruption, for which England hears ill abroad, than household gluttony: who shall be the rectors of our daily rioting? And what shall be done to inhibit the multitides that frequent those houses where drunkenness is sold and harboured? Our garments also should be referred to the licensing of some more sober workmasters to see them cut into a less wanton garb. Who shall regulate all the mixed conversation of our youth, male and female together, as is the fashion of this country? Who shall still appoint what shall be discoursed, what presumed, and no further? Lastly, who shall forbid and separate all idle resort, all evil company? These things will be, and must be; but how they shall be least hurtful, how least enticing, herein consists the grave and governing wisdom of a state . . .

They are not skilful considers of human things, who imagine to remove sin by removing the matter of sin; for, besides that it is a huge heap increasing under the very act of diminishing, though some part of it may for a time be withdrawn from some persons, it cannot from all, in such a universal thing as books are; and when this is done, yet the sin remains entire. Though ye take from a covetous man all his treasure, he has yet one jewel left, ye cannot bereave him of his covetousness. Banish all objects of lust, shut up all youth into the severest discipline that can be exercised in any hermitage, ye cannot make them chaste, that came not thither so: such great care and wisdom is required to the right managing of this point. Suppose we could expel sin by this means; look how much we thus expel of sin, so much we expel of virtue: for the matter of them both is the same; remove that, and ye remove them both alike . . .

I cannot set so light by all the invention, the art, the wit, the grave and solid judgment which is in England, as that it can be comprehended in any twenty capacities how good soever, much less that it should not pass except their superintendence be over it, except it be sifted and strained with their strainers, that it should be uncurrent without their manual stamp. Truth and understanding are not such wares as to be monopolized and traded in by tickets and statutes and standards. We must not think to make a staple commodity of all the knowledge in the land, to mark and license it like our broadcloth and our woolpacks. What is it but a servitude like that imposed by the Philistines, not to be allowed the sharpening of our own axes and coulters, but we must repair from all quarters to twenty licensing forges? . . .

Nor is it to the common people less than a reproach; for if we be so jealous over them, as that we dare not trust them with an English pamphlet, what do we but censure them for a giddy, vicious, and ungrounded people; in such a sick and weak state of faith and discretion, as to be able to take nothing down but through the pipe of a licenser? . . .

Where there is much desire to learn, there of necessity will be much arguing, much writing, many opinions; for opinion in good men is but knowledge in the making . . .

Methinks I see in my mind a noble and puissant nation rousing herself like a strong man after sleep, and shaking her invincible locks. Methinks I see her as an eagle mewing her mighty youth, and kindling her undazzled eyes at the full midday beam; purging and unscaling her long-abused sight at the fountain itself of heavenly radiance; while the whole noise of timorous and flocking birds, with those also that love the twilight, flutter about, amazed at what she means, and in their envious gabble would prognosticate a year of sects and schisms.

What would ye do then? should ye suppress all this flowery crop of knowledge and new light sprung up and yet springing daily in this city? should ye set an obligarchy of twenty engrossers over it, to bring a famine upon our minds again, when we shall know nothing but what is measured to us by their bushel? Believe it, Lords and Commons, they who counsel ye to such a suppressing do as good as bid ye suppress yourselves; and I will soon show how. If it be desired to know the immediate cause of all this free writing and free speaking, there cannot be assigned a truer than your own mild and free and humane government. It is the liberty, Lords and Commons, which your own valorous and happy counsels have purchased us, liberty which is the nurse of all great wits; this is that which hath rarefied and enlightened our spirits like the influence of heaven; this is that which hath enfranchised, enlarged and lifted up our apprehensions degrees above themselves.

Ye cannot make us now less capable, less knowing, less eagerly pursuing of the truth, unless ye first make yourselves, that made us so, less the lovers, less the founders of our true liberty. We can grow ignorant again, brutish, formal and slavish, as ye found us; but you then must first become that which ye cannot be, oppressive, arbitrary and tyrannous, as they were from whom ye have freed us. That our hearts are now more capacious, our thoughts more erected to the search and expectation of greatest and exactest things, is the issue of your own virtue propagated in us; ye cannot suppress that, unless ye reinforce an abrogated and merciless law, that fathers may dispatch at will their own children. And who shall then stick closest to ye, and excite others? not he who takes up arms for coat and conduct, and his four nobles of Danegelt. Although I dispraise not the defence of just immunities, yet love my peace better, if that were all. Give me the liberty to know, to utter, and to argue freely according to conscience, above all liberties.

From *Areopagitica* by John Milton, 1644; directed against an Act of Parliament (1643) that said that 'no book . . . [could] be printed unless approved of and licensed' by an appointee of the government.

'The Wooing Rogue'

Come live with me and be my Whore,
And we will beg from door to door
Then under a hedge we'l sit and louse us,
Until the Beadle come to rouse us
And if they'l give us no relief;
  Thou shalt turn Whore and I'l turn Thief.
  Thou shalt turn Whore and I'l turn Thief.

If thou canst rob, then I can steal,
And we'l eat Roast-meat every meal:
Nay, we'l eat white-bread every day
And throw our mouldy crusts away,
And twice a day we will be drunk,
  And then at night I'l kiss my Punk,
  And then at night I'l kiss my Punk.

And when we both shall have the Pox,
We then shall want both Shirts and Smocks,
To shift[1] each others mangy hide,
That is with Itch so pockifi'd;

We'l take some clean ones from a hedge,
And leave our old ones for a pledge.
And leave our old ones for a pledge.

[1] Clothe

Anon., *c.* 1660

The Gaiety of Her Dress

Elizabeth West daughter of William West of Gate Burton having been overtaken in the sin of fornication with her father's servant that is no Friend, and since both gone with him and married with a priest: She having seen into the sin and follie she hath run into both in this and also in the gaiety of her dress hath given forth a paper of condemnation for the same which was satisfactory to Friends at this Meeting which is as followeth . . .

Record of a Quaker meeting, Lincoln, 1717

Riots are the language of the unheard.

Martin Luther King

To Real Lovers of Liberty

To all real lovers of Liberty. Be assured that Liberty and Freedom will at last prevail. Tremble O thou the Oppressor of the People that reigneth upon the throne and ye Ministers of State, weep for ye shall fall. Weep ye who grind the face of the poor, oppress the People and starve the Industrious Mechanic. My friends, you are oppressed, you know it. Lord Buckingham who died the other day had thirty thousand pounds yearly for setting his arse in the House of Lords and doing nothing. Liberty calls aloud, ye who will hear her Voice, may you be free and happy. He who does not, let him starve and be DAMNED.
N.B. Be resolute and you shall be happy. He who wishes well to the cause of Liberty let him repair to Chapel Field at Five O'Clock this afternoon, to begin a Glorious Revolution.

Leaflet circulated in response to Burke's condemnation of the French Revolution, 1793

In Support of the Luddites

You call these men a mob, desperate, dangerous, and ignorant; and seem to think that the only way to quiet the '*Bellua multorum capitum*' is to lop off a few of its superfluous heads. But even a mob may be better reduced to reason by a mixture of conciliation and firmness, than by additional irritation and redoubled penalties. Are we aware of our obligations to a mob? It is the mob that labour in your fields and serve in your houses, – that man your navy, and recruit your army, – that have enabled you to defy all the world, and can also defy you when neglect and calamity have driven them to despair! You may call the people a mob; but do not forget that a mob too often speaks the sentiments of the people. And here I must remark, with what alacrity you are accustomed to fly to the succour of your distressed allies, leaving the distressed of your own country to the care of Providence or – the parish. When the Portuguese suffered under the retreat of the French, every arm was stretched out, every hand was opened, from the rich man's largess to the widow's mite, all was bestowed, to enable them to rebuild their villages and replenish their granaries. And at this moment, when thousands of misguided but most unfortunate fellow-countrymen are struggling with the extremes of hardships and hunger, as your charity began abroad it should end at home. A much less sum, a tithe of the bounty bestowed on Portugal, even if those men (which I cannot admit without inquiry) could not have been restored to their employments, would have rendered unnecessary the tender mercies of the bayonet and the gibbet. But doubtless our friends have too many foreign claims to admit a prospect of domestic relief; though never did such objects demand it. I have traversed the seat of war in the Peninsula, I have been in some of the most oppressed provinces of Turkey; but never under the most despotic of infidel governments did I behold such squalid wretchedness as I have seen since my return in the very heart of a Christian country. And what are your remedies? After months of inaction, and months of action worse than inactivity, at length comes forth the grand specific, the never-failing nostrum of all state physicians, from the days of Draco to the present time. After feeling the pulse and shaking the head over the patient, prescribing the usual course of warm water and bleeding, – the warm water of your mawkish police, and the lancets of your military, – these convulsions must terminate in death, the sure consummation of the prescriptions of all political Sangrados. Setting aside the palpable injustice and the certain inefficiency of the Bill, are there not capital punishments sufficient in your statutes? Is there not blood enough upon your penal code, that more must be poured forth to ascend to Heaven and testify against you? How will you carry the Bill into effect? Can you commit a whole county to their own prisons? Will you erect a gibbet in every field, and hang up men like scarecrows? or will you proceed (as you must to bring this measure into effect) by decimation? Place the county under martial law? depopulate and lay waste all around you? and restore Sherwood Forest as an acceptable gift to the crown, in its former condition of a royal chase and an asylum for outlaws? Are these the remedies for a starving and desperate populace? Will the famished wretch who has braved your bayonets be appalled by your gibbets? When death is a relief, and the only relief it appears that you will afford him, will he be dragooned into tranquillity? Will that which could not be effected by your grenadiers be accomplished by your executioners? If you proceed by the forms of law, where is your evidence? Those who have refused to impeach their accomplices when transportation only was the punishment, will hardly be tempted to witness against them when death is the penalty.

From George Gordon, Lord Byron's maiden speech in the House of Lords, 27 February 1812

Luddite Ballad

Welcome Ned Ludd, your case is good
Make Perceval[1] your aim
For by this Bill 'tis understood
It's death to break a frame

With dextrous skill, the Hosiers kill
For they are quite as bad
And die you must by the late Bill
Go on my bonny lad

You might as well be hung for death
As breaking a machine
So now my lad your sword unsheath
And make it sharp and keen.

We are ready now your cause to join
Whenever you may call
So make foul blood run clear and fine
Of tyrants great and small.

[1] Prime Minster = Spencer Perceval

Poster, Nottingham, 1812

'The Mask of Anarchy'

I

As I lay asleep in Italy
There came a voice from over the Sea,
And with great power it forth led me
To walk in the visions of Poesy.

II

I met Murder on the way –
He had a mask like Castlereagh –
Very smooth he looked, yet grim;
Seven blood-hounds followed him:

III

All were fat; and well they might
Be in admirable plight,
For one by one, and two by two,
He tossed them human hearts to chew
Which from his wide cloak he drew.

IV

Next came Fraud, and he had on,
Like Eldon, an ermined gown;
His big tears, for he wept well,
Turned to mill-stones as they fell.

V

And the little children, who
Round his feet played to and fro,
Thinking every tear a gem,
Had their brains knocked out by them.

VI

Clothed with the Bible, as with light,
And the shadows of the night,
Like Sidmouth, next, Hypocrisy
On a crocodile rode by.

VII

And many more Destructions played
In this ghastly masquerade,
All disguised, even to the eyes,
Like Bishops, lawyers, peers, or spies.

VIII

Last came Anarchy: he rode
On a white horse, splashed with blood;
He was pale even to the lips,
Like Death in the Apocalypse.

IX

And he wore a kingly crown;
And in his grasp a sceptre shone;
On his brow this mark I saw –
'I AM GOD, AND KING, AND LAW!'

X

With a pace stately and fast,
Over English land he passed,
Trampling to a mire of blood
The adoring multitude.

XI

And a mighty troop around,
With their trampling shook the
ground,
Waving each a bloody sword,
For the service of their Lord.

XII

And with glorious triumph, they
Rode through England proud and
gay,
Drunk as with intoxication
Of the wine of desolation.

XIII

O'er fields and towns, from sea to
sea,
Passed the Pageant swift and free,
Tearing up, and trampling down;
Till they came to London town.

XIV

And each dweller, panic-stricken,
Felt his heart with terror sicken
Hearing the tempestuous cry
Of the triumph of Anarchy.

XV

For with pomp to meet him came,
Clothed in arms like blood and
flame,
The hired murderers, who did sing
'Thou art God, and Law, and
King.

XVI

'We have waited, weak and lone
For thy coming, Mighty One!
Our purses are empty, our swords
are cold.
Give us glory, and blood, and
gold.'

XVII

Lawyers and priests, a motley
crowd,
To the earth their pale brows
bowed;
Like a bad prayer not over loud,
Whispering – 'Thou art Law and
God.' –

XVIII

Then all cried with one accord,
'Thou art King, and God, and
Lord;
Anarchy, to thee we bow,
Be thy name made holy now!'

XIX

And Anarchy, the Skeleton,
Bowed and grinned to every one,
As well as if his education
Had cost ten millions to the
nation.

XX

For he knew the Palaces
Of our Kings were rightly his;
His the sceptre, crown, and globe,
And the gold-inwoven robe.

XXI

So he sent his slaves before
To seize upon the Bank and
Tower,
And was proceeding with intent
To meet his pensioned Parliament

XXII

When one fled past, a maniac
maid,
And her name was Hope, she said:
But she looked more like Despair,
And she cried out in the air:

XXIII

'My father Time is weak and gray
With waiting for a better day;
See how idiot-like he stands,
Fumbling with his palsied hands!

XXIV

'He has had child after child,
And the dust of death is piled
Over every one but me –
Misery, oh, Misery!'

XXV

Then she lay down in the street,
Right before the horses' feet,
Expecting, with a patient eye,
Murder, Fraud, and Anarchy.

XXVI

When between her and her foes
A mist, a light, an image rose,
Small at first, and weak, and frail
Like the vapour of a vale:

XXVII

Till as clouds grow on the blast,
Like tower-crowned giants
striding fast,
And glare with lightnings as they
fly,
And speak in thunder to the sky,

XXVIII

It grew – a Shape arrayed in mail
Brighter than the viper's scale,
And upborne on wings whose
grain
Was as the light of sunny rain.

XXIX

On its helm, seen far away,
A planet, like the Morning's, lay;
And those plumes its light rained
through
Like a shower of crimson dew.

XXX

With step as soft as wind it passed
O'er the heads of men – so fast
That they knew the presence
there,
And looked, – but all was empty
air.

XXXI

As flowers beneath May's footstep
waken,
As stars from Night's loose hair
are shaken,
As waves arise when loud winds
call,
Thoughts sprung where'er that
step did fall.

XXXII

And the prostrate multitude
Looked – and ankle-deep in blood,
Hope, that maiden most serene,
Was walking with a quiet mien:

XXXIII

And Anarchy, the ghastly birth,
Lay dead earth upon the earth;
The Horse of Death tameless as
wind
Fled, and with his hoofs did grind
To dust the murderers thronged
behind.

XXXIV

A rushing light of clouds and
  splendour,
A sense awakening and yet tender
Was heard and felt – and at its
  close
These words of joy and fear arose

XXXV

As if their own indignant Earth
Which gave the sons of England
  birth
Had felt their blood upon her
  brow,
And shuddering with a mother's
  throe

XXXVI

Had turnèd every drop of blood
By which her face had been
  bedewed
To an accent unwithstood, –
As if her heart had cried aloud:

XXXVII

'Men of England, heirs of Glory,
Heroes of unwritten story,
Nurslings of one mighty Mother,
Hopes of her, and one another;

XXXVIII

'Rise like Lions after slumber
In unvanquishable number,
Shake your chains to earth like
  dew
Which in sleep had fallen on
  you –
Ye are many – they are few.

XXXIX

'What is Freedom? – ye can tell
That which slavery is, too well –
For its very name has grown
To an echo of your own.

XL

' 'Tis to work and have such pay
As just keeps life from day to day
In your limbs, as in a cell
For the tyrants' use to dwell,

XLI

'So that ye for them are made
Loom, and plough, and sword, and
  spade,
With or without your own will
  bent
To their defence and nourishment.

XLII

' 'Tis to see your children weak
With their mothers pine and peak,
When the winter winds are
  bleak, –
They are dying whilst I speak.

XLIII

' 'Tis to hunger for such diet
As the rich man in his riot
Casts to the fat dogs that lie
Surfeiting beneath his eye;

XLIV

' 'Tis to let the Ghost of Gold
Take from Toil a thousandfold
More than e'er its substance could
In the tyrannies of old.

XLV

'Paper coin – that forgery
Of the title-deeds, which ye
Hold to something of the worth
Of the inheritance of Earth.

XLVI

' 'Tis to be a slave in soul
And to hold no strong control
Over your own wills, but be
All that others make of ye.

XLVII

'And at length when ye complain
With a murmur weak and vain
'Tis to see the Tyrant's crew
Ride over your wives and you –
Blood is on the grass like dew.

XLVIII

'Then it is to feel revenge
Fiercely thirsting to exchange
Blood for blood – and wrong for
wrong –
Do not thus when ye are strong.

XLIX

'Birds find rest, in narrow nest
When weary of their wingèd
quest;
Beasts find fare, in woody lair
When storm and snow are in the
air.

L

'Asses, swine, have litter spread
And with fitting food are fed;
All things have a home but one –
Thou, Oh, Englishman, hast none!

LI

'This is Slavery – savage men,
Or wild beasts within a den
Would endure not as ye do –
But such ills they never knew.

LII

'What art thou Freedom? O! could
slaves
Answer from their living graves
This demand – tyrants would flee
Like a dream's dim imagery:

LIII

'Thou art not, as impostors say,
A shadow soon to pass away,
A superstition, and a name
Echoing from the cave of Fame.

LIV

'For the labourer thou art bread,
And a comely table spread
From his daily labour come
In a neat and happy home.

LV

'Thou art clothes, and fire, and
food
For the trampled multitude –
No – in countries that are free
Such starvation cannot be
As in England now we see.

LVI

'To the rich thou art a check,
When his foot is on the neck
Of his victim, thou dost make
That he treads upon a snake.

LVII

'Thou art Justice – ne'er for gold
May thy righteous laws be sold
As laws are in England – thou
Shield'st alike the high and low.

LVIII

'Thou art Wisdom – Freemen never
Dream that God will damn for ever
All who think those things untrue
Of which Priests make such ado.

LIX

'Thou art Peace – never by thee
Would blood and treasure wasted be
As tyrants wasted them, when all
Leagued to quench thy flame in Gaul.

LX

'What if English toil and blood
Was poured forth, even as a flood?
It availed, Oh, Liberty,
To dim, but not extinguish thee.

LXI

'Thou art Love – the rich have kissed
Thy feet, and like him following Christ,
Give their substance to the free
And through the rough world follow thee,

LXII

'Or turn their wealth to arms, and make
War for thy belovèd sake
On wealth, and war, and fraud – whence they
Drew the power which is their prey.

LXIII

'Science, Poetry, and Thought
Are thy lamps; they make the lot
Of the dwellers in a cot
So serene, they curse it not.

LXIV

'Spirit, Patience, Gentleness,
All that can adorn and bless
Art thou – let deeds, not words, express
Thine exceeding loveliness.

LXV

'Let a great Assembly be
Of the fearless and the free
On some spot of English ground
Where the plains stretch wide around.

LXVI

'Let the blue sky overhead,
The green earth on which ye tread,
All that must eternal be
Witness the solemnity.

LXVII

'From the corners uttermost
Of the bounds of English coast;
From every hut, village, and town
Where those who live and suffer moan
For others' misery or their own,

LXVIII

'From the workhouse and the
prison
Where pale as corpses newly
risen,
Women, children, young and old
Groan for pain, and weep for
cold –

LXIX

'From the haunts of daily life
Where is waged the daily strife
With common wants and common
cares
Which sows the human heart with
tares –

LXX

'Lastly from the palaces
Where the murmur of distress
Echoes, like the distant sound
Of a wind alive around

LXXI

'Those prison halls of wealth and
fashion,
Where some few feel such
compassion
For those who groan, and toil, and
wail
As must make their brethren
pale –

LXXII

'Ye who suffer woes untold,
Or to feel, or to behold
Your lost country bought and sold
With a price of blood and gold –

LXXIII

'Let a vast assembly be,
And with great solemnity
Declare with measured words that
ye
Are, as God has made ye, free –

LXXIV

'Be your strong and simple words
Keen to wound as sharpened
swords,
And wide as targets let them be,
With their shade to cover ye.

LXXV

'Let the tyrants pour around
With a quick and startling sound,
Like the loosening of a sea,
Troops of armed emblazonry.

LXXVI

'Let the charged artillery drive
Till the dead air seems alive
With the clash of clanging wheels,
And the tramp of horses' heels.

LXXVII

'Let the fixèd bayonet
Gleam with sharp desire to wet
Its bright point in English blood
Looking keen as one for food.

LXXVIII

'Let the horsemen's scimitars
Wheel and flash, like sphereless
stars
Thirsting to eclipse their burning
In a sea of death and mourning.

LXXIX

'Stand ye calm and resolute,
Like a forest close and mute,
With folded arms and looks which
are
Weapons of unvanquished war,

LXXX

'And let Panic, who outspeeds
The career of armèd steeds
Pass, a disregarded shade
Through your phalanx
undismayed.

LXXXI

'Let the laws of your own land,
Good or ill, between ye stand
Hand to hand, and foot to foot,
Arbiters of the dispute,

LXXXII

'The old laws of England – they
Whose reverend heads with age
are gray,
Children of a wiser day;
And whose solemn voice must be
Thine own echo – Liberty!

LXXXIII

'On those who first should violate
Such sacred heralds in their state
Rest the blood that must ensue,
And it will not rest on you.

LXXXIV

'And if then the tyrants dare
Let them ride among you there,
Slash, and stab, and maim, and
hew, –
What they like, that let them do.

LXXXV

'With folded arms and steady eyes,
And little fear, and less surprise,
Look upon them as they slay
Till their rage has died away.

LXXXVI

'Then they will return with shame
To the place from which they
came,
And the blood thus shed will
speak
In hot blushes on their cheek.

LXXXVII

'Every woman in the land
Will point at them as they stand –
They will hardly dare to greet
Their acquaintance in the street.

LXXXVIII

'And the bold, true warriors
Who have hugged Danger in wars
Will turn to those who would be
free,
Ashamed of such base company.

LXXXIX

'And that slaughter to the Nation
Shall steam up like inspiration,
Eloquent, oracular;
A volcano heard afar.

XC

'And these words shall then
become
Like Oppression's thundered
doom
Ringing through each heart and
brain,
Heard again – again – again –

XCI

'Rise like Lions after slumber
In unvanquishable number –
Shake your chains to earth like
  dew
Which in sleep had fallen on
  you –
Ye are many – they are few.'

Percy Bysshe Shelley, 1819 (published 1832); written on the occasion of the Peterloo Massacre

Convict Mutiny – 'Seizure of the Cyprus Brig *in Recherche Bay'*

Come all you sons of Freedom, a chorus join with me,
I'll sing a song of heroes, and glorious liberty.
Some lads condemned from England sailed to Van Diemen's shore,
Their country, friends and parents perhaps never to see more.

When landed in this Colony to different Masters went,
For trifling offences, to Hobart town jail were sent;
A second sentence being incurred we were ordered for to be
Sent to Macquarie Harbour, that place of tyranny.

The hardships we'd to undergo are matters of record,
But who believes the convict, or who regards his word?
For starved and flogged and punished, deprived of all redress,
The Bush our only refuge, with death to end distress.

Hundreds of us were shot down, for daring to be free,
Numbers caught and banished to life-long slavery.
Brave Swallow, Watt, and Davis, were in our noble band
Determined at the first slant to quit Van Diemen's Land.

Marched down in chains and guarded, on the *Cyprus Brig* conveyed
The topsails being hoisted, the anchor being weighed,
The wind it blew sou'-sou'-west and on we went straightway,
Till we found ourselves wind-bound, in gloomy Recherche Bay.

Twas August eighteen twenty-nine, with thirty-one on board,
Lieutenant Carew left the brig, and soon we passed the word
The Doctor too was absent, the soldiers off their guard:
A better opportunity could never have occurred.

Confined within a dismal hole, we soon contrived a plan,
To capture now the *Cyprus*, or perish every man.
But thirteen turned faint-hearted and begged to go ashore,
So eighteen boys rushed daring, and took the brig and store.

We first addressed the soldiers, 'For liberty we crave!
Give up your arms this instant, or the sea will be your grave.
By tyranny we've been oppressed, by your Colonial laws,
But we'll bid adieu to slavery, or die in freedom's cause.'

We next drove off the Skipper, who came to help his crew,
Then gave three cheers for liberty, 'twas answered cheerly too.
We brought the sailors from below, and rowed them to the land,
Likewise the wife and children of Carew in command.

Supplies of food and water we gave the vanquished crew,
Returning good for evil, as we'd been taught to do.
We mounted guard with watch and ward, then hauled the boat
aboard;
We elected William Swallow, and obeyed our Captain's word.

The morn broke bright, the wind was fair, we headed for the sea
With one cheer more for those on shore and glorious liberty.
For navigating smartly Bill Swallow was the man,
Who laid a course out neatly to take us to Japan.

Then sound your golden trumpets, play on your tuneful notes,
The *Cyprus Brig* is sailing, how proudly now she floats.
May fortune help the noble lads, and keep them ever free
From Gags, and Cats, and Chains, and Traps, and Cruel Tyranny.

'Frank the Poet', *c.* 1820

The Fight for the Free Press

1. *SELLERS WANTED.*

Some hundreds of Poor Men out of employ who have nothing to risk, some of those unfortunate wretches to whom Distress has made a Prison a desirable Home.

An honest and moral way of finding head and gaol shelter, and moreover of earning the thanks of their fellow countrymen, now presents itself to such patriotic Englishmen as will, in defiance of the most odious 'laws' of a most odious Tyranny, imposed upon an enslaved and oppressed people, to sell to the poor and ignorant *The Poor Man's Guardian*, a weekly Newspaper for the People, published contrary to 'Law' to try the power of Might against Right.

NB A subscription is opened for the relief, support and reward of all such persons as may become Victims of the Whig Tyranny.

Henry Hetherington in *The Poor Man's Guardian*, *c.* 1820

2. BENCH: Hold your tongue a moment.

DEFENDANT: I shall not! for I wish every man to read these publications (*pointing to the 'Poor Man's Guardian', 'Hunt's Address', etc.*).

BENCH: You are insolent; therefore you are committed to three months' imprisonment in Knutsford House of Correction, to Hard Labour.

DEFENDANT: I've nothing to thank you for; and whenever I come out, I'll hawk them again. And mind you, the first that I hawk shall be to your house (*looking at Captain Clarke*).

BENCH: Stand down.

DEFENDANT: No! I shall not stand down for you.

(He was then forcibly removed from the dock and back to the New Bailey.)

The prosecution of J. Swann (who had already been imprisoned for the same offence), *c.* 1820

Epitaph

Posterity will ne'er survey
A nobler grave than this:
Here lie the bones of Castlereagh:
Stop, traveller, and piss.

George Gordon, Lord Byron, 1821

A Miner's Protest

I was at yor hoose last neet and meyd mysel very comfortable. Ye hey nee family and yor just won man on the colliery, I see ye hev a greet lot of rooms and big cellars and plenty wine and beer in them which I got ma share on. Noo I naw some at wor colliery that has three of fower lads and lasses and they live in won room not half as gude as yor cellar. I dont pretend to naw very much but I naw there shudnt be that much difference. The only place we can gan to o the week ends is the yel hoose and hev a pint. I dinna pretend to be a profit, but I naw this, and lots of ma marrows na's te, that were not tret as we owt to be, and a great filosopher says, to get noledge is to naw yer ignerent. But weve just begun to find that oot, and ye maisters and owners may luk oot, for yor not gan to get se much o yor own way, wer gan to hev some o wors now . . .

From a letter left in the house of a colliery manager in the North-east, broken into during a riot in 1831

Swing's Revolution

The assembled Council is the place formerly called the House of Lords; Lords and Bishops on the right hand; Delegates of the People on the left. Archbishop of Canterbury led in between Swing and Richard Jones; the Archbishop places Swing on the Throne.

ARCHBISHOP: My Lords and Gentlemen, but to be Lords no more;
The Revolution, that all good men wished
And bad men feared – the People's Revolution –
Has come upon us; the first Revolution
That ever yet, in all the tide of time,
Proposed the People's good. For 'tisn't enough
That we have banished James, and Swing now sits
On England's throne – but we must banish, too,
All tyrannous notions from our own hearts, all scorn
Of those we called the swinish multitude,
And recognise them henceforth by the title of
THE SOVEREIGN PEOPLE. Say, our Citizen-King, what is't
That the good People of England, do petition for?
SWING [*descending from the throne*]: Nothing.
The good People of England
Will never again be petitioners;
The agricultural labourers, whose voice
Doth speak in mine, have tried petition
Upon petition, prayer on prayer, entreaty on entreaty,
All in vain; denied sufficiency
Of the fruits of the earth, which their own labour tilled,
Till extreme want, and agonizing hunger,

Drave them to madness – madness gave them strength,
Where reason had been weak.
ARCHBISHOP: What strength mean ye?
SWING: The strength of the first rick-burner, the inspired
    Samson, –
Who, when his Philistine tyrants had put his eyes out,
As you, ye priests, put out the eyes of the people,
And bound him in the temple of their god
Dagon – as your temples are to this day
But forges for welding fetters for the People –
Made him their scoff and jeer, the mighty man
Found that his injuries had given him back
His native strength, and with a giant's grasp
He pulled th' whole edifice upon himself
And them, and crushed god and his priests together:
He died i' th' act himself, but died revenged.
JONES: And now, my Lords, a power
Greater than that of Samson hath passed
Over into the People's hands – a power with which
Your bayonets, your gunpowder, your prisons,
Your legal murders, can compete no longer.
If you would have that power sleep innocent,
Do justice to the People.
ARCHBISHOP: Do it? As how?
JONES: Visit the poor man's cottage throughout the land,
Not with your vile religious balderdash
And Gospel tracts, to fool him into cowardice,
And tame submission to distresses, which
His wisdom might avert, or his virtue might redress;
Not with deceitful promises of Heaven
Hereafter, to reconcile him to a Hell on earth:
But i' the spirit of honesty and love,
The proper feelings of man's heart to man;
See that he hath the good sufficient meal
His nature craves; nor let your own be sweet to you
Till you are sure your every brother man
Hath a sufficiency. Do this, and ye shall
Possess yourselves of a power greater than
That of fire-balls. Do this, and ye shall
Be fortified in a security – compared to which
Th' array of bayonets and the power of arms
Is but a house of wafers –

Ye shall invest yourselves in triple adamant –
The love of grateful millions.
[ALL CRY OUT]: We will, we will!
SWING: Then Swing resigns his Kingship,
And will return, a British Cincinnatus,
To the plough, from whence he sprang;
Happy to have taught the world, tho' by a fiery lesson –
The noblest moral Heaven itself could give,
'WHO'D LIVE HIMSELF, MUST LET HIS
NEIGHBOUR LIVE.'

From *Swing or, Who are the Incendiaries?* by Robert Taylor, 1831

'The Unions of England, Huzza!'

Come all you bold Britons attend to my rhymes
I am just going to give you a sketch of the times.
So give ear high and low, you will find by these lines
The strength of the famed British Union
The Unions of England, Huzza.

There's the Tailors and Shoe-makers, Masons likewise,
The Plasterers and Bricklayers strongly do rise
The nobs of this country are struck with surprise
To behold the brave men of the Unions
The true British Union, Huzza.

There's the Carpenters, Sawyers and Labourers too
Tanners and Painters and Glaziers a few
All bravely minted, courageous and true
To stick up for the right of their trades sir
Success to the Unions, Huzza.

All over Great Britain they're nobly combined
And some great alteration we shortly may find
They are liberal, generous, valiant and kind
Hurrah for the true British Unions
The Unions of England, Huzza.

Tho' the six men of Dorchester sails o'er the deep
The Unions will not see their families weep
They will prosper, alas, when oppressors shall sleep
And their names shall henceforth be recorded
By the Unions of England, Huzza.

By the Whigs and the Tories we've long been oppressed
Crushed down by taxation and drove to distress
Their motto is 'Shall we from slavery rest?'
'We will' cries the true British Unions
The Unions of England, Huzza.

See the shamrock and rose and the thistle unite,
Like the true sons of freedom stick up for their right
All the threats they hold forward will never affright
The true British sons of the Unions
The Unions of England, Huzza

There is Manchester, Birmingham, Liverpool too
Derby, Leicester, Nottingham valiant and true
From the Lands End of England to Scotland through
The numbers are daily increasing
The Unions of England, Huzza

England, Ireland and Scotland united shall be
Till from bondage and slavery Britons are free
Here's the shamrock, the rose and the thistle all three
So bravely combined in the Union
The Unions of freedom, Huzza

Three cheers for the brave men of Dorchester give
Three groans for the Tories and two for the Whigs
Let every true Briton as long as they live
Give three cheers for the true British Unions
The Unions of England, Huzza!

Anon., 1834; written for the great demonstration at Copenhagen Fields, Islington, called to secure the release of the Tolpuddle Martyrs, published here for the first time since

Sunday Restrictions in Sheffield

No manufacturing town in England is worse situated for places for public or healthful recreation than Sheffield. Thirty years ago it had numbers of places as common land where youths and men could have taken exercise at cricket, quoits, football, and other exercises . . . Scarce a foot of all these common wastes remain for the enjoyment of the industrial classes. It is true we have a noble cricket-ground, but access to this must be purchased. We have also perhaps as beautiful botanical gardens as any in the kingdom, but these are opened only once or twice a year to the poorer classes, and they are admitted for sixpence each; and hermetically sealed on a Sunday . . . the only day when members of the working classes have leisure to enjoy them. Many attempts have been made to open them in summer after service, but in vain; the X X X consider it would be a desecration of the Sabbath to permit the hard-toiled mechanic or tradesman to walk through these beautiful gardens on that day to view the beauties of creation in plants and flowers, such as the Saviour of mankind said that Solomon in all his glory was not to be compared with.

John Wardle, a cutler, 1843

'Get Drunk'

It is essential to be drunk all the time. That is all: there's no other problem. If you do not want to feel the appalling weight of Time which breaks your shoulders and bends you to the ground, get drunk, and drunk again.

What with? Wine, poetry, or being good, please yourself. But get drunk.

And if now and then, on the steps of a palace, on the green grass of a ditch, in the glum loneliness of your room, you come to, your drunken state abated or dissolved, ask the wind, ask the wave, the star, the bird, the clock, ask all that runs away, all that groans, all that wheels, all that sings, all that speaks, what time it is; and the wind, the wave, the star, the bird, the clock, will tell you: 'It is time to get drunk!' If you do not want to be the martyred slaves of Time, get drunk, always get drunk! With wine, with poetry or with being good. As you please.

Charles Baudelaire, *c.* 1866

Déculottez vos phrases pour être à la hauteur des sans culottes

Graffito, Paris, 1968

The Communist Manifesto

A spectre is haunting Europe – the spectre of Communism. All the powers of old Europe have entered into a holy alliance to exorcise this spectre: Pope and Tsar, Metternich and Guizot, French Radicals and German police-spies.

Where is the party in opposition that has not been decried as communistic by its opponents in power? Where is the Opposition that has not hurled back the branding reproach of Communism, against the more advanced opposition parties, as well as against its reactionary adversaries?

Two things result from this fact:

I. Communism is already acknowledged by all European powers to be itself a power.

II. It is high time that Communists should openly, in the face of the whole world, publish their views, their aims, their tendencies, and meet this nursery tale of the spectre of Communism with a manifesto of the party itself.

To this end, Communists of various nationalities have assembled in London, and sketched the following manifesto, to be published in the English, French, German, Italian, Flemish and Danish languages . . .

The Communists disdain to conceal their views and aims. They openly declare that their ends can be attained only by the forcible overthrow of all existing social conditions. Let the ruling classes tremble at a Communist revolution. The proletarians have nothing to lose but their chains. They have a world to win.

Working men of all countries, unite!

Karl Marx and Friedrich Engels, 1848

The Crofter's War

The enemy is the landlord, the agent, the capitalist, and the Parliament which makes and maintains inhuman and iniquitous laws.

Cut down the telegraph wires and posts, carry away the wires and instruments! Stop the mail-carts, destroy the letters.

Burn the property of all obnoxious landlords, agents, etc. Set fire to the heather to destroy the game; disturb the deer; poison game-dogs!

Manifesto, c. 1880

The Docker's Tanner

Sing a song of sixpence
Dockers on the strike,
Guinea pigs as greedy
As a hungry pike,
Till the docks are opened
Burns for you will speak –
Courage lads! And you'll win
Well within the week!
Norwood's in his counting house, counting up his money;
Says he finds his life now isn't sweet as honey!
Ships are in the river lying there in rows –
But the tardy tanner's coming, everybody knows!

Song for the first organized strike by unskilled London workers, 1889

Aboriginal Australians' Rejection of Wage-Slavery

Often in those early days, did I return from a brief absence to find the whole of the labourers stretched like black shadows on the ground, I tried upbraiding them. It was no use. I tried ridiculing – saying scornfully that they worked like women or children, that they had neither strength nor endurance. That was no use either . . . There were, in fact, no means by which I could persuade them into sudden acceptance of a daily routine of toil.

Jack McLaren – Memoirs, 1900

The Dock Strike

It just grew out of despair, the very madness of despair: almost hysterically the human cry of protest broke out. We smothered it for a month, we 'leaders,' we 'dictators' for we had not realised the hot resentment and stubborn determination of the men.

The employers scoffed at our exasperation. We simply told the men what the employers thought of them. The men grew restive, then angry, and then the thought came to them like an inspiration: they would no longer labour. Sulkily, by scores of thousands, they left their work. The work stopped – dead. Milk, ice, eggs, meat, vegetables, fruit, all manner of foods and necessaries lay there, out of the public reach. The stream of London's food supplies was stopped . . .

How often and with what a haughty unctuousness it had been demonstrated to Park Lane, and Change Alley, and Stockwell Park, and the New Cut, and the Mile End Road that Labour was dependent upon Capital; that the iron law of wages was as immutable as the force of gravity, and that the great and gifted captains of Industry made the wheels go round. And the clock stopped; and the Captains of Industry could not set it going, but sat supine and sulky, looking exceedingly foolish. Labour had said 'No.' Labour had put its 'No' into action, and the immutable laws of economics were as futile as the empty barrows, the unfired engines, and the moveless cranes along the blank sides of the deserted docks . . .

'Mob law in London! Police helpless! Government impotent! Demagogues as dictators! Wolf at our doors! Men compelled to leave their honest toil! Sufferings of the poor! Reign of terror! Where are the respectable leaders of Labour? Where is the Cabinet? Where are the troops?' Heaven in its mercy leaves us always the Press in all our afflictions.

But the action of the Press is typical. The Press might scold, and rant and sneer; but the Press wanted paper! What would the world do without its half-penny oracles? What could the oracles do without paper? What would the advertiser say? The Press swanked and blustered and bluffed; but the Press did not go to the Government, nor to the troops, nor to the captains of industry for its paper; it went to the Strike committee of the working men. The Press, being a thing of wind and words, understood that wind and words will not lift and load and carry tons of paper reels: that must be done by hands: common, hard, vulgar hands. So the Press ambled off to Tower Hill, and craved permission of Mob law. It was a lesson: it was a take down. It was, as the Press too well perceived, a portent. The Press swallowed the dose, but did not like it: made the most damnable faces, said rude words about the paid agitator, and the tyrannical Sansculotte, lording it on Tower Hill. But the Press had felt a draught.

A hard world, my masters, but we demagogues manage to live in it; and to live virilly, pugnaciously, agitating, and winning; to the disgusted amazement of hireling slanderers and refined futilities.

But the fight's the thing: the strike.

Ben Tillett, 1911

Strike Benefit

By closing up *Those Who Walk in Darkness* and *Oh, What a Girl!* the Equity Association undoubtedly did a big thing towards ameliorating conditions among theater-goers; but the great achievement of the actors' strike is the series of benefit performances which it has brought about. The striking actors chartered the Lexington Opera House, gave their services to the cause, and showed what they could do in the way of giving a performance without managerial aid. And from the way the public has flocked to the opera house, it looks to even the most casual observer as if only their own relatives can be backing up the managers.

Aside from the excellence of the bill, there is such a nice, homey atmosphere about these benefit performances. You can stand out in the lobby and be jostled by actors and actresses just as if you were one of them. You can buy a program – and get your change back – from one of a large flock of eminent ingenues. It is, undoubtedly, an evening to send night letters to the dear ones about. Marie Dressler, Eddie Cantor, W. C. Fields, Ivy Sawyer and Joseph Santley, Van and Schenck, John Charles Thomas – you can see for yourself that it is considerable entertainment. Frank Tinney was funnier than ever in a little scene with Pearl White, who proves to be an excellent feeder for him, and a newcomer, Jim Barton, simply drove everybody wild with his comedy dances. The big event of the bill was, of course, the second act of *The Lady of the Camellias*, done by Ethel and Lionel Barrymore, with Conway Tearle and Doris Rankin in the supporting company. The Barrymores can never fail to be the big event of any bill on which they appear.

Unfortunately, the bill closes with what was classed as an oration, entitled 'Equity,' passionately delivered by Brandon Tynan, and written by Hassard Short and Perceval Knight, who based it on Mark Antony's speech in *Julius Caesar*. A little of it might have been a good idea, but it seems to last for three or four hours. Far more effective propaganda for the actors' cause was the brief speech which, in response to the insistent audience, Lionel

Barrymore made on behalf of himself and his sister: 'We're proud to be here. We'll be here forever, if necessary.'

Review of New York Equity strike benefit in *Vanity Fair* by Dorothy Parker, 1919

How could I indifferently stand by, and behold some of the very best of my fellow-creatures cruelly treated by some of the very worst?

Richard Parker, leader of the Nore Mutiny, executed 1797

'Which Side Are You On?'

Come all of you good workers,
Good news to you I'll tell
Of how the good old union
Has come in here to dwell.

Which side are you on?
Which side are you on?
Which side are you on?
Which side are you on?

My daddy was a miner
And I'm a miner's son,
And I'll stick with the union
Till ev'ry battle's won.

They say in Harlan County
There are no neutrals there;
You'll either be a union man
Or a thug for J. H. Blair.

Oh, workers, can you stand it?
Oh, tell me how you can.
Will you be a lousy scab
Or will you be a man?

Don't scab for the bosses,
Don't listen to their lies,
Us poor folks haven't got a chance
Unless we organize.

Mrs Reece, wife of a miner during a coal strike in Harlan, Kentucky, 1931

The Making of The Week

From the standpoint of *The Week*[1] an interesting aspect of the whole business was the fact that almost up to the last moment the British press was still purveying the preposterous pieces of optimism being peddled from No. 10 Downing Street. As so often happened in the Thirties, this type of deception boomeranged. In this particular case it boomeranged much to the advantage of *The Week*. The list of its subscribers was still of course pitifully small. On the other hand it had got itself talked about. And then the kind of thing happened which makes one feel that if *surréalisme* had not existed it would have been necessary to invent it. MacDonald[2] himself suddenly gave *The Week* world publicity.

There was, as there usually is in such situations, a dotty kind of logic about the way things turned out. And to Claud at least it was a confirmation of his theory that the more people tried to suppress the facts, the greater is the explosive effect of even the smallest detonation, disclosing reality. MacDonald came to the conclusion that all the *sotto voce* rumours about impending disaster at the conference, all the cynical chat which never got into the columns of the British press, were in fact inspired by *The Week*. One morning he went down to the Geological Museum and called a special conference in the crypt. Leading journalists from the press of the entire world were present. A special conference of this kind naturally suggested that something momentous was about to be said.

As though under the guidance of some peculiarly diabolic theatrical director, MacDonald placed himself on a small temporary podium against a background of the bones of prehistoric animals, so worn, broken or unidentifiable that they were useless for exhibition in the museum itself and had been relegated to the crypt. After a few opening words of hope and glory MacDonald swept himself into a tirade against evil influences which he said were gnawing at 'the very foundations of the noblest aspirations'. He then reached into his pocket and produced a document. He waved it about his head. He held it in front of him and punched at it with his fist. 'This, this,' he choked, 'is where you will find that all this sort of thing is coming from.'

He even read a line or two from the document and then paused to give an elaborately sarcastic laugh.

Claud could barely believe his eyes. For the document consisted of the familiar brown-on-buff pages of *The Week* which he had himself written only a few hours before. Since the passage which MacDonald had chosen to read exactly expressed what was known or suspected by at least a majority of the journalists present, his laughter did not get the response he had expected. Only a minority had up to that time even heard of *The Week*. They jostled forward to peer at whatever it was MacDonald was holding in his hand and to ask questions. MacDonald was only too happy to hand out not just one copy but two. The second he had apparently brought along for this very purpose – that is to say to give the journalists of the world ocular proof of the kind of villainy which was being manufactured in an obscure office in Victoria Street.

The journalists of course were not trying to read *The Week*, there was no time for that. They were simply scribbling down its address and the rates of subscription. By late that evening or the following morning the circulation of *The Week* had trebled. But more important and interesting from Claud's point of view was that the quality of the subscription list had also been profoundly changed. It now included the London bureau of every principal newspaper and news agency in the world, the press secretaries of most of the embassies and legations in London, and the representatives of a large number of foreign banking houses in the City of London.

[1] A broadsheet of exposés
[2] The Prime Minister

From *The Years of The Week*, by Patricia Cockburn, 1967 describing 1933

Blathering

Blather Is Here

> As we advance to make our bow, you will look in vain for signs of servility or for any evidence of a slavish desire to please. We are an arrogant and a depraved body of men. *Blather* doesn't care. A sardonic laugh escapes us as we bow, cruel and cynical hounds that we are. It is a terrible laugh, the laugh of lost men. Do you get the smell of porter?

Blather, its editorial said, was a 'publication of the Gutter' which would achieve 'entirely new levels in everything that is contemptible, despicable and unspeakable in contemporary journalism.' *Blather* had 'no principles, no honour, no shame'; its objects were 'the fostering of graft and corruption in public life, the furtherance of cant and hypocrisy, the encouragement of humbug and hysteria, the glorification of greed and gombeenism' . . .

> In regard to politics all our rat-like cunning will be directed towards making Ireland fit for the depraved readers of *Blather* to live in. In the meantime, anything that distortion, misrepresentation and long-distance lying can do to injure and wreck the existing political parties, one and all, *Blather* will do it. Much in the way of corruption has already been done. We have de Valera and the entire Fianna Fáil Cabinet in our pocket; we have O'Duffy in a sack. Michael Hayes lies, figuratively speaking, bound and gagged in our hen-house. Colonel Broy has lent us a Guard to post our letters.

Founding editorial of the Dublin *Blather*, by Flann O'Brien, *c.* 1934

'The Börgermoor Song'

As far as the eye can see nothing but moor and heath all around, no bird-song regales us, oak-trees stand bare and crooked.
We are the moor-soldiers who march out to the moors with their spades

Here in this bleak heath the camp has been built. Far from pleasures of any kind we are stowed behind barbed-wire.
(Refrain)

Every morning the columns march out to work on the moors.
They dig in the heat of the sun, but their thoughts turn to home.
(Refrain)

Homewards, homewards, goes their longing, to parents, wife and child. Many a breast heaves a sigh, because we are prisoners here.
(Refrain)

Up and down go the guards, nobody, but nobody can escape.
Flight can cost your life, for the prison has a fourfold fence.
(Refrain)

Yet we do not complain, winter cannot last for ever.
One day we'll rejoice and say: home, you're mine again!
Then the moor-soldiers, will *not* march
out to the moors with their spades.

Composed in the Prussian State Concentration Camp, Börgermoor/Tapenburg, by an actor, Wolfgang Langhoff, and a miner, Johann Esser, *c.* 1935

Invading the Ritz

As a follow-up to this action, we decided to invade the Ritz Hotel in Piccadilly. Everything was well planned. The press – that is, the London and national newspapers (and in those days before the swallowing up of the little fish by the big 'uns under free enterprise there was quite a number of them) were all informed in advance. At the appointed time about 150 of our unemployed members, all dressed up in such remnants of our best suits as had escaped the pawnbroker, walked quietly into the Grill and sat down. This did not have quite the hoped-for effect, for due to a mistake – the only organisational mistake I can remember on the part of the campaign committee – we had overlooked the fact that the Grill was never open in the afternoons, only in the evenings. However, we continued as planned, took our places at the tables which were being set by waiters in readiness for the evening, and then pulled out our posters from beneath our coats, with slogans calling for an end to the Means Test and more winter relief for the aged pensioners.

Can you imagine the looks on the faces of the waiters! They stood still in their tracks. Up rushed the management supervisor demanding to know what it was all about. He was politely told by our elected speaker, Wal Hannington, that we would like to be served with some tea and sandwiches because we were very tired and hungry, but he was not to be anxious and could present the bill which would be paid on the spot.

When the supervisor regained his breath he said, in a very cultured, precise Oxford-English voice: 'I cannot permit you to be served. You are not our usual type of customer. You know full well that you are not accustomed to dine in an establishment of this quality. If you do not leave I shall have to send for the police.' (This had already been done.) In reply, our spokesman informed him that many was the Saturday when wealthy clients of the Ritz would drive down to the East End workmen's caffs in their Rollses and Daimlers and have a jolly hot saveloy, old boy, what! Slumming, they called it, and they too were in unusual attire and frequenting establishments that were not accustomed to such a clientele; nevertheless, said our spokesman, these gentlemen were treated with courtesy and civility and nobody sent for the police. The Ritz, he added, was not a private members' club but a public restaurant; he requested the supervisor to give orders to the staff to serve us with the refreshment we had asked for.

The appeal might just as well have been addressed to the chandelier which hung from the ceiling. The supervisor stood there with a look of scorn, waiting for the police to come and throw us out. We refused to budge, insisting on our right as members of the general public, with legal tender in our pockets, to be served with what we had ordered. Meanwhile Wally had mounted the orchestra-platform to address us; waiters and kitchen staff stood around dumbfounded at our temerity. But our speaker was incensed and in good form, and the issue of class privilege was clearly put. I noticed several of the staff members nodding their heads as the speaker touched on salient points. His speech was never finished, however, for the Grill was soon surrounded by police. A couple of Inspectors came over and consulted our organisers; we were ordered to leave, and did so in an orderly manner. As we filed out several of the waiters came to wish us luck in our campaign, and pressed money into our hands.

Jack Dash of the National Unemployed Workers Movement, from *Good Morning, Brothers*, 1969 referring to 1938

The imaginary is that which tends to become real.

André Breton

The Appalling War

The battle goes on. It will go on, both because men believe in just or fair-play, but because it is in the nature of things that one terror should provoke another. This is the end of the world as we have known it. From now on naked terror will be fought with naked terror. The Moors who crucify the Republicans, the Fascists who drop the bodies of our comrades from aeroplanes on to our lines, the hostages who are slaughtered, the girls who are violated, demand vengeance. It is as simple as that. And yet it is not so simple. There are some spirits in the world who possess the quality of mercy. This is what I have been trying to describe in my play Pastor Hall.

I am not sure that I entirely understand mercy, but I believe that it is only through mercy that we can prevent the whole of Europe from disappearing from the map. Europe will die. She may be reborn. . . . Four times they have tried to assassinate me. Once in Paris, once in Switzerland, once in Stockholm, once here. And yet I am no longer very important to the future of the world. My books still sell, they are translated in many languages, but they are not read. I belong to an early generation, and now there is a generation which is physically strong and mentally courageous above everything which was produced in the revolution in Bavaria . . . The war of the future will be a war fought by the implacable young against the implacable young, and this is what is so terrible, and breaks my heart . . .

Ernst Toller, the playwright who headed the short-lived communist republic of Bavaria, written in 1938

The Swing Movement

The dance music was all English and American. Only swing dancing and jitterbugging took place. At the entrance to the hall stood a notice on which the words 'Swing prohibited' had been altered to 'Swing requested'. The participants accompanied the dances and songs, without exception, by singing the English words. Indeed, throughout the evening they attempted only to speak English; at some tables even French.

The dancers were an appalling sight. None of the couples danced normally; there was only swing of the worst sort. Sometimes two boys danced with one girl; sometimes several couples formed a circle, linking arms and jumping, slapping hands, even rubbing the backs of their heads together; and then, bent double, with the top half of the body hanging loosely down, long hair flopping into the face, they dragged themselves round practically on their knees. When the band played a rumba, the dancers went into wild ecstasy. They all leaped around and joined in the chorus in broken English. The band played wilder and wilder items; none of the players was sitting down any longer, they all 'jitterbugged' on the stage like wild creatures. Several boys could be observed dancing together, always with two cigarettes in the mouth, one in each corner . . .

The predominant form of dress consisted of long, often checked English sports jackets, shoes with thick light crepe soles, showy scarves, Anthony Eden hats, an umbrella on the arm whatever the weather, and, as an insignia, a dress-shirt button worn in the buttonhole, with a jewelled stone.

The girls too favoured a long overflowing hair style. Their eyebrows were pencilled, they wore lipstick and their nails were lacquered.

The bearing and behaviour of the members of the clique resembled their dress.

From an internal Hitler Youth report, 1940

Gulag Song

Three times a day we go for gruel,
The evenings we pass in song,
With a contraband prison needle
We sew ourselves *bags* for the road.

We don't care about ourselves any more,
We signed – just to be quicker!
And when will we ever return here again
From the distant Siberian camps?

Anon., *c.* 1940

'Manifesto of the Poles'

Poles, citizens, soldiers of Freedom! Through the din of German cannon, destroying the homes of our mothers, wives and children: through the noise of their machine-guns, seized by us in the fight against the cowardly German police and SS men; through the smoke of the Ghetto, that was set on fire, and the blood of its mercilessly killed defenders, we, the slaves of the Ghetto, convey heartfelt greetings to you.

We are well aware that you have been witnessing breathlessly, with broken hearts, with tears of compassion, with horror and enthusiasm, the war that we have been waging against every brutal occupant these past few days.

Every doorstep in the Ghetto has become a stronghold and shall remain a fortress until the end! All of us will probably perish in the fight, but we shall never surrender! We, as well as you, are burning with the desire to punish the enemy for all his crimes, with a desire for vengeance. It is a fight for our freedom, as well as yours; for our human dignity and national honour, as well as yours! We shall avenge the gory deeds of Oswiecim, Treblinka, Belzec and Majdanek!

Long live the fraternity of blood and weapons in a fighting Poland!

Long live freedom!

Death to the hangmen and the killer!

We must continue our mutual struggle against the occupant until the very end!

Produced by ZOB, a Jewish armed resistance movement, April 1943; during the Warsaw Ghetto Rising

Franz Otto Colliery

We wish to inform you herewith of an incident which occurred underground here on 9.10 in Franz Otto Colliery, Duisburg Neuenkamp.

At the end of a shift the foreman S[. . .], Karl, b. 24.10.03 in Duisburg, who is in charge of coal-extraction from the faces of one district of the pit, ordered one of the Russian prisoners of war employed there to stay on longer and help extract a wedge of coal that had remained in the rock.

Since the Russian refused, despite repeated requests, to comply with this instruction, S[. . .] attempted forcibly to compel him to perform this task.

In the course of the altercation the apprentice face-worker Lapschieß, Max, b. 24.4.03 in Gelsenkirchen, resident here at Essenbergerstr. 127, turned on the foreman and defended the POW in a manner such as to encourage the latter to strike the foreman on the head with his lamp. S[. . .] received a gaping wound on the face which has required stitches, and he has since been on sick leave. He is a diligent man and a member of the colliery Political Action Squad.

We should be grateful if you could make it clear to Lapschieß, who has already been in a concentration camp (1935–9), that his interference with instructions issued to the Russian prisoners of war constitutes a disturbance of the colliery's operation and that he may under no circumstances take the part of a POW.

This morning Lapschieß declared in impudent fashion to my face that he would continue to intervene if Russian prisoners of war were assaulted. No previous instances of ill-treatment or any other kinds of dispute with Russian prisoners of war have occurred here.

Memorandum from Franz Otto Colliery to Duisburg Gestapo, 13 October 1943

Ted Bramley

He played a leading role in organising the squatters' movement, when [in 1946] hundreds of families took over empty blocks of luxury flats, demanding that local councils use their powers to requisition all such empty properties.

Tried with four others at the Old Bailey on a catch-all charge of 'conspiracy to incite to trespass', he conducted his own political defence, challenging the crowded court with a characteristic personal appeal to heart and conscience. 'Those among you who have the good fortune to enjoy shelter, warmth and the comfort of a good home, I would ask you to consider just one thing: what would you do if you saw your wife and children condemned to live for years in a single room? I know what you would do. You would move heaven and earth to get something done, and if you knew there were large numbers of empty places which could be used you would protest against it by every means within your power, and so would I. That is what we have done . . . I, with thousands of other Londoners, want to see something better for our people, and what we claim for ourselves we feel it our duty to find for anyone else.'

The defendants were found guilty, but surprisingly were only bound over instead of the prison sentences they had expected, and the requisitioning of buildings for the homeless notably increased.

From his obituary by Margot Heinemann, February 1991

The Un-American Activities Committee

(The Chair called for the next witness – Alvah Bessie.)

THOMAS: Mr. Bessie, while there is some doubt that your statement is pertinent to the inquiry, as will be very evident when you read it –

BESSIE: I would still like to have permission to read it –

THOMAS: Just a minute. Nevertheless, the Committee is willing that you read the statement. We were just wondering, in order to save time, if you couldn't read the first couple paragraphs and then let us put it in the record . . .

BESSIE: In accordance with your request, I will read the first two paragraphs and the last two . . .

'It is my understanding of the First Amendment to our Constitution that it expressly forbids Congress to pass any law which shall abridge freedom of speech or opinion. And it is my understanding of the function of congressional committees that they are set up by the Congress for the express purpose of inquiring into matters that may lead to the initiation of legislation in the Congress.

'Now either the Constitution and its Bill of Rights mean what they say or they do not mean what they say. Either the First Amendment is binding upon Congress and all legislative bodies of our government or it means nothing at all. I cannot agree with this so-called committee in its implied belief that the Bill of Rights means whatever this body chooses it to mean or is applicable only to those with whose opinions this committee is in agreement . . .' Those are the first two paragraphs. Now, the last two:

'In calling me from my home, this body hopes also to rake over the smoldering embers of the war that was fought in Spain from 1936 to 1939. This body, and all its previous manifestations, is on record as believing that support of the Spanish Republic was and is subversive, un-American, and Communist-inspired. That lie was originally spawned by Hitler and Franco, and the majority of the American people – in fact, the majority of the people of the world – never believed it. And I want it on the record at this point that I not only supported the Spanish Republic but that it was my high privilege and the greatest honor I have ever enjoyed to have been a volunteer soldier in the ranks of its International Brigades throughout 1938. And I shall continue to support the Spanish Republic until the Spanish people in their majesty and power remove Francisco Franco and all his supporters and re-establish the legal government Franco and his Nazi and Italian Fascist soldiers overthrew.

'The understanding that led me to fight in Spain for that republic, and my experience in that war, teaches me that this committee is engaged in precisely the identical activities engaged in by un-Spanish committees, un-German committees, and un-Italian committees which preceded it in every country which eventually succumbed to fascism. I will never aid or abet such a committee in its patent attempt to foster the sort of intimidation and terror that is the inevitable precursor of a Fascist regime. And I therefore restate my conviction that this body has no legal authority to pry into the mind or activities of any American who believes, as I do, in the Constitution and who is willing at any time to fight to preserve it – as I fought to preserve it in Spain.'

(After the usual identifying questions, Stripling got right to the point:)

STRIPLING: Are you a member of the Screen Writers' Guild?

BESSIE: This is the same sort of question that was asked of other witnesses. It involves a question of my associations.

STRIPLING: Do you refuse to answer the question?

BESSIE: I have not refused to answer the question, but I must answer the question in the only way in which I know how, and that is that I believe that such a question violates my right of association and is not properly falling – I do not believe it falls properly within the scope of this committee's inquiry.

STRIPLING: We will move on to the $64 question, Mr. Bessie. Are you now, or have you ever been, a member of the Communist Party?

BESSIE: Mr. Stripling and gentlemen of the Committee, unless it has been changed since yesterday, in our country we have a secret ballot; and I do not believe this Committee has any more right to inquire into my political affiliations than I believe an election official has the right to go into the voting booth and examine the ballot which has been marked by the voter. General Eisenhower himself has refused to reveal his political affiliations, and what is good enough for General Eisenhower is good enough for me.

(Laughter, applause – and some booing.)

STRIPLING: Mr. Bessie, this Committee has officially found that the Communist Party in the United States is not a political party but is, in fact, the agent of a foreign government. I will ask you again: Are you now, or have you ever been, a member of the Communist Party?

BESSIE: Mr. Stripling, if you did not understand my answer to your question –
STRIPLING: I understood your answer.
BESSIE: I suggest you have the secretary read it back to you.
STRIPLING: Mr. Bessie, there have been charges made before this Committee that you are a Communist. I didn't notice anywhere in your statement that you denied that charge. You are now being given an opportunity to deny whether or not you are a member of the Communist Party. You have not answered whether or not you are a member of the Communist Party.
BESSIE: In the statement which you were kind enough to permit me to read, I stated I stand on the Bill of Rights on this issue; and I think either the Bill of Rights means something or it doesn't; and if it doesn't mean anything, it is news to me, and I think it would be great news to the majority of the American people.

(Stripling then requested Thomas to order the witness to answer the question, and Thomas attempted to clarify matters for the witness, who obviously did not understand the question:)

THOMAS: Mr. Bessie, in order to save a lot of time, we would like to know whether you are or have ever been a member of the Communist Party. We would like a very frank answer. You can answer it 'yes' or 'no'; or if you don't care to answer it, just say so.
BESSIE: Mr. Thomas, with whatever respect is due this Committee, I now state I have given you my answer to this question. I have not attempted to evade the question. I have given you the answer to the question, according to my understanding of what protections are offered the American people, and I object violently to the procedure this Committee engages in, in an attempt to make people state what they think, believe, with whom they associate, whom they go to dinner with, or what have you.
THOMAS: The only part of your answer I can remember is that part about General Eisenhower, and I don't think that is a –
BESSIE: May I ask if you would have General Eisenhower here and ask him –
STRIPLING: Just a minute.
THOMAS: Just a minute.
BESSIE: – ask him whether he is a member of the Republican or Democratic Party?
THOMAS: I don't think that was a responsive answer to the question. What we are attempting to do – what this Committee of Congress is attempting to do – is to ascertain the extent of Communist infiltration in the moving-picture industry.
BESSIE: I don't believe that that is what the Committee is trying to do.
THOMAS: Just a minute –
BESSIE: I believe what this Committee is trying to do –

(Thomas pounds gavel.)

BESSIE: – is to do exactly the same thing –
THOMAS: I am telling you what the Committee is trying to do. We know exactly what the Committee is trying to do.
BESSIE: I have my own opinion of it.

THOMAS: That is all right; you can have any opinion you want.
BESSIE: Thank you.
THOMAS: The Committee would like to know whether you have ever been a member of the Communist Party or whether you are a member of the Communist Party now?
BESSIE: I have given you several answers to that question, and that is the best I can do for you, Mr. Chairman.
THOMAS: Then do you –
BESSIE: Because I believe you are violating my rights as an American citizen.
THOMAS: So you refuse?
BESSIE: I am not refusing. I have told you that is the answer I have given you. The answer is now recorded several times. I don't believe you have the right to ask this question of anybody.
THOMAS: It is very apparent that you are following the same line of these other witnesses.
BESSIE: I am following no line –
THOMAS: Which is definitely the Communist line.
BESSIE: – I am using my own head, which I am privileged to do.
THOMAS: You are excused. If you want to make a speech, go out there under a big tree.
BESSIE: Thank you.

(Laughter)

CHAIRMAN: May we have order, please?

From *Inquisition in Eden* by Alvah Bessie, 1967 describing 1947

'Transform the world,' Marx said; 'change life,' Rimbaud said. These two watchwords are one for us.

André Breton

Laughter and Freedom

Medieval laughter is directed at the same object as medieval seriousness. Not only does laughter make no exception for the upper stratum, but indeed it is usually directed toward it. Furthermore, it is directed not at one part only, but at the whole. One might say that it builds its own world versus the official world, its own church versus the official church, its own state versus the official state. Laughter celebrates its masses, professes its faith, celebrates marriages and funerals, writes its epitaphs, elects kings and bishops.

Even the smallest medieval parody is always built as part of a whole comic world.

From *Rabelais and His World* by Mikhail Bakhtin, 1966

Czech Dissidents

I met Hrabal under circumstances that sound like one of his own stories. In the early Fifties when I was an editor at a publishing house, one of my duties was delivering obsolete galley proofs to the scrap-paper salvage centre. The fellow in the patched overalls there would examine my proofs with interest. Then he would launch into a fluent discussion of literature; Breton's *Najda*, I think, was his subject that day. Later we met at the flat of the poet and artist Jiri Kolár (best known in the West for his collages), a typical centre of the Czech avant-garde, where we discussed abstract expressionism or whatever was in the air. We also read aloud our verses and stories.

Josef Skvorecky, *c.* 1950

'Rule Britannia'

Rule Britannia
two tanners make a bob.
Good King Henry
never shaved his knob.

Anon., *c.* 1950

A Letter from an Old Communist

Here is what the old communist, Comrade Kedrov, wrote to the Central Committee through Comrade Andreyev (Comrade Andreyev was then a Central Committee secretary):

'I am calling to you for help from a gloomy cell of the Lefortovsky prison. Let my cry of horror reach your ears; do not remain deaf; take me under your protection; please, help remove the nightmare of interrogations and show that this is all a mistake.

I suffer innocently. Please believe me. Time will testify to the truth. I am not an *agent provocateur* of the Tsarist Okhrana; I am not a spy; I am not a member of an anti-Soviet organization of which I am being accused on the basis of denunciations. I am also not guilty of any other crimes against the party and the government. I am an old Bolshevik, free of any stain: I have honestly fought for almost forty years in the ranks of the party for the good and prosperity of the nation . . .

. . . Today I, a 62-year-old-man, am being threatened by the investigative judges with more severe, cruel and degrading methods of physical pressure. They (the judges) are no longer capable of becoming aware of their error and of recognizing that their handling of my case is illegal and impermissible. They try to justify their actions by picturing me as a hardened and raving enemy and are demanding increased repressions. But let the party know that I am innocent and that there is nothing which can turn a loyal son of the party into an enemy, even right up to his last dying breath.

But I have no way out. I cannot divert from myself the hastily approaching new and powerful blows.

Everything, however, has its limits. My torture has reached the extreme. My health is broken, my strength and my energy are waning, the end is drawing near. To die in a Soviet prison, branded as a vile traitor to the Fatherland – what can be more monstrous for an honest man? And how monstrous all this is! Unsurpassed bitterness and pain grips my heart. No! No! This will not happen; this cannot be, I cry. Neither the party, nor the Soviet government, nor the People's Commissar, L. P. Beria, will permit this cruel, irreparable injustice. I am convinced that, given a quiet, objective examination, without any foul rantings, without any anger and without the fearful tortures, it would be easy to prove the baselessness of the charges. I believe deeply that truth and justice will triumph. I believe. I believe.'

From the speech to the 20th Party Congress by Krushchev, 1956

'In Place of a Foreword'

In the years of the Yezhov Terror I have spent seventeen months standing in queues in front of the prisons of Leningrad.*

Once, someone recognized me.

In that moment, a woman standing behind me – who in all probability had never heard of my name – suddenly came to her senses from the overpowering numbness affecting us all, and with her lips blue from cold whispered into my ears (everybody whispered there), 'Can you describe this?'

And I answered, 'Yes, I can.' And something of a smile appeared there where her face once was.

*trying to free her son

Anna Akhmatova, 1957

Launch Speech of the Campaign for Nuclear Disarmament

That is the function of the campaign which we are launching here tonight: to make every individual reassume the moral responsibility for opposing public insanity. The issue is one for direct action by every one of us.

We are not at the mercy of the Government, nor of events, nor of the policy of other nations, nor of the world situation, if we are prepared as a public to be sufficiently combative.

I would remind you that once already in the last two years we have seen public opinion assert itself on a moral issue through the sheer force of unorganised indignation. The response which we have received from you tonight is of that same order.

Within the coming weeks we intend to raise throughout the country a solid body of opposition to the whole strategy of moral bankruptcy and ceremonial suicide which the hydrogen bomb epitomises, to all the mentally under-privileged double-talk by which it has been justified.

I would urge every one of us at this meeting to go home determined to become a living focus of that opposition. Some of us are going to march to Aldermaston on Good Friday, whether the Minister of Works likes it or not. Some of us live in areas which have been selected to receive American guided missile bases.

The Government is intensely anxious about public reaction to those bases, and is trying to keep their location secret.

If there are no local committees in your area, keeping their eyes open for base building activity, form one. If there is no focus for public opposition to nuclear tests and nuclear weapons in your district, in your church, among your neighbours, become one. If you are not already exerting pressure on your Member, on the Prime Minister, on the Press, on any scientists involved in unethical projects whose addresses you can get, begin to do so now, by letter and by lobbies.

It is high time we held some atomic tests of our own – in Downing Street.

Much has been said about a summit conference. Sanity is always hardest to restore at the summit – the air there is rarefied. It seems to affect the brain. We can reassert it at the base.

The people must take over – you must take over. The leaders of all the parties are waiting, as they always wait on any issue of principle, to follow public opinion. We can coerce them.

Gaitskell and Bevan say they will not abandon the H-bomb unilaterally. If they were here tonight, they would see that in this issue their party is abandoning them unilaterally.

We can make Britain offer the world something which is virtually forgotten – moral leadership. Let us make this country stand on the side of human decency and human sanity – alone if necessary. It has done so before. If it does so again I do not think we need fear the consequences.

Alex Comfort, 1958

'I Have a Dream'

I say to you today, my friends, though . . . even though we face difficulties today and tomorrow . . . I still have a dream. It is a dream that . . . one day this nation will rise up, live out the true meaning of its creed: 'We hold these truths to be self-evident . . . that all men are created equal . . .'

I have a dream . . . that one day on the red hills of Georgia, sons of former slaves and sons of former slave-owners . . .

. . . will be able to sit down together at the table of brotherhood.

I have a dream . . . that one day even the State of Mississippi . . . a state sweltering with the heat of injustice . . . sweltering with the heat of oppression . . . will be transformed into an oasis of freedom and justice.

I have a dream . . . that my four little children will one day live in a nation where they will not be judged by the color of their skin, but by the content of their character.

When we let freedom ring, black men and white men . . . Jews and Gentiles . . . Protestants and Catholics . . . will be able to join hands and sing . . . in the words of the old Negro spiritual . . . 'Free at last! Free at last! Great God Almighty, we are free at last!'

From a speech by Martin Luther King to 250,000 people at a Civil Rights March, Washington, 28 August 1963

I am pleased at the Revolution, particularly on this account, that it makes the working classes see their real importance, and those who despise them see it too.

William Cobbett

Strike Breaking in Brooklyn

The men on the picket line were startled when the trucks turned into the runway leading to the loading platform, but only for a second. They yelled at the drivers of the trunks that they were on strike and the drivers yelled fuck you. A few of the men tried to jump on the hoods of the trucks, but fell; a few others picked up stones and tin cans and threw them at the drivers but they just bounced off the cabs. When the men tried to follow the trucks to the platform the police grabbed them and held them back. The yelling of the men on the picket line was heard by the others hanging around the office and they came running; and a call was made from one of the police cars for additional men. Some of the police formed a line across the runway while the others pushed the men back. Soon there were hundreds of men yelling and pushing; those in the rear shouting to shove the fuckin cops outta the way and get those fuckinscabs; the men in front screaming in the faces of the cops and being shoved by the mob behind them into the line of police that was slowly weakening. For many minutes the amoeba like mass flowed forward, backward and around, arms and signs bobbing up and down over heads; white gloves and clubs raised; red infuriated faces almost pressed together, words and spit bouncing off faces; anger clouding and watering eyes. Then more police arrived by the carsfull. Then a firetruck. Men leaped from the cars and were assimilated by the mass. A fire hose was quickly unravelled and connected; a loudspeaker screeched and told the men to breakitup. FUCKYOU FLATFOOT GO AND FUCKYASELF YASONOFABITCH IF YOU MEN DONT BREAKITUP WE'LL RUN YOU ALL IN NOW GET BACK FROM THAT RUNWAY YEAH, SURE, AFTA WE BREAK THOSE FUCKINSCABSHEADS DERE TAKIN THE BREAD FROM OUR MOUTHS IM TELLING YOU FOR THE LAST TIME, BREAKITUP OR I'LL TURN THE HOSE ON YOU WHO PAID YAOFF YASONOFABITCH. The line of police had been extended and was pushing as hard as it could against the mob, but the men became more incensed as more cops fought them and the voice threatened them and they felt the power of their numbers and the frustration and lost hope of fruitless months on the picket and food lines finally found the release it had been looking for. Now there was something tangible to strike at. And the police who had been standing, bored, for months as the men walked up and down, telling them to keep moving, envying them because they at least could do something tangible to get more money while all they could do was put in a request to the mayor and be turned down by the rotten politicians, finally found the outlet they too had been waiting for and soon the line became absorbed by the mass and two and three went down to their knees and then others too, strikers and cops, and a sign swooped through the air and thudded against a head and a white gloved hand went up and then a club thudded and hands, clubs, signs, rocks, bottles were lifted and thrown as if governed by a runaway eccentric rod and the mass spread out, some falling over others and heads popped out of windows and doorways and peered and a few cars parked cautiously or slowed and observed for a moment and the mass continued to wallow along and across 2nd avenue as a galaxy through the heavens with the swooshing of comets and meteors and the voice that screeched now directed itself to the firemen and they walked slowly toward the grinding mass and a white glove clutched at a head and the glove turned red and occasionally a bloody body would be exuded from the mass and roll a foot or two and just lie there or perhaps wriggle slightly and four or five beaten and bloodied cops managed to work their way free from the gravity of the mass and stood side by side and walked back to the mass swinging their clubs and screaming and a sign was broken over one of their heads but the cop only screamed louder and continued to swing, still walking, until his club was broken over a head and he picked up the broken sign without breaking rank and continued and the thudding of the clubs on heads was only slightly audible and the sound not at all unpleasant as it was muted by the screams and curses and they stepped over a few bodies until a line of strikers was somehow formed and they charged the cops not stopping as the clubs were methodically pounded on their heads and the two lines formed a whirling heated nebula that spun off from the galaxy to disintegrate as the strikers overwhelmed them and kicked the cops as they tried to regain their feet or roll away and sirens screeched but were unheard and more police jumped from cars and trucks and another fire hose was unravelled and aimed the order given to open the hydrants and not wait until the police who were whirling with the strikers could extricate themselves and a few of the strikers noticed the second hose being readied and then noticed the first hose and charged the firemen but the water leaped forth in an overpowering gush and one of the men took the full force in his abdomen and his mouth jutted open but if a sound came out it was unheard and he doubled over and spun like a gyroscope runamuck bouncing off the men behind him and bouncing to the curb and those who were behind him were knocked and spun and a few policemen ran frantically to the various street corners trying to direct and divert traffic but all of the cars moved slowly no matter how urgently the police waved them on not wanting to miss any of the excitement and the voice screeched again giving directions and the two powered battering rams were directed with knowledge and precision and soon the mass was a chaos of colliding particles that bounced tumbled and whirled around against and over each other and soon it was quiet enough to hear the ambulance sirens and the louder moans that spewed from the mass and soon too the street was clear of the smaller debris and even the blood had been washed away.

From *Last Exit to Brooklyn* by Hubert Selby, 1965

Louis he was King of France
before the revolution.
Then he had his head chopped off
which spoiled his constitution.

Sea shanty

Kesey's Capture

Then the Haight-Ashbury heads held the first big 'be-in,' the Love Festival on October 7, on the occasion of the California law against LSD going into effect. Thousands of heads piled in, in high costume, ringing bells, chanting, dancing ecstatically, blowing their minds one way and another and making their favorite satiric gesture to the cops, handing them flowers, burying the bastids in tender fruity petals of love. Oh christ, Tom, the thing was fantastic, a freaking mind-blower, thousands of high-loving heads out there messing up the minds of the cops and everybody else in a fiesta of love and euphoria. And who pops up in the middle of it all, down in the panhandle strip of the Golden Gate Park, but the Pimpernel, in Guadalajara boots and cowboy suit, and just as the word gets to ricocheting through the crowd real good – *Kesey's here! Kesey's here!* – he vanishes, accursed Pimpernel.

Just in case there was anybody left who didn't get the Gestalt here, Kesey made his big move in the press. He met with Donovan Bess, a reporter for the San Francisco *Chronicle*, and gave him the story of his flight to Mexico and his plans, as The Fugitive. The story was a real barn burner, Secret Interview with Fugitive Wanted by FBI, with all the trimmings, awash in screamers all across the San Francisco *Chronicle*. The line that captured all imaginations was where Kesey said:

'I intend to stay in this country as a fugitive, and as salt in J. Edgar Hoover's wounds.'

Then – this next prank was beautiful. A TV interview. The Fugitive on TV, while all, F. B. Eyes and everyone, watch helpless as the full face of the Fugitive, Kesey, beams forth into every home and bar and hospital and detective bureau in the Bay Area. It was beautiful even to think about, this prank. It was set up, much sly planning, with Roger Grimsby, a San Francisco television personality, on Station KGO, the local CBS outlet. The fantasy was that Grimsby would tape an interview with Kesey in a hideaway in the Portrero section of San Francisco, which was far away from both Haight-Ashbury and North Beach, and then put it on the air a couple of days later, October 20, a Friday. This fantasy came off like a dream. Grimsby taped the interview, and all was cool, and on Friday afternoon Kesey's face beamed into every home, bar, hospital and detective bureau, saying it all again, in person:

'I intend to stay in this country as a fugitive, and as salt in J. Edgar Hoover's wounds . . .'

See the very hunted coons
Salt J. Edgar Hoover's wounds!
Yah! the cops and robbers game. . . .

right right right right an even even even even even world twenty-five minutes after the Grimsby TV show Friday afternoon, October 20, Kesey and Hassler driving out of San Francisco on the Harbor Freeway, toward Palo Alto, in an old red panel truck. The current fantasy . . . this movie is too *real*, mommy – but they have actually pulled it off. They have just been in town in the hideaway watching Kesey the Fugitive on TV, and this prank was too beautiful. The FBI and all cops everywhere *shucked* in the most public galling way. The sun slants down on the Harbor Freeway in the afternoon and all the shiny black-shoe multitudes are out in their 300-horsepower fantasy cars heading into the rush hour, out the freeway, toward the waiting breezeway slots. It's actually peaceful, this rush hour

WE PULLED IT OFF

thousands of cars sailing up the swooping expressway like so many Salt Flat Futur-o-matics with taillight bands like hard red candy . . . It's relaxing, the rush hour is, and hypnotic, it drones, and it winks like red hard candy with the sun shining through it, and the sun shines in Kesey's side of the panel truck, very relaxing, and he takes off his disguise, the cowboy hat and dark glasses

SEE THE VERY HUNTED COONS
SALT J. EDGAR HOOVER'S WOUNDS

From *The Electric Kool-Acid Test* by Tom Wolfe, 1968

Whither China?

The bourgeoisie always represent the form of political power of their rule as the most perfect, flawless thing in the world that serves the whole people. The new bureaucratic bourgeoisie and the brutes of the Right-Wing of the petty bourgeoisie who depend on them are doing exactly that . . .

We really believe that ninety per cent of the senior cadres should stand aside, that at most they can only be objects to be educated and united. This is because they have already constituted a decaying class with its own particular 'interests.' Their relation with the people has changed from the relation between the leaders and the led in the past to that between exploiters and the exploited, the oppressors and the oppressed. Most of them consciously or unconsciously yearn for the capitalist road, and protect and develop capitalist things. The rule of their class has completely blocked the development of history . . . However they (the bureaucrats) hit back at and carry out counter-reckoning against the revolutionary people with increasing madness, pushing themselves nearer and nearer the guillotine. All this proves that no decaying class in history would voluntarily make an exit from the stage of history.

In the new society of the Paris Commune type this class will be overthrown . . .

If dictatorship by the revolutionary committee is regarded as the ultimate object of the first great cultural revolution, then China will inevitably go the way of Soviet Union and the people may again return to the fascist bloody rule of the capitalists. The revolutionary committee's road of bourgeois reformism is impracticable . . .

The commune of the 'Ultra-Left faction' will not conceal its viewpoints and intentions. We publicly declare that our object of establishing the 'People's Commune of China' can be attained only by overthrowing the bourgeois dictatorship and revisionist system of the revolutionary committee with brute force . . .

The China of tomorrow will be the world of the 'Commune.'

From the *Manifesto* of the Sheng-wu-Lien Group in Hunan, 1968

When the last socialist has been strangled with the guts of the last bureaucrat, will we still have 'problems'?

Graffito, Paris, 1968

Solzhenitsyn Protests Against Expulsion

Shamelessly trampling underfoot your own statutes, you have expelled me in my absence, as at the sound of a fire-alarm, without even sending me a summons by telegram, without even giving me the four hours I needed to come from Ryazan and be present at the meeting. You have shown openly that the RESOLUTION preceded the 'discussion'. Was it less awkward for you to invent new charges in my absence? Were you afraid of being obliged to grant me ten minutes for my answer? I am compelled to substitute this letter for those ten minutes.

Blow the dust off the clock. Your watches are behind the times. Throw open the heavy curtains which are so dear to you – you do not even suspect that the day has already dawned outside. It is no longer that stifling, that sombre, irrevocable time when you expelled Akhmatova in the same servile manner. It is not even that timid, frosty period when you expelled Pasternak, whining abuse at him. Was this shame not enough for you? Do you want to make it greater? But the time is near when each of you will seek to erase his signature from today's resolution.

Blind leading the blind! You do not even notice that you are wandering in the opposite direction from the one you yourselves announced. At this time of crisis you are incapable of suggesting anything constructive, anything good for our society, which is gravely sick – only your hatred, your vigilance, your 'hold on and don't let go'.

Your clumsy articles fall apart; your vacant minds stir feebly – but you have no arguments. You have only your voting and your administration. And that is why neither Sholokhov nor any of you, of all the lot of you, dared reply to the famous letter of Lydia Chukovskaya, who is the pride of Russian publicistic writing. But the administrative pincers are ready for her: how could she allow people to read her book (*The Deserted House*) when it has not been published? Once the AUTHORITIES have made up their minds not to publish you – then stifle yourself, choke yourself, cease to exist, and don't give your stuff to anyone to read!

They are also threatening to expel Lev Kopelev, the frontline veteran, who has already served ten years in prison although he was completely innocent. Today he is guilty: he intercedes for the persecuted, he revealed the hallowed secrets of his conversation with an influential person, he disclosed an OFFICIAL SECRET. But why do you hold conversations like these which have to be concealed from the people? Were we not promised fifty years ago that never again would there be any secret diplomacy, secret talks, secret and incomprehensible appointments and transfers, that the masses would be informed of all matters and discuss them openly?

'The enemy will overhear' – that is your excuse. The eternal, omnipresent 'enemies' are a convenient justification for your functions and your very existence. As if there were no enemies when you promised immediate openness. But what would you do without 'enemies'? You could not live without 'enemies'; hatred, a hatred no better than racial hatred, has become your sterile atmosphere. But in this way a sense of our single, common humanity is lost and its doom is accelerated. Should the antarctic ice melt tomorrow, we would all become a sea of drowning humanity, and into whose heads would you then be drilling your concepts of 'class struggle'? Not to speak of the time when the few surviving bipeds will be wandering over radioactive earth, dying.

It is high time to remember that we belong first and foremost to humanity. And that man has distinguished himself from the animal world by THOUGHT and SPEECH. And these, naturally, should be FREE. If they are put in chains, we shall return to the state of animals.

OPENNESS, honest and complete OPENNESS – that is the first condition of health in all societies, including our own. And he who does not want this openness for our country cares nothing for his fatherland and thinks only of his own interest. He who does not wish this openness for his fatherland does not want to purify it of its diseases, but only to drive them inwards, there to fester.

Letter by Alexander Solzhenitsyn to the Secretariat of the Soviet Writers' Union, 12 November 1969

The Ford Strike

Believe Us –
and Here's Proof

Ford have spent a lot of money in newspaper adverts saying that their workers are earning far more than they actually are.

Why do they do this?

It's not for the benefit of the men who work for them, because they know the truth anyway. We believe it must be to try and convince those people who don't work in Fords – who might be called the public in this instance – that the Ford worker is an unreasonable fellow who wants more money than he's worth. Fords are also backing the Government in their campaign to keep wages down whilst letting prices rise at will.

We at Fords have never said that we are the lowest paid in the country, but what we DO say is that working on the assembly line of other car factories earns more money than Fords pay. And that Fords can afford to pay at least as much as them.

Now, we can't afford the tens of thousands needed to buy newspaper adverts but we have a right for our point to be said. [Here the pamphlet reproduces a typical Ford worker's pay slip, showing: gross pay £25.1.8d; net pay £20.8.0d; hours 40.]

Above is a copy of an actual wage slip of an assembly worker. Ford said in their adverts that he gets £35.6.0d. a week average. But this is indisputable proof of what a man earns for a week of 40 hours, *providing* he has over 4 years of service with the company (take £2 off without service).

THERE ARE NO BONUSES OR EXTRAS PAID AT FORDS.

TO GET MORE THAN THIS HE MUST WORK NIGHTSHIFT OR OVERTIME, BUT EVERYONE DOESN'T DO THIS.

WE CHALLENGE ANYONE TO DISPUTE THIS PAY SLIP AND WE CAN PROVIDE 20,000 MORE LIKE IT

Leaflet by Ford Halewood Shop Stewards' Committee, 1972

'Chile Stadium'

There are five thousand of us here
In this little part of the city.
We are five thousand.
I wonder how many we are in all
In the cities and in the whole country?
Here alone
are ten thousand hands which plant seeds
and make the factories run.
How much humanity
exposed to hunger, cold, panic, pain,
moral pressures, terror and insanity?
Six of us were lost
as if into starry space.
One dead, another beaten as I could never have believed
a human being could be beaten.
The other four wanted to end their terror –
one jumping into nothingness,
another beating his head against a wall,
but all with the fixed look of death.
What horror the face of fascism creates!
They carry out their plans with knife-like precision.

Nothing matters to them,
For them blood equals medals,
slaughter is an act of heroism.
Oh God, is this the world that you created?
For this, your seven days of wonder and work?
Within these four walls only a number exists
which does not progress.
Which slowly will wish more and more for death.
But suddenly my conscience awakes
and I see this tide with no heartbeat,
only the pulse of machines
and the military showing their midwives' faces
full of sweetness.
Let Mexico, Cuba and the world
cry out against this atrocity!
We are ten thousand hands
which can produce nothing.
How many of us in the whole country?
The blood of our compañero Presidente
will strike with more strength than bombs and machine guns!
So will our fist strike again.

How hard it is to sing
When I must sing of horror.
Horror which I am living
Horror which I am dying.
To see myself among so much
and so many moments of infinity
in which silence and screams
are the end of my song.
What I see I have never seen
What I have left and what I feel
will give birth to the moment . . .

Victor Jara, 1973; composed in the football stadium where supporters of President Allende were imprisoned and many, including Jara, were murdered

'If I Had a Gun'

I'd shoot the man who pulled up slowly in his hot car this morning
I'd shoot the man who whistled from his balcony
I'd shoot the man with things dangling over his creepy chest in the park when I was contemplating the universe
I'd shoot the man who can't look me in the eye
who stares at my boobs when we're talking
who rips me off in the milk-bar and smiles his wet purple smile
who comments on my clothes. I'm not a fucking painting that needs to be told what it looks like.
who tells me where to put my hands, who wrenches me into position like a meccano-set, who drags you round like a war
I'd shoot the man who couldn't live without me
I'd shoot the man who thinks it's his turn to be pretty flashing his skin passively like something I've got to step into, the man who says *John's a chemistry Phd and an ace cricketer, Jane's got rotten legs*
who thinks I'm wearing perfume for him
who says *Baby you can really drive* like it's so complicated, male, his fucking highway, who says *ah but you're like that* and pats you on the head, who kisses you at the party because everybody does it, who shoves it up like a nail
I'd shoot the man who can't look after himself
who comes to me for wisdom
who's witty with his mates about heavy things that wouldn't interest you, who keeps a little time to be human and tells me, female, his ridiculous private thoughts.
Who sits up in his moderate bed and says *Was that good* like a menu who hangs onto you sloppy and thick as a carpet
I'd shoot the man last night who said *Smile honey don't look so glum* with money swearing from his jacket and a 3-course meal he prods lazily
who tells me his problems: his girlfriend, his mother, his wife, his daughter, his sister, his lover because women will listen to that sort of rubbish
Women are full of compassion and have soft soggy hearts
you can throw up in and no-one'll notice and they won't complain.
I'd shoot the man who thinks he can look like an excavation-site but you can't, who thinks what you look like's for him to appraise, to sit back, to talk his intelligent way.
I've got eyes in my fucking head.

Who thinks if he's smart he'll get it in.
I'd shoot the man who said
Andrew's dedicated and works hard, Julia's ruthlessly ambitious who says *I'll introduce you to the ones who know* with their inert alcoholic eyes that'll get by, sad, savage, and civilised
who say *you can* like there's a law against it
I'd shoot the man who goes stupid in his puny abstract how-could-I-refuse-she-needed-me taking her tatty head in his neutral arms like a pope
I'd shoot the man who pulled up at the lights who rolled his face articulate as an asylum and revved the engine, who says *you're paranoid* with his educated born-to-it calm
who's standing there wasted as a rifle and explains the world to me.
I'd shoot the man who says *Relax honey come and kiss my valium-mouth blue.*

Gig Ryan, *c.* 1975

I Want my Freedom

This is how Mrs Desai* put it at the Inquiry, held in a basement of the Piccadilly Hotel, ten months later.

'I say, "Look, Mr Alden, why you bring me in the office? I am here to explain something and I want to know what is going on. If you want to shout at me I am not prepared to listen to what you are talking about. If you are prepared to listen to me I am prepared to listen to you as well, but if you shout like that to me I am not talking to you.'

'Then he started to threaten me and warn me, he said, "Look, Mrs Desai, I warn you." I know that they are the tactics they always use; they give a warning the first time and they sack you, because they do not have any evidence as to why they have sacked you.

'As soon as I heard that "I warn you", I stopped him in the middle and said, "Look, I do not want to work with you; I do not want your warning. I respect you all the time and expect the same respect from you, and in this condition I am not prepared to work with you. Please give me my cards straight away. I am leaving."'

And this is Mr Alden's [Personnel Manager] version; given at the same Inquiry:

'She was obviously a little excited but she was constantly interrupting me and I must admit I did not find it terribly easy to understand what she was saying, but she did interrupt me and I could not finish a single sentence without getting some interruption. This was all, just a few seconds, but the impression I have all these months later is that I could not simply finish one sentence without her interrupting.'

Asked by his counsel, Mr Heald, 'Then did the subject seem to change after a little bit?' Mr Alden went on:

'All of a sudden she kind of exploded and said: "I want my freedom. I am going. I have had enough."'

'When you say she exploded, what effect did that have on the tone of voice she was using?'

'She shouted. She shouted very loudly.'

'Thereafter did she leave Mr Duffy's office and go into . . .'

'She immediately stormed out of Mr Duffy's office and Mr Duffy followed her out and we trailed down the office behind whilst she was shouting.'

'What language was she shouting in?'

'At that stage it was a mixture of Gujerati and English. She was obviously lapsing into Gujerati but also shouting some phrases in English.'

'Could you understand what she was shouting about?'

'"I want my freedom" is the phrase that stands out in my mind as being the one that she used a number of times.'

*leader of a strike for union recognition

From *Grunwick* by Joe Rogaly, 1977

'Ode to Democracy Wall'

A white stone brick wall at Xidan,
calmly stands by Changan Street.
Accompanied by chimes from the Telegraph Building,
it closely watches people's trends.
Even if you are not grand and imposing,
nor magnificent and beautiful,
you're extremely ordinary, ordinary.

In the China of the Seventies,
you send out the calls of the times!
The cry of a new arrival
echoes all around, forcefully.
'We want democracy!'
'We want science!'
'We want a legal system!'
'We want the Four Modernizations!'

These cries already old, pressed on people's chests,
these desires buried for years in people's hearts!
People hail them.
Because you,
express people's ideals.
Here
one can finally breathe the air of freedom,
Here
one can finally feel the power of the masses.

Some are astounded, frightened.
Traditional ignorance still binds their thoughts.
Here they carefully inspect the new world.
Sometimes they close their eyes for fear,
but don't see the itch in their hearts.

Some are in a fury, panic.
You are a sharp sword,
Ruthlessly you stab at demons and monsters.
You burn the raging flames of revolution,
glistening with the radiance of truth.
You are a mirror to the society of China,
impartially reflect the appearance of society.
All hideous things are revealed,
all beautiful things receive praise.

People with grievances come here to tell,
at pains come and talk before you,
People with opinions put them to you
unconcernedly they can present their ideas on governing as well.
Here the darkness of society is exposed,
Here the livers of Lin Biao and the Gang of Four are dissected.
Here the robe of religion is cast off;
Here the throne of despotism is set on fire;
Immortals smashed images of emperors and kings!

The soldiers of the Paris Commune
falling held on to the 'Wall of the Commune',
the already awakened Chinese giant
in his blood writes
compositions about communes on 'Democracy Wall'.

Although blue ghosts wander amongst the masses,
and the sound of handcuffs resounds in people's ears;
Although closed chains already smothered countless lives,
the claws of Fascism again stretched out to burning chests.
The people did not yield,
in the high song of freedom of Democracy Wall.

Cry out! – Democracy Wall,
the trend of the times is gathering in front of you,
rolling forward! No man can stop it!
Fight! – Democracy Wall.
People stand in front of you arm in arm,
to fight for a lofty ideal,
fearless against blood-stained weapons!
I praise you Democracy Wall,
you symbolize the light of China,
stand for man's hopes,
Forever you will be in people's hearts,
imprinted in the nation's glorious history!

Anon., 1978; Democracy Wall, Beijing, was where people
put up posters, poster-poems and slogans

'Après Nous le Déluge'

There's a land of stones and molotovs
And Tel-Aviv seethes with night-clubs and orgies
There's a land of resisters where they bind the wounds
And Tel-Aviv celebrates – eat, drink and be merry.
No, don't tell me of a child who lost her eye
It only makes me sick, sick, sick
It only makes me sick.

I've no time for the oppressed and the suffering
And I don't care what's going on 'over there'
Don't tell me about 'Yellow Wind', about detainees and rioters
Let's make love and live our lives
Tel-Aviv – that's the life!
No, don't tell me of a child who lost her home
It only makes me sick, sick, sick
It only makes me sick.

I've no time for pious moralisers
Let's drink-in the busy streets of Tel-Aviv
No, don't tell me of a child who lost her childhood
It only makes me sick, sick, sick
It only makes me sick.

Let's live here in Tel-Aviv
Après nous le déluge
The fed don't understand the hungry
Tel-Aviv – c'est la vie!

A Jewish Israeli woman's song banned on Israeli radio for 'lowering morale', written in response to the Intifada; Nurit Galron, 1984

'May the Force be With You'

If allyu want to keep yu carnival,
Wid yu jump-up, yu fete, yu roti,
An a chance to meet up wid yu key spar
Yu macumere an ting,
Who yu ain see for years,
You must remember –
Any gathering of Black people in dis town,
Dus make dem nervous.
De only Blacks who ain criminals,
Is entertainers, is sportsmen, or is police.

So.

Next year, we go bring out a band.
An we go have a maas, to end all maas.
Two hundred tousand Black man, woman and chile
Dress in dark blue.
Yes, de maas we playing is 'Police'
An de theme of we band is
'Law an Order!'

So when dey turn on de telly,
To hear about how many Blacks riot for carnival,
All dey go see is
Two hundred tousand *police* going dung de road,

Singing, drinking rum,
Whining, dancing.
Dey ain go be able to tell,
Who is de real police,
An who is de maas police.

De press gon' go mad,
(Cos yu know how dey dus love take same fucking picture every year
Of police dancing up at carnival)
De Commissioner, Home Secretr'y an Prime Minister
Go declare how 'community policing'
Is a big success, an dey go be right,
(Because, of course, for dat day
De whole community go turn policeman!)

An, we Black people,
Go get to keep we carnival.

Marsha Prescod, 1985

'Tramp the Dirt Down'

I saw a newspaper picture from the political campaign
A woman was kissing a child, who was obviously in pain
She spills with compassion as that young child's face in her hands she
  grips
Can you imagine all that greed and avarice coming down on that
  child's lips

Well I hope I don't die too soon
I pray the Lord my soul to save
Oh I'll be a good boy, I'm trying so hard to behave
Because there's one thing I know, I'd like to live long enough to
  savour
That's when they finally put you in the ground
I'll stand on your grave and tramp the dirt down

When England was the whore of the world
Margaret was her madam
And the future looked as bright and as clear as the black tarmacadam

Well I hope that she sleeps well at night, isn't haunted by every tiny detail
'Cos when she held that lovely face in her hands all she thought of was betrayal

And now the cynical ones say that it all ends the same in the long run
Try telling that to the desperate father who just squeezed the life from his only son
And how it's only voices in your head and dreams you never dreamt
Try telling him the subtle difference between justice and contempt
Try telling me she isn't angry with this pitiful discontent
When they flaunt in your face as you line up for punishment
And then expect you to say 'Thank you', straighten up, look proud and pleased
Because you've only got the symptoms, you haven't got the whole disease
Just like a schoolboy, whose head's like a tin-can, filled up with dreams then poured down the drain
Try telling that to the boys on both sides, being blown to bits or beaten and maimed
Who takes all the glory and none of the shame
Well I hope you live long now, I pray the Lord your soul to keep
I think I'll be going before we fold our arms and start to weep
I never thought for a moment that human life could be so cheap
'Cos when they finally put you in the ground
They'll stand there laughing and tramp the dirt down

Elvis Costello, 1990

'Deng, where are you hiding?'

Deng, where are you hiding?
Have you really stepped down?
The state is in crisis by your will.
How can you dodge the blame?

We call to the earth: 'Deng where are you?'
The earth rings back: 'He's just moved on.
He's gone to Wuhan to mobilise the troops,
The Military Committee is full of killing ideas.'

We call to the mountains:
'Deng where are you?'
The hills and gullies ring back:
'He's just moved on.

He's having a banquet in
Emeishan,
The tables are loaded with mao-
tai, the floor with cigarette
butts,'

We call to the sea: 'Deng where
are you?'
The pounding waves reply: 'He's
just moved on.
He's in his seaside villa playing
bridge,
Blood pressure dangerously high
with excitement.'

We call to the forests: 'Deng
where are you?'
The forests reply: 'He's just
moved on.
He's teaching his son Pufang
how to arrange things,
How to get profit from foreign
loans.'

We call out to the whole of
China.
'Hey, Chairman Deng!
Second Empress Dowager
behind the curtain!
Your 'stupid' children wait for
you in jail,
No matter where you are
hiding.'

We return to the heart of the
motherland,
And cry out loud before
Tiananmen.
'Chairman – Deng!'
The great square replies: 'A little
quieter, please,
Don't disturb his inventive spirit.
He's here, working out where he
went wrong.'

'I should not have let myself be
persuaded.
In 1985 they cheered me to the
skies.
Then a comet appeared and
brought me bad luck.
A vicious dog appeared and took
advantage.

'Facing the masses I can only
weep helplessly.
Many years ago they shed blood
for me on Tiananmen.
Last year I plunged them in a
pool of gore.

'Brother Hu Yaobang, I beg
pardon.
You treated me honestly, I
snuffed out your breath.
Mao Zedong, I cheated you.
I forgot my promise never to
upset the Cultural Revolution.'

'Chairman Deng,' his friends
respond,
'Don't fear the world will spit on
you.
You still have bosom friends.
Come now, come now.
Let's carry on just as we please.'

'Ah,' he replies, 'the Spirit of
Doom!
Do not strike the bell of death.
Do not lop my limbs.
Save me! Save me!'

Shi Xiang, 1990

Two

WORDS MUST BE GIVEN THEIR TRUE MEANING

John Ball's Speech Before the Peasants' Revolt, 1381

'Ah, ye good people, the matters goeth not well to pass in England, nor shall do till everything be common, and that there be no villains nor gentlemen, but that we may be all united together [*tout-unis*], and that the lords be no greater masters than we be. What have we deserved, or why should we be kept thus in servage? We be all come from one father and one mother, Adam and Eve: whereby can they say or shew that they be greater lords than we be, saving by that they cause us to win and labour for that they dispend? They are clothed in velvet and camlet[1] furred with grise,[2] and we be vestured with poor cloth: they have their wines, spices and good bread, and we have the drawing out of the chaff and drink water: they dwell in fair houses, and we have the pain and travail, rain and wind in the fields; and by that that cometh of our labours they keep and maintain their estates: we be called their bondmen and without we do readily them service, we be beaten; and we have no sovereign to whom we may complain, nor that will hear us nor do us right. Let us go to the king, he is young, and shew him what servage we be in, and shew him how we will have it otherwise, or else we will provide us of some remedy; and if we go together, all manner of people that be now in any bondage will follow us to the intent to be made free; and when the king seeth us, we shall have some remedy, either by fairness or otherwise.'

Thus John Ball said on Sundays, when the people issued out of the churches in the villages; wherefore many of the mean people loved him, and such as intended to no goodness said how he said truth; and so they would murmur one with another in the fields and in the ways as they went together, affirming how John Ball said truth.

[1] A costly Eastern fabric
[2] A kind of grey fur

From the chronicles of Jean Froissart (*c.* 1337–*c.* 1410)

Society is a World Turned Upside Down

Society, as constituted, is truly a world turned upside down:

For the nation has accepted as a fundamental principle the rule that the poor should be generous to the rich, and that, consequently, those worst off should be deprived each day of a part of their necessities in order to augment the superfluity of the great proprietors . . .

For, in a word, in all kinds of occupations, the incompetent people are charged with directing the competent; with regard to morality, the most immoral are expected to train citizens in virtue; and with regard to administrative justice, the big crooks are chosen to punish the faults of the petty delinquents.

Claude-Henri de Rouvroy, Comte de Saint-Simon, 1819

The Political House that Jack Built

THESE ARE
THE PEOPLE
all tatter'd and torn,
Who curse the day
wherein they were born,
On account of Taxation
too great to be borne,
And pray for relief,
from night to morn;
Who, in vain, Petition
in every form,
Who, peaceably Meeting
to ask for Reform,
Were sabred by Yeomanry Cavalry,
who,
Were thank'd by THE MAN,
all shaven and shorn,
All cover'd with Orders –
and all forlorn;
THE DANDY OF SIXTY,
who bows with a grace,
And has *taste* in wigs, collars,
cuirasses, and lace;
Who, to tricksters, and fools,
leaves the State and its treasure,
And when Britain's in tears,
sails about at his pleasure;
Who spurn'd from his presence
the Friends of his youth,
And now has not one
who will tell him the truth;

Who took to his counsels, in evil hour,
The Friends to the Reasons of lawless Power,
That back the Public Informer, who
Would put down the *Thing*, that, in spite of new Acts,
And attempts to restrain it, by Soldiers or Tax,
Will *poison* the Vermin, that plunder the Wealth,
That lay in the House, that Jack built.

William Hone, from *The Political House that Jack Built*, 1819; Hone was tried for blasphemous libel and won a celebrated case.
The Man, the *Dandy of Sixty* was the Prince Regent, *The Thing* was the printing press, *The Public Informer* was Robert Clifford, Attorney-General.

A Chartist Speech

On Sunday morning, in company with these Chartist friends, I went and spoke in the open air at Fenton, and in the afternoon at Longton. In the evening I addressed an immense crowd at Hanley, standing on a chair in front of the Crown Inn: such ground being called the Crown Bank by the natives. I took for a text the sixth commandment: 'Thou shalt do no murder' – after we had sung Bramwich's hymn, 'Britannia's sons, though slaves ye be,' and I had offered up a short prayer.

I showed how kings, in all ages, had enslaved the people, and spilt their blood in wars of conquest, thus violating the precept, 'Thou shalt do no murder.'

I described how the conquerors of America had nearly exterminated the native races, and thus violated the precept, 'Thou shalt do no murder.'

I recounted how English and French and Spanish and German wars, in modern history, had swollen the list of the slaughtered and had violated the precept, 'Thou shalt do no murder.'

I described our own guilty Colonial rule, and still guiltier rule of Ireland; and asserted that British rulers had most awfully violated the precept, 'Thou shalt do no murder.'

I showed how the immense taxation we were forced to endure, to enable our rulers to maintain the long and ruinous war with France and Napoleon, had entailed indescribable suffering on millions, and that thus had been violated the precept, 'Thou shalt do no murder.'

I asserted that the imposition of the Bread Tax was a violation of the same precept; and that such was the enactment of the Game Laws; that such was the custom of primogeniture and keeping of land in the possession of the privileged classes; and that such was the enactment of the infamous new Poor Law.

The general murmur of applause now began to swell into loud cries; and these were mingled with execrations of the authors of the Poor Law. I went on.

Thomas Cooper, 1842

Discretion is the polite word for hypocrisy.

Christine Keeler

'What is a Peer?'

What is a peer? A useless thing;
A costly toy, to please a king;
  A bauble near a throne;
A lump of animated clay;
A gaudy pageant of a day;
  An incubus; a drone!

What is a peer? A nation's curse –
A pauper on the public purse;
  Corruption's own jackal:
A haughty, domineering blade;
A cuckold at a masquerade;
  A dandy at a ball.

Ye butterflies, whom kings create;
Ye caterpillars of the state;
  Know that your time is near!
This moral learn from nature's plan,
That in creation God made man;
  But never made a peer.

Anon., 1842

Man is a dupable animal. Quacks in medicine,
quacks in religion, and quacks in politics know this,
and act upon that knowledge.

Robert Southey

Paroxysms of Frantic Coercion

. . . your authorised system of medicine is nothing but a debased survival of witchcraft. Your schools are machines for forcing spurious learning on children in order that your universities may stamp them as educated men when they have finally lost all power to think for themselves. The tall silk hats and starched linen fronts which you force me to wear, and without which I cannot successfully practise as a physician, clergyman, schoolmaster, lawyer or merchant, are inconvenient, unsanitary, ugly, pompous and offensive. Your temples are devoted to a God in whom I do not believe; and . . . your popular forms of worship [are] . . . only redeemed from gross superstition by their obvious insincerity . . . Under color of protecting my person and property you forcibly take my money to support an army of soldiers and policemen for the execution of barbarous and detestable laws; for the waging of wars which I abhor, and for the subjection of my person to those legal rights of property which compel me to sell myself for a wage to a class the maintenance of which I hold to be the greatest evil of our time. Your tyranny makes my very individuality a hindrance to me: I am outdone and outbred by the mediocre, the docile, the time-serving. Evolution under such conditions means degeneracy . . .

. . . your slaves are beyond caring for your cries: they breed like rabbits; and their poverty breeds filth, ugliness, dishonesty, disease, obscenity, drunkenness, and murder. In the midst of the riches which their labor piles up for you, their misery rises up too and stifles you. You withdraw in disgust to the other end of the town from them; you appoint special carriages on your railways and special seats in your churches and theatres for them; you set your life apart from theirs by every class barrier you can devise; and yet they swarm about you still: your face gets stamped with your habitual loathing and suspicion of them: your ears get so filled with the language of the vilest of them that you break into it when you lose your self-control: they poison your life as remorselessly as you have sacrificed theirs heartlessly. You begin to believe intensely in the devil. Then comes the terror of their revolting; the drilling and arming of bodies of them to keep down the rest; the prison, the hospital, paroxysms of frantic coercion, followed by paroxysms of frantic charity. And in the meantime, the population continues to increase!

From a speech by George Bernard Shaw, *c.* 1889

If we feel the least degradation in being amorous,
or merry or hungry, or sleepy, we are so far
bad animals and miserable men.

William Morris

Dung-Eating Descendant of an Outhouse Maggot

JUDGE ROY BEAN: : You have been tried by twelve good men and true who are as high above you as heaven is of hell. Time will pass and seasons will come and go. Spring will come with its wavin' green grass and heaps of sweet-smellin' flowers on every hill. Then sultry Summer with her shimmerin' heat-waves and Fall with her yeller harvest moon and the hills a-growin' brown and golden under a sinkin' sun. And finally Winter with all the land mantled with snow. But you won't be here to see any of 'em; not by a damned sight because it's the order of this court that you be took to the nearest tree and hanged by the neck until you're dead, dead, dead, you olive-colored, chili-eatin', sheep-stealin' son of a bitch.

MEXICAN SHEEP THIEF: : I admit I'm a thief, but so eager was this court to add another to its already long list of slaughtered victims that you remind me more of a lot of buzzards hovering over a carcass than men supposed to dispense justice. You half-starved hyena, you've sat through this trial with devilish glee written all over your hellish face. You talk about Spring with its sweet smelling blossoms and Fall with its yellow moon, you damned offspring of a diseased whore. You say that I'm to be hanged and as I gaze into your bloated, whisky-soaked face, I'm not surprised at the pretended gravity and the evil sarcasm with which you send me to my death. You haven't even the grace to call down the mercy of God on my soul, you dirty-nosed, pot-bellied, dung-eating descendant of an outhouse maggot. I defy you to the end. You can hang me by the neck until I'm dead, dead, dead, and you can also kiss my ass until it's red, red, red, and God damn your foul old soul.

Court proceedings, Langtry, *c.* 1882; ex-jailbird Bean was appointed Justice of the Peace by the Southern Pacific railroad in 1879, and regularly acquitted killers of Chinese and Mexicans – 'There's no law makin' it illegal to shoot a damn chink or greaser.'

Les murs ont des oreilles. Vos oreilles ont des murs.

Graffito, Paris 1968

How the Miners are Robbed

A case of heartless robbery was exposed the other day when the Duke of Hamilton, a local coalmaster named Frederick Michael Thomas Andrew Sucker, and several others were charged with having conspired together and robbed an old miner named Dick M'Gonnagle. Great interest was manifested in the case, the Court being densely crowded. The Magistrate, in opening the proceedings, said that owing to the very grave nature of the charge, and its immense interest to the community, he had decided to adopt the French mode of procedure and would commence by asking the prisoners to submit themselves to examination.

The Coalmaster then entered the witness box to be examined by the Magistrate.

MAG: What is your name?
PRIS: Frederick Michael Thomas Andrew Sucker, sir.
MAG: You have a great many names.
PRIS: I protest, sir.
MAG: I did not ask you your occupation. I desire to know how you came to be possessed of so many names?
PRIS: I can't answer your question, sir.
MAG: Ah! That sounds suspicious. Now will you kindly tell us how much wealth you possess?
PRIS: (*proudly*) One million pounds, sir.

MAG: You must be an extremely able man. How did you come to have a million pounds?
PRIS: I made it, sir.
MAG: Ah! do you plead guilty to manufacturing coin?
PRIS: (*indignantly*) No, sir.
MAG: Then will you please tell us what you mean by saying you made it?
PRIS: I earned it in business, sir.
MAG: How long have you been in business?
PRIS: Twenty years, sir.
MAG: You must be a very capable worker to have earned such a huge sum in such a short time?
PRIS: (*indignantly*) I don't work, sir.
MAG: Ah! this is interesting. You don't work and yet you have told us that in twenty years you have earned one million pounds?
PRIS: I own a colliery, sir.
MAG: What is a colliery?
PRIS: A shaft sunk perhaps a hundred fathoms in the earth; also various buildings and machinery for the production of coal.
MAG: Did you sink the shaft?
PRIS: No, sir. I got men to do it.
MAG: Did you manufacture the machinery and erect the buildings?
PRIS: No, sir. I am not a workman. I got others to work.
MAG: This is an extraordinary case. You say other men erected the buildings, and manufactured the machinery, and sunk the shaft and yet you own the colliery? Have the workmen no share in it?
PRIS: No, sir. I am the sole owner.
MAG: I confess I can't understand. Do you mean to tell me that those men put a colliery in full working order, and then handed it over to you without retaining even a share of it for themselves?
PRIS: Certainly, sir.
MAG: They must have been very rich and generous, or very foolish! Were they rich men?
PRIS: Oh no, sir.
MAG: Had they many collieries?
PRIS: Oh, none at all, sir. They were merely workmen.
MAG: What do you mean by merely workmen?
PRIS: Merely people who work for others.
MAG: Surely they must be generous people. Don't they require collieries themselves?
PRIS: They do, sir.
MAG: And they own no collieries?
PRIS: No, sir; but I allow them to work in mine.

MAG: That is very kind of you, but of course not nearly so kind as their act in giving the colliery to you. Do you find you don't require the whole colliery yourself, that you can allow others also to use it?

PRIS: Oh, you don't understand sir. I don't work in my colliery. I allow the workmen to do so.

MAG: Oh, I see. After those men handed over the colliery to you, you found you had no use for it, and so returned it to save them erecting another?

PRIS: Oh no, no, sir. The colliery is still mine, but they work in it.

MAG: Really, this is very confusing. You own a pit which you did not sink, and plant which you did not manufacture nor erect. You do not work in this colliery because you do not want to work. Those who do want to work own no colliery, and yet they gave one to you. Did you beg of them to come and work in your colliery, as you had no use for it?

PRIS: Oh, not at all, sir. They begged me to allow them to work.

MAG: But why beg leave to use your colliery? Why not make one for themselves, as they had done for you?

PRIS: I beg pardon, sir, but they could only do that by electing their own men to the County Councils and Parliament, and getting those bodies to do it, and *that* would never do. That would be Socialism.

MAG: Seems to me it would be ordinary common sense.

From *How the Miners are Robbed* by John Wheatley, 1907

Q. What is the difference between capitalism and communism?
A. Capitalism is the exploitation of man by man.
Communism is the other way round.

Radio Armenia

Acts Alone

I also wish my friends to speak little or not at all about me, because idols are created when men are praised, and this is very bad for the future of the human race. Acts alone, no matter by whom committed, ought to be studied, praised, or blamed. Let them be praised in order that they may be imitated when they seem to contribute to the common weal; let them be censured when they are regarded as injurious to the general well-being, so that they may not to be repeated.

I desire that on no occasion, whether near or remote, nor for any reason whatsoever, shall demonstrations of a political or religious character be made before my remains, as I consider the time devoted to the dead would be better employed in improving the condition of the living, most of whom stand in great need of this.

> From the will of Francisco Ferrer, educator and radical executed after the Barcelona riots, 1909

L'anarchie c'est je.

Graffito, Paris, 1968

A New and Beautiful Life?

'Comrades, we are going to build a new and beautiful life,' thus spoke and wrote the Communists. 'We are going to destroy the world of violence and build a new socialist world filled with beauty.' Thus they sang to the people. Let us see what the reality is.

All the best houses, all the best apartments are requisitioned for the offices of Communist institutions. Thus only the bureaucrats find themselves living in a comfortable, agreeable and spacious manner. The number of habitable lodgings has diminished, and the workers have remained where they were before. They live crowded together in worse conditions than ever.

For the houses, not being kept in repair, are dilapidated. The heating is out of order. Broken windowpanes are not replaced. Roofs are full of holes which let the water in. Fences are falling down. Half the chimneys are broken. The toilets do not work and their contents flow all over the apartments, forcing citizens to relieve themselves in the yard or at a neighbour's house. The staircases are unlit and full of rubbish. The yards are piled with excrement, since the slit trenches, the privies, the drains and the sewers are neither cleaned nor emptied. The streets are filthy. The sidewalks are never repaired and they are uneven and slippery. It is dangerous to walk in the streets.

To obtain lodging, one must have influence at a housing bureau.

Without that nothing can be done; only the favourites have decent apartments.

As for food, it is even worse. Irresponsible and ignorant officials let tons of produce spoil. The potatoes which are distributed are always frozen. In spring and summer the meat is always rotten. At one time we would hardly feed pigs with what the citizens now get from the 'builders of the beautiful new life'. The 'honest Soviet fish', the herring, has saved the situation for a long time now, but even that is getting scarce. The Soviet shops are worse than the old factory shops of unhappy memory, where the bosses kept all kinds of junk and the worker-slaves could say nothing about it.

In order to destroy family life, our rulers have invented collective restaurants. What is the result? The food is still inedible. The produce is stolen in various ways before it even reaches the citizens, who get only the leavings. The nourishment of the children is a little better, but still very inadequate. Milk especially is lacking. The Communists have requisitioned all the dairy cows from the peasants for their own *sovkhoz* [state farms]. Moreover, half of these animals die before reaching their destinations, and the milk of the surviving cows goes first to the rulers and then to the functionaries. Only what is left after that goes to the children.

But the hardest things to obtain are clothing and shoes. One wears, or exchanges, second-hand suits. Hardly anything is distributed. For example, one of the unions is now distributing buttons – a button and a half per person. Is this not laughable? As for shoes, they are unprocurable.

The road to the Communist paradise is beautiful. But can one traverse it barefooted?

There are plenty of cracks through which everything necessary flows. The clientele of the so-called 'co-operatives' and the rulers possess everything. They have their own restaurants and special rations as well. They also have at their disposal the 'Goods Bureau', which distributes products according to the wishes of the commissars.

We have finally realised that this 'Commune' has sapped and completely demoralised productive work. All desire to work, all interest in work has disappeared. Shoemakers, tailors, plumbers, etc., have all quit and dispersed. They are serving as guards, messengers, etc. Such is the paradise which the Bolsheviks have tried to build.

In place of the old régime, a new régime of despotism, insolence, favouritism, theft and speculation has been established, a terrible régime in which one must hold out his hand to the authorities for every piece of bread, for every button, a régime in which one does not belong to himself, where one cannot dispose of his own labour, a régime of slavery and degradation.

Article produced by the Kronstadt Mutiny, 1921

From 'Vladimir Ilyich Lenin'

To the Russian
Communist Party
I dedicate this poem

The time has come.
I begin
the story of Lenin.
Not
because the grief
is on the wane,
but because
the shock of the first moment
has become
a clear-cut,
weighed and fathomed pain.
Time,
speed on,
spread Lenin's slogans in your whirl!
Not for us
to drown in tears,
whatever happens.
There's no one
more alive
than Lenin in the world,
our strength,
our wisdom,
surest of our weapons.
People
are boats,
although on land.
While life
is being roughed
all species
of trash
from the rocks and sand
stick
to the sides of our craft.
But then,
having broken
through the storm's mad froth,

one sits
in the sun
for a time
and cleans off
the tousled seaweed growth
and oozy
jellyfish slime.
I
go to Lenin
to clean off mine
to sail on
with the revolution.
I fear
these eulogies
line upon line
like a boy
fears falsehood and delusion.
They'll rig up an aura
round any head;
the very idea –
I abhor it,
that such a halo
poetry-bred
should hide
Lenin's real,
huge,
human forehead.
I'm anxious lest rituals,
mausoleums
and processions,
the honeyed incense
of homage and publicity
should
obscure
Lenin's essential
simplicity.
I shudder
as I would
for the apple of my eye
lest Lenin
be falsified
by tinsel beauty.

Vladimir Mayakovsky, 1924

[Untitled]

We exist, without sensing our country beneath us.
Ten steps away our words can't be heard.

But where there are enough of us for half a conversation
They always commemorate the Kremlin mountaineer.

His fat fingers slimy as worms,
His words dependable as weights of measure.

The cockroach moustaches chuckle,
His top-boots gleam.

And round him a riff-raff of scraggy-necked chiefs;
He plays with these half men, lackeys,

Who warble, or miaow, or whimper.
He alone prods and probes.

He forges decree after decree like horseshoes:
In the groin, brain, forehead, eye.

Whoever's being executed – there's raspberry compote
And the gigantic torso of the Georgian.

Osip Mandelstam, 1933; poem on Stalin that caused Mandelstam's persecution, imprisonment and eventual death

---

Whoever you vote for, the government will get in.

Graffito

Learning Stalinism

Managed literature and science permit the organization of festivities at which solemnity is mingled with the mirth of banquets, with ordered ovations, and with ridiculous things that are at once amusing and saddening. The surgeons assembled in congress swear eternal devotion to the Leader. The gynaecologists declare that they want to draw their inspiration for ever from his teachings. The writers, whom he has called the 'engineers of the soul', declaim litanies to him and adopt the canons of 'socialistic realism', which is actually neither realist nor socialist, since it rests on the suppression of all freedom of opinion and expression . . .

From *Destiny of a Revolution* by Victor Serge, 1937

Wrong Members in Control

England is a family with the wrong members in control. Almost entirely we are governed by the rich, and by people who step into positions of command by right of birth. Few if any of these people are consciously treacherous, some of them are not even fools, but as a class they are quite incapable of leading us to victory. They could not do it, even if their material interests did not constantly trip them up. As I pointed out earlier, they have been artificially stupefied. Quite apart from anything else, the rule of money sees to it that we shall be governed largely by the old – that is, by people utterly unable to grasp what age they are living in or what enemy they are fighting. Nothing was more desolating at the beginning of this war than the way in which the whole of the older generation conspired to pretend that it was the war of 1914–18 over again. All the old duds were back on the job, twenty years older, with the skull plainer in their faces. Ian Hay was cheering up the troops, Belloc was writing articles on strategy, Maurois doing broadcasts, Bairnsfather drawing cartoons. It was like a tea-party of ghosts. And that state of affairs has barely altered. The shock of disaster brought a few able men like Bevin to the front, but in general we are still commanded by people who managed to live through the years 1931–9 without ever discovering that Hitler was dangerous. A generation of the unteachable is hanging upon us like a necklace of corpses.

As soon as one considers any problem of this war – and it does not matter whether it is the widest aspect of strategy or the tiniest detail of home organization – one sees that the necessary moves cannot be made while the social structure of England remains what it is. Inevitably, because of their position and upbringing, the ruling class are fighting for their own privileges, which cannot possibly be reconciled with the public interest. It is a mistake to imagine that war aims, strategy, propaganda and industrial organization exist in watertight compartments. All are interconnected. Every strategic plan, every tactical method, even every weapon will bear the stamp of the social system that produced it. The British ruling class are fighting against Hitler, whom they have always regarded and whom some of them still regard as their protector against Bolshevism. That does not mean that they will deliberately sell out; but it does mean that at every decisive moment they are likely to falter, pull their punches, do the wrong thing.

Until the Churchill Government called some sort of halt to the process, they have done the wrong thing with an unerring instinct ever since 1931. They helped Franco to overthrow the Spanish Government, although anyone not an imbecile could have told them that a Fascist Spain would be hostile to England. They fed Italy with war materials all through the winter of 1939–40, although it was obvious to the whole world that the Italians were going to attack us in the spring. For the sake of a few hundred thousand dividend-drawers they are turning India from an ally into an enemy. Moreover, so long as the moneyed classes remain in control, we cannot develop any but a *defensive* strategy. Every victory means a change in the *status quo*. How can we drive the Italians out of Abyssinia without rousing echoes among the coloured peoples of our own Empire? How can we ever smash Hitler without the risk of bringing the German Socialists and Communists into power? The left-wingers who wail that 'this is a capitalist war' and that 'British Imperialism' is fighting for loot have got their heads screwed on backwards. The last thing the British moneyed class wish for is to acquire fresh territory. It would simply be an embarrassment. Their war aim (both unattainable and unmentionable) is simply to hang on to what they have got.

Internally, England is still the rich man's Paradise. All talk of 'equality of sacrifice' is nonsense. At the same time as factory-workers are asked to put up with longer hours, advertisements for 'Butler. One in family, eight in staff' are appearing in the press. The bombed-out populations of the East End go hungry and homeless while wealthier victims simply step into their cars and flee to comfortable country houses. The Home Guard swells to a million men in a few weeks, and is deliberately organized from above in such a way that only people with private incomes can hold positions of command. Even the rationing system is so arranged that it hits the poor all the time, while people with over £2,000 a year are practically unaffected by it. Everywhere privilege is squandering good will. In such circumstances even propaganda becomes almost impossible. As attempts to stir up patriotic feeling, the red posters issued by the Chamberlain Government at the beginning of the war broke all depth-records. Yet they could not have been much other than they were, for how could Chamberlain and his followers take the risk of rousing strong popular feeling *against Fascism*? Anyone who was genuinely hostile to Fascism must also be opposed to

Chamberlain himself and to all the others who had helped Hitler into power. So also with external propaganda. In all Lord Halifax's speeches there is not one concrete proposal for which a single inhabitant of Europe would risk the top joint of his little finger. For what war aim can Halifax, or anyone like him, conceivably have, except to put the clock back to 1933?

It is only by revolution that the native genius of the English people can be set free. Revolution does not mean red flags and street fighting, it means a fundamental shift of power. Whether it happens with or without bloodshed is largely an accident of time and place. Nor does it mean the dictatorship of a single class. The people in England who grasp what changes are needed and are capable of carrying them through are not confined to any one class, though it is true that very few people with over £2,000 a year are among them. What is wanted is a conscious open revolt by ordinary people against inefficiency, class privilege and the rule of the old. It is not primarily a question of change of government. British governments do, broadly speaking, represent the will of the people, and if we alter our structure from below we shall get the government we need. Ambassadors, generals, officials and colonial administrators who are senile or pro-Fascist are more dangerous than Cabinet ministers whose follies have to be committed in public. Right through our national life we have got to fight against privilege, against the notion that a half-witted public-schoolboy is better for command than an intelligent mechanic. Although there are gifted and honest *individuals* among them, we have got to break the grip of the moneyed class as a whole. England has got to assume its real shape. The England that is only just beneath the surface, in the factories and the newspaper offices, in the aeroplanes and the submarines, has got to take charge of its own destiny.

From *The Lion and the Unicorn* by George Orwell, 1941

The Deep South Observed

I spoke of this piece of work we were doing as 'curious.' I had better amplify this.

It seems to me curious, not to say obscene and thoroughly terrifying, that it could occur to an association of human beings drawn together through need and chance and for profit into a company, an organ of journalism, to pry intimately into the lives of an undefended and appallingly damaged group of human beings, an ignorant and helpless rural family, for the purpose of parading the nakedness, disadvantage and humiliation of these lives before another group of human beings, in the name of science, of 'honest journalism' (whatever that paradox may mean), of humanity, of social fearlessness, for money, and for a reputation for crusading and for unbias which, when skillfully enough qualified, is exchangeable at any bank for money (and in politics, for votes, job patronage, abelincolnism, etc.[1]); and that these people could be capable of meditating this prospect without the slightest doubt of their qualification to do an 'honest' piece of work, and with a conscience better than clear, and in the virtual certitude of almost unanimous public approval. It seems curious, further, that the assignment of this work should have fallen to persons having so extremely different a form of respect for the subject, and responsibility toward it, that from the first and inevitably they counted their employers, and that Government likewise to which one of them was bonded, among their most dangerous enemies, acted as spies, guardians, and cheats,[2] and trusted no judgment, however authoritative it claimed to be, save their own: which in many aspects of the task before them was untrained and uninformed. It seems further curious that realizing the extreme corruptness and difficulty of the circumstances, and the unlikelihood of achieving in any untainted form what they wished to achieve, they accepted the work in the first place. And it seems curious still further that, with all their suspicion of and contempt for every person and thing to do with the situation, save only for the tenants and for themselves, and their own intentions, and with all their realization of the seriousness and mystery of the subject, and of the human responsibility they undertook, they so little questioned or doubted their own qualifications for this work.

All of this, I repeat, seems to me curious, obscene, terrifying, and unfathomably mysterious.

[1] Money.
[2] Une chose permise ne peut pas être pure.
L'illégal me va.
Essai de Critique Indirecte.

From *Let Us Now Praise Famous Men* by James Agee, 1941

'The State that Can't be Found on any Map'

Back in the barracks, the man on duty told me that Sasha Weber had been looking for me and wanted to see me right away. It was still too early to get my dinner, so I went to visit Sasha in his barracks. He rushed up to me. 'How did it go?'

'As you see, I didn't get a death sentence.'

'That's the main thing; you'll be absolved in due time.'

'I'm sure I'll have to serve those ten years, every one of them.'

We sat down on the bunk. Sasha had saved my lunch for me. After I had eaten, he asked: 'Do you still think nothing will change after Germany loses the war?'

'As long as Stalin's in power, the camps and prisons are going to be full of millions of people, and we'll be among them.'

'I wonder why they're doing this. Why is it necessary to deprive so many people of their freedom? I can't help thinking that this is a childhood disease of the new society.'

'This is not a childhood disease; it's the society itself.'

'In a socialist state, this can only be a transitional phase,' he said.

'Sasha, do you still refuse to understand that after Lenin's death and after Stalin's accession to power everything socialist in this country has been stamped out? It began with the dissolution of the Society of Old Bolsheviks and ended with the deliberate wiping out of every trace of genuine socialism.'

'But why? It would be so much better to let people work in freedom. That's the way to make use of them, not grinding them down till they're wrecks.'

'A lot of people get to be wrecks here, but you can be sure they bring in a handsome profit.'

'Do you really think the whole idea is to get cheap labor into this wasteland?'

'It's certainly not the only reason. Another motive is social control, keeping the whole population in check by terror. Under ordinary conditions, terror has a damaging effect on the economy, but Stalin has come up with a totally new economic system. There has never been anything like it in the history of man.'

'You mean a kind of serfdom?'

'No, I don't. Serfdom was about as different from this system as the first steam engine from a locomotive. It was primitive and comparatively humane, while the Stalinist system represents barbarity in its most modern and technically perfect form.'

'Most people believe that forced labor is not profitable. You don't think so?'

'Whoever says that the labor of Soviet prisoners is not profitable does not understand the significance of these camps. They are the very basis of Soviet economy. Not only are the camps profitable; they're practically the only enterprises that bring in any gain. Most of the so-called free industrial plants are producing at a loss, and let's not even talk about the farms. Billions of rubles are spent every year in subsidies to industry and agriculture. Where does this money come from? It's very simple: it's the clean profit from the camps.'

'You can claim that, but how can you prove it?' Sasha said, shaking his head.

'Let's start with Nolrisk. To house and feed a hundred thousand prisoners, the Soviet government spends two hundred and forty rubles a month per prisoner: that includes the cost of administration, supervision, etc. The prisoners' food is supplied by the labor of prisoners in agricultural camps. The fish we get here is caught by prisoners in Murmansk. The coal we heat our barracks with was mined by prisoners. The railroad that transports coal and food to our camp was built and is operated by prisoners. The clothes we wear were sewn by prisoners. Even the material they're made of and the thread they're sewn with were produced in the women's camps of Potyma and Yaya. For the little bit of food we get, we produce thousands of tons of nickel, copper, hundreds of tons of cobalt, not to mention uranium. Most of these products are sold on the foreign market for millions of dollars. And still there are people who compare this system with serfdom and claim that Soviet prison labor is not profitable!'

From *7000 Days in Siberia* by Karlo Stajner, a Yugoslav socialist who was imprisoned in a Gulag

'The Solution'

After the uprising of the 17th June
The Secretary of the Writers' Union
Had leaflets distributed in the Stalinallee
Stating that the people
Had forfeited the confidence of the government
And could win it back only
By redoubled efforts. Would it not be easier
In that case for the government
To dissolve the people
And elect another?

Bertolt Brecht, *c.* 1952

Two Muscovites meet.
'How's life?'
'Fantastic.'
'Do you read the papers?'
'Of course! How else would I know?'

'Little boxes'

Little boxes on the hillside,
Little boxes made of ticky tacky,
Little boxes on the hillside,
Little boxes all the same;
There's a green one and a pink one
And a blue one and a yellow one
And they're all made out of ticky tacky
And they all look just the same.

And the people in the houses
All went to the university;
Where they were put in boxes
And they came out all the same,
And there's doctors and there's lawyers,
And business executives,
And they're all made out of ticky tacky
And they all look just the same.

And they all play on the golf course
And drink their martinis dry,
And they all have pretty children
And the children go to school,
And the children go to summer camp
And then to the university,
Where they are put in boxes
And they come out all the same.

And the boys go into business
And marry and raise a family
In boxes made of ticky tacky
And they all look just the same.

Song by Malvina Reynolds, 1962

Like all the other officers at Group Headquarters except Major Danby, Colonel Cathcart was infused with the democratic spirit: he believed that all men were created equal, and he therefore spurned all men outside Group Headquarters with equal fervor. Nevertheless, he believed in his men. As he told them frequently in the briefing room, he believed they were at least ten missions better than any other outfit and felt that any who did not share this confidence he had placed in them could get the hell out. The only way they could get the hell out, though, as Yossarian learned when he flew to visit ex-P.F.C. Wintergreen, was by flying the extra ten missions.

'I still don't get it,' Yossarian protested. 'Is Doc Daneeka right or isn't he?'

'How many did he say?'

'Forty.'

'Daneeka was telling the truth,' ex-P.F.C. Wintergreen admitted. 'Forty missions is all you have to fly as far as Twenty-seventh Air Force Headquarters is concerned.'

Yossarian was jubilant. 'Then I can go home, right? I've got forty-eight.'

'No, you can't go home,' ex-P.F.C. Wintergreen corrected him. 'Are you crazy or something?'

'Why not?'

'Catch-22.'

'Catch-22?' Yossarian was stunned. 'What the hell has Catch-22 got to do with it?'

'Catch-22,' Doc Daneeka answered patiently, when Hungry Joe had flown Yossarian back to Pianosa, 'says you've always got to do what your commanding officer tells you to.'

'But Twenty-seventh Air Force says I can go home with forty missions.'

'But they don't say you have to go home. And regulations do say you have to obey every order. That's the catch. Even if the colonel were disobeying a Twenty-seventh Air Force order by making you fly more missions, you'd still have to fly them, or you'd be guilty of disobeying an order of his. And then Twenty-seventh Air Force Headquarters would really jump on you.'

Yossarian slumped with disappointment. 'Then I really do have to fly the fifty missions, don't I?' he grieved.

'The fifty-five,' Doc Daneeka corrected him.

'What fifty-five?'

'The fifty-five missions the colonel now wants all of you to fly.'

Hungry Joe heaved a huge sigh of relief when he heard Doc Daneeka and broke into a grin. Yossarian grabbed Hungry Joe by the neck and made him fly them both right back to ex-P.F.C. Wintergreen.

'What would they do to me,' he asked in confidential tones, 'if I refused to fly them?'

'We'd probably shoot you,' ex-P.F.C. Wintergreen replied.

'We?' Yossarian cried in surprise. 'What do you mean, we? Since when are you on their side?'

'If you're going to be shot, whose side do you expect me to be on?' ex-P.F.C. Wintergreen retorted.

Yossarian winced. Colonel Cathcart had raised him again.

From *Catch-22* by Joseph Heller, 1962

Everybody is somebody's bore.

Edith Sitwell

Cured of a Long Bitter-sweet Madness

I was taught Bible history, the Gospel and the catechism without being given the means of believing: the result was a disorder which became my private order. There were some puckers and a considerable shift; levied on Catholicism, the sacred settled into Belles-Lettres and the writer appeared, an *ersatz* of the Christian I could not be: his only concern was salvation, the one aim of his stay here below was to earn for himself posthumous bliss through trials endured worthily. Death was reduced to a transitory rite and earthly immortality presented itself as a substitute for eternal life. To reassure myself that the human race would perpetuate me it was agreed in my mind that it would not come to an end. To extinguish myself in it was to be born and to become infinite, but if anyone had advanced the theory in front of me that some cataclysm might one day destroy the planet, even fifty thousand years hence, I would have been terrified. Today, in my disillusion, I still cannot envisage the cooling of the sun without fear: it matters little to me if my fellow-creatures forget me the day after my burial; while they live, I shall haunt them, elusive, nameless, present in each one like the thousands of millions of dead of whom I know nothing and yet whom I preserve from annihilation. But should humanity ever disappear, it will kill off its dead for good.

The myth was a very simple one and I swallowed it without difficulty. Protestant and Catholic, my twin denominational adherence preserved me from believing in the Saints, the Virgin and eventually in God while they were still called by their names. But a vast collective power had penetrated me; lodged in my heart, it was keeping watch, it was the Faith of others. It is enough to debaptize and modify superficially its normal object: faith recognized it beneath the disguises which deceived me, threw itself on it and enclosed it in its tendrils. I thought I was giving myself to Literature when I was, in fact, taking holy orders. In me the certainty of the humblest believer became the proud evidence of my predestination. Why not predestined? Is not every Christian one of the elect? I grew up, a rank weed, on the compost-heap of catholicity; my roots sucked up its juices, and from them I made my sap. This was the cause of that lucid blindness from which I suffered for thirty years. One morning, in 1917, at La Rochelle, I was waiting for some companions who were supposed to accompany me to the *lycée*; they were late. Soon I could think of nothing more to distract myself, and I decided to think about the Almighty. He at once tumbled down into the blue sky and vanished without explanation: He does not exist, I said to myself, in polite astonishment, and I thought the matter was settled.

From *Words* by Jean-Paul Sartre, 1964

Punctuality, regularity, discipline, industry, thoroughness, are a set of 'slave' virtues.

G. D. H. Cole

'Emperor'

Once upon a time there was an Emperor. He had yellow eyes and a predatory jaw. He lived in a palace full of statuary and policemen. Alone. At night he would wake up and scream. Nobody loved him. Most of all he liked hunting game and terror. But he posed for photographs with children and flowers. When he died, nobody dared to remove his portraits. Take a look, perhaps still you have his mask at home.

Zbigniew Herbert, Poland, *c.* 1965

GROSS: As I've just discovered, any staff member who has recently received a memorandum in Ptydepe can only be granted a translation of a Ptydepe text after his memorandum has been translated. But what happens if the Ptydepe text which he wishes translated is precisely that memorandum? It can't be done, because it hasn't yet been translated officially. In other words, the only way to learn what is in one's memo, is to know it already. An extraordinary paradox, when you come to think of it. Ladies and gentlemen, do you come to think of it? I ask you, what must an employee of our organization – whoever he may be – do in order to escape this vicious, vicious circle?

(For a second there is dead silence.)

BALLAS: He must learn Ptydepe, Mr Gross. (*To the others.*) You may sit down.

(They all sit down at once. MARIA, *still hiding the slip behind her, runs fearfully to her desk.)*

GROSS (*faintly*): Are you here?

BALLAS: Yes, we are.

GROSS: Have you been here long?

BALLAS: Not long.

GROSS: I didn't hear you come.

BALLAS: We entered quietly.

GROSS: Excuse me, I –

BALLAS: There are things, Mr Gross, that cannot be excused. And when, at the very time in which the whole organization is conducting a courageous struggle for the introduction and establishment of Ptydepe, an official, referring to the activities of our employees, speaks with such malicious innuendo and mean irony about – I quote – 'a vicious, vicious circle', then it cannot be excused at all.

GROSS: I'm sorry, Mr Ballas, but the circumstance I've allowed myself to point out is simply a fact.

BALLAS: What of it? We won't be bullied by facts!

(Long pause.)

GROSS (*in a quiet, broken voice*): I plead guilty. I acknowledge the entire extent of my guilt, while fully realizing the consequences resulting from it. Furthermore, I wish to enlarge my confession by the following self-indictment. I issued an illegal order which led to the fraudulent authentication of my own, personal copy-book. By this action I abused my authority. I did this in order to avert attention from the fact that I'd appropriated a bank endorsement stamp improperly for my private use. I request myself the most severe punishment.

BALLAS: I think that under these circumstances it is no longer possible for him to remain in our organization. What do you say, Mr P?

(PILLAR *shakes his head.*)

BALLAS: Certainly not. Come to my office tomorrow morning. We'll settle the formalities connected with your dismissal. (*Calls.*) George, come out of there! You'll be my deputy. (*To the others.*) You may leave now. Mr P., let's go.

From *The Memorandum* by Vaclav Havel, 1966; Ptydepe is a new language that all bureaucrats must learn and use

'Footnotes to the Book of the Setback'

1

Friends,
The ancient word is dead.
The ancient books are dead.
Our speech with holes like worn-out shoes is dead.
Dead is the mind that led to defeat.

2

Our poems have gone sour.
Women's hair, nights, curtains and sofas
Have gone sour.
Everything has gone sour.

3

My grieved country,
In a flash
You changed me from a poet who wrote love poems
To a poet who writes with a knife.

4

What we feel is beyond words:
We should be ashamed of our poems.

5

Stirred
By Oriental bombast,
By Antaric* swaggering that never killed a fly,
By the fiddle and the drum,
We went to war
And lost.

6

Our shouting is louder than our actions,
Our swords are taller than us,
This is our tragedy.

7

In short
We wear the cape of civilization
But our souls live in the stone age.

8

You don't win a war
With a reed and a flute.

9

Our impatience
Cost us fifty thousand new tents.

10

Don't curse heaven
If it abandons you,
Don't curse circumstances.
God gives victory to whom He wishes.
God is not a blacksmith to beat swords.

11

It's painful to listen to the news in the morning.
It's painful to listen to the barking of dogs.

12

Our enemies did not cross our borders
They crept through our weaknesses like ants.

**Antaric:* Antar (525–615), a pre-Islamic poet and hero of a popular epic bearing his name, is the symbol of the unbeaten knight.

13

Five thousand years
Growing beards
In our caves.
Our currency is unknown,
Our eyes are a haven for flies.
Friends,
Smash the doors,
Wash your brains,
Wash your clothes.
Friends,
Read a book,
Write a book,
Grow words, pomegranates and grapes,
Sail to the country of fog and snow.
Nobody knows you exist in caves.
People take you for a breed of mongrels.

14

We are a thick-skinned people
With empty souls.
We spend our days practising witchcraft,
Playing chess and sleeping.
Are we the 'Nation by which God blessed mankind'?

15

Our desert oil could have become
Daggers of flame and fire.
We're a disgrace to our noble ancestors:
We let our oil flow through the toes of whores.

16

We run wildly through the streets
Dragging people with ropes,
Smashing windows and locks.
We praise like frogs,
Swear like frogs,
Turn midgets into heroes,
And heroes into scum:
We never stop and think.
In mosques
We crouch idly,

Write poems,
Proverbs
And beg God for victory
Over our enemy.

17

If I knew I'd come to no harm.
And could see the Sultan,
I'd tell him:
'Sultan,
Your wild dogs have torn my clothes
Your spies hound me
Their eyes hound me
Their noses hound me
Their feet hound me
They hound me like Fate
Interrogate my wife
And take down the names of my friends.
Sultan,
When I came close to your walls
And talked about my pains,
Your soldiers beat me with their boots,
Forced me to eat my shoes.
Sultan,
You lost two wars.
Sultan,
Half of our people are without tongues,
What's the use of a people without tongues?
Half of our people
Are trapped like ants and rats
Between walls.'
If I knew I'd come to no harm
I'd tell him:
'You lost two wars
You lost touch with children.'

18

If we hadn't buried our unity
If we hadn't ripped its young body with bayonets
If it had stayed in our eyes
The dogs wouldn't have savaged our flesh.

19

We want an angry generation
To plough the sky
To blow up history
To blow up our thoughts.
We want a new generation
That does not forgive mistakes
That does not bend.
We want a generation
Of giants.

20

Arab children,
Corn ears of the futures,
You will break our chains.
Kill the opium in our heads,
Kill the illusions.
Arab children,
Don't read about our windowless generation,
We are a hopeless case.
We are as worthless as water-melon rind.
Don't read about us,
Don't ape us,
Don't accept us,
Don't accept our ideas,
We are a nation of crooks and jugglers.
Arab children,
Spring rain,
Corn ears of the future,
You are the generation
That will overcome defeat.

Written after the Six Day War and banned throughout the Middle East;
Nizar Qabbani, 1967

Pigasus

Another case in point is the Pig. Introduced fairly early in the game by Hugh Romney, spiritual leader of the Hogfarm, a commune outside Los Angeles, the Pig gravitated to the center of the myth. It took a long time, probably because of Hugh's vacillation about coming, and the fact that he was bringing the Pig probably held the myth back. During the week before the thing happened we noticed the media picking up on the Pig; with the cold-bloodedness of Madison Avenue we rammed in the Pigshit. It took only four days. When I went out to get the Pig on some American farm in Northern Illinois, the Pig had already become famous.

This particular pig was finally rejected by the myth – with a good deal of help from Jerry Rubin and Stu Albert. The meeting at which this decision was made was quite heated and actually our only 'meeting' in Chicago. They wanted a meaner pig. I thought it didn't matter, sort of liked the pig we had, was worried about the technical problems of managing a large pig, and had doubts that Jerry, Stu, and Phil Ochs could find another pig in time. They were not the resource people, who were all in my gang by that time. Jerry and I had a huge fight and didn't speak to each other the rest of the time. Which upset everybody except probably Jerry and me, since we were both so determined to make our Chicago in our own style. We would not let a personal fight upset anything. Besides, we were both so dedicated that I, at least, realized that Jerry would cry at my funeral and make the right speech and that I would do the same at his. But I deliberately told my police tail and everyone else except the reporters about the fight we had. I wanted to destroy a charge of conspiracy and thought this was the best way. It fitted my pattern of Not Getting Caught. Even though we fought, we were all together.

The first blood I saw in Chicago was the blood of Stu Albert, Jerry's closest friend. It happened in the first Sunday afternoon police riot in Lincoln Park. I embraced Stu, crying and swearing – sharing his blood. I went up to the cops and shook my fist. I made a haranguing speech, standing between rows of pig cops and scared spectators of the music festival, which of course by now was over. That kind of unity that Stu and I have, even though he is a Marxist-Leninist and I am a fuck-off, is impossible to explain. We are united in our determination to smash this system by using any means at our disposal and build a new world. In any event it didn't matter. Jerry's big Pig hit the Civic Center and Mrs Pig was let loose in the park hours later, screaming that her thirty sons would avenge her husband's arrest. I dropped the hint that we were considering running a lion. In the end thousands of pigs were used, real pigs, pig buttons, nice pigs like Mr and Mrs Pig (see wonderful photo in Chicago *Daily News* entitled 'Mr & Mrs Pig Re-United in the Pokey') and bad pigs like the cops, Daley, Humphrey and the politicians. It was shades of Animal Farm and you couldn't tell the pigs from the farmers or the farmers from the pigs. On the last day, I knew we had won when I saw Humphrey and Daley on TV and in photos. Everyone could see they were coming up Pig as all hell.

From *Revolution For The Hell Of It* by Abbie Hoffmann, 1968;
the Yippies ran a pig as their Presidential candidate

A politician is a fellow who will lay down your life
for his country.

Texas Guinan, nightclub hostess

The Vandals' Committee of Public Safety

In the struggle against alienation, words must be given their true meaning and must cover their original force:

so don't say:	*say instead:*
society	racket
professor	COPS
psychologist	"
poet	"
sociologist	"
militants (of all kinds)	"
conscientious objector	"
trade unionist	"
priest	"
family	"
(to mention just a few)	
information	deformation (on the scale of the world-wide racket and its mystifications)
work	forced labour
art	how much does it cost?
dialogue	masturbation
culture	shit gargled over a long period by pedantic cretins (see: professor)
my sister	my love
Professor, sir	crève, salope!*
good evening, papa	crève, salope!
excuse me, officer	crève, salope!
thank you, doctor	crève, salope!
legality	'booby-trap'
civilization	sterilization
urbanism	police control

*fuck off, bastard

villages, 1, 2, 3, 4	strategic hamlets
structuralism	the last chance for neo-capitalism, the outstanding failure of which is covered up by *official* lies inexpertly woven over the most flagrant contradictions

Students, you are all impotent cunts (that much we already know) and you will stay so until you have:

– beaten up your teachers
– buggered all your priests
– set fire to the faculty

NO, Nicholas, the Commune is not dead.

THE VANDALS' COMMITTEE OF PUBLIC SAFETY

Anon., Bordeaux, 1968

Alexander Woollcott, a leader of the Algonquin 'Round Table' (which prided itself on its sophistication and witty conversation) had invited Tallulah to attend one of their luncheons. After taking it all in for a few moments she turned to him and said: 'Mr Woollcott, there is less here than meets the eye.'

Tallulah Bankhead

'How to Blame the Victim'

Twenty years ago, Zero Mostel used to do a sketch in which he impersonated a Dixiecrat Senator conducting an investigation of the origins of World War II. At the climax of the sketch, the Senator boomed out, in an excruciating mixture of triumph and suspicion, 'What was Pearl Harbor *doing* in the Pacific?' This is an extreme example of Blaming the Victim.

Twenty years ago, we could laugh at Zero Mostel's caricature. In recent years, however, the same process has been going on every day in the arena of social problems, public health, anti-poverty programs, and social welfare. A philosopher might analyze this process and prove that, technically, it is comic. But it is hardly ever funny.

Consider some victims. One is the miseducated child in the slum school. He is blamed for his own miseducation. He is said to contain within himself the causes of his inability to read and write well. The shorthand phrase is 'cultural deprivation,' which, to those in the know, conveys what they allege to be inside information: that the poor child carries a scanty pack of intellectual baggage as he enters school. He doesn't know about books and magazines and newspapers, they say. (No books in the home: the mother fails to subscribe to *Reader's Digest*.) They say that if he talks at all – an unlikely event since slum parents don't talk to their children – he certainly doesn't talk correctly. (Lower-class dialect spoken here, or even – God forbid! – Southern Negro. *Ici on parle nigra*.) If you can manage to get him to sit in a chair, they say, he squirms and looks out the window. (Impulsive-ridden, these kids, motoric rather than verbal.) In a word he is 'disadvantaged' and 'socially deprived,' they say, and this, of course, accounts for his failure (*his* failure, they say) to learn much in school.

Note the similarity to the logic of Zero Mostel's Dixiecrat Senator. What is wrong with the victim? In pursuing this logic, no one remembers to ask questions about the collapsing buildings and torn textbooks; the frightened, insensitive teachers; the six additional desks in the room; the blustering, frightened principals; the relentless segregation; the callous administrator; the irrelevant curriculum; the bigoted or cowardly members of the school board; the insulting history book; the stingy taxpayers; the fairy-tale readers; or the self-serving faculty of the local teachers' college. We are encouraged to confine our attention to the child and to dwell on all his alleged defects. Cultural deprivation becomes an omnibus explanation for the educational disaster area known as the inner-city school. This is Blaming the Victim.

From *Blaming the Victim* by William Ryan, 1971

'A Question of Definition'

Is a democracy
in which one may not say
that it is not
a real democracy
really
a real democracy?

Erich Fried, *c.* 1975

'Oz' on Trial

As for the general public, which of them are unaware of cheerful obscenities, and how many think these harmful? In this holiday season, our resorts are garlanded with festoons of 'comic cards' whose obscenity is removed only in degree from that of *Oz* 28. Millions must have heard, and enjoyed, obscene variety performances. Whose ears are deaf to saloon bar stories, or barrack-room tales and songs? And who, that hears and sees all these things, would consider himself depraved thereby? It is surprising (by which I of course mean it is not) that no prosecution witness and, in particular, no juvenile, was called to declare himself corrupted by *Oz* 28. . . .

What may the consequences of the trial be – apart from those to the defendants? In the short term, an encouragement to harassing of minority expression, to sterile public busybodies, and even to additional prudence among 'respectable' publishers in all media. For the prosecution is one manifestation among many of the new morality of the 'silent majority' – whose chief characteristic, both here and in the United States, is its vociferous clamour to deny.

In the longer term, I would guess the result will be the opposite to that intended. By younger generations the trial will be seen as yet another proof of their elders' mistrust and dislike of them, which they will increasingly reciprocate. Nor do I believe many schoolkids will alter their life-styles because of this trial – rather the contrary. Nor yet do I think that these legal fingers stuck in a shaky dyke to withhold the flood of what the old call 'permissiveness', and the young call living, will hold back the rising waters. . . .

Though the prosecution pored, like scholars studying a codex, over every line and image of *Oz* 28, there's one picture I didn't hear referred to. It is, as it happens, the largest in the magazine, covering two pages just inside the cover. It's a photograph of the schoolkids editorial team, surrounding headmaster Neville in a garden. Mr Leary taught us, in the trial, that you can read much into images, and so let's try with this one. These twenty young men and women look to me bright, healthy, handsome and irreverent; and if that's what corruption and depravity do to them, I hope a lot more get hooked.

From 'Trial of a Trial' by Colin MacInnes, 1971

To have printed liberties, and not to have liberties in truth and realities, is but to mock the kingdom.

John Pym

Awful Australia

You big ugly. You too empty. You desert with your nothing nothing nothing. You scorched suntanned. Old too quickly. Acres of suburbs watching the telly. You bore me. Freckle silly children. You nothing much. With your big sea. Beach beach beach. I've seen enough already. You dumb dirty city with bar stools. You're ugly. You silly shoppingtown. You copy. You too far everywhere. You laugh at me. When I came this woman gave me a box of biscuits. You try to be friendly but you're not very friendly. You never ask me to your house. You insult me. You don't know how to be with me. Road road tree tree. I came from crowded and many. I came from rich. You have nothing to offer. You're poor and spread thin. You big. So what. I'm small. It's what's in. You silent on Sunday. Nobody on your streets. You dead at night. You go to sleep too early. You don't excite me. You scare me with your hopeless. Asleep when you walk. Too hot to think. You big awful. You don't match me. You burnt out. You too big sky. You make me a dot in the nowhere. You laugh with your big healthy. You want everyone to be the same. You're dumb. You do like anybody else. You engaged Doreen. You big cow. You average average. Cold day at school playing around at lunchtime. Running around for nothing. You never accept me. For your own. You always ask me where I'm from. You always ask me. You tell me I look strange. Different. You don't adopt me. You laugh at the way I speak. You think you're better than me. You don't like me. You don't have any interest in another country. Idiot centre of your own self. You think the rest of the world walks around without shoes or electric light. You don't go anywhere. You stay at home. You like one another. You go crazy on Saturday night. You get drunk. You don't like me and you don't like women. You put your arm around men in bars. You're rough. I can't speak to you. You burly burly. You're just silly to me. You big man. Poor with all your money. You ugly furniture. You ugly house. Relaxed in your summer stupor. All year. Never fully awake. Dull at school. Wait for other people to tell you what to do. Follow the leader. Can't imagine. Work horse. Thick legs. You go to work in the morning. You shiver on a tram.

Anna Walwicz, *c.* 1985

1938 and 1988

1938

'First they came for the Jews
And I did not speak out –
Because I was not a Jew.

Then they came for the communists
And I did not speak out –
Because I was not a communist.

Then they came for the trade unionists
And I did not speak out –
Because I was not a trade unionist.

Then they came for me –
And there was no one left
To speak out for me.'

Pastor Niemöller

1988

SPEAK OUT NOW FOR LESBIANS AND GAYS

STOP CLAUSE 28

Clause 28 of the Local Government Bill
is an attack on *everyone's* freedom

Leaflet, 1988

Life

You start as somebody's sperms
end, being eaten by worms.
And the part in between
is, as you've seen
full of diseases and germs.

Anon., 1990

Three

FIE ON THE FALSEHOODE OF MEN

Lilith

God formed Lilith the first woman just as He had formed Adam except that he used filth and impure sediment instead of dust or earth. Adam and Lilith never found peace together. She disagreed with him in many matters, and refused to lie beneath him in sexual intercourse, basing her claim for equality on the fact that each had been created from earth. When Lilith saw that Adam would overpower her, she uttered the ineffable name of God and flew up into the air of the world. Eventually, she dwelt in a cave in the desert on the shores of the Red Sea. There she engaged in unbridled promiscuity, consorted with lascivious demons, and gave birth to hundreds of *Lilim* or demonic babies, daily . . .

It is said that soon after Lilith left Adam he stood in prayer before his creator and said: 'God of the World, the woman that you gave me has run away from me.' Immediately God, the Holy One, dispatched the three angels, Sanvai, Sansanvai, and Semangelof to bring her back. They caught up with her in the desert near the Red Sea. 'Return to Adam without delay,' the angels said, 'or we will drown you!' Lilith asked: 'How can I return to Adam and be his woman, after my stay beside the Red Sea?' 'It would be death to refuse!'; they answered. 'How can I die,' Lilith asked again, 'when God has ordered me to take charge of all newborn children: boys up to the eighth day of life, that of circumcision; girls up to the twentieth day? Nevertheless,' she said, "I swear to you in the name of God, El, who is living and exists, that if ever I see your three names on likenesses displayed in an amulet above a newborn child, I promise to spare it.' To this day they agreed; however, God punished Lilith by making one hundred of her demon children perish daily, and if Lilith could not destroy a human infant, because of the angelic amulet, she would spitefully turn against her own.

From the *Alpha Bet Ben Sira*, ninth century

The trouble with some women is they get all excited
about nothing – and then marry him.

Cher

'Fie on the Falsehoode of Men'

TO ALL WOMEN IN GENERALL AND GENTLE
READER WHATSOEVER

Fie on the falsehoode of men,
Whose minds goe oft a madding
And whose tongues can not so soone bee wagging
But straight they fal a railing.
Was there ever any so abused,
So slaundered, so railed upon,
Or so wickedly handeled
Undeservedly, as are we women?

Jane Anger, 1589

Dallyance with an Indian

Mary, the wyfe of Robert Mandame, of Duxbarrow, for useing dallyance divers tymes with Tinsin, an Indian, and after committing the act of uncleanesse with him, as by his owne confession by severall interpretors is made apparent, the Bench doth therefore censure the said Mary to be whip through the townes streets, and to wear a badge upon her left sleeve during her aboad in this government; and if shee shalbe found without it abroad, then to be burned in the face with a hott iron; and the said Tinsin, the Indian, to be well whipt with a halter about his neck at the post, because it arose through the allurement & enticement of the said Mary, that hee was drawne thereunto.

From court proceedings at Plymouth, New England, 1639

Shall we Sit Still?

[Women] appeare so despicable in your eyes as to be thought unworthy to petition or represent our grievances . . . Can you imagine us to be so sottish or stupid, as not to perceive, or not to be sensible when daily those strong defences of our Peace and Welfare are broken down and trod underfoot by force or arbitrary power? Would you have us keep at home in our houses while men . . . are fetched out of their beds and forced from their houses by souldiers, to the affrighting and undoing of themselves, and their wives, children and families . . . Shall we sit still and keep at home.

From a petition in favour of the release of Lilburne, the Leveller, 1647

'Ah, Rot it – 'tis a Women's Comedy'

MRS GWIN.

I here and there o'erheard a Coxcomb cry,
'Ah, Rot it – 'tis a Women's Comedy,
One, who because she lately chanc'd to please us.
With her damn'd Stuff, will never cease to teeze us.'
What has poor Woman done, that she must be
Debar'd from Sense, and sacred Poetry?
Why in this Age has Heaven allow'd you more,
And Women less of Wit than heretofore?
We once were fam'd in story, and could write
Equal to Men; cou'd govern, nay, cou'd fight.
We still have passive Valour, and can show,
Wou'd Custom give us leave, the active too,
Since we no Provocations want from you.
For who but we cou'd your dull Fopperies bear,
Your saucy Love, and your brisk Nonsense hear;
Indure your worse than womanish Affectation,
Which renders you the Nusance of the Nation;
Scorn'd even by all the Misses of the Town,
A Jest to Vizard Mask, the *Pit-Buffoon*;
A Glass by which the admiring Country Fool
May learn to dress himself *en Ridicule*:
In Leudness, Foppery, Nonsense, Noise and Show.
And yet to these fine things we must submit
Our Reason, Arms, our Laurels, and our Wit.
Because we do not laugh at you, when leud,
And scorn and cudgel ye when ye are rude.
That we have nobler Souls than you, we prove,
By how much more we're sensible of Love;
Quickest in finding all the subtlest ways
To make your Joys, why not to make you Plays?
We best can find your foibles, know our own,
And Jilts and Cuckolds now best please the Town;
Your way of Writing's out of fashion grown.

Method and Rule – you only understand;
Pursue that way of Fooling and be damn'd.
Your learned Cant of Action, Time and Place,
Must all give way to the unlabour'd Farce.
To all the Men of Wit we will subscribe –
But for your half Wits, ye unthinking Tribe
We'll let you see, whate'er besides we do,
How artfully we copy some of you –
And if you're drawn to th' Life pray tell me then,
Why Women should not write as well as Men.

Epilogue to the play *Sir Patient Fancy* by Aphra Behn, 1678

Woman's Place

'Tis hard we should be by the men despised,
Yet kept from knowing what would make us prized;
Debarred from knowledge, banished from the schools,
And with the utmost industry bred fools;
Laughed out of reason, jested out of sense,
And nothing left but native innocence;
Then told we are incapable of wit,
And only for the meanest drudgeries fit;
Made slaves to serve their luxury and pride,
And with innumerable hardships tried,
Till pitying heaven release us from our pain,
Kind heaven, to whom alone we dare complain.
Th' ill-natured world will no compassion show:
Such as are wretched it would still have so.
It gratifies its envy and its spite:
The most in others' miseries take delight.
While we are present, they some pity spare,
And feast us on a thin repast of air;
Look grave and sigh, when we our wrongs relate,
And in a compliment accuse our fate;
Blame those to whom we our misfortunes owe,
And all the signs of real friendship show,
But when we're absent, we their sport are made,
They fan the flame, and our oppressors aid;
Join with the stronger, the victorious side,
And all our sufferings, all our griefs deride.

Those generous few whom kinder thoughts inspire,
And who the happiness of all desire,
Who wish we were from barbarous usage free,
Exempt from toils and shameful slavery,
Yet let us, unreproved, mis-spend our hours,
And to mean purposes employ our nobler powers.
They think, if we our thoughts can but express,
And know but how to work, to dance and dress,
It is enough, as much as we should mind,
As if we were for nothing else designed,
But made, like puppets, to divert mankind.
O that my sex would all such toys despise,
And only study to be good and wise;
Inspect themselves, and every blemish find,
Search all the close recesses of the mind,
And leave no vice, no ruling passion there,
Nothing to raise a blush, or cause a fear;
Their memories with solid notions fill,
And let their reason dictate to their will;
Instead of novels, histories peruse,
And for their guides the wiser ancients choose;
Through all the labyrinths of learning go,
And grow more humble, as they more do know.
By doing this they will respect procure,
Silence the men, and lasting fame secure;
And to themselves the best companions prove,
And neither fear their malice, nor desire their love.

From *The Ladies' Defence* by Mary, Lady Chudleigh, 1701;
provoked by a savagely anti-feminist wedding sermon
by the Rev. John Sprint

Down with Marriage

'Down with marriage! It's out of date;
It exhausts the stock and cripples the state.
The priest has failed with whip and blinker,
Now give a chance to Tom the Tinker,
And mix and mash in Nature's can
The tinker and the gentleman!
Let lovers in every lane extended

Struggle and strain as God intended
And locked in frenzy bring to birth
The morning glory of the earth;
The starry litter, girl and boy
Who'll see the world once more with joy.
Clouds will break and skies will brighten,
Mountains bloom and spirits lighten,
And men and women praise your might,
You who restore the old delight.'

From *The Midnight Court* by Bryan Merryman, 1780

Deplorable!

BRID'OISON: And if we looked at it carefully enough, no one would marry anybody.

BARTHOLO: Faults so notorious. A deplorable youth –

MARCELINE [*warming to it by degrees*]: Ay! Deplorable! More so than you think! I won't attempt to deny my faults – they have been fully exposed today! But it's hard to have to expiate them after thirty years of decent living. I was by nature good and so remained as long as I was allowed to do so, but just at the age when we are beset by illusions, inexperience, and necessity, when seducers besiege us and want stabs in the back, what can a young girl do against the serried ranks of her enemies? The very man who judges us so severely now has probably compassed the ruin of a dozen such unfortunates himself!

FIGARO: Those who are most blameworthy are the least generous themselves. That's always the way!

MARCELINE: You men, lost to all sense of obligation, who stigmatize with your contempt the playthings of your passions – your unfortunate victims! It's you who ought to be punished for the errors of our youth – you and your magistrates so vain of their right to judge us, you who by your culpable negligence allow us to be deprived of all honest means of existence. What is there for these unhappy girls to do? They had a natural right to make all feminine apparel and yet they let thousands of men be trained to it.

FIGARO [*furiously*]: They even set soldiers to embroidery!

MARCELINE [*carried away by her own eloquence*]: Even in the more exalted walks of life you accord us women no more than a derisory consideration. In a state of servitude behind the alluring pretences of respect, treated as children where our possessions are concerned we are punished as responsible adults where our faults are in question! Ah! Whatever way one looks at it your conduct towards us must provoke horror or compassion!

FIGARO: She's right!

THE COUNT [*aside*]: All too much so.

BRID'OISON: My God! How right she is!

MARCELINE: But what if an unjust man denies us justice, my son? Think no more about whence you came but whither you are bound. That is all that matters to any of us. Within a few months your fiancée will be her own mistress: she'll accept you: that I'll answer for. Live, then, henceforward in company of a loving wife and mother who will be rivals only in affection for you. Be indulgent towards them and rejoice in your happiness, my son; be gay, free, open-hearted with all the world: your mother will seek no other happiness.

FIGARO: You speak wonderfully persuasively, Mother, but I hold to my own opinion. What fools we are indeed! Here the world's been turning for thousands and thousands of years, and in face of that ocean of time, from which I've chanced to snatch some miserable thirty years or so that will never come again, I'm tormenting myself over the question of whom I owe them to. So much the worse for those who bother about such things! Spending one's life on such trivial worries means pulling against the collar with never a break, like the miserable horses on the tow-paths of our rivers: even when they come to a halt they still keep on pulling. We'll take what comes to us.

From *The Marriage of Figaro* by Pierre Augustin Caron de Beaumarchais, 1784, omitted in the original production at the insistence of the actors

The Ladies of Llangollen

Miss Butler and Miss Ponsonby have retired from society into a certain Welch Vale.

Both Ladies are daughters of the great Irish families whose names they retain.

Miss Butler, who is of the Ormonde family had several offers of marriage, all of which she rejected. Miss Ponsonby, her particular friend and companion, was supposed to be the bar to all matrimonial union, it was thought proper to separate them, and Miss Butler was confined.

The two Ladies, however found means to elope together. But being soon overtaken, they were each brought back by their respective relations. Many attempts were renewed to draw Miss Butler into marriage. But upon her solemnly and repeatedly declaring that nothing could induce her to wed any one, her parents ceased to persecute her by any more offers.

Not many months after, the Ladies concerted and executed a fresh elopement. Each having a small sum with them, and having been allowed a trifling income the place of their retreat was confided to a female servant of the Butler family, who was sworn to secrecy as to the place of their retirement. She was only to say that they were well and safe and hoped that their friends would without further enquiry, continue their annuities, which has not only been done but increased.

The beautiful above-mentioned vale is the spot they fixed on where they have resided for several years unknown to the neighbouring villages by any other appellation than *the Ladies of the Vale*!

About a twelve month since three ladies and a Gentleman stopping one night at an inn in the village, not being able to procure beds, the inhabitants applied to the Female Hermits for accommodation to some foreign strangers. This was readily granted – when lo! in these foreigners they described some of their own relations! But no entreaties could prevail on the Ladies to quit their sweet retreat.

Miss Butler is tall and masculine, she wears always a riding habit, hangs her hat with the air of a sportsman in the hall, and appears in all respects as a young man, if we except the petticoats which she still retains.

Miss Ponsonby, on the contrary, is polite and effeminate, fair and beautiful. In Mr Secretary Steel's list of Pensions for 1788, there are the names of Elinor Butler and Sarah Ponsonby, for annuities of fifty pounds each. We have many reasons to imagine that these pensioners are the ladies of the Vale; their female confidante continues to send them their Irish annuities beside.

They live in neatness, elegance and taste. Two females and their only servants.

Miss Ponsonby does the duties and honours of the house, while Miss Butler superintends the gardens and the rest of the grounds.

From the *Evening Post*, 1787

'Declaration of the Rights of Woman and Citizen'

The mothers, daughters, sisters, representatives of the nation, ask to constitute a National Assembly. Considering that ignorance, forgetfulness or contempt of the rights of women are the sole causes of public miseries, and of corruption of governments, they have resolved to set forth in a solemn declaration, the natural, unalterable and sacred rights of woman, so that this declaration, being ever present to all members of the social body, may unceasingly remind them of their rights and their duties; in order that the acts of women's power, as well as those of men, may be judged constantly against the aim of all political institutions, and thereby be more respected for it, in order that the complaints of women citizens, based henceforth on simple and indisputable principles, may always take the direction of maintaining the Constitution, good morals and the welfare of all.

In consequence, the sex superior in beauty and in courage in maternal suffering recognizes and declares, in the presence of and under the auspices of the Supreme Being, the following rights of woman and of the woman citizen:

ARTICLE I

Woman is born free and remains equal to man in rights. Social distinctions can be based only on common utility.

ARTICLE II

The aim of every political association is the preservation of the natural and imprescriptible rights of man and woman. These rights are liberty, prosperity, security and above all, resistance to oppression.

ARTICLE III

The source of all sovereignty resides essentially in the Nation, which is nothing but the joining together of Man and Woman; no body, no individual, can exercise authority that does not emanate expressly from it.

ARTICLE IV

Liberty and justice consist in giving back to others all that belongs to them; thus the only limits on the exercise of woman's natural rights are the perpetual tyranny by which man opposes her; these limits must be reformed by the laws of nature and of reason.

ARTICLE V

The laws of nature and reason forbid all actions that are harmful to society; all that is not forbidden by these wise and divine laws cannot be prevented, and no one can be constrained to do what they do not prescribe.

ARTICLE VI

Law must be the expression of the general will: all citizens, men and women alike, must personally or through their representatives concur in its formation; it must be the same for all; all citizens, men and women alike, being equal before it, must be equally eligible for all high offices, positions and public employments, according to their abilities, and without distinctions other than their virtues and talents.

ARTICLE VII

No woman can be an exception: she will be accused, apprehended and detained in cases determined by law; women, like men, will obey this rigorous rule.

ARTICLE VIII

The law must establish only those penalties which are strictly and clearly necessary, and no woman can be punished by virtue of a law established and promulgated prior to the offence, and legally applied to women.

ARTICLE IX

When a woman is declared guilty, full severity is exercised by the law.

ARTICLE X

No one ought to be disturbed for one's opinions, however fundamental they are; since a woman has the right to mount the scaffold, she must also have the right to address the House, provided her interventions do not disturb the public order as it has been established by law.

ARTICLE XI

The free communication of ideas and opinions is one of the most precious rights of woman, since this freedom ensures the legitimacy of fathers toward their children. Every woman citizen can therefore say freely: I am the mother of a child that belongs to you, without being forced to conceal the truth because of a barbaric prejudice; except to be answerable for abuses of this liberty as determined by law.

ARTICLE XII

The guarantee of the rights of woman and of the woman citizen is a necessary benefit; this guarantee must be instituted for the advantage of all, and not for the personal benefit of those to whom it is entrusted.

ARTICLE XIII

For the upkeep of public forces and for administrative expenses, the contributions of woman and man are equal; a woman shares in all the labors required by law, in the painful tasks; she must therefore have an equal share in the distribution of offices, employments, trusts, dignities and work.

ARTICLE XIV

Women and men citizens have the right to ascertain by themselves or through their representatives the necessity of public taxes. Women citizens will not only assume an equal part in providing the wealth but also in the public administration and in determining the quota, the assessment, the collection and the duration of the impost.

ARTICLE XV

The mass of women, joined together to contribute their taxes with those of men, have the right to demand from every public official an accounting of his administration.

ARTICLE XVI

Any society in which the guarantee of rights is not assured, nor the separation of powers determined, has no Constitution; the Constitution is null if the majority of the individuals of whom the nation is comprised have not participated in its drafting.

ARTICLE XVII

Ownership of property is for both sexes, mutually and separately; it is for each a sacred and inviolable right; no one can be deprived of it as a true patrimony from nature, unless a public necessity, legally established, evidently demands it, and with the condition of a just and prior indemnity.

AFTERWORD

Woman, wake up! The alarm bell of reason is making itself heard throughout the universe; recognize your rights. The powerful empire of nature is no longer beset by prejudices, fanaticism, superstition and lies. The torch of truth has dispelled all clouds of stupidity and usurpation. The enslaved man multiplied his forces but has had to resort to yours to break his chains. Once free he became unjust to his female companion. O women! women, when will you stop being blind? What advantages have you received from the Revolution? A more pronounced scorn, a more marked contempt? During the centuries of corruption, your only power was over the weaknesses of men. Your empire is destroyed, what then is left to you? The conviction that men are unjust. The claiming of your patrimony based on the wise laws of nature. The good word of the Lawgiver of the Marriage at Cana? Are you afraid that our French lawmakers, correctors of this morality, so long tied up with the politics which is no longer in style will say to you: 'Women, what is there in common between you and us?' – Everything, you would have to reply. If they persisted in their weakness, in putting forth this inconsistency which is a contradiction of their principles, you should courageously oppose these hale pretensions of superiority with the force of reason; unite under the banner of philosophy, unfold all the energy of your character and you will soon see these proud men, your servile adorers, crawling at your feet, but proud to share with you the treasures of the Supreme Being. Whatever the obstacles that oppose us may be, it is in your power to free us, you have only to will it . . .

Since it is now a question of national education, let us see if our wise lawmakers will think wisely about the education of women.

Olympe de Gouges, 1790

Make them Free

One class presses on another, for all are aiming to procure respect on account of their property; and property once gained will procure the respect due only to talents and virtue. Men neglect the duties incumbent on man, yet are treated like demi-gods. Religion is also separated from morality by a ceremonial veil, yet men wonder that the world is almost, literally speaking, a den of sharpers or oppressors.

I mean therefore to infer that the society is not properly organised which does not compel men and women to discharge their respective duties by making it the only way to acquire that countenance from their fellow-creatures, which every human being wishes some way to attain.

In short, in whatever light I view the subject, reason and experience convince me that the only method of leading women to fulfil their peculiar duties is to free them from all restraint by allowing them to participate in the inherent rights of mankind.

Make them free, and they will quickly become wise and virtuous, as men become more so, for the improvement must be mutual, or the injustice which one-half of the human race are obliged to submit to retorting on their oppressors, the virtue of man will be worm-eaten by the insect whom he keeps under his feet.

From *A Vindication of the Rights of Woman* by Mary Wollstonecraft, 1792

What Men Would Have Women to Be

I could here enumerate numberless instances, of WHAT MEN WOULD HAVE WOMEN TO BE, under circumstances the most trying and the most humiliating; but as I neither wish to tire out the reader nor myself with what may be well imagined without repetition, I shall only say; that though they are allowed, and even expected, to assume upon proper occasions, and when it happens to indulge the passions, or fall in with the humors of men, all that firmness of character, and greatness of mind commonly esteemed masculine; yet this is in so direct opposition, and so totally inconsistent with that universal weakness, which men first endeavour to affix upon women for their own convenience, and then for their own defence affect to admire; that really it requires more than female imbecility and credulity to suppose that such extremes can unite with any degree of harmony, in such imperfect beings as we all of us, men and women, must acknowledge ourselves to be. And therefore, except a woman has some schemes of her own to accomplish by this sort of management, – which necessity is most galling to an ingenuous mind; or except she is herself a mere nothing, – in which case her merit is next to nothing; these violent extremes, – these violent exertions of the mind, – are by no means natural or voluntary ones; but are on the contrary at variance with nature, with reason, and with common sense.

Indeed by preparatory tortures any mode of conduct, however unnatural, may be forced upon individuals.

Even inferior animals are taught not only to dance, but to dance to appearance in time, and with alacrity, when their tyrant pipes. Bears and Turkeys for example. But we ought not to forget, that to produce these wonderful exertions; the first have had their eyes put out, to render them more docile to the cruel caprice of man; and that nothing less than hot iron applied to the feet of the latter, had furnished that singular spectacle, with which many had the barbarity to be amused.

So alas! women often go through scenes with apparent cheerfulness, that did the most indifferent spectators, but consider what such appearances must have previously cost them, they would execrate the mean and sordid system; and join in endeavouring to expel from society those errors in theory, which produce such consequences in practice. For, from exertions made under such circumstances; – against nature, – against reason, – and against common sense; – can good be expected? Can such mend the understanding, or purify the heart? No, never! On the contrary they debase the one, and they corrupt the other. But it is a melancholy truth, that the whole system raised and supported by the men, tends to, nay I must be honest enough to say hangs upon, degrading the understandings, and corrupting the hearts of women; and yet! they are unreasonable enough to expect, discrimination in the one, and purity in the other.

From *Appeal to the Men of Great Britain in Behalf of Women*, ascribed to Mary Hays, 1798

The Remedy

To the Married of Both Sexes of the Working People.

'This paper is addressed to the most reasonable and considerate among you, the most numerous and most useful class of society. It is not intended to produce vice and debauchery, but to destroy vice and put an end to debauchery.

'It is a great truth, often told and never denied, that where there are too many working people in any trade or manufacture, they are worse paid than they ought to be paid, and are compelled to work more hours than they ought to work. When the number of working people in any trade or manufacture has for some years been too great, wages are reduced very low, and the working people become little better than slaves. When wages have been thus reduced to a very small sum, working people can no longer maintain their children as all good and respectable people wish to maintain their children, but are compelled to neglect them; to send them to different employments; to Mills and Manufactories, at a very early age. The misery of these poor children cannot be described, and need not be described to you, who witness them and deplore them every day of your lives.

'Many indeed among you are compelled for a bare subsistence to labour incessantly from the moment you rise in the morning to the moment you lie down again at night, without even the hope of ever being better off.

'The sickness of yourselves and your children, the privation and pain and premature death of those you love but cannot cherish as you wish, need only be alluded to. You know all these evils too well.

'And what, you will ask, is the remedy? How are we to avoid these miseries? The answer is short and plain: the means are easy. Do as other people do, to avoid having more children than they wish to have, and can easily maintain.

'What is done by other people is this. A piece of soft sponge is tied by a bobbin or penny ribbon, and inserted before the sexual intercourse takes place, and is withdrawn again as soon as it has taken place. Many tie a piece of sponge to each end of the ribbon, and they take care not to use the same sponge again until it has been washed. If the sponge be large enough, that is, as large as a green walnut, or a small apple, it will prevent conception, and thus, without diminishing the pleasures of married life, or doing the least injury to the health of the most delicate woman, both the woman and her husband will be saved from all the miseries which having too many children produces.

'By limiting the number of children, the wages both of children and of grown up persons will rise; the hours of working will be no more than they ought to be; you will have some time for recreation, some means of enjoying yourselves rationally, some means as well as some time for your own and your children's moral and religious instruction . . .

'But when it has become the custom here as elsewhere, to limit the number of children, so that none need have more than they wish to have, no man will fear to take a wife, all will be married while young – debauchery will diminish – while good moral and religious duties will be promoted.

'You cannot fail to see that this address is intended solely for your good. It is quite impossible that those who address you can receive any benefit from it, beyond the satisfaction which every benevolent person, every true Christian, must feel, at making you comfortable, healthy, and happy.'

Handbill circulated after Richard Carlile's article in *The Republican*, *c.* 1820

Women's Rights

Workers, in 1791 your fathers proclaimed the immortal Declaration of the Rights of Man, and it is thanks to that solemn Declaration that you are today free and equal men before the law. All honour to your fathers for this great achievement, but there remains for you men of 1843, a task no less great to accomplish. In your turn, free the last slaves remaining in France; proclaim the Rights of Woman, and, using the same terms as your fathers did, say: 'We, the proletariat of France, after fifty-three years' experience, acknowledge having been duly convinced that the ways in which the natural rights of women have been disregarded are the sole causes of the world's misfortunes, and we have resolved to include in our Charter woman's sacred and inalienable rights. We desire that men should give to their wives and mothers liberty and absolute equality which they enjoy themselves.'

From *L'Union Ouvrière* by Flora Tristan, 1843

'Nobody knows how many rebellions . . .'

Anybody may blame me who likes, when I add further, that, now and then, when I took a walk by myself in the grounds; when I went down to the gates and looked through them along the road; or when, while Adèle played with her nurse, and Mrs Fairfax made jellies in the store-room, I climbed the three staircases, raised the trap-door of the attic, and having reached the leads, looked out afar over sequestered field and hill, and along dim skyline: that then I longed for a power of vision which might overpass that limit; which might reach the busy world, towns, regions full of life I had heard of but never seen: that then I desired more of practical experience than I possessed; more of intercourse with my kind, of acquaintance with variety of character, than was here within my reach. I valued what was good in Mrs Fairfax, and what was good in Adèle; but I believed in the existence of other and more vivid kinds of goodness, and what I believed in I wished to behold.

Who blames me? Many no doubt; and I shall be called discontented. I could not help it: the restlessness was in my nature; it agitated me to pain sometimes. Then my sole relief was to walk along the corridor of the third storey, backwards and forwards, safe in the silence and solitude of the spot, and allow my mind's eye to dwell on whatever bright visions rose before it – and certainly they were many and glowing; to let my heart be heaved by the exultant movement which, while it swelled it in trouble, expanded it with life; and best of all, to open my inward ear to a tale that was never ended – a tale my imagination created, and narrated continuously; quickened with all of incident, life, fire, feeling, that I desire and had not in my actual existence.

It is in vain to say human beings ought to be satisfied with tranquillity: they must have action; and they will make it if they cannot find it. Millions are condemned to a stiller doom than mine, and millions are in silent revolt against their lot. Nobody knows how many rebellions besides political rebellions ferment in the masses of life which people earth. Women are supposed to be very calm generally: but women feel just as men feel; they need exercise for their faculties, and a field for their efforts as much as their brothers do; they suffer from too rigid a restraint, too absolute a stagnation, precisely as men would suffer; and it is narrow-minded in their more privileged fellow-creatures to say that they ought to confine themselves to making puddings and knitting stockings, to playing on the piano and embroidering bags. It is thoughtless to condemn them, or laugh at them, if they seek to do more or learn more than custom has pronounced necessary for their sex.

From *Jane Eyre* by Charlotte Brontë, 1847

What If I am a Prostitute?

Now, what if I am a prostitute, what business has society to abuse me? Have I received any favours at the hands of society? If I am a hideous cancer in society, are not the causes of the disease to be sought in the rottenness of the carcass? Am I not its legitimate child; no bastard, Sir? Why does my unnatural parent repudiate me, and what has society ever done for me, that I should do anything for it, and what have I ever done against society that it should drive me into a corner and crush me to the earth? I have neither stolen (at least since I was a child), nor murdered, nor defrauded. I earn my money and pay my way, and try to do good with it, according to my ideas of good. I do not get drunk, nor fight, nor create uproar in the streets or out of them. I do not use bad language. I do not offend the public eye by open indecencies. I go to the Opera, I go to Almack's, I go to the theatres, I go to quiet, well-conducted casinos, I go to all the places of public amusement, behaving myself with as much propriety as society can exact. I pay business visits, to my tradespeople, the most fashionable of the West-end. My milliners, my silk-mercers, my bootmakers, know, all of them, who I am and how I live, and they solicit my patronage as earnestly and cringingly as if I were Madam, the Lady of the right rev. patron of the Society for the Suppression of Vice. They find my money as good and my pay better (for we are robbed on every hand) than that of Madam, my Lady; and, if all the circumstances and conditions of our lives had been reversed, would Madam, my Lady, have done better or been better than I?

I speak of others as well as for myself, for the very great majority, nearly all the real undisguised prostitutes in London, spring from my class, and are made by and under pretty much such conditions of life as I have narrated, and particularly by untutored and unrestrained intercourse of the sexes in early life. We come from the dregs of society, as our so-called betters term it. What business has society to have dregs – such dregs as we? You railers of the Society for the Suppression of Vice, you the pious, the moral, the respectable, as you call yourselves, who stand on your smooth and pleasant side of the great gulf you have dug and keep between yourselves and the dregs, why don't you bridge it over, or fill it up, and by some humane and generous process absorb us into your leavened mass, until we become interpenetrated with goodness like yourselves? What have we to be ashamed of, we who do not know what shame is – the shame you mean?

From an anonymous letter to *The Times*, 24 February 1858

What Working Women Want

Yet, what is it we working women ask? What is it we are made to think and feel through every fibre of the frame with which it has pleased God to endow us as well as men, and for the maintenance of which in health, ease, and comfort, we, with men, have equal rights?

It is work we ask, room to work, encouragement to work, an open field with a fair day's wages for a fair day's work; it is injustice we feel, the injustice of men, who arrogate to themselves all profitable employments and professions, however unsuited to the vigorous manhood they boast, and thus, usurping women's work, drive women to the lowest depths of penury and suffering.

We are sick to our hearts of being told 'women cannot do this; women must not do that; they are not strong enough for this, and that, and the other' while we know and see every hour of our lives that these arguments are but shams; that some of the hardest and coarsest work done in this weary world is done by women, while, in consequence of usurped and underpaid labor, they are habitually consigned to an amount of physical endurance and privation from which the hardiest man would shrink appalled.

Society for Promoting the Employment of Women, 1860

Testimony Against the Contagious Diseases Acts

We have abundant suggestions by which the State may check profligacy, not with the object of curing disease only, but to check the vice which is the cause of the disease . . . Legislation alone will not do it. Seduction must be punished.

At present for the purpose of seduction, and of seduction only, our law declares every female child a woman at 12 years of age. I am ashamed to have to confess to such a shameful state of the law before you gentlemen, but a child is a woman, for that purpose alone, at 12 years of age. I know from my experience amongst this class of women, how many have become so from that cause. The law of bastardy must be altered. At present the responsibility of illegitimate children is thrown on the mothers only, the fathers are irresponsible. Better laws in this direction would aid in diminishing the causes of prostitution. A higher standard of public opinion as to the vice of men – that is a thing in which we women are most deeply interested; we have had enough to do with the reclamation of women, we know about that, but we know now that nothing can be done until the vices of men are attacked and checked. Above all things a higher standard with regard to the morality of men is needed, and we, thousands of us, are banded together to attain that if possible. The laws which we shall claim shall be constituted, they shall not be a breach of the Constitution, they shall be moral in their tendency, and above all they shall be just; that is, they shall be laws which shall tend to repress crimes which we abhor equally in both sexes and which shall deal with the vice itself, and not merely with its physical effects. Our measures will be directed against prostitution itself, and, with your permission, I will just call your attention to this, that whereas all legislation hitherto which is at all of the right kind has been directed against one sex only, we insist that it shall be directed against both sexes, and whereas it has been directed against the poor only, we insist, and the working men insist, that it shall also apply to the rich profligate. Partial laws, however excellent, will not effect the purification of society. It is quite the fashion, I find, in London, among the upper classes, to talk of this subject as if women were tempters, harpies, devils, while men are wholly innocent, and in every case the tempted, and legislation, following out this idea, has in almost all cases been protective for men and punitive for women. It cannot be said that men, in our own days, are entirely innocent and entirely the victims, while women are the sole assailants of purity. It cannot be said there is no such thing as seduction of young girls by gentlemen of the upper classes. It cannot be said there is no such thing as profuse patronage of houses of ill-fame by rich profligate men. I could tell you much of that from my own experience. Therefore we are profoundly convinced, and thousands among the working classes share our convictions in the matter, that legislation, however pure its aim, which is directed against the weaker sex only, will fail to accomplish any reduction in the amount of misery and sin there is amongst us.

Josephine Butler, 1871

To be Married is to be a Slave

'Marriage, *citoyennes*, is the greatest error of ancient humanity. To be married is to be a slave. Will you be slaves?' – 'No, no!' cried all the female part of the audience, and the orator, a tall gaunt woman with a nose like the beak of a hawk, and a jaundice-coloured complexion, flattered by such universal applause, continued, 'Marriage, therefore, cannot be tolerated any longer in a free city. It ought to be considered a crime, and suppressed by the most severe measures. Nobody has the right to sell his liberty, and thereby to set a bad example to his fellow citizens. The matrimonial state is a perpetual crime against morality. Don't tell me that marriage may be tolerated, if you institute divorce. Divorce is only an expedient, and, if I may be allowed to use the word, an Orleanist expedient! (*Thunders of applause*).

'Therefore, I propose to this assembly, that it should get the Paris Commune to modify the decree which assures pensions to the legitimate or illegitimate companions of the National Guards, killed in the defence of our municipal rights. No half measures. We, the illegitimate companions, will no longer suffer the legitimate wives to usurp rights they no longer possess, and which they ought never to have had at all. Let the decree be modified. All for the free women, none for the slaves!'

Report of a meeting of a women's club during the Paris Commune, 1871

Mr Dooley on Women's Suffrage

Don't ask f'r rights. Take thim. An' don't let anny wan give thim to ye. A right that is handed to ye f'r nawthin' has somethin' the matter with it. It's more than likely it's on'y a wrong turned inside out.

c. 1890

The Love that Dare not Speak its Name

The 'Love that dare not speak its name' in this century is such a great affection of an elder for a younger man as there was between David and Jonathan, such as Plato made the very basis of his philosophy, and such as you find in the sonnets of Michelangelo and Shakespeare. It is that deep, spiritual affection that is as pure as it is perfect. It dictates and pervades great works of art like those of Shakespeare and Michelangelo, and those two letters of mine, such as they are. It is in this century misunderstood, so much misunderstood that it may be described as the 'Love that dare not speak its name,' and on account of it I am placed where I am now. It is beautiful, it is fine, it is the noblest form of affection. There is nothing unnatural about it. It is intellectual, and it repeatedly exists between an elder and a younger man, when the elder man has intellect, and the younger man has all the joy, hope and glamour of life before him. That it should be so the world does not understand. The world mocks at it and sometimes puts one in the pillory for it.

Oscar Wilde in court, 1895

The Life Sentence of Marriage

As long as man is only half-grown, and woman is a serf or a parasite, it can hardly be expected that Marriage should be particularly successful. Two people come together, who know but little of each other, who have been brought up along different lines, who certainly do not understand each other's nature; whose mental interests and occupations are different, whose worldly interest and advantage are also different; to one of whom the subject of sex is probably a sealed book, to the other perhaps a book whose most dismal page has been opened first. The man needs an outlet for his passion; the girl is looking for a 'home' and a proprietor. A glamor of illusion descends upon the two, and drives them into each other's arms. It envelops in a gracious and misty halo all their differences and misapprehensions. They marry without misgiving; and their hearts overflow with gratitude to the white-surpliced old gentleman who reads the service over them.

But at a later hour, and with calmer thought, they begin to realise that it is a life-sentence which he has so suavely passed upon them – not reducible (as in the case of ordinary convicts) even to a term of 20 years. The brief burst of their first satisfaction has been followed by satiety on the physical plane, then by mere vacuity of affection, then by boredom, and even nausea. The girl, full perhaps of a tender emotion, and missing the sympathy and consolation she expected in the man's love, only to find its more materialistic side – 'This, this then is what I am wanted for;' the man, who looked for a companion, finding he can rouse no mortal interest in his wife's mind save in the most exasperating trivialities; – whatever the cause may be, a veil has fallen from before their faces, and there they sit, held together now by the least honorable interests, the interests which they themselves can least respect, but to which Law and Religion lend all their weight. The monetary dependence of the woman, the mere sex-needs of the man, the fear of public opinion, all form motives, and motives of the meanest kind, for maintaining the seeming tie; and the relation of the two hardens down into a dull neutrality, in which lives and characters are narrowed and blunted, and deceit becomes the common weapon which guards divided interests.

From *Love's Coming-Of-Age* by Edward Carpenter, 1896

Women have to go through such a tremendous struggle
before they are free in their own minds that freedom
is more precious to them than men.

Angelica Balabanov

Wasted Energy

How much energy and time we wasted in all our endless love tragedies and their complications! But it was also we, the women of the 1890s, who taught ourselves and those younger than we that love is not the most important thing in a woman's life. And that if she must choose between love and work, she should never hesitate: it is work, a woman's own creative work, that gives her the only real satisfaction and makes her life worth living.

Alexandra Kollontai, *c.* 1900

A Dissatisfied Mother

Dear Doctor! I realize that in all probability I will invite your vigorous condemnation by writing this letter today but the sincere interest which you take in us [mothers] merits to be candidly repaid and should not be answered with just a few banal and hypocritical phrases.

You consider me very fortunate. Married, if not in the best of circumstances, with a rosy one-year-old to whom I can dedicate all my motherly care. What greater fortune could one ask for? – So you think, as a man.

I think and feel otherwise. I am dissatisfied, nervous, and exhausted.

'Oh yes, for your nervousness,' I hear you say, 'you must refrain from all excitement, get plenty of good, refreshing sleep and avoid coffee, tea and alcohol.' – I know all that already, before you even order it. I follow all the rules which are supposed to be compatible with the occupation of mother. And yet nothing helps. The causes of my discontent, my anxiety, my neurasthenia, lie much deeper; they lie in the unavoidable circumstances which nature has conferred upon me as a consequence of motherhood. Oh yes, be amazed, horrified, whatever you want, but believe me, we women, we who have thoughts and aspirations, we who through serious intellectual activities have come to a higher state of civilization – we are so far removed from contact with nature that the so-called sweet joys of motherhood cause us more tortures than a quiet, normal thinking man can imagine.

I know for certain that for many women the moment a child is born their whole world dissolves, their own ego no longer exists, their selflessness goes so far that they no longer know any of their own pleasures, and since they continuously descend to the level of the child's intelligence, they are ultimately lost to any other kind of intellectual activity. As the child begins to develop his mental powers and widen his circle of interest, he sets an intellectual standard for the mother educating him. Then he is left to his own devices, because other children follow whose care and protection now completely consume the already mentioned mothers. These are the mothers who through tradition, education and talent have become 'true women,' who personify all the attributes so highly treasured by the male consumer: resignation, sacrifice and an absence of 'ego.' . . .

From the Austrian magazine *Dokumenteder Frauen*, 1899

Take Up Arms

Autobiography – self-purification. One should stay away from it and yet I can't do that. Why not? Well, because I've been challenged repeatedly to serve the cause of truth. But I'm alone and afraid, very afraid.

I am by no means one of those who considers herself unlucky or who is ashamed of her situation and says to everybody – 'Oh, we poor lesbians. Forgive us for existing in this world.' No, I'm proud of my exceptional orientation. I hold my head high, stamp my feet and say boldly: 'See, that's what I am.'

I was born in a small capital city, the daughter of a scholar, and I'm the oldest of eight children. Whether I was congenitally tainted or not will not be discussed here, for though I know something about the noble science of medicine, I am not inclined to write a scholarly treatise . . .

I decided on medicine as my major, along with astronomy and ancient languages, and was determined not to do any less well than my male colleagues. So I did very well on my examination and I chose to become a scholar. I settled in an idyllic region of our country; I have lived there with 'her' until this day and we lead a life that cannot be any less divine or happy than Eden.

But that requires courage, a great deal of courage. You can have the same thing, my dear sisters, and it will show that you are justified in living a happy life and loving like the 'normal' world. And in spite of the way you are, people will tolerate you, people will acknowledge you, people will envy you. Take up arms! We must and we will succeed. I've done it. Why shouldn't all of you? . . .

You poor, poor people! When will the hour of deliverance come? When will it come for our brothers who share our fate as we exceptions from the usual mold and the ancient, eternal law of nature. Should we make generalizations about us [homosexuals], our special talents and such things? Couldn't we be part of a design rather than an accident? . . .

Take up arms until this legal clause [against homosexuality] is abolished.

It has already caused so much misery and brought so much sorrow. Why should, why must the innocent suffer; they were created by the heavens with feelings, which when expressed in their own way, are not understood by the everyday world. That is taken for granted! I don't demand a code of morals just for homosexuals. What I demand is humane treatment, impartiality and equal rights for all . . .

From *Jahrbuch für sexuelle Zwischenstufen* by E. Kranse, 1901

Bigamy is having one husband too many.
Monogamy is the same.

Erica Jong

Here Lies A Poor Woman

Here lies a poor woman who always was tired;
She lived in a house where help was not hired,
Her last words on earth were: 'Dear friends, I am going
Where washing ain't done, nor sweeping, nor sewing.
But everything there is exact to my wishes,
For where they don't eat, there's no washing of dishes
I'll be where loud anthems will always be ringing
But having no voice, I'll be clear of the singing.
Don't mourn for me now, don't mourn for me never,
I'm going to do nothing for ever and ever.'

Self-composed epitaph by Catherine Alsopp, 1905

A Nation is not conquered
Until the hearts of its women
Are on the ground.

Cheyenne proverb

We Do Not Want Condescension

Men say when we become educated we shall push them out of work and abandon the role for which God has created us. But, isn't it rather men who have pushed women out of work? Before, women used to spin and to weave cloth for clothes for themselves and their children, but men invented machines for spinning and weaving and put women out of work. In the past, women sewed clothes for themselves and their households but men invented the sewing machine. The iron for these machines is mined by men and the machines themselves are made by men. Then men took up the profession of tailoring and began to make clothes for our men and children. Before women winnowed the wheat and ground flour on grinding stones for the bread they used to make with their own hands, sifting flour and kneading dough. Then men established bakeries employing men. They gave us rest but at the same time pushed us out of work. We or our female servants, used to sweep our houses with straw brooms and then men invented machines to clean that could be operated by a young male servant. Poor women and servants used to fetch water for their homes or the homes of employers but men invented pipes and faucets to carry water into houses . . .

Work at home now does not occupy more than half the day. We must pursue an education in order to occupy the other half of the day but that is what men wish to prevent us from doing under the pretext of taking their jobs away. Obviously, I am not urging women to neglect their home and children to go out and become lawyers or judges or railway engineers. But if any of us wish to work in such professions our personal freedom should not be infringed. It might be argued that pregnancy causes women to leave work, but there are unmarried women, others who are barren or have lost their husbands or are widowed or divorced or those whose husbands need their help in supporting the family. It is not right that they should be forced into lowly jobs. These women might like to become teachers or doctors with the same academic qualifications. Is it just to prevent women from doing what they believe is good for themselves and their support? If pregnancy impedes work outside the house it also impedes work inside the house. Furthermore, how many able-bodied men have not become sick from time to time and have had to stop work?

Men say to us categorically, 'You women have been created for the house and we have been created to be breadwinners.' Is this a God-given dictate? How are we to know this since no holy book has spelled it out? Political economy calls for a division of labour but if women enter the learned professions it does not upset the system. The division of labour is merely a human creation . . .

Specialised work for each sex is a matter of convention. It is not mandatory. We women are now unable to do hard work because we have not been accustomed to it. If the city woman had not been prevented from doing hard work she would have been as strong as the man. Isn't the country woman like her city sister? Why then is the former in better health and stronger than the latter? Do you have any doubt that a woman from Minufiya (a town in the Delta) would be able to beat the strongest man from al-Ghuriya (a section of Cairo) in a wrestling match? If men say to us that we have been created weak we say to them, 'No it is you who made us weak through the path you made us follow.' After long centuries of enslavement by men, our minds rusted and our bodies weakened. Is it right that they accuse us of being created weaker than them in mind and body? Women may not have to their credit great inventions but women have excelled in learning and the arts and politics. Some have exceeded men in courage and valour, such as Hawla bint al-Azwar al-Kindi who impressed Umar ibn al-Khattab with her bravery and skill in fighting when she went to Syria to free her brother held captive by the Byzantines . . .

Nothing irritates me more than when men claim they do not wish us to work because they wish to spare us the burden. We do not want condescension, we want respect. They should replace the first with the second.

From a lecture by Bahithat al-Badiya, 1909

I soon noticed that the feelings I expressed were turned into jests, and that my intelligence was silenced, as if it were improper for a woman to have any.

Mme de Staël

Force-Feeding Suffragettes

The prisoner is at her weakest this morning – her physical powers are at their lowest ebb – her mouth, which has been so tortured, is ulcerated, and shrinking from the slightest touch.

In his right hand the man holds an instrument they call a gag, partly covered with India rubber, which part the prisoner never feels, and the moment of battle has come.

The prisoner refuses to unclose her teeth – the last defense against the food she out of principle, refuses to take – the doctor has his 'duty' to perform – his dignity also to maintain before five women and a tall junior doctor. His temper is short – has already been ruffled. So he sets about his job in a butcherly fashion – there is no skill required for this job – only brutality. He puts his great fingers along her teeth – feels a gap at the back, rams the tool blindly and with evident intention to hurt her, and cause the helpless woman to wince – along the shrinking flesh – how long will it take before superior strength triumphs? Tears start in the prisoner's eyes – uncontrollable tears – tears she would give anything to control.

It is still dark in the cell and the man strains at her mouth blindly, without result. 'Can you see?' asks the junior doctor. 'No,' blusters the other, 'better bring a light.' But he does not wait until the taper is brought – ah – at last he has forced the tool in, and with leverage the jaw opens.

He has still to hold it for twenty minutes or so while the food is being poured or pushed or choked down her throat – unluckily the gag has been forced in so carelessly that it has caught in the cheek, between it and the sharp teeth below.

The pain is maddening – she strains at her hands – her feet are in a vice – her head is held – she tries to speak – her jaw is forced to its widest. They pour the food down – it is a mince of meat and brown bread and milk – too dry – too stiff – they hold her nose [so] that she cannot breathe, and so she must breathe with her mouth and swallow at the same time, the doctors helping it in with hot hands that have handled a pipe and heaven knows how many patients – scraping their fingers clean on her teeth from the horrible mess.

It would seem they were not doctors, for they force it down so heedlessly that the prisoner chokes and gasps for breath, the tears pouring from her eyes. The young doctor is called away – the pain is too much for her – she moves her head – the doctor gives another twist, and the nurse, to get it over sooner, pours the food quicker.

The limit is reached, and for the first time the prisoner gives way – great sobs of pain and breathlessness come faster and faster – she cannot bear it – she tries to call out 'Stop!' with that tortured wide-open mouth – and with one wrench she frees her hands and seizes the gag.

The doctor says to the officers – 'She says it is hot.' 'No,' they cry – the horror of the scene upon them – 'she said stop.'

He waits, gloomily with irritation, and in a moment free from the restraint of his fellow physician, without a word he drags her head back and she is held down again.

A short quick thrust and her mouth is gagged again – the prisoner tries to control herself – her sobs increase – her breathlessness also – there is nothing but the pain and the relentless forcing of food down her throat – her choking despair, and the bitter draught of tonic and digestive medicine which is also poured down her throat.

From *The Prisoner* by Helen Gordon Liddle, 1911

In the Strange New World

Thrown into strict logical form, our demand is this: We do not ask that the wheels of time should reverse themselves, or the stream of life flow backward. We do not ask that our ancient spinning-wheels be again resuscitated and placed in our hands; we do not demand that our old grindstones and hoes be returned to us, or that man should again betake himself entirely to his ancient province of war and the chase, leaving to us all domestic and civil labor. We do not even demand that society shall immediately so reconstruct itself that every woman may be again a childbearer (deep and overmastering as lies the hunger for motherhood in every virile woman's heart!); neither do we demand that the children we bear shall again be put exclusively into our hands to train. This, we know, cannot be. The past material conditions of life have gone for ever; no will of man call recall them. But *this* is our demand: We demand that, in that strange new world that is arising alike upon the man and the woman, where nothing is as it was, and all things are assuming new shapes and relations, that in this new world we also shall have our share of honored and socially useful human toil, our full half of the labor of the Children of Woman. We demand nothing more than this, and will take nothing less. *This is our* 'WOMAN'S RIGHT!'

From *Woman and Labour* by Olive Schreiner, 1911

A Call to Women

From many countries appeals have come asking us to call together an International Women's Congress to discuss what the women of the world can do and ought to do in the dreadful times in which we are now living.

We women of the Netherlands, living in a neutral country, accessible to the women of all other nations, therefore take upon ourselves the responsibility of calling together such an International Congress of Women. We feel strongly that at a time when there is so much hatred among nations, we women must show that we can retain our solidarity and that we are able to maintain a mutual friendship.

Women are waiting to be called together. The world is looking to them for their contribution towards the solution of the great problems of to-day.

Women, whatever your nationality, whatever your party, your presence will be of great importance.

The greater the number of those who take part in the Congress, the stronger will be the impression its proceedings will make.

Your presence will testify that you, too, wish to record your protest against this horrible war, and that you desire to assist in preventing a recurrence of it in the future . . .

War, the ultima ratio of the statesmanship of men, we women declare to be a madness, possible only to a people intoxicated with a false idea; for it destroys everything the constructive powers of humanity have taken centuries to build up.

From the *Declaration* of the International Congress of Women, 1915

Lecturing on Homosexuality

My tour this year [1915] met with no police interference until we reached Portland, Oregon, although the subjects I treated were anything but tame: anti-war topics, the gift for Caplan and Schmidt, freedom in love, birth-control, and the problem most tabooed in polite society, homosexuality. Nor did [Anthony] Comstock and his purists try to suppress me, although I openly discussed methods of contraception before various audiences.

Censorship came from some of my own comrades because I was treating such 'unnatural' themes as homosexuality. Anarchism was already enough misunderstood, and anarchists considered depraved; it was inadvisable to add to the misconceptions by taking up perverted sex-forms, they argued. Believing in freedom of opinion, even if it went against me, I minded the censors in my own ranks as little as I did those in the enemy's camp. In fact, censorship from comrades had the same effect on me as police persecution; it made me surer of myself, more determined to plead for every victim, be it one of social wrong or of moral prejudice.

The men and women who used to come to see me after my lectures on homosexuality, and who confided to me their anguish and their isolation, were often of finer grain than those who had cast them out. Most of them had reached an adequate understanding of their differentiation only after years of struggle to stifle what they had considered a disease and a shameful affliction. One young woman confessed to me that in the twenty-five years of her life she had never known a day when the nearness of a man, her own father and brothers even, did not make her ill. The more she had tried to respond to sexual approach, the more repungnant men became to her. She had hated herself, she said, because she could not love her father and her brothers as she loved her mother. She suffered excruciating remorse, but her revulsion only increased. At the age of eighteen she had accepted an offer of marriage in the hope that a long engagement might help her grow accustomed to a man and cure her of her 'disease.' It turned out a ghastly failure and nearly drove her insane. She could not face marriage and she dared not confide in her fiancé or friends. She had never met anyone, she told me, who suffered from a similar affliction, nor had she ever read books dealing with the subject. My lecture had set her free; I had given her back her self-respect.

This woman was only one of the many who sought me out. Their pitiful stories made the social ostracism of the invert seem more dreadful than I had ever realized before. To me anarchism was not a mere theory for a distant future; it was a living influence to free us from inhibitions, internal no less than external, and from the destructive barriers that separate man from man.

From *Living My Life* by Emma Goldman, published 1931

'Breed, Women, Breed'

Breed, little mothers,
With tired backs and tired hands,
Breed for the owners of mills and the owners of mines,
Breed a race of danger-haunted men,
A race of toiling, sweating, miserable men,
Breed, little mothers,
Breed for the owners of mills and the owners of mines,
Breed, breed, breed!

Breed, little mothers,
With the sunken eyes and the sagging cheeks,
Breed for the bankers, the crafty and terrible masters of men,
Breed a race of machines,
A race of anaemic, round-shouldered, subway-herded machines!

Breed, little mothers,
With a faith patient and stupid as cattle,
Breed for the war lords,
Offer your woman flesh for incredible torment,
Wrack your frail bodies with the pangs of birth
For the war lords who slaughter your sons!

Breed, little mothers,
Breed for the owners of mills and the owners of mines,
Breed for the bankers, the crafty and terrible masters of men,
Breed for the war lords, the devouring war lords,
Breed, women, breed!

Lucia Trent, *c.* 1920

Frankly, Gaily or Not At All

In my opinion as a Feminist and a Communist, the fundamental importance and value of birth control lie in its widening of the scope of human freedom and choice, its *self-determining* significance for women. For make no mistake about this: Birth Control, the diffusion of the knowledge and possibility of Birth Control, means freedom for women, social and sexual freedom, and that is why it is so intensely feared and disliked in many influential quarters to-day. For thousands of years births and the rearing – and often the losing – of unlimited broods of babies were considered to be women's business *par excellence*. But that women should *think* about this business, that they should judge and examine it, that they should look at their future and their children's future . . . this is, indeed, camouflage it as you may, the beginning of the end of a social system and a moral code.

Let me develop very briefly and sketchily my assertion that Birth Control means sexual freedom. The ostensible reasons for the established form of patriarchal marriage have always been (a) the inheritance of property, and (b) the protection ensured to the young children and to their mother during her child-bearing period. But when marriage no longer means the subjection of unlimited motherhood and the economic dependence of mothers, the main social reasons for its retention as a stereotyped monogamous formula will be at an end. Observe, I do not say that Birth Control will abolish or diminish real monogamy: there will probably always be as much, or rather as little, monogamy as there has always been. But it will no longer be *stereotyped* as the one lifelong and unvarying form of legally recognised expression for anything so infinitely variable and individual as the sexual impulse.

Now the demand for Birth Control has long ago ceased to be academic. It is becoming very urgent and more widespread than many persons, even among those interested and sympathetic, quite realise. This demand touches the lives of the majority of women in this and every country very acutely. Any one who knows the lives and work of the wives and mothers of the working class – or, as I, a Communist, would prefer to style it, the exploited class – who has helped them and striven to teach them, not in the spirit of a schoolmistress, but as a fellow-woman and a friend – knows that these women are in no doubt as to the essential righteousness of their claim to control their own maternity. But how? Hardly any of these women, if she can speak to you fully and frankly as a friend, but will admit that – often more than once – she has, on finding herself, in the hideously significant phrase they use, 'caught,' had recourse either to drugs or to most violent internal operative methods in order to bring about a miscarriage. And these operative methods have, of course, been applied absolutely without antiseptic or aseptic precautions, and without any of the rest which is as essential after such an experiment as after a normal confinement at full term. Yet it ought not to be beyond the powers of medical and chemical science to invent an absolutely reliable contraceptive! Think of the marvels of destruction in the shape of asphyxiating and corrosive gases all ready for the next great war for liberty and civilization. Think of the knowledge we have already attained of the structure and functions of the endocrine glands, and the work which has been done in the direction of modifying, renewing or transforming sexuality and procreative power . . . Surely a science which can perform such wonders, though the technique is obviously only in its first stages, should be able to prevent conception without injuring health or impairing natural pleasure! . . .

Now I am *not* concerned here to vindicate the moral right to abortion, though I am profoundly convinced that it is a woman's right, and have argued the case for that right in the Press, both in England and America. I am told, however, by one of the leaders of our movement, to whose penetrating judgement and wide nursing experience I give the highest honour, that abortion is *physiologically injurious* and to be deprecated. It is open, perhaps, to question whether the effects of abortion itself have been sufficiently separated from the appalling bad conditions of nervous terror, lack of rest and lack of surgical cleanliness in which it is generally performed. But *granted that it is injurious per se*, the demand for effective contraception is all the stronger. The ancient codes, the decaying superstitions and prejudices of an old theoretical morality which has never been thoroughly accepted in practice, are losing all the sanctity they ever had.

For an increasing number of persons throughout the world, including all the most mentally capable and physically vigorous, *they mean just nothing at all.*

It is up to science to meet the demands of humanity; and one of the most urgent of those demands is that of true eugenics (not privilege and property defence) that shall be given as Anna Wickham says, 'frankly, gaily,' or – not at all. Which shall it be?

From 'The Feminine Aspect of British Culture', by F. W. Stella Browne, 1922

It is quite true that are no limits to masculine
egotism in ordinary life.

Leon Trotsky

I Can Only Love You

Mary got up, and just for a moment their eyes met, then Stephen looked away quickly: 'Good night, Mary.'

'Stephen . . . won't you kiss me good night? It's our first night together here in your home. Stephen, do you know that you've never kissed me?'

The clock chimed ten, a rose on the desk fell apart, its overblown petals disturbed by that almost imperceptible vibration. Stephen's heart beat thickly.

'Do you want me to kiss you?'

'More than anything else in the world,' said Mary.

Then Stephen suddenly came to her senses, and she managed to smile: 'Very well, my dear.' She kissed the girl quietly on her cheek. 'And now you really must go to bed, Mary.'

After Mary had gone she tried to write letters; a few lines to Anna, announcing her visit; a few lines to Puddle and to Mademoiselle Duphot – the latter she felt that she had shamefully neglected. But in none of these letters did she mention Mary. Brockett's effusion she left unanswered. Then she took her unfinished novel from its drawer, but it seemed very dreary and unimportant, so she laid it aside again with a sigh, and locking the drawer put the key in her pocket.

And now she could no longer keep it at bay, the great joy, the great pain in her heart that was Mary. She had only to call and Mary would come, bringing all her faith, her youth and her ardour. Yes, she had only to call, and yet – would she ever be cruel enough to call Mary? Her mind recoiled at that word; why cruel? She and Mary loved and needed each other. She could give the girl luxury, make her secure so that she need never fight for her living; she should have every comfort that money could buy. Mary was not strong enough to fight for her living. And then she, Stephen, was no longer a child to be frightened and humbled by this situation. There was many another exactly like her in this very city, in every city; and they did not all live out crucified lives, denying their bodies, stultifying their brains, becoming the victims of their own frustrations. On the contrary, they lived natural lives – lives that to them were perfectly natural. They had their passions like everyone else, and why not? They were surely entitled to their passions? They attracted too, that was the irony of it, she herself had attracted Mary Llewellyn – the girl was quite simply and openly in love. 'All my life I've been waiting for something . . .' Mary had said that, she had said: 'All my life I've been waiting for something . . . I've been waiting for you.'

Men – they were selfish, arrogant, possessive. What could they do for Mary Llewellyn? What could a man give that she could not? A child? But she would give Mary such a love as would be complete in itself without children. Mary would have no room in her heart, in her life, for a child, if she came to Stephen. All things they would be the one to the other, should they stand in that limitless relationship; father, mother, friend and lover, all things – the amazing completeness of it; and Mary, the child, the friend, the belovèd. With the terrible bonds of her dual nature, she could bind Mary fast, and the pain would be sweetness, so that the girl would cry out for that sweetness, hugging her chains always closer to her. The world would condemn but they would rejoice; glorious outcasts, un-ashamed, triumphant! . . .

Then Stephen must tell her the cruel truth, she must say: 'I am one of those whom God marked on the forehead. Like Cain, I am marked and blemished. If you come to me, Mary, the world will abhor you, will persecute you, will call you unclean. Our love may be faithful even unto death and beyond – yet the world will call it unclean. We may harm no living creature by our love; we may grow more perfect in understanding and in charity because of our loving; but all this will not save you from the scourge of a world that will turn away its eyes from your noblest actions, finding only corruption and vileness in you. You will see men and women defiling each other, laying the burden of their sins upon their children. You will see unfaithfulness, lies and deceit among those whom the world views with approbation. You will find that many have grown hard of heart, have grown greedy, selfish, cruel and lustful; and when you will turn to me and will say: "You and I are more worthy of respect than these people. Why does the world persecute us, Stephen?" And I shall answer: "Because in this world there is only toleration for the so-called normal." And when you come to me for protection, I shall say: "I cannot protect you, Mary, the world has deprived me of my right to protect; I am utterly helpless, I can only love you."'

From *The Well of Loneliness* by Radclyffe Hall, 1928

Women and Poverty

Professors, schoolmasters, sociologists, clergymen, novelists, essayists, journalists, men who had no qualification save that they were not women, chased my simple and single question – Why are women poor? – until it became fifty questions; until the fifty questions leapt frantically into mid-stream and were carried away. Every page in my notebook was scribbled over with notes. To show the state of mind I was in, I will read you a few of them, explaining that the page was headed quite simply, WOMEN AND POVERTY, in block letters; but what followed was something like this:

Condition in Middle Ages of,
Habits in the Fiji Islands of,
Worshipped as goddesses by,
Weaker in moral sense than,
Idealism of,
Greater conscientiousness of,
South Sea Islanders, age of puberty among,
Attractiveness of,
Offered as sacrifice to,
Small size of brain of,
Profounder sub-consciousness of,
Less hair on the body of,
Mental, moral, and physical inferiority of,
Love of children of,
Greater length of life of,
Weaker muscles of,
Strength of affections of,
Vanity of,
Higher education of,
Shakespeare's opinion of,
Lord Birkenhead's opinion of,
Dean Inge's opinion of,
La Bruyère's opinion of,
Dr Johnson's opinion of,
Mr Oscar Browning's opinion of, . . .

Here I drew breath and added, indeed, in the margin, Why does Samuel Butler say, 'Wise men never say what they think of women?' Wise men never say anything else apparently. But, I continued, leaning back in my chair and looking at the vast dome in which I was a single but by now somewhat harassed thought, what is so unfortunate is that wise men never think the same thing about women. Here is Pope:

> Most women have no character at all.

And here is La Bruyère:

> Les femmes sont extrêmes; elles sont meilleures ou pires que les hommes –

a direct contradiction by keen observers who were contemporary. Are they capable of education or incapable? Napoleon thought them incapable. Dr Johnson thought the opposite.[1] Have they souls or have they not souls? Some savages say they have none. Others, on the contrary, maintain that women are half divine and worship them on that account.[2] Some sages hold that they are shallower in the brain; others that they are deeper in the consciousness. Goethe honoured them; Mussolini despises them. Wherever one looked men thought about women and thought differently. It was impossible to make head or tail of it all, I decided, glancing with envy at the reader next door who was making the neatest abstracts, headed often with an A or a B or a C, while my own notebook rioted with the wildest scribble of contradictory jottings. It was distressing, it was bewildering, it was humiliating. Truth had run through my fingers. Every drop had escaped.

[1] '"Men know that women are an overmatch for them, and therefore they choose the weakest or the most ignorant. If they did not think so, they never could be afraid of women knowing as much as themselves." . . . In justice to the sex, I think it but candid to acknowledge that, in a subsequent conversation, he told me that he was serious in what he said.' – Boswell, *The Journal of a Tour to the Hebrides*.

[2] 'The ancient Germans believed that there was something holy in women, and accordingly consulted them as oracles.' – Frazer, *Golden Bough*.

From *A Room of One's Own* by Virginia Woolf, 1929

A WOMAN'S WORK IS NEVER DONE BY MEN

What Is Sexual Chaos?

It is to resort, in the conjugal bed, to the law of conjugal duty.

It is to contract a lifelong sexual liaison without having sexual knowledge of one's partner beforehand.

It is to sleep with a proletarian girl because she is not worth anything more, while one would never ask the same of a decent girl.

It is the lubricity of a life of sordid prostitution, or to abstain until the wedding night.

It is to consider it the height of potency to deprive a girl of her virginity.

It is to mentally paw every picture of a half-naked woman from top to bottom at the age of fourteen, and at the age of twenty to intervene as a nationalist in favour of woman's purity and honour.

It is to tolerate the pornography industry and to excite teenagers with erotic films.

What is not sexual chaos?

It is to desire sexual abandon through mutual love, without considering the established laws and moral principles, and to act accordingly.

It is to give birth to children only when one desires to have them and is able to bring them up.

It is to have no intercourse with prostitutes.

It is to get married or to establish a lasting relationship only when one has an exact sexual knowledge of one's partner.

It is not to demand from anybody a right to love and sexual abandon.

From *Sexpol*, by Wilhelm Reich, 1932

Love for the Invert

Very well – what is this love we have for the invert, boy or girl? It was they who were spoken of in every romance that we ever read. The girl, lost, what is she but the Prince found? The Prince on the white horse that we have always been seeking. And the pretty lad who is a girl, what but the prince-princess in point lace – neither one and half the other, the painting on the fan! We love them for that reason. We were impaled in our childhood upon them as they rode through our primers, the sweetest lie of all, now come to be in boy or girl, for in the girl it is the prince, and in the boy it is the girl that makes a prince a prince – and not a man. They go far back in our lost distance where what we never had stands waiting; it was inevitable that we should come upon them, for our miscalculated longing has created them.

They are our answer to what our grandmothers were told love was, and what it never came to be; they, the living lie of our centuries. When a long lie comes up, sometimes it is a beauty; when it drops into dissolution, into drugs and drink, into disease and death, it has at once a singular and terrible attraction. A man can resent and avoid evil on his own plane, but when it is the thin blown edge of his reverie, he takes it to his heart, as one takes to one's heart the dark misery of the close nightmare, born and slain of the particular mind; so that if one of them were dying of the pox, one would will to die of it too, with two feelings, terror and joy, welded somewhere back again into a formless sea where a swan (would it be ourselves, or her or him, or a mystery of all) sinks crying.

From *Nightwood* by Djuna Barnes, 1936

Manifesto for Bachelors Anonymous

The group is described as 'a service and welfare organization devoted to the protection and improvement of Society's Androgynous Minority.' The reasons for the group's formation are listed as follows:

encroaching American Fascism . . . seeks to bend unorganized and unpopular minorities into isolated fragments . . .

. . . the Androgynous Minority was . . . stampeded into serving as hoodlums, stool pigeons . . . hangmen, before it was ruthlessly exterminated [a reference to the Nazi extermination of homosexuals];

. . . government indictment of Androgynous Civil Servants . . . [legally establishes] GUILT BY ASSOCIATION;

. . . under the Government's announced plans for eventual 100% war production all commerce . . . would be conducted under government contract . . . making it impossible for Androgynes to secure employment;

. . . Guilt of Androgynity BY ASSOCIATION, equally with Guilt of Communist sympathy, . . . can be employed as a threat against . . . every man and woman in our country . . . to insure thought control and political regimentation;

. . . in order to earn for ourselves any place in the sun, we must . . . work collectively on the side of peace, . . . in the spirit . . . of the United Nations Charter, for the full-class citizenship participation of Minorities everywhere, including ourselves;

WE, THE ANDROGYNES OF THE WORLD, HAVE FORMED THIS RESPONSIBLE CORPORATE BODY TO DEMONSTRATE BY OUR EFFORTS THAT OUR PHYSIOLOGICAL AND PSYCHO-

LOGICAL HANDICAPS NEED BE NO DIFFERENT IN INTEGRATING 10% OF THE WORLD'S POPULATION TOWARDS THE CONSTRUCTIVE SOCIAL PROGRESS OF MANKIND.

'Henry Hay' (Eann Macdonald), 1950; for the first North American gay organisation

'Unfortunate Coincidence'

By the time you swear you're his,
Shivering and sighing
And he vows his passion is
Infinite, undying –
Lady, make a note of this:
One of you is lying.

Dorothy Parker, *c.* 1955

A Difficult Feat for a Cambridge Male

'Guess Where It's Heaven to be a Girl!' the Woman's Sunday Mirror gushed a short while back; we couldn't, so read on. Cambridge University, it seems, is this very green Eden, offering women students 'a crazy mixed-up social whirl, with an average of 500 bottle parties per eight-week term.' Slightly staggered by such statistics as, 'In her five weeks at Cambridge she has had 180 dates with 45 different men', we skimmed through an account of dating life that would have made the Alpha maidens in Brave New World take to soma, wild with envy.

The magazine Varsity, admitting that the Mirror account contained nothing 'specifically untrue', cleverly criticised the exaggerated effect arising from the 'subtle technique of leaving out'. Leaving out, no doubt, those bluestockinged Cambridge women who brood in the university library until closing time. Or also, the advice given by the main speaker at a women's college dinner: cloister yourself in 'research' during these three precious academic years; avoid, if possible, anything so distracting as summer jobs; 'You can always get out in the world later.'

Fresh from the easy-going, co-educational school system in America, where boys and girls are not immured in segregated public schools during adolescence until they came upon the 'opposite sex' with some of the self-consciousness and awe of an amateur anthropologist confronting, for the first time, a mob of orang-utans (or vice versa), we paused to reflect upon the position of women in Cambridge, upon the man/woman relationship, even.

Apparently, the most difficult feat for a Cambridge male is to accept a woman not merely as feeling, not merely as thinking, but as managing a complex, vital interweaving of both. Men here are inclined to treat women in one of two ways: either (1) as pretty, beagling, frivolous things (or devastating bohemian things) worthy of May Balls and suggestive looks over bottles of Chablis by candlelight, or, more rarely, (2) as esoteric opponents on an intellectual tennis court where the man, by law of kind, always wins.

Is this drastic split in the functions of a whole woman (matter versus mind, one might say) a flaw in the male approach, or does it stem from some lack on the woman's side? Perhaps a little of both. We shall deal, however, with the former. A debonair Oxford PPE man demurred, laughing incredulously: 'But really, talk about philosophy with a *woman*!' A poetic Cambridge chap maintains categorically: 'As soon as a woman starts talking about intellectual things, she loses her feminine charm for me.' By complaining about such remarks here, we are not advocating abstruse discussions about the animal symbolism in The Garden of Delights, by Hieronymous Bosch, but only a more natural and frequent commerce between male and female minds on their favourite subjects; perhaps in supervisions, perhaps in coffee shops: a sense of fun, not artificial posturing, in playing with ideas where a woman keeps her female status while being accepted simultaneously as an intelligent human being.

In a society where men outnumber women 10 to one, women are, admittedly, in an artificial position; competition is keen, even deadly, and the difficulty of acquiring a date induces many Cambridge men to draw on the reservoir of blonde, monosyllabic Scandinavian girls at the English schools, favouring what is often the prettier, less complicated side of the pass.

Perhaps a restoration of the old French salon, with each Cambridge girl presiding like Madame Récamier over her ratio of 10 men, would enrich male/female relationships. More likely, co-educational public schools would make intelligent sharing of ideas easier, less self-conscious from an earlier age. At least co-ed university activities such as political clubs, newspaper work, and acting, make it possible for men and women to meet on a sounder basis than the superficial sherry party where a girl is just that, and, alas, not much more.

Article in *Isis* magazine by Sylvia Plath while she was at Cambridge University, 1956

Never despise what it says in women's magazines:
it may not be subtle but neither are men.

Zsa Zsa Gabor

The Yoke of So-Called Legitimacy

The time came when I had to go after a job; I was assigned one in Marseille, and felt scared stiff. I had envisaged worse exiles than this, but I had never really believed in them. Now, suddenly, it was all true. On 2 October, I would find myself over five hundred miles from Paris. Faced with my state of panic, Sartre proposed to revise our plans. If we got married, he said, we would have the advantages of a double post, and in the long run such a formality would not seriously affect our way of life. This prospect took me unawares. Hitherto we had not even considered the possibilities of submitting ourselves to the common customs and observances of our society, and in consequence the notion of getting married had simply not crossed our minds. It offended our principles. There were many points over which we hesitated, but our anarchism was as deep-dyed and aggressive as that of the old libertarians, and stirred us, as it had done them, to withstand any encroachment by society on our private affairs. We were against institutionalism, which seemed incompatible with freedom, and likewise opposed to the bourgeoisie, from whom such a concept stemmed. We found it normal to behave in accordance with our convictions, and took the unmarried state for granted. Only some very serious consideration could have made us bow before conventions which we found repellent.

But such a consideration had now, in fact, arisen, since the thought of going away to Marseille threw me into a state of great anxiety: in these circumstances, Sartre said, it was stupid to martyr oneself for a principle. I may say that not for one moment was I tempted to fall in with his suggestion. Marriage doubles one's domestic responsibilities, and, indeed, all one's social chores. Any modification of the relationship we maintained with the outside world would have fatally affected that existing between the two of us. The task of preserving my own independence was not particularly onerous; I would have regarded it as highly artificial to equate Sartre's absence with my own freedom – a thing I could only find, honestly, within my own head and heart. But I could see how much it cost Sartre to bid farewell to his travels, his own freedom, his youth – in order to become a provincial academic, now finally and forever grown-up. To have joined the ranks of the married men would have meant an even greater renunciation. I knew he was incapable of bearing a grudge against me; but I knew, too, how vulnerable I was to the prick of conscience, and how greatly I detested it. Mere elementary caution prevented my choosing a future that might be poisoned by remorse. I did not even have to think it over: the decision was taken without any effort on my part – no hesitations, no weighing the pros and cons.

There was only one consideration that could have carried sufficient weight to make us pass under the yoke of so-called legitimacy: the desire for children. This we did not possess. I have so often been taken up on this point, and have been asked so many questions concerning it, that an explanation is, perhaps, desirable. I had not then, and have not now, any prejudice against motherhood as such. Small babies had never interested me, but I often found slightly older children charming, and had intended to have some of my own when I was thinking of marrying my cousin Jacques. If now I turned aside from such a scheme it was, primarily, because my happiness was too complete for any new element to attract me. A child would not have strengthened the bonds that united Sartre and me; nor did I want Sartre's existence reflected and extended in some other being. He was sufficient both for himself and for me. I too was self-sufficient: I never once dreamed of rediscovering myself in the child I might bear. In any case, I felt such absence of affinity with my own parents that any sons or daughters I might have I regarded in advance as strangers; from them I expected either indifference or hostility – so great had been my own aversion to family life. So I had no dreams urging me to embrace maternity; and to look at the problem another way, maternity itself seemed incompatible with the way of life upon which I was embarking. I knew that in order to become a writer I needed a great measure of time and freedom. I had no rooted objection to playing at long odds, but this was not a game: the whole value and direction of my life lay at stake. The risk of compromising it could only have been justified had I regarded a child as no less vital a creative task than a work of art, which I did not. I have recounted elsewhere how shocked I was by Zaza's declaration – we were both fifteen at the time – that having babies was just as important as writing books: I still failed to see how any common ground could be discovered between two such objects in life. Literature, I thought, was a way of justifying the world by fashioning it anew in the pure context of imagination – and, at the same time, of preserving its own existence from oblivion. Childbearing, on the other hand, seemed no more than a purposeless and unjustifiable increase of the world's population. It is hardly surprising that a Carmelite, having undertaken to pray for all mankind, also renounces the engendering of individual human beings. My vocation likewise would not admit impediments and stopped me from pursuing any plan alien to its needs. Thus the way of life I had chosen forced me to assume an attitude that would not be shaken by any of my impulses, and which I would never be tempted to discard. I never felt as though I were holding out against motherhood; it simply was not my natural lot in life, and by remaining childless I was fulfilling my proper function.

All the same, we did revise our original pact, inasmuch as we abandoned the idea of a provisional mutual 'surety' between us. Our relationship had become closer and more demanding than at first; it could allow brief separations, but not vast solitary escapades. We did not swear oaths of eternal fidelity; but we did agree to postpone any possibility of separation until the distant time when we reached our thirties.

From *The Prime of Life* by Simone de Beauvoir, 1960

A Terminal Note

In its original form, which it still almost retains, *Maurice* dates from 1913. It was the direct result of a visit to Edward Carpenter at Milthorpe. Carpenter had a prestige which cannot be understood today. He was a rebel appropriate to his age. He was sentimental and a little sacramental, for he had begun life as a clergyman. He was a socialist who ignored industrialism and a simple-lifer with an independent income and a Whitmannic poet whose nobility exceeded his strength and, finally, he was a believer in the Love of Comrades, whom he sometimes called Uranians. It was this last aspect of him that attracted me in my loneliness. For a short time he seemed to hold the key to every trouble. I approached him through Lowes Dickinson, and as one approaches a saviour.

It must have been on my second or third visit to the shrine that the spark was kindled and he and his comrade George Merrill combined to make a profound impression on me and to touch a creative spring. George Merrill also touched my backside – gently and just above the buttocks. I believe he touched most people's. The sensation was unusual and I still remember it, as I remember the position of a long vanished tooth. It was as much psychological as physical. It seemed to go straight through the small of my back into my ideas, without involving my thoughts. If it really did this, it would have acted in strict accordance with Carpenter's yogified mysticism, and would prove that at that precise moment I had conceived.

I then returned to Harrogate, where my mother was taking a cure, and immediately began to write *Maurice*. No other of my books has started off in this way. The general plan, the three characters, the happy ending for two of them, all rushed into my pen. And the whole thing went through without a hitch. It was finished in 1914. The friends, men and women, to whom I showed it liked it. But they were carefully picked. It has not so far had to face the critics or the public, and I have myself been too much involved in it, and for too long, to judge.

A happy ending was imperative. I shouldn't have bothered to write otherwise. I was determined that in fiction anyway two men should fall in love and remain in it for the ever and ever that fiction allows, and in this sense Maurice and Alec still roam the greenwood. I dedicated it 'To a Happier Year' and not altogether vainly. Happiness is its keynote – which by the way has had an unexpected result: it has made the book more difficult to publish. Unless the Wolfenden Report becomes law, it will probably have to remain in manuscript. If it ended unhappily, with a lad dangling from a noose or with a suicide pact, all would be well, for there is no pornography or seduction of minors. But the lovers get away unpunished and consequently recommend crime. Mr Borenius is too incompetent to catch them, and the only penalty society exacts is an exile they gladly embrace . . .

Note in conclusion on a word hitherto unmentioned. Since *Maurice* was written there has been a change in the public attitude here: the change from ignorance and terror to familiarity and contempt. It is not the change towards which Edward Carpenter had worked. He had hoped for the generous recognition of an emotion and for the reintegration of something primitive into the common stock. And I, though less optimistic, had supposed that knowledge would bring understanding. We had not realized that what the public really loathes in homosexuality is not the thing itself but having to think about it. If it could be slipped into our midst unnoticed, or legalized overnight by a decree in small print, there would be few protests. Unfortunately it can only be legalized by Parliament, and Members of Parliament are obliged to think or to appear to think. Consequently the Wolfenden recommendations will be indefinitely rejected, police prosecutions will continue and Clive on the bench will continue to sentence Alec in the dock. Maurice may get off.

From an addition to *Maurice* by E. M. Forster, 1960;
published (as stipulated) after his death in 1970

'If Men Could Menstruate'

So what would happen if suddenly, magically, men could menstruate and women could not?

Clearly, menstruation would become an enviable, boast-worthy, masculine event:

Men would brag about how long and how much.

Young boys would talk about it as the envied beginning of manhood.

Gifts, religious ceremonies, family dinners, and stag parties would mark the day.

To prevent monthly work loss among the powerful, Congress would fund a National Institute of Dysmenorrhea. Doctors would research little about heart attacks, from which men were hormonally protected, but everything about cramps.

Sanitary supplies would be federally funded and free. Of course, some men would still pay for the prestige of such commercial brands as Paul Newman Tampons, Muhammad Ali's Rope-a-Dope Pads, John Wayne Maxi Pads, and Joe Namath Jock Shields – 'For Those Light Bachelor Days'.

Gloria Steinem, *c.* 1965

When I'm good, I'm very very good,
but when I'm bad, I'm better.

Mae West

'An Interview'

[I. = Interviewer]

I. Do you need any particular environment in which to work?

ME. I like a room without a view, preferably a closet. Oddly enough, I've never worked in the attic. The front of our attic has a view, you see, and then the back part is jammed with old toys.

I. Do you need seclusion?

ME. I wish I could say I'd been locked in a room. It's pedestrian not to have a tyrannical husband. My work is, in this way, deprived of pathetic circumstance.

I. Never mind, perhaps you have a writer's costume.

ME. Only a navy blue woollen bathrobe. An effortlessly drab garment, I hate answering the phone in it. But I just don't have any faded dungarees or open-necked sport shirts. They're for men.

I. They're for men?

ME. They're for men.

I. I see. Well, speaking of men, could you explain why you are writing about women?

ME. I didn't want to overreach. Right from the start I thought: ME, you must limit yourself to *half* of the human race.

I. Then you were not prompted by feminism?

ME. Please.

I. Oh. Feminism is out, isn't it?

ME. Well, yes, in the way principles all go out before they're practiced. Say a bride gets locked in the bathroom. The guests have gone home from the wedding, they've already forgotten their sanction of this event – which, as it happens, hasn't quite happened. Still, people can't go on throwing rice forever.

I. But think of the poor bride.

ME. It's better for her to gnaw at the door than to argue in the mirror about her right to get out.

I. Then you do not have a female program of your own?

ME. You phrase things peculiarly.

I. I scarcely know what word will not offend you. I will try again. You don't have a program for women?

ME. No. No program.

I. Ah! But perhaps you will define the attitude of the woman toward the gun, the ship and the helicopter?

ME. Impossible.

I. It's been done. A man has done it for men.

ME. Indeed.

I. Then have you something to contribute to our knowledge of human sexual responses?

ME. You mean with wires and thermometers and all.

I. Yes.

ME. No.

I. This is fun, isn't it? Now tell me, is your work concerned with the status of American women?

ME. You make everything sound like a symposium.

I. Forgive me once again. Nonetheless, a good deal of work has been done on this subject. And it looks as though their status is slipping.

ME. I applaud this work. I deplore this slipping.

I. But have you studied the statistics on it?

ME. You touch on a personal matter which I am of course willing to reveal to the public. My internist has asked me to cut down gradually on my consumption of statistics about American women.

I. Why?

ME. It's sort of sad. Say I read that only nineteen American women became orthodontists in 1962. I am humiliated, depressed. I cry easily. It's days before I think to be glad that so few *wanted* to be orthodonists, do you see?

I. I think so. You like only statistics of success.

ME. Perhaps. But I think it's worse than that. I am afflicted by miscomprehension, the failures often seem to me successes. For example, we know exactly how many American women interrupted their husbands' anecdotes at dinner parties in 1966. Quite a few, as a matter of fact – 204,648 wives. But of course just to *count* them is to say they have failed at the table. This complicated thing, interruption, is made quite simply bad. And yet all dialogue, like you and me, might be defined as the prevention of monologue. And think of the other guests – how can we hope that they wanted to hear the husbands out? Perhaps these wives are socialists who place the liveliness of the party before their own favor with their husbands.

I. I think perhaps you might say *Yes* or *No* for a while again.

From *Thinking About Women* by Mary Ellmann, 1968

Why Do We Stand for It?

The first question is why do we stand for it? The oppressed are mysteriously quiet. The conservative answer is 'because they like it like that'. But the revolutionary can't afford to be so sure. He has learned to be doubtful about the 'happiness' of the exploited. He knows that containment cannot be directly related to quietness. The subordination of women only achieves perspective when it is seen in relation to the mechanism of domination. The way in which we are contained only really becomes comprehensible when it is seen as part of the general situation of the oppressed. In order to understand why those in control stay on top and the people they use don't shake them off it is necessary to trace the way in which the outward relationship of dominator to dominated becomes internalised.

'But they are happy like that.'

'Can't you see they enjoy it?'

Superficially there is a complicity between the subordinated and the authority figure. But this is in fact the mutuality of whore and pimp. They associate because of the way the game is rigged. She continually keeps back a percentage, he continually steals her clothes and beats her to survive. Deceit and violence are the basis of their relationship, and continue to be so until the external situation is changed. However the conception of change is beyond the notions of the oppressed. They are confined within the limits of their imagination of the possible. For the dominated without hope the relationship is habitual. There is neither the memory of a different condition in the past, nor the possibility of difference in the future, but an always world of dominating and dominated without moral belief in change or the means of effecting it.

The oppressed in their state before politics lack both the idea and practice to act upon the external world. Both coherent protest and organised resistance is inconceivable. They do not presume to alter things, they are timid. Life is cyclical, weary, events happen, disaster impinges, there is no rational order in the universe, to the authorities properly belong the business and responsibilities of government. They play dumb and the superior people assume they have nothing to say, nothing to complain of. Those in power conclude their 'inferiors' must be a different order of people. This justifies their subjugation. The impression is confirmed by their inability to take the advantage offered to them, by the shrugging off of responsibilities, by the failure to take initiatives. They refuse to help themselves, they are their own worst enemy. But meanwhile they survive. They are skilled in collaboration and subterfuge. They do not compete, they resort to indirect, sly methods. Like Br'er Rabbit they lie low.

All these characteristics can be detected amongst oppressed groups before they have created a political movement. They are also most common among those women completely dependent on men. The same mistake has been made about these traditional women as the rest. Because they do not articulate their complaints in terms recognised by those in control, they are presumed to be happy.

Women have been lying low for so long most of us cannot imagine how to get up. We have apparently acquiesced always in the imperial game and are so perfectly colonised that we are unable to consult ourselves. Because the assumption does not occur to us, it does not occur to anyone else either. We are afraid to mention ourselves in case it might disturb or divert some important matter he has in hand. We are the assistants, the receivers, the collaborators, dumb, lacking in presumption, not acting consciously upon the external world, much given to masochism. We become sly – never trust a woman – we seek revenge, slighted we are terrible; we are trained for subterfuge, we are natural creatures of the underground. Within us there are great gullies of bitterness, but they do not appear on the surface. Our wrapped-up consciousness creeps along the sewers, occasionally emerging through a manhole. After death, hag-like spirits roam the earth, the symbols of frustrated unfulfilled desires. But in life our spirits are contained.

From *Women's Liberation and the New Politics*, by Sheila Rowbotham, 1968

SCUM

SCUM is too impatient to hope and wait for the debrainwashing of millions of assholes. Why should the swinging females continue to plod dismally along with the dull male ones? Why should the fates of the groovy and the creepy be intertwined? Why should the active and imaginative consult the passive and dull on social policy? Why should the independent be confined to the sewer along with the dependent who need Daddy to cling to?

A small handful of SCUM can take over the country within a year by systematically fucking up the system, selectively destroying property and murder:

SCUM will become members of the unwork force, the fuck-up force; they will get jobs of various kinds and unwork. For example, SCUM salesgirls will not charge for merchandise; SCUM telephone operators will not charge for calls; SCUM office and factory workers, in addition to fucking up their work, will secretly destroy equipment. SCUM will unwork at a job until fired, then get a new job to unwork at.

SCUM will forcibly relieve bus drivers, cab drivers and subway token sellers of their jobs and run buses and cabs and dispense free tokens to the public.

SCUM will destroy all useless and harmful objects – cars, store windows, 'Great Art,' etc.

Eventually, SCUM will take over the airwaves – radio and TV networks – by forcibly relieving of their jobs all radio and TV employees who would impede SCUM's entry into the broadcasting studios.

SCUM will couple-bust – barge into mixed (male-female) couples, wherever they are, and bust them up.

SCUM will kill all men who are not in the Men's Auxiliary of SCUM. Men in the Men's Auxiliary are those men who are working diligently to eliminate themselves, men who, regardless of their motives, do good, men who are playing ball with SCUM. A few examples of the men in the Men's Auxiliary are: men who kill men; biological scientists who are working on constructive programs, as opposed to biological warfare; journalists, writers, editors, publishers and producers who disseminate and promote ideas that will lead to the achievement of SCUM's goals; faggots, who by their shimmering, flaming example encourage other men to de-man themselves, and thereby make themselves relatively inoffensive; men who consistently give things away – money, things, services; men who tell it like it is (so far not one ever has), who put women straight, who reveal the truth about themselves, who give the mindless male females correct sentences to parrot, who tell them a woman's primary goal in life should be to squash the male sex (to aid men in this endeavour SCUM will conduct Turd Sessions, at which every male present will give a speech beginning with the sentence: 'I am a turd, a lowly, abject turd,' then proceed to list all the ways in which he is. His reward for so doing will be the opportunity to fraternize after the session for a whole, solid hour with the SCUM who will be present. Nice, clean-living male women will be invited to the sessions to help clarify any doubts and misunderstandings they may have about the male sex); makers and promoters of sex books and movies, etc., who are hastening the day when all that will be shown on the screen will be Suck and Fuck (males, like the rats following the Pied Piper, will be lured by Pussy to their doom, will be overcome and submerged by and will eventually drown in the passive flesh that they are); drug pushers and advocates, who are hastening the dropping out of men.

SCUM will keep on destroying, looting, fucking-up and killing until the money/work system no longer exists and automation is completely instituted or until enough women co-operate with SCUM to make violence unnecessary to achieve these goals, that is, until enough women either unwork or quit work, start looting, leave men and refuse to obey all laws inappropriate to a truly civilized society. Many women will fall into line, but many others, who surrendered long ago to the enemy, who are so adapted to animalism, to maleness, that they like restrictions and restraints, don't know what to do with freedom, will continue to be toadies and doormats, just as peasants in rice paddies remain peasants in rice paddies as one regime topples another. A few of the more volatile will whimper and sulk and throw their toys and dishrags on the floor, but SCUM will continue to steamroller over them.

Prior to the institution of automation, to the replacement of males by machines, the male should be of use to the female, wait on her, cater to her slightest whim, obey her every command, be totally subservient to her, exist in perfect obedience to her will, as opposed to the completely warped, degenerate situation we have now of men, not only existing at all, cluttering up the world with their ignominious presence, but being pandered to and groveled before by the mass of females, millions of women piously worshipping the Golden Calf, the dog leading the master on the leash, when in fact the male, short of being a drag queen, is least miserable when abjectly prostrate before the female, a complete slave. Rational men want to be squashed, stepped on, crushed and crunched, treated as the curs, the filth that they are, have their repulsiveness confirmed.

The sick, irrational men, those who attempt to defend themselves against their disgustingness, when they see SCUM barreling down on them, will cling in terror to Big Mama with her Big Bouncy Boobies, but Boobies won't protect them against SCUM; Big Mama will be clinging to Big Daddy, who will be in the corner shitting in his forceful, dynamic pants. Men who are rational, however, won't kick or struggle or raise a distressing fuss, but will just sit back, relax, enjoy the show and ride the waves to their demise.

From the *SCUM (Society for Cutting Up Men) Manifesto*
by Valerie Solanas, 1969

No More Miss America

WE Protest:

1 The degrading Mindless-Boob-Girlie Symbol. The Pageant contestants epitomize the roles we are all forced to play as women. The parade down the runway blares the metaphor of the 4-H Club county fair, where the nervous animals are judged for teeth, fleece, etc., and where the best 'specimen' gets the blue ribbon. So are women in our society forced daily to compete for male approval, enslaved by ludicrous 'beauty' standards we ourselves are conditioned to take seriously.

2 Racism with Roses. Since its inception in 1921, the Pageant has not had one Black finalist, and this has not been for a lack of test-case contestants. There has never been a Puerto Rican, Alaskan, Hawaiian, or Mexican-American winner. Nor has there ever been a *true* Miss America – an American Indian.

3 Miss America as Military Death Mascot. The highlight of her reign each year is a cheerleader-tour of American troops abroad – last year she went to Vietnam to pep-talk our husbands, fathers, sons and boyfriends into dying and killing with a better spirit. She personifies the 'unstained patriotic American womanhood our boys are fighting for'. The Living Bra and the Dead Soldier. We refuse to be used as Mascots for Murder.

4 The Consumer Con-Game. The Pageant is sponsored by Pepsi-Cola, Toni, and Oldsmobile – Miss America is a walking commercial. Wind her up and she plugs your product on promotion tours and TV – all in an 'honest objective' endorsement. What a shill.*

5 Competition Rigged and Unrigged. We deplore the encouragement of

an American myth that oppresses men as well as women: the win-or-you're-worthless competitive disease. The 'beauty contest' creates only one winner to be 'used' and forty-nine losers who are 'useless'.

6 The Woman as Pop Culture Obsolescent Theme. Spindle, mutilate and then discard tomorrow. What is so ignored as last year's Miss America? This only reflects the gospel of our society, according to Saint Male: women must be young, juicy, malleable – hence age discrimination and the cult of youth. And we women are brain-washed into believing this ourselves!

7 The Unbeatable Madonna-Whore Combination. Miss America and Playboy's centrefold are sisters over the skin. To win approval, we must be both sexy and wholesome, delicate but able to cope, demure yet titillatingly bitchy. Deviation of any sort brings, we are told, disaster: 'You won't get a man!!'

8 The Irrelevant Crown on the Throne of Mediocrity. Miss America represents what women are supposed to be: unoffensive, bland, apolitical. If you are tall, short, over or under what weight the Man prescribes you should be, forget it. Personality, articulateness, intelligence, commitment – unwise. Conformity is the key to the crown – and, by extension, to success in our society.

9 Miss America as Dream Equivalent to – ? In this reputedly democratic society, where every little boy supposedly can grow up to be President, what can every little girl hope to grow to be? Miss America. That's where it's at. Real power to control our own lives is restricted to men, while women get patronizing pseudo-power, an ermine cloak and a bunch of flowers; men are judged by their actions, women by their appearance.

10 Miss America as Big Sister Watching You. The Pageant exercises Thought Control, attempts to sear the Image into our minds, to further make women oppressed and men oppressors; to enslave us all the more in high-heeled, low-status roles; to inculcate false values in young girls; to use women as beasts of buying; to seduce us to prostitute ourselves before our own oppression.

*A confidence trickster's female assistant

Leaflet distributed at the Miss World Contest, 1970

IT BEGINS WHEN YOU SINK INTO HIS ARMS AND ENDS WITH YOUR ARMS IN HIS SINK

'While You'

While you
come home
open a beer
and watch TV
while you
settle down in the same old chair
and say how tough things are at the office
you don't say how often you
  asked the secretary for a date
how often you and your drinking pals
  made passes at the girls in the bar
while you
decide what café you'll head for today
or submerge in the commercial and wait for dinner
she
tries to forget the tasteless flirting
she put up with on her way to work
how she was propositioned by the customers and by the boss
she
tries to prepare dinner
fix up the house
smile at the kids
and tell herself that your escapades
are just a passing fancy
that your whims are just a passing notion
and that she in spite of everything is
  a happily married woman.

Bessy Reyna, *c.* 1970

I have three pets at home that answer the same purpose as a husband. I have a dog that growls every morning, a parrot that swears all afternoon and a cat that comes home late at night.

Marie Corelli

We Fight

HELEN [*to the audience*]: You don't count as a woman without a husband so you get married. But you're not much of a wife without kids so you stay at home. But you can't be a good mother without money so you go out to work. But you can't be a good worker and a good mother so you stay, underpaid, untrained and you do a second shift at home. But you're not a good wife when you're tired so you don't count as a woman.

We fight against all these things and what we've achieved is a beginning. But the fight won't end while we keep asking for crumbs. We've got to fight for something different. A world where children can grow up under decent conditions, where women can choose when to have kids, where we have free contraception and, when we need it, abortion. Where women can choose not to have kids and that's just as natural as having them. A world where women really are men's equals, not just with equal pay – that's just equal exploitation – but a world with no exploitation. This means big changes and only you and I can make them. But if they're needed, can you say we're asking too much?

From *Strike While the Iron is Hot* by Red Ladder Theatre, 1973

'I am a Dangerous Woman'

I am a dangerous woman
Carrying neither bombs nor babies
Flowers or Molotov cocktails.
I confound all your reason, theory, realism
Because I will neither lie in your ditches
Nor dig your ditches for you
Nor join your armed struggle
For bigger and better ditches.
I will not walk with you nor walk for you,
I won't live with you
And I won't die for you
But neither will I try to deny you
Your right to live and die.
I will not share one square foot of this earth with you
While you're hell-bent on destruction
But neither will I deny that we are of the same earth,
born of the same Mother

I will not permit
You to bind my life to yours
But I will tell you that our lives
Are bound together
And I will demand
That you live as though you understand
This one salient fact.

I am a dangerous woman
because I will tell you, sir,
whether you are concerned or not,
Masculinity has made of this world a living hell
A furnace burning away at hope, love, faith, and justice,
A furnace of My Lais, Hiroshimas, Dachaus.
A furnace which burns the babies
You tell us we must make,
Masculinity made Femininity
Made the eyes of our women go dark and cold,
sent our sons – yes sir, *our* sons –
To War
Made our children go hungry
Made our mothers whores
Made our bombs, our bullets, our 'Food for Peace,'
  our definitive solutions and first strike policies
Yes sir
Masculinity broke women and men on its knee
Took away our futures
Made our hopes, fears, thoughts and good instincts
'irrelevant to the larger struggle.'
And made human survival beyond the year 2000
An open question.
Yes sir
And it has possessed you.

I am a dangerous woman
because I will say all this
lying neither to you nor with you
Neither trusting nor despising you.
I am dangerous because
I won't give up, shut up, or put up
  with your version of reality.
You have conspired to sell my life quite cheaply

Because I will never forgive nor forget
Or ever conspire
To sell yours in return.

Joan Cavanagh, *c.* 1975

'What-I'm-Not Song'

I'm not your Little Woman
I'm not your Better Half
I'm not your nudge, your snigger
Or your belly laugh.

I'm not Jezebel
And I'm not Delilah
I'm not Mary Magdalen
Or the Virgin Mary either.

Not a Novice or a Nun.
Nor a Hooker or a Stripper.
Not Super Shirley Conran.
Not Jill the Ripper.

No I'm no Scissor-Lady –
I won't snip at your . . . locks.
I'm not a siren, you're not obliged
To get off my rocks.

Not Medusa, not Medea
And, though my tongue may be
salty
I'm not the Delphic Sybil –
Or Sybil Fawlty

I'm not Poison Ivy
You can throw away the lotion
I'm not your Living Doll
I'm not Poetry in Motion.

And if selling Booze and Cars
Involves my body being used.
Well . . .
I'm not Queen Victoria
But I'm not amused.

And if you don't like my Body
You can sodding well lump it –
I'm not a Tart-with-a-Golden-Heart
Or Thinking Man's Crumpet.

I'm not your Woman of Achievement
Not your Slimmer Of The Year
I'm not Princess Diana . . .
No Frog Princes 'Ere!

I'm not little Ms. Midler
I'm not little Miss Muffet
Make me An Offer I Can't Refuse –
And I'll tell you to stuff it!

'Cos I'm not your Little woman
I'm not your Lady Wife
I'm not your Old Bag
Or the Love of Your Life

No, I'm not your Little Woman
Not your Better Half
I'm not your Nudge, your Snigger
Or your Belly-Laugh!

Liz Lochhead, 1985

Medallion Man

Bar. Tracey Ullman sitting at table, reading book. David Copperfield (wearing open shirt, medallion, i.d. bracelet, flares, etc.) comes and stands over her.

DAVID: Haven't I seen you somewhere before?

TRACEY: Yeah, you've been staring at me for half an hour.

DAVID: Can I sit down, babe?

TRACEY: I doubt it, in those trousers . . .

DAVID: Oh, groovy. Yeah, what a girl!

(Sits down in discomfort. Leans over.)

DAVID: So, what are you having, dream child?

TRACEY: A lot of aggravation . . .

DAVID: Hey groovy. Barman! Two martinis!

TRACEY: One with ground glass in it please.

DAVID: Hey, those pretty lips of yours could be put to much better use. How about showing me what they can do?

(Tracey blows raspberry at him.)

DAVID: Yeah, nice sound. Come on now, babe. You and me. Me and you. We could work magic together.

TRACEY: We could work magic?

DAVID: Yeah.

TRACEY: Well, let's start with your disappearing trick.

DAVID: Babe. Easy now. Look into my face.

TRACEY: How can I? You're sitting on it.

DAVID: Look, all I want to do is have a nice time. We could go back to my pad, turn the dimmer switch down low, pop on a Tony Christie LP and swing, swing, swing . . .

TRACEY: Oh, I'd like to see you swing.

DAVID: Hey, hey, hey, so what do you say?

TRACEY: Get stuffed!

DAVID: Hang loose, babe. I'm the company's number one rep . . .

TRACEY: Short for reptile?

DAVID: No, you're talking to money here. You're talking to ten thou plus commission and petrol. You're talking to a Ford Sierra with heated rear window. You babe, are talking to a circular bed and a sunken bath.

TRACEY: And you are talking to a brick wall, so shove off.

(Lenny Henry appears in a suit and tie.)

LENNY: I'm the manager, miss. Is this jerk bothering you?

TRACEY: Yeah, he really is.

LENNY: O.K. mate, hop it. Out.

DAVID: Yeah? What are you going to do about it? . . . O.K.!

(David exits.)

TRACEY: Phew, thanks. It's lucky you came over.

LENNY: (*sits in David's seat.*) Yeah, it's your lucky night tonight, all right.

(Sits down and rips off tie to reveal medallion.)

Sketch by Andrea Solomons in *Three of a Kind*, *c.* 1985

WHEN GOD MADE MAN SHE WAS ONLY TESTING

Graffito

Enema

'She felt the soft bud of him within her stirring, and strange rhythms flushing up into her with a strange rhythmic growing motion, swelling and swelling till it filled all her cleaving consciousness, and then began again with the unspeakable motion that was not really motion, but pure deepening whirlpools of sensation swirling deeper and deeper through all her tissue and consciousness, till she was one perfect concentric fluid of feeling . . .'

An enema under the influence of Ecstasy would probably feel much like this. . . .

Germaine Greer on *Lady Chatterley's Lover*, 1990

'Blow Jobs'

You'd get more protein from the average egg;
the taste's a tepid, watery nothingness –
skimmed milk? weak coffee? puréed cucumber?

Fellation's not a woman's idea of fun.
Just doing it as foreplay is OK.
You kiss me, I'll kiss you's a quid pro quo –
but carrying on until the buggers come –
suck, suck, suck, suck for half a bloody hour!
(I haven't timed it but it feels that way.)

There's nothing in the act for us. Our mouths
are better stimulated by a kiss.
The sucked lie back (with beatific smiles),
forget our bodies in their private dreams,
while we grow cold, detached, unloved, untouched,
our heads like 3-D sporrans on their groins,
bored out of mind, with aching jaws and cheeks,
like kids that Santa gave a plastic flute,
still trying to get a tune on Boxing Day.

'Toothless George' sucked all comers to the rocks
in a secluded Jersey cove each June.
(He'd come from Blackpool for his yearly treat.)
Men love that act, sucking and being sucked.
Most women wish they'd keep it to themselves.

Fiona Pitt-Kethley, 1991

Four

OPULENCE IS ALWAYS THE RESULT OF THEFT

A Peasant is not Called a Man

The carpenter who wields an adze,
He is wearier than a field-laborer;
His field is the timber, his hoe the adze.
There is no end to his labor,
He does more than his arms can do,
Yet at night he kindles light.

The jewel-maker bores with his chisel
In hard stone of all kinds;
When he has finished the inlay of the eye,
His arms are spent, he's weary;
Sitting down when the sun goes down,
His knees and back are cramped.

The barber barbers till nightfall,
He betakes himself to town,
He sets himself up in his corner,
He moves from street to street,
Looking for someone to barber.
He strains his arms to fill his belly,
Like the bee that eats as it works.

The reed-cutter travels to the Delta to get arrows;
When he has done more than his arms can do,
Mosquitoes have slain him,
Gnats have slaughtered him,
He is quite worn out.

The potter is under the soil,
Though as yet among the living;
He grubs in the mud more than a pig,
In order to fire his pots.
His clothes are stiff with clay,

His girdle is in shreds;
If air enters his nose,
It comes straight from the fire.
He makes a pounding with his feet,

And is himself crushed;
He grubs the yard of every house
And roams the public places. . . .

The bird-catcher suffers much
As he watches out for birds;
When the swarms pass over him,
He keeps saying, 'had I a net!'
But the god grants it not,
And he's angry with his lot.

I'll speak of the fisherman also,
His is the worst of all the jobs;
He labors on the river,
Mingling with crocodiles.
When the time of reckoning comes,
He is full of lamentations;
He does not say, 'There's a crocodile,'
Fear has made him blind.
[Coming from] the flowing water
He says, 'Mighty god!'

See, there's no profession without a boss,
Except for the scribe; he is the boss.
Hence if you know writing,
It will do better for you
Than those professions I've set before you,
Each more wretched than the other.
A peasant is not called a man,
Beware of it!

From the *Satire of the Trades*, Ancient Egypt, *c.*1550 BCE

Poverty

A beggar to the graveyard hied
And there 'Friend corpse, arise,' he cried;
'One moment lift my heavy weight
Of poverty; for I of late
Grow weary and desire instead
Your comfort; you are good and dead.'

The corpse was silent. He was sure
'Twas better to be dead than poor.

From the Sanskrit story-cycle, *The Panchatantra*, *c.* 1000 BCE

Trampling the Poor

They hate him who reproves in the gate,
and they abhor him who speaks the truth.
Therefore:
Because you trample the poor
and take from him exactions of wheat,
you have built houses of hewn stone,
but you shall not dwell in them.
You have planted pleasant vineyards,
but you shall not drink their wine.
For I know how many are your transgressions,
and how great are your sins –
you who afflict the righteous, who take a bribe,
and turn aside the needy in the gate . . .
Hear this,
you who trample upon the needy,
and bring the poor of the land to an end,
saying,
'When will the new moon be over,
that we may sell grain?
And the sabbath,
that we may offer wheat for sale,
that we may make the ephah small and the shekel great,
and deal deceitfully with false balances,
that we may buy the poor for silver
and the needy for a pair of sandals,
and sell the refuse of the wheat?'
The Lord has sworn by the pride of Jacob:
'Surely I will never forget any of their deeds.
Shall not the land tremble on this account,
and every one mourn who dwells in it?'

Amos 5:10–12 and 8:4–8, eighth century BCE

Money is like Muck, not good except it be spread.

Francis Bacon

Money Cloaks Iniquity

Money wins friendship, honour, place and power,
and sets man next to the proud tyrant's throne.
All trodden paths and paths untrod before
are scaled by nimble riches, where the poor
can never hope to win the heart's desire.
A man ill-formed by nature and ill-spoken,
Money shall make him fair to eye and ear.
Money earns man his health and happiness
and only money cloaks iniquity.

From *Antigone* by Sophocles, 443 BCE

Howl Rich

Come now, you rich, weep and howl for the miseries that are coming upon you. Your riches have rotted and your garments are moth-eaten. Your gold and silver have rusted, and their rust will be evidence against you and will eat up your flesh like fire . . .

Behold, the wages of the labourers who moved your fields, which you kept back by fraud, cry out; and the cries of the harvesters have reached the ears of the Lord of hosts. You have lived on the earth in luxury and in pleasure; you have fattened your hearts in a day of slaughter. You have condemned, you have killed the righteous man; he does not resist you.

James 5:1–6, first century

Early Christians and the Rich

I know that God has given us the use of goods, but only as far as is necessary; and He has determined that the use be common. It is absurd and disgraceful for one to live magnificently and luxuriously when so many are hungry.

Clement of Alexandria (150–215)

No man shall be received into our commune who sayeth that the land may be sold. God's footstool is not property.

St Cyprian (200–258)

Which things, tell me, are yours? Whence have you brought your goods into life? You are like one occupying a place in a theatre, who should prohibit others from entering, treating that as his own which was designed for the common use of all. Such are the rich. Because they preoccupy common goods, they take these goods as their own. If each one would take that which is sufficient for his needs, leaving what is superfluous to those in distress, no one would be rich, no one poor . . . The rich man is a thief.

St Basil (329–379)

How far, O rich, do you extend your senseless avarice? Do you intend to be the sole inhabitants of the earth? Why do you drive out the fellow sharers of nature, and claim it all for yourselves? The earth was made for all, rich and poor, in common. Why do you rich claim it as your exclusive right? The soil was given to the rich and poor in common – wherefore, oh, ye rich, do you unjustly claim it for yourselves alone? Nature gave all things in common for the use of all; usurpation created private rights. Property hath no rights. The earth is the Lord's, and we are his offspring. The pagans hold earth as property. They do blaspheme God.

St Ambrose (340–397)

All riches come from iniquity, and unless one has lost, another cannot gain. Hence that common opinion seems to me to be very true, 'the rich man is unjust, or the heir an unjust one.' Opulence is always the result of theft, if not committed by the actual possessor, then by his predecessor.

St Jerome (340–420)

Tell me, whence are you rich? From whom have you received? From your grandfather, you say; from your father. Are you able to show, ascending in the order of generation, that that possession is just throughout the whole series of preceding generations? Its beginning and root grew necessarily out of injustice. Why? Because God did not make this man rich and that man poor from the beginning. Nor, when He created the world, did He allot much treasure to one man, and forbid another to seek any. He gave the same earth to be cultivated by all. Since, therefore, His bounty is common, how comes it that you have so many fields, and your neighbor not even a clod of earth? . . . The idea we should have of the rich and covetous – they are truly as robbers, who, standing in the public highway, despoil the passers.

St John Chrysostom (347–407)

Small thieves lie in towers fastened to wooden blocks; big ones strut about in gold and silver.

Cato the censor, *c.* 200 BCE

One law for the poor and one for the rich

One man owns a large mansion with costly marbles, another has not so much as a small hut to keep out the cold and heat. One man has vast territories, another has a little bit of turf to sit on and call his own . . . Did God will universal inequality? Does this poor man feel the sun less keenly than the rich? Should there be one law for the poor and one for the rich? . . .

When does your prosperous man remember the frailty of his condition? Listen to the rich man calling the beggar 'wretch', 'beggar', 'rabble', because he dares to open his mouth in 'our' presence . . .

Magistrates have under their very eyes the bodies of men like you in nature beaten with whips of lead, broken with clubs, burnt in the flames.

Pelagian Briton, fourteenth century

Piers Plowman's Lament

Lo, lords, lo, and ladies! witness
That the sweet liquor lasts but a little season,
Like peapods, and early pears, plums and cherries,
What lances up lightly lasts but a moment,
And what is readiest to ripen rots soonest.
A fat land full of dung breeds foul weeds rankly,
And so are surely all such bishops,
Earls and archdeacons and other rich clerics

Who traffic with tradesmen and turn on them if they are beaten,
And have the world at their will to live otherwise.
As weeds run wild on ooze or on the dunghill,
So riches spread upon riches give rise to all vices.
The best wheat is bent before ripening
On land that is overlaid with marle or the dungheap.
And so are surely all such people:
Overplenty feeds the pride which poverty conquers.

The wealth of this world is evil to its keeper,
Howsoever it may be won, unless it be well expended.
If he is far from it, he fears often
That false men or felons will fetch away his treasure.
Moreover wealth makes men on many occasions
To sin, and to seek out subtlety and treason,
Or from coveting of goods to kill the keepers.
Thus many have been murdered for their money or riches,
And those who did the deed damned forever,
And he himself, perhaps, in hell for his hard holding;
And greed for goods was the encumbrance of all together.
Pence have often purchased both palaces and terror;
Riches are the root of robbery and of murder;
He who so gathers his goods prizes God at little.

William Langland, *c.* 1350

Woe to the Lords
'Balade'

I fear sore that dear times will come, and that we shall have an evil year, when I see many men gather corn together and store it apart. I see the fields fail, the air corrupted, the land in disarray, evil plowing and rotting seed, weakling horses whose labour drags; on the other hand the rich man crieth 'Check!' Wherefore poor folk must needs go begging, for no man careth but to fill his bags.

Each man is selfish and covetous in his own fashion; their lives are disordered; all is snatched away by violence of great men, nor doth any creature under the sun seek the common good. Do men govern the land according to reason? Nay! for law is perished, Truth faileth, I see Lying reign among us, and the greatest men are drowned in this lake [of sin]; the earth is ruined by covetise, for no man careth but to fill his bags.

Therefore the innocent must die of hunger, with whom these great wolves daily fill their maw; those who heap up false treasures by the hundred and the thousand. This grain, this corn, what is it but the blood and bones of the poor folk who have ploughed the land? wherefore their spirit crieth on God for vengeance. Woe to the lords, the councillors, and all who steer us thus, and woe to all such as are of their party; for no man careth now but to fill his bags.

L'ENVOY

Prince, short is the span of this Life, and a man dieth as suddenly as one may say 'clac'; whither will the poor abashed soul go? for no man careth now but to fill his bags.

Eustache Deschamps (1346–1406)

Civil war is only another name for class war.

Rosa Luxemburg

'Sir Penny'

In earth it is a little thing,
And reigns also a rich king,
  Where he is lent in land;
Sir Penny is his name called,
He makes both young and old
  Bow unto his hand.

Popes, kings, and emperors,
Bishops, abbots, and priors,
  Parson, priest, and knight,
Dukes, earls, and each baron,
To serve him are they full bound,
  Both by day and night.

He may buy both heaven and hell,
And each thing that is to sell,
  In earth he has such grace;
He may loose and he may bind;
The poor are aye put behind,
  Where he comes in place.

Anon., *c.* 1400

The Sheep-thief's Message

Mr. Pratt, your sheep are very fat,
  And we thank you for that;
We have left you the skins to pay your wife's pins,
  And you must thank us for that.

Anon., medieval

The Fatte Priestes

Nevertheles even as in the time of oure greatest errour and ignoraunce, the fatte priestes wold never confesse that any thing concerninge our religion was amis, worthy to be reformed, even so now at this daye there be many fatte marchauntes which wold have no reformation in the comon wealth affirming that therin al thinges be wel, but he that wyll be conversaunt with the comen sorte of the poore comens, shal (if he stop not his eares, nor hyde not his eyes) both heare se and perceyve the case to be farre other wise. He shal heare tel that a fewe richemen have ingrossed up so many fermes and shepe pastures, and have decayed so many whole townes, that thousands of the poore comens can not get so muche as one ferme, nor scant any litell house to put their head in. It is not agreable with the gospel that a fewe parsons shall lyve in so great aboundaunce of wealth and suffer so many their christen brothers to lyve in extreme povertie.

From *Pyers Plowmans Exhortation unto the Lordes, Knightes and Burgoysses of Parlyamenthouse*, anon., 1550

On Enclosures

The more sheep, the dearer is the wool.
The more sheep, the dearer is the mutton.
The more sheep, the dearer is the beef.
The more sheep, the dearer is the corn.
The more sheep, the scanter is the white meat.
The more sheep, the fewer eggs for a penny.

Anon., *c.* 1600

Widow Want

Diggers and dikers, drudges, carters, swains,
Shepherds and cowards, friend thee at thy need,
The poorest persons work thy richest gains,
Thy dropsy with commodity to feed,
  Cobblers and curriers, tinkers and tanners all
  Support thy state, else would thy fortress fall.

It's work time-worthy to observe the ways
Of worldlings, how prepost'rously they live,
That will not help, yet want helps all their days,
That without gifts live not, yet will not give.
  O brazen fronts, o iron-mettled hearts,
  Whose quivers surfeit with discourteous darts.

The widow Want sojourns at low-streets end,
While monster Money purchaseth a place,
His consistory midst the town to spend,
'mongst magistrates, monarchs of greatest grace;
  While to the rich the world a Lor'ship gives,
  Poverty always undertenant lives.

Nature, that first gave life, decreed a law,
That mortals earth's-fruits should in common hold,
When time's corruption private profit saw,
Things *gratis* given must be bought and sold,
  And then division strived for a store,
  To mar what Golden Age had made before.

These fatlings feast, while as I poorly fast,
They dine, I pine; they sweetly sleep, I wake:
They leave, I lack; I want, they plenty waste:
I seek a crumb, while choice of cates they make,
  Their fast is dearth of stomach, not of meat,
  Mine is because I have not what to eat.

Verses 26, 27, 31, 44, and 109 from *The Poor Man's Passions* by Arthur Warren, 1605, and reprinted here for the first time since

The Fruit of Other Men's Labours

When the earth was first bought and sold, many gave no consent: as when our crown lands and bishops' lands were sold, some foolish soldiers yielded, and covetous officers were active in it, to advance themselves above their brethren; but many who paid taxes and free-quarter for the purchase of it gave no consent but declared against it as an unrighteous thing, depriving posterity of their birthrights and freedoms.

Therefore this buying and selling did bring in, and still doth bring in, discontent and wars, which have plagued mankind sufficiently for so doing. And the nations of the world will never learn to beat their swords into ploughshares, and their spears into pruning hooks, and leave off warring, until this cheating device of buying and selling be cast out among the rubbish of kingly power.

'But shall not one man be richer than another?'

There is no need of that; for riches make men vain-glorious, proud, and to oppress their brethren; and are the occasion of wars.

No man can be rich, but he must be rich either by his own labours, or by the labours of other men helping him. If a man have no help from his neighbour, he shall never gather an estate of hundreds and thousands a year. If other men help him to work, then are those riches his neighbours' as well as his; for they may be the fruit of other men's labours as well as his own.

But all rich men live at ease, feeding and clothing themselves by the labours of other men, not by their own; which is their shame, and not their nobility; for it is a more blessed thing to give than to receive. But rich men receive all they have from the labourer's hand, and what they give, they give away other men's labours, not their own. Therefore they are not righteous actors in the earth.

From *The Law of Freedom in a Platform* by Gerald Winstanley, 1652

Mr Badman

Extortion is a screwing from men more than by the law of God or men is right; and it is committed sometimes by them in office, about fees, rewards, and the like: but it is most commonly committed by men of trade, who without all conscience, when they have the advantage, will make a prey of their neighbour. And thus was Mr Badman an extortioner; for although he did not exact, and force away, as bailiffs and clerks have used to do, yet he had his opportunities, and such cruelty to make use of them, that he would often, in his way, be extorting and forcing of money out of his neighbour's pockets.

He that sells as dear as he can, offereth violence to the law of nature, for that saith,

Do unto all men even as ye would that they should do unto you.

From *The Life and Death of Mr Badman* by John Bunyan, 1680

A House She Hath

A house she hath, it's made of such good fashion
The tenant ne'er shall pay for reparation:
Nor will the Landlord ever raise the rent,
Or turn her out of doors for non-payment
From chimney money too, this cell is free
To such a house as this who would not tenant be.

Rebecca Rogers' epitaph, Folkestone, 1688

Dick Turpin wore a mask to rob the poor, but Ford spare the nicety.

Ford striker, 1972

The Interest of the Great

Now the great, who were tyrants themselves before the election of one tyrant, are naturally averse to a power raised over them, and whose weight must ever lean heaviest on the subordinate orders. It is the interest of the great, therefore, to diminish kingly power as much as possible; because, whatever they take from that is naturally restored to themselves; and all they have to do in the state is to undermine the single tyrant, by which they resume their primeval authority.

Now the state may be so circumstanced, or its laws may be so disposed, or its men of opulence so minded, as all to conspire in carrying on this business of undermining monarchy. For, in the first place, if the circumstances of our state be such as to favour the accumulation of wealth, and make the opulent still more rich, this will increase their ambition. An accumulation of wealth, however, must necessarily be the consequence, when, as at present, more riches flow in from external commerce than arise from internal industry; for external commerce can only be managed to advantage by the rich, and they have also at the same time all the emoluments arising from internal industry; so that the rich, with us, have two sources of wealth, whereas the poor have but one. For this reason, wealth, in all commercial states, is found to accumulate; and all such have hitherto in time become aristocratical.

From *The Vicar of Wakefield* by Oliver Goldsmith, 1766

The first lesson one learns in Parliament is that the two
great parties generally forget their political differences
when the just claims of the people threaten their pockets.

Will Crooks

A Crab is a Crab

O' lordling acquaintance ne'er boast,
Nor Duke that ye dined wi' yestreen;
A crab-louse is still but a crab
Tho' perch'd on the cunt o' a Queen.

Robert Burns, *c.* 1780

Epitaph

Underneath Lieth the Body of Robert Comonly Called Bone Phillip who died July 27th 1793 Aged 63 Years At whose request the following lines are here inserted

Here lie I at the Chancel door
Here lie I because I'm poor
The farther in the more you'll pay
Here lie I as warm as they.

From a tomb at Kingsbridge, Devon

Such Heat

Some of these lords of the loom have in their employ thousands of miserable creatures. In the cotton-spinning work, these creatures are kept, fourteen hours in each day, locked up, summer and winter, in a heat of from *eighty to eighty-four degrees*. The rules which they are subjected to are such as no negroes were ever subjected to . . .

Very seldom do we feel such a heat as this in England. The 31st of last August, and the 1st, 2nd, and 3rd of last September, were very hot days. The newspapers told us that men had dropped down dead in the harvest fields, and that many horses had fallen dead upon the road; and yet the heat during those days never exceeded eighty-four degrees in the *hottest part of the day*. We were retreating to the coolest rooms in our house; we were pulling off our coats, wiping the sweat off our faces, puffing, blowing, and panting, and yet we were living in a heat nothing like eighty degrees.

What, then, must be the situation of the poor creatures who are doomed to toil day after day, for three hundred and thirteen days in the year, fourteen hours in each day, in an average heat of eighty-two degrees? Can any man, with a heart in his body, and a tongue in his head, refrain from cursing a system that produces such slavery and such cruelty?

Observe, too, that these poor creatures have no cool room to retreat to, not a moment to wipe off the sweat, and not a breath of air to come and interpose itself between them and infection. The 'door of the place wherein they work, *is locked, except half an hour*, at tea-time, the workpeople are not allowed to send for water to drink, in the hot factory; even *the rain water is locked up*, by the master's order, otherwise they would be happy to drink even that. If any spinner be found with his *window open*, he is to pay a fine of a shilling! Mr Martin, of Galway, has procured acts of parliament to prevent *cruelty* to *animals*. If horses or dogs were shut up in a place like this, they would certainly be thought worthy of Mr Martin's attention.

'Not only is there not a breath of sweet air in these truly infernal scenes, but, for a large part of the time, there is the abominable and pernicious stink of the *gas* to assist in the murderous effects of the heat. In addition to the noxious effluvia of the gas, mixed with the steam, there are the dust, and what is called cotton-flying or fuz, which the unfortunate creatures have to inhale; and the fact is, the notorious fact is, that well constitutioned men are rendered old and past labour at forty years of age, and that children are rendered decrepit and deformed, and thousands upon thousands of them slaughtered by consumptions, before they arrive at the age of sixteen . . .

'Nine hundred and ninety-nine thousandths of the people of England have not the most distant idea that such things are carried on, in a country calling itself free; in a country whose Minister for Foreign Affairs is everlastingly teasing and bothering other Powers to emulate England in 'her humanity', in abolishing the slave trade in the blacks. The blacks, when carried to the West Indies, are put into a paradise compared with the situation of these poor white creatures in Lancashire, and other factories of the North . . .

'Then the immoralities engendered in these pestiferous scenes are notorious . . . All experience proves, that the congregating of people together in great masses, is sure to be productive of impurity of thought and of manners. The country lad, who becomes a soldier, has a new soul in him by the time that he has passed a year in a barrack-room. Even in great schools, all experience tells us how difficult it is to prevent contagious immoralities. This is universally acknowledged. What, then, must be the consequences of heaping these poor creatures together in the cotton-factories? But, what more do we want; what other proof of the corrupting influence of these assemblages; what more than the following regulation, which I take from a list of fines, imposed at the factory of Tyldesley, in Lancashire? 'Any two spinners, *found together* in the *necessary*, each man . . . Is.'

One is almost ashamed to put the thing on paper, though for the necessary purpose of exposing it to just indignation. To what a pitch must things have come; how familiar people must have become with infamy, before a master manufacturer could put such a thing into writing, and stick it up in his factory! . . .

From the *Political Register* by William Cobbett, 1824

Ye gods above, send down your love,
With swords as sharp as sickles,
To cut the throats of gentlefolks,
Who rob the poor of victuals.

'Captain Swing'

Britons Blush

The very streets which received the droppings of an 'Anti-Slavery Society' are every morning wet with the tears of innocent victims at the accursed shrine of avarice, who are compelled (not by the cartwhip of the negro slave-driver) but by dread of the equally appalling thong or strap of the overlooker, to hasten half-dressed, but not half-fed, to those magazines of British Infantile Slavery – the Worsted Mills in the town and neighbourhood of Bradford!

Thousands of little children, both male and female, but principally female, from seven to fourteen years, are daily compelled to labour from six o'clock to seven in the evening with only – Britons, blush whilst you read it! – with only thirty minutes allowed for eating and recreation.

From a letter to the *Leeds Mercury* by Richard Oastler, 1830

A Flax Mill in Dundee

Alexander Dean, overlooker in a flax-mill at Dundee; age, going on for 27; having no parents to take care of him, he obtained his first job at the age of twelve in a flax mill in Dundee, where they worked not less than 17 hours a day, exclusive of meals, and for wages 'sometimes we got the clothes which were taken from others who had deserted the service'. Was beaten very often. His story continued:

One time I was struck by the master on the head with his clenched first, and kicked, when I was down. I saw one girl trailed by the hair of her head, and kicked by him, when she was down, till she roared 'Murder!' several times. The girl told me that the master had wished to use familiarities with her, and she had refused the night before; and he found a small deficiency in her work, and he took that opportunity of abusing her.

From the *Report* of Sadler's Committee, 1832

The parents who surrender their children to this infantile slavery may be separated into two classes. The first, and I trust by far the most numerous one, consists of those who are obliged, by extreme indigence, so to act, but who do it with great reluctance and bitter regret: themselves perhaps out of employment, or working at very low wages, and their families in a state of great destitution; – what can they do? The overseer refuses relief if they have children capable of working in factories whom they object to send thither. They choose therefore what they probably deem the lesser evil, and reluctantly resign their offspring to the captivity and pollution of the mill; they rouse them in the winter morning, which, as poor father says before the Lords Committee, they 'feel very sorry to do'; they receive them fatigued and exhausted, many a weary hour after the day has closed; they see them droop and sicken, and in many cases become cripples and die, before they reach their prime: and they do all this, because they must otherwise suffer unrelieved, and starve amidst their starving children. It is a mockery to contend that these parents have a choice . . . Free agents! To suppose that parents are free agents while dooming their own flesh and blood to this fate, is to believe them monsters! . . .

Then, in order to keep the children awake, and to stimulate their exertions, means are made use of, to which I shall now advert . . . Sir, children are beaten with thongs prepared for the purpose. Yes, the females of this country, no matter whether children or grown up, – I hardly know which is the more disgusting outrage – are beaten upon the face, arms, and bosom – beaten in your 'free market of labour', as you term it, like slaves! These are the instruments. – (*Here the honourable member exhibited some black, heavy, leathern thongs, – one of them fixed in a sort of handle, the smack of which, when struck upon the table, resounded through the House.*) – They are quite equal to breaking an arm, but that the bones of the young are pliant. The marks, however, of the thong are long visible; and the poor wretch is flogged before its companions; flogged, I say, like a dog, by the tyrant overlooker. We speak with execration of the cart-whip of the West Indies – but let us see this night an equal feeling rise against the factory-thong of England . . .

I wish I could bring a group of these little ones to that bar – I am sure their silent appearance would plead more forcibly on their behalf than the loudest eloquence . . . At this late hour, while I am thus feebly, but earnestly, pleading the cause of these oppressed children, what numbers of them are still tethered to their toil, confined in heated rooms, bathed in perspiration, stunned with the roar of revolving wheels, poisoned with the noxious effluvia of grease and gas, till, at last, weary and exhausted, they turn out, almost naked, into the inclement air, and creep, shivering, to beds from which a relay of their young work-fellows have just risen.

From a speech in the House of Commons by M. T. Sadler MP, 1832

The Rich Man and the Pauper

Alas! that New Year's Day was one of strange contrasts in the social sphere of London.

And as London is the heart of this empire, the disease which prevails in the core is conveyed through every vein and artery over the entire national frame.

The lowest step in the ladder is occupied by that class which is the most numerous, the most useful, and which ought to be the most influential.

The average annual incomes of the individuals of each class are as follows:-

The Sovereign	£500,000.
The member of the Aristocracy	£30,000.
The Priest	£7,500.
The member of the middle classes	£300.
The member of the industrious classes	£20.

Is this reasonable? is this just? is this even consistent with common sense?

It was New Year's Day, 1839.

The rich man sat down to a table crowded with every luxury: the pauper in the workhouse had not enough to eat. The contrast may thus be represented:-

Turtle, venison, turkey, hare, pheasant, perigord-pie, plum-pudding, mince-pies, jellies, blanc-manger, trifle, preserves, cakes, fruits of all kinds, wines of every description.	½ lb. bread. 4 oz. bacon. ½ lb. potatoes. 1½ pint of gruel.

And this was New Year's Day, 1839!

Broadside, anon., 1839

Midas's Touch

Midas, they say, possessed the art of old,
Of turning whatsoe'er he touch'd to gold;
This modern statesmen can reverse with ease;
Touch them with gold, they'll turn to what you please.

Sir John Byrom, *c.* 1760

The Common and the Goose

The law locks up the man or woman
Who steals the goose from off the common
But leaves the greater felon loose
Who steals the common from the goose.

Anon, *c.* 1800

The rich man, who, in point of fact, pays nothing, receives everything, while the poor man, who, in point of fact, pays everything, receives nothing.

John Gray.

No Distinction Noticed

If God sent the rich into the world with combs on their heads like fighting cocks, if He sent the poor into the world with humps on their backs like camels, then I would say it was predestinated that the rich should be born booted and spurred, ready to ride over the poor; but when I see that God has made no distinction between rich and poor – when I see that all men are sent into this working world without silver spoons in their mouths or shirts on their backs, I am satisfied that all must labour in order to get themselves fed and clothed.

Bronterre O'Brien, *c.* 1840

The Sore Spot of England

The condition of the working class is the condition of the vast majority of the English people. The question: what is to become of those destitute millions, who consume today what they earned yesterday; who have created the greatness of England by their inventions and their toil; who become with every passing day more conscious of their might, and demand, with daily increasing urgency, their share of the advantages of society? – this, since the Reform Bill, has become the national question. All Parliamentary debates of any importance may be reduced to this; and, though the English middle class will not as yet admit it, though they try to evade this great question, and to represent their own particular interests as the truly national ones, their attitude is utterly useless. With every session of Parliament the working class gains ground, the interests of the middle class diminish in importance; and, in spite of the fact that the middle class diminish in importance; and, in spite of the fact that the middle class is the chief, in fact, the only power in Parliament, the last session of 1844 was a continuous debate upon subjects affecting the working class, the Poor Relief Bill, the Factory Act, the Masters' and Servants' Act; and Thomas Duncombe, the representative of the working men in the House of Commons, was the great man of the session; while the Liberal middle class with its motion for repealing the Corn Laws, and the Radical middle class with its resolution for refusing the taxes, played pitiable roles. Even the debates about Ireland were at bottom debates about the Irish proletariat, and the means of coming to its assistance. It is high time, too, for the English middle class to make some concessions to the working men who no longer plead but threaten; for in a short time it may be too late.

In spite of all this, the English middle class, especially the manufacturing class, which is enriched directly by the poverty of the workers, persists in ignoring this poverty. This class, feeling itself the mighty representative class of the nation, is ashamed to lay the sore spot of England bare before the eyes of the world; will not confess, even to itself, that the workers are in distress, because it, the property-holding, manufacturing class, must bear the moral responsibility for this distress. Hence the scornful smile which intelligent Englishmen (and they, the middle class, alone are known on the Continent) assume when anyone begins to speak of the condition of the working class; hence the utter ignorance on the part of the whole middle class of everything which concerns the workers; hence the ridiculous blunders which men of this class, in and out of Parliament, make when the position of the proletariat comes under discussion; hence the absurd freedom from anxiety, with which the middle class dwells upon a soil that is honeycombed, and may any day collapse, the speedy collapse of which is as certain as a mathematical or mechanical demonstration; hence the miracle that the English have as yet no single book upon the condition of their workers, although they have been examining and mending the old state of things no one knows how many years. Hence also the deep wrath of the whole working class, from Glasgow to London, against the rich, by whom they are systematically plundered and mercilessly left to their fate, a wrath which before too long a time goes by, a time almost within the power of man to predict, must break out into a revolution in comparison with which the French Revolution, and the year 1794, will prove to have been child's play.

From *The Condition of the Working Class in England* by Friedrich Engels, 1845

'The Speculators'

The night was stormy and dark,
The town was shut up in sleep:
Only those were abroad who were out on a lark,
Or those who'd no beds to keep.

I pass'd through the lonely street,
The wind did sing and blow;
I could hear the policeman's feet
Clapping to and fro.

There stood a potato-man
In the midst of all the wet;
He stood with his 'tato-can
In the lonely Haymarket.

Two gents of dismal mien,
And dank and greasy rags,
Came out of a shop for gin,
Swaggering over the flags:

Swaggering over the stones,
These shabby bucks did walk;
And I went and followed those seedy ones,
And listened to their talk.

Was I sober or awake?
Could I believe my ears?
Those dismal beggars spake
Of nothing but railroad shares.

I wondered more and more:
Says one – 'Good friend of mine,
How many shares have you wrote for?
In the Diddlesex Junction line?'

'I wrote for twenty,' says Jim,
'But they wouldn't give me one;'
His comrade straight rebuked him
For the folly he had done:

'O Jim, you are unawares
Of the ways of this bad town;
I always write for five hundred
  shares,
And *then* they put me down.'

'And yet you got no shares,'
Says Jim, 'for all your boast;'
'I *would* have wrote,' says Jack,
  'but where
Was the penny to pay the
  post?'

'I lost, for I couldn't pay
That first instalment up;
But here's taters smoking hot –
  I say
Let's stop, my boy, and sup.'

And at this simple feast
The while they did regale,
I drew each ragged capitalist
Down on my left thumb-nail.

Their talk did me perplex,
All night I tumbled and tost,
And thought of railroad specs.,
And how money was won and
  lost.

'Bless railroads everywhere,'
I said, 'and the world's advance;
Bless every railroad share
In Italy, Ireland, France;
For never a beggar need now
  despair,
And every rogue has a chance.'

William Makepeace Thackeray, *c.* 1850

Work put up for Auction

What is competition, from the point of view of the workman? It is work put up to auction. A contractor wants a workman; three present themselves.

'How much for your work?'

'Half a crown; I have a wife and children.'

'Well; and how much for yours?'

'Two shillings; I have no children, but I have a wife.'

'Very well; and now how much for yours?'

'One and eightpence are enough for me; I am single.'

'Then you shall have the work.'

It is done; the bargain is struck. And what are the other two workmen to do? It is to be hoped they will die quietly of hunger. But what if they take to thieving? Never fear; we have the police. To murder? We have the hangman. As for the lucky one, his triumph is only temporary. Let a fourth workman make his appearance, strong enough to fast every other day, and his price will run down still lower; there will be a new outcast, perhaps a new recruit for the prison.

Louis Blanc, *c.* 1850

'The Song of the Low'

We're low – we're low – we're very, very low,
As low as low can be;
The rich are high – for we make them so –
And a miserable lot are we!
And a miserable lot are we! are we!
A miserable lot are we!

We plough and sow – we're so very, very low,
That we delve in the dirty clay,
Till we bless the plain with the golden grain,
And the vale with the fragrant hay.
Our place we know – we're so very low,
'Tis down at the landlord's feet:
We're not too low – the bread to grow
But too low the bread to eat.

We're low, we're low, etc.

Down, down we go – we're so very, very low,
To the hell of the deep sunk mines.
But we gather the proudest gems that glow,
When the crown of a despot shines;
And whenever he lacks – upon our backs
Fresh loads he deigns to lay,
We're far too low to vote the tax
But we're not too low to pay.

We're low, we're low, etc.

We're low, we're low – mere rabble, we know,
But at our plastic power,
The mould at the lordling's feet will grow
Into palace and church and tower –
Then prostrate fall – in the rich man's hall,
And cringe at the rich man's door,
We're not too low to build the wall,
But too low to tread the floor.

We're low, we're low, etc.

We're low, we're low – we're very, very low
Yet from our fingers glide
The silken flow – and the robes that glow,
Round the limbs of the sons of pride.
And what we get – and what we give,
We know – and we know our share.
We're not too low the cloth to weave –
But too low the cloth to wear.

We're low, we're low, etc.

We're low, we're low – we're very, very low,
And yet when the trumpets ring,
The thrust of a poor man's arm will go
Through the heart of the proudest king!
We're low, we're low – our place we know,
We're only the rank and file,
We're not too low – to kill the foe,
But too low to touch the spoil.

We're low, we're low, etc.

Ernest Jones, 1852

We will free ourselves by the aid of that large and respectable class of the community – the men of no property.

Wolfe Tone

The Grinders

The Sheffield grinder's a terrible blade.
Tally hi-o, the grinder!
He sets his little 'uns down to trade.
Tally hi-o, the grinder!
He turns his baby to grind in the hull,
Till his body is stunted and his eyes are dull,
And the brains are dizzy and dazed in his skull.
Tally hi-o, the grinder!

He shortens his life and he hastens his death.
    Tally hi-o, the grinder!
Will drink steel dust in every breath.
    Tally hi-o, the grinder!
Won't use a fan as he turns his wheel.
Won't wash his hands ere he eats his meal.
But dies as he lives, as hard as steel.
    Tally hi-o, the grinder!

These Sheffield grinders of whom we speak.
    Tally hi-o, the grinder!
Are men who earn a pound a week.
    Tally hi-o, the grinder!
But of Sheffield grinders another sort
Methinks ought to be called in court,
And that is the grinding Government Board.
    Tally hi-o, the grinder!

At whose door lies the blacker blame?
    Tally hi-o, the grinder!
Where rests the heavier weight of shame?
    Tally hi-o, the grinder!
On the famine-price contractor's head,
Or the workman's, under-taught and -fed,
Who grinds his own bones and his child's for bread?
    Tally hi-o, the grinder!

Trad., *c.* 1860

Fat Oxen! Starving Men!

Within the last few days the walls of London have been placarded with large posters, bearing the following remarkable announcement: 'Fat oxen! Starving men! The fat oxen from their palace of glass have gone to feed the rich in their luxurious abode, while the starving men are left to rot and die in their wretched dens.'

The placards bearing these ominous words are put up at certain intervals. No sooner has one set been defaced or covered over, than a fresh set is placarded in the former, or some equally public place.

At this moment, while English workmen with their wives and children are dying of cold and hunger, there are millions of English gold – the produce of English labour – being invested in Russian, Spanish, Italian, and other foreign enterprises.

From a report in *Reynolds News*, 20 January 1867

Fellow Citizens

FELLOW CITIZENS, – We come before you as a body advocating the principles of Revolutionary International Socialism; that is, we seek a change in the basis of Society – a change which would destroy the distinctions of classes and nationalities.

As the civilised world is at present constituted, there are two classes of Society – the one possessing wealth and the instruments of its production, the other producing wealth by means of those instruments but only by the leave and for the use of the possessing classes.

These two classes are necessarily in antagonism to one another. The possessing class, or non-producers, can only live as a class on the unpaid labour of the producers – the more unpaid labour they can wring out of them, the richer they will be; therefore the producing class – the workers – are driven, to strive to better themselves at the expense of the possessing class, and the conflict between the two is ceaseless. Sometimes it takes the form of open rebellion, sometimes of strikes, sometimes of mere widespread mendicancy and crime; but it is always going on in one form or other, though it may not always be obvious to the thoughtless looker-on . . .

The profit-grinding system is maintained by competition, or veiled war, not only between the conflicting classes, but also within the classes themselves: there is always war among the workers for bare subsistence, and among their masters, the employers and middle-men for the share of the profit wrung out of the workers; lastly, there is competition always, and sometimes open war, among the nations, of the civilised world for their share of the world-market. For now, indeed, all the rivalries of nations have been reduced to this one – a degrading struggle for their share of the spoils of barbarous countries to be used at home for the purpose of increasing the riches of the rich and the poverty of the poor . . .

Moreover, the whole method of distribution under this system is full of waste; for its employ whole armies of clerks, travellers, shopmen, advertisers, and what not, merely for the sake of shifting money from one person's pocket to another's; and this waste in production and waste in distribution, added to the maintenance of the useless lives of the possessing and non-producing class, must all be paid for out of the products of the workers, and is a ceaseless burden on their lives.

Therefore the necessary results of this so-called civilization are only too obvious in the lives of its slaves, the working-class – in the anxiety and want of leisure amidst which they toil, in the squalor and wretchedness of those parts of our great towns where they dwell; in the degradation of their bodies, their wretched health, and the shortness of their lives; in the terrible brutality so common among them, and which is indeed but the reflection of the cynical selfishness found among the well-to-do classes, a brutality as hideous as the other; and lastly, in the crowd of criminals who are as much manufacturers of our commercial system as the cheap and nasty wares which are made at once for the consumption and the enslavement of the poor.

From *The Manifesto of the Socialist League* by William Morris, 1885

Atrocities

Talk about the atrocities of the Revolution! All the atrocities of the democracy heaped together ever since the world began would not equal, if we had any gauge by which to measure them, the atrocities perpetrated in a week upon the poor, simply because they are poor; and the marvel rather is, not that there is every now and then a September massacre at which the world shrieks, but that such horrors are so infrequent. Again, I say, let no man judge communist or anarchist *till he has asked for leave to work*, and a 'Damn your eyes!' has rung in his ears.

From *The Revolution in Tanner's Lane* by
'Mark Rutherford' (William White), 1887

Song of a South African Herd Boy

We just take care of the cattle,
But they belong to other people.
The one who cooks does not eat the food.

Anon., *c.* 1890

Boris won an award for his tremendous achievements on the labour front. The whole factory was summoned together to witness the presentation ceremony. The factory director and the local Party secretary praised him lavishly, and then handed him the Order of Labour Hero of the Soviet Union, Second Class.

At the end of the ceremony the hall emptied, but Boris continued to hang around at the foot of the stage.

'What are you waiting for?' asked the director.

'The money, comrade.'

'What money?'

'Don't you get any money when you become a labour hero?'

'Of course not. The award itself is sufficient.'

'What? No money? Just the shame of it?'

'Labor'

I saw that you fed the loom; but who fed you?
I saw that you fueled the fire; but who fueled you?
History put up big signs, but they never bore your name,
History set great feasts, but you were never invited.

You go to work in the morning with your dinner pail on your arm.
Does that pail contain your dinner alone and provide only for your simple day?
Millions of mouths to come hereafter are to be fed by that pail you carry on your arm.

When you go home at night after the day's work the universe goes home with you,
When you strike against the injustice of the master the sun strikes with you.

Horace Traubel, *c.* 1890

The Production of Frippery

Poverty means disease and crime, ugliness and brutality, drink and violence, stunted bodies and unenlightened minds. Riches heaped up in idle hands mean flunkeyism and folly, insolence and servility, bad example, false standards of worth, and the destruction of all incentive to useful work in those who are best able to educate themselves for it. Poverty and riches together mean the perversion of our capital and industry to the production of frippery and luxury whilst the nation is rotting for want of good food, thorough instruction, and wholesome clothes and dwellings for the masses. What we want in order to make true progress is more bakers, more schoolmasters, more wool-weavers and tailors, and more builders: what we get instead is more footmen, more gamekeepers, more jockeys, and more prostitutes.

From 'What Socialism Is' by George Bernard Shaw, 1890

Machinery must work for us

Up to the present, man has been, to a certain extent, the slave of machinery, and there is something tragic in the fact that as soon as man had invented a machine to do his work he began to starve. This, however, is, of course, the result of our property system and our system of competition. One man owns a machine which does the work of five hundred men. Five hundred men are, in consequence, thrown out of employment, and, having no work to do, become hungry and take to thieving. The one man secures the produce of the machine and keeps it, and has five hundred times as much as he should have, and probably, which is of much more importance, a great deal more than he really wants. Were that machine the property of all, everybody would benefit by it. It would be an immense advantage to the community. All unintellectual labour, all monotonous, dull labour, all labour that deals with dreadful things, and involves unpleasant conditions, must be done by machinery. Machinery must work for us in coal mines, and do all sanitary services, and be the stoker of steamers, and clean the streets, and run messages on wet days, and do anything that is tedious or distressing. At present machinery competes against man. Under proper conditions machinery will serve man. There is no doubt at all that this is the future of machinery; and just as trees grow while the country gentleman is asleep, so while Humanity will be amusing itself, or enjoying cultivated leisure – which, and not labour, is the aim of man – or making beautiful things, or reading beautiful things, or simply contemplating the world with admiration and delight, machinery will be doing all the necessary and unpleasant work. The fact is, that civilization requires slaves. The Greeks were quite right there. Unless there are slaves to do the ugly, horrible, uninteresting work, culture and contemplation become almost impossible. Human slavery is wrong, insecure and demoralizing. On mechanical slavery, on the slavery of the machine, the future of the world depends. And when scientific men are no longer called upon to go down to a depressing East End and distribute bad cocoa and worse blankets to starving people, they will have delightful leisure in which to devise wonderful and marvellous things for their own joy and the joy of everyone else. There will be great storages of force for every city, and for every house if required, and this force man will convert into heat, light or motion, according to his needs. Is this Utopian? A map of the world that does include Utopia is not worth even glancing at, for it leaves out the one country at which Humanity is always landing. And when Humanity lands there, it looks out and, seeing a better country, sets sail. Progress is the realization of Utopias.

From *The Soul of Man under Socialism* by Oscar Wilde, 1891

Going to Paris

Tis a sthrange thing whin we come to think iv it that th' less money a man gets f'r his wurruk, th' more nicissary it is to th' wurruld that he shud go on wurrukin'. Ye'er boss can go to Paris on a combination wedding an' divoorce thrip an' no wan bothers his head about him. But if ye shud go to Paris – excuse me f'r laughin' mesilf black in th' face – th' industhrees iv the counthry pines away.

'Mr Dooley' (probably Finley Peter Dunne), *c.* 1900

'Golf Links'

The golf links lie so near the mill
That almost every day
The laboring children can look out
And see the men at play.

Sarah Cleghorn, *c.* 1900

Ignorant Acquiescence

At present, it is not too much to say that the average citizen of the middle or upper class takes for granted the constantly recurring destitution among wage-earning families due to unemployment, as part of the natural order of things, and as no more to be combated than the east wind.

In the same way the eighteenth-century citizen acquiesced in the horrors of the contemporary prison administration, and in the slave trade; just as, for the first decades of the nineteenth century, our grandfathers accepted as inevitable the slavery of the little children of the wage-earners in mines and factories, and the incessant devastation of the slums by 'fever'.

Fifty years hence we shall be looking back with amazement at the helpless and ignorant acquiescence of the governing classes of the United Kingdom, at the opening of the twentieth century, in the constant debasement of character and *physique*, not to mention the perpetual draining away of the nation's wealth, that idleness combined with starvation plainly causes . . .

From the *Minority Report of the Royal Commission on the Poor Laws and Relief of Distress*, 1905–1909

'Ilda

I'm sick of it, I tell yer straight,
I'm at it early hours and late;
Up with the lark it ain't much cop,
Feels by eleven fit to drop.
And it's 'ave yer done this, and 'ave yer done that?
Didn't I tell yer to shake the mat?
Quick, there's the milkman at the door.
Now use some Ronuk to polish the floor.
Come, it's time the washing was done –
Now, my girl, you've some errands to run.

'Oh, 'Ilda, 'Ilda, 'Ilda,
Go and tidy yer 'air.
Oh, 'Ilda, 'Ilda, 'Ilda,
Here, there and everywhere.
Have yer me boots? Where's the 'ot water?
Stop carryin' on as yer didn't oughter.

Use yer brain. Are yer sane?
Oh, 'Ilda, 'Ilda, 'Ilda!'

When the beds is made and sweeping done,
Off for some fish I 'as ter run,
Or else ter fetch a bottle of stout,
Or take the kids fer a short walk out.
If the washing's out it's sure ter rain,
Then I 'as ter lug it in again.
I'm running about all over the show,
Why ever I does it, I don't know.
I'd like ter lay me down and die,
But I gets no chance, 'cause they always cry:

'Oh, 'Ilda, 'Ilda, 'Ilda,
Go and tidy yer 'air,
Oh, 'Ilda, 'Ilda, 'Ilda,
Here, there and everywhere.
Wash yerself – you're stale and musty,
Sneeze, my girl, for yer brains are dusty,
Use yer eyes – don't catch flies –
Oh, 'Ilda, 'Ilda, 'Ilda!'

I'm a slave, and it's a shame,
Why should *I* get all the blame?
I wouldn't mind so much if they smiled,
But, lumme! their looks near drive me wild.
They shoves on that superior face,
As if they was a-saying their grace.
I'm sorry I'm not a bit quicker – it's true,
But I'm not blaming meself, would you?
No, as I says when I thinks it all out,
It strengthens their lungs to 'ave to shout:

'Oh, 'Ilda, 'Ilda, 'Ilda,
Go and tidy yer 'air,
Oh, 'Ilda, 'Ilda, 'Ilda,
Here, there and everywhere.
Go to the door – there's someone knocking,
Clean yer teeth, pull up yer stocking,
'Pon my soul, you're up the pole –
Oh, 'Ilda, 'Ilda, 'Ilda!'

English music-hall song by Marie Makino, *c.* 1910

THE ECONOMY IS THE SECRET POLICE OF YOUR SENSE(S)

Graffito

'The Riveter'

The steam-shovels had sunk their teeth
 Through earth and rock until a hole
Yawned like a black hell underneath,
 Like a coal-crater with all the coal
Torn out of her: the shovels bit
The stinking stony broth – and spit.

The Wops went up and down; they spilled
 Cement like a groggy soup in chutes;
They mixed the mortar and they filled
 The gash with it . . . Short, swarthy brutes
They were, who reeked of rock and wet
Lime and accumulated sweat.

At first the work was tame enough:
 Only another foundation like
Hundreds before and just as tough
 To stand under a ten-ton spike.
But it was different when a whir
Of steel announced the riveter.

One long lad of them took the crowd
 As he straddled the girders and hooked the nuts
Livid-white hot: and we allowed
 He was the lunatic for guts;
The sidewalk bleachers yelled as he
Speared a sizzler dizzily.

They got to call him the 'Rivet Ruth'
 That crisp corn shock of gusty hair,
That blue hawk-eye and devil of youth
 Juggling with death on a treacherous stair,

Tipping his heart on a beam of steel
That made his pavement audience reel.

The riveting hammers stuttered and kicked;
  The ten-ton trestles whined in the winch;
And still this golden Icarus picked
  The hissing rivets by half an inch,
Twirled and nailed them on the spin
Out of the air and rocked them in.

And one fine sun-splashed noon he lunged
  Over the stark deadline – and missed!
Swung for an instant and then plunged
  While the lone insane rivet hissed
Him all the way down from truss to truss
And dropped beside its Icarus!

The old strap-hanger thumbed his paper;
  Feet shuffled sidewalks; traffic roared . . .
Icarus had performed his caper –
  Little New York minced by bored;
Leave the lads with the broken backs,
Soiled feathers and some melted wax!

Joseph Auslander, *c.* 1920

'Winnsboro Cotton Mill Blues'

Old man Sargent, sittin' at the desk,
The damned old fool won't give us no rest,
He'd take the nickels off a dead man's eyes
To buy Coca Colas and Eskimo Pies.

I got the blues, I got the blues,
I got the Winnsboro Cotton Mill Blues,
Lordy, Lordy spoolin's hard,
You know and I know, I don't have to tell,
You work for Tom Watson, got to work like hell.
I got the blues. I got the blues.
I got the Winnsboro Cotton Mill Blues.

When I die, don't bury me at all,
Just hang me up on the spool room wall,
Place a knotter in my hand,
So I can spool in the Promised Land.

When I die, don't bury me deep,
Bury me down on 600 Street,
Place a bobbin in each hand,
So I can doff* in the Promised Land.

*take bobbins off a carding machine.

Anon., *c.* 1922

'Poor Man's Blues'

Mister rich man, rich man, open up your heart and mind,
Mister rich man, rich man, open up your heart and mind;
Give the poor man a chance, help stop these hard, hard times.

While you're living in your mansion, you don't know what hard
times mean,
While you're living in your mansion, you don't know what hard
times mean;
Poor working man's wife is starving; your wife is living like a queen.

Please listen to my pleadin', 'cause I can't stand these hard times long,
Aw, listen to my pleadin', can't stand these hard times long;
They'll make an honest man do things that you know is wrong.

Now the war is over, poor man must live the same as you,
Now the war is over, poor man must live the same as you;
If it wasn't for the poor man, mister rich man, what would you do?

Bessie Smith, 1928

'Depression Hits Robinson Crusoe's Island'

'Friday,' said Robinson Crusoe, 'I'm sorry, I fear I must lay you off.'
'What do you mean, Master?'
'Why, you know there's a big surplus of last year's crop. I don't need you

to plant another this year. I've got enough goatskin coats to last me a lifetime. My house needs no repairs. I can gather turtle eggs myself. There's an overproduction. When I need you I will send for you. You needn't wait around here.'

'That's all right, Master, I'll plant my own crop, build up my own hut and gather all the eggs and nuts I want myself. I'll get along fine.'

'Where will you do all this, Friday?'

'Here on this island.'

'This island belongs to me, you know. I can't allow you to do that. When you can't pay me anything I need I might as well not own it.'

'Then I'll build a canoe and fish in the ocean. You don't own that.'

'That's all right, provided you don't use any of my trees for your canoe, or build it on my land, or use my beach for a landing place, and do your fishing far enough away so you don't interfere with my riparian rights.'

'I never thought of that, Master. I can do without a boat, though. I can swim over to that rock and fish there and gather sea-gull eggs.'

'No you won't, Friday. The rock is mine. I own riparian rights.'

'What shall I do, Master?'

'That's your problem, Friday. You're a free man, and you know about rugged individualism being maintained here.'

'I guess I'll starve, Master. May I stay here until I do? Or shall I swim beyond your riparian rights and drown or starve there?'

'I've thought of something, Friday. I don't like to carry my garbage down to the shore each day. You may stay and do that. Then whatever is left of it, after my dog and cat have fed, you may eat. You're in luck.'

'Thank you, Master. That is true charity.'

'One more thing, Friday. This island is overpopulated. Fifty percent of the people are unemployed. We are undergoing a severe depression, and there is no way that I can see to end it. No one but a charlatan would say that he could. So keep a lookout and let no one land here to settle. And if any ship comes don't let them land any goods of any kind. You must be protected against foreign labor. Conditions are fundamentally sound, though. And prosperity is just around the corner.'

Mary Atterbury in the *Industrial Worker*, 1932

'I Want You Women Up North to Know'

I want you women up north to know
how those dainty children's dresses you buy
    at macy's, wanamakers, gimbels, marshall fields,

are dyed in blood, are stitched in wasting flesh,
down in San Antonio, 'where sunshine spends the winter.'

I want you women up north to see
the obsequious smile, the salesladies trill
   'exquisite work, madame, exquisite pleats'
vanish into a bloated face, ordering more dresses,
   gouging the wages down,
dissolve into maria, ambrosa, catalina,
   stitching these dresses from dawn to night,
   in blood, in wasting flesh.

Catalina Rodriguez, 24,
   body shrivelled to a child's at twelve,
catalina rodriguez, last stages of consumption,
   works for three dollars a week from dawn to midnight.
A fog of pain thickens over her skull, the parching heat
   breaks over her body.
and the bright red blood embroiders the floor of her room.
   White rain stitching the night, the bourgeois poet would say,
   white gulls of hands, darting, veering,
   white lightning, threading the clouds,
this is the exquisite dance of her hands over the cloth,
and her cough, gay, quick, staccato,
   like skeleton's bones clattering,
is appropriate accompaniment for the esthetic dance of her fingers,
and the tremolo, tremolo when the hands tremble with pain.
Three dollars a week,
two fifty-five,
seventy cents a week,
no wonder two thousands eight hundred ladies of joy
are spending the winter with the sun after he goes down –
for five cents (who said this was a rich man's world?) you can get all
   the lovin you want
'clap and syph aint much worse than sore fingers, blind eyes, and t.m.'

Maria Vasquez, spinster,
   for fifteen cents a dozen stitches garments for children she has
   never had,
Catalina Torres, mother of four,
   to keep the starved body starving, embroiders from dawn to night.
Mother of four, what does she think of,

as the needle pocked fingers shift over the silk –
of the stubble-coarse rags that stretch on her own brood,
and jut with the bony ridge that marks hunger's landscape
of fat little prairie-roll bodies that will bulge in the
silk she needles?
(Be not envious, Catalina Torres, look!
on your own children's clothing, embroidery,
more intricate than any a thousand hands could fashion,
there where the cloth is ravelled, or darned,
designs, multitudinous, complex and handmade by Poverty
herself.)

Ambrosa Espinoza trusts in god,
'Todos es de dios, everything is from god,'
through the dwindling night, the waxing day, she bolsters herself
up with it –
but the pennies to keep god incarnate, from ambrosa,
and the pennies to keep the priest in wine, from ambrosa,
ambrosa clothes god and priest with hand-made children's dresses.

Her brother lies on an iron cot, all day and watches,
on a mattress of rags he lies
For twenty-five years he worked for the railroad, then they laid him
off.
(racked days, searching for work; rebuffs; suspicious eyes of
policemen.)
goodbye ambrosa, mebbe in dallas I find work; desperate swing for
a freight,
surprised hands, clutching air, and the wheel goes over a leg,
the railroad cuts it off, as it cut off twenty-five years of his life.)
She says that he prays and dreams of another world, as he lies there,
a heaven (which he does not know was brought to earth in 1917 in
Russia, by workers like him).

Women up north, I want you to know
when you finger the exquisite hand made dresses
what it means, this working from dawn to midnight,
on what strange feet the feverish dawn must come
to maria, catalina, ambrosa,
how the malignant fingers twitching over the pallid faces jerk them to
work,
and the sun and the fever mounts with the day –

long plodding hours, the eyes burn like coals, heat jellies the flying fingers,
down comes the night like blindness.
long hours more with the dim eye of the lamp, the breaking back,
weariness crawls in the flesh like worms, gigantic like earth's in winter.
And for Catalina Rodriguez comes the night sweat and the blood embroidering the darkness.
for Catalina Torres the pinched faces of four huddled children,
the naked bodies of four bony children,
the chant of their chorale of hunger.
And for twenty eight hundred ladies of joy the grotesque act gone over – the wink – the grimace – the 'feeling like it baby?'
And for Maria Vasquez, spinster, emptiness, emptiness.
flaming with dresses for children she can never fondle.
And for Ambrosa Espinoza – the skeleton body of her brother on his mattress of rags, boring twin holes in the dark with his eyes to the image of christ remembering a leg, and twenty-five years cut off from his life by the railroad.

Women up north, I want you to know,
I tell you this can't last forever.

I swear it won't.

Tillie Olsen, 1934; Olsen was jailed in 1932 for handing out pamphlets to packing-house workers

---

The essence of a satisfactory health service is that the rich and the poor are treated alike, that poverty is not a disability, and wealth is not advantaged.

Aneurin Bevan

'Song of the Deportees'

The crops are all in and the peaches are rotting.
The oranges are piled in their creosote dumps.
You're flying them back to the Mexico border,
To pay all their money to wade back again.

Goodbye to my Juan, goodbye Rosalita,
Adios, mi amigos, Jesus and Maria,
You won't have a name when you ride the big airplane,
And all they will call you will be 'deportee'.

My father's own father, he waded that river,
They took all the money he made in his life;
My brothers and sisters come working the fruit trees.
And they rode the truck till they took down and died.

Some of us are illegal, and some are not wanted,
Our work contract's out and we have to move on;
Six hundred miles to that Mexican border,
They chase us like outlaws, like rustlers, like thieves.

We died in your hills, we died in your deserts,
We died in your valleys and died on your plains,
We died 'neath your trees and we died in your bushes,
Both sides of the river, we died just the same.

The sky plane caught fire over Los Gatos Canyon,
A fireball of lightning, and shook al' our hills.
Who are all these friends, all scattered like dry leaves?
The radio says they are just deportees.

Is this the best way we can grow our big orchards?
Is this the best way we can grow our good fruit?
To fall like dry leaves to rot on my topsoil
And be called by no name except deportees?

Woody Guthrie, 1959

'Measure for Measure'

go measure the distance from cape town to pretoria
and tell me the prescribed area i can work in

count the number of days in a year
and say how many of them i can be contracted around

calculate the size of house you think good for me
and ensure the shape suits tribal tastes

measure the amount of light into the window
known to guarantee my traditional ways

count me enough wages to make certain that i
grovel in the mud for more food

teach me just so much of the world that i
can fit into certain types of labour

show me only those kinds of love
which will make me aware of my place at all times

and when all that is done
let me tell you this
you'll never know how far i stand from you

Sipho Sepamla, *c.* 1960

Why People Like Me are What You Would Call Bloody-Minded

Sir, – You have had a lot of letters about people being bloody minded. You have not had any that I have seen about why people like me are what you would call bloody minded.

I read your paper in the public library – I can't afford to purchase it every day. It is the same for a lot of ordinary working people like me. So you don't get much of what we think.

I am 50 years of age. I started work at 15 years of age. I will work, if I am lucky, until I am 65 years of age. I might live to 70, but I will be lucky if I can work to 70 because, even if I am able and willing, the bosses don't want us. So I shall have the old-age pension. I have not been able to save. In all my working life the money I have got will amount to about £60,000. That is the highest it could be.

I saw in your paper that the Chairman of Bowring's insurance gets £57,000 a year. And of course he gets a free car, free drinks, trips abroad with his wife, etc. He gets in a year as much as I get in all my working life. The differential is a bit wrong somewhere. Or what about your reports about wills? Often you see someone, a stockbroker, for example, leaving £500,000. That is his savings, not what he lived on. It would take me 500 years to earn that little lot. Something wrong with the differential there too.

The Tory Party goes on about competition. How much competition was there when Brooke Bond put up their prices and all the others did the same. They didn't want to, they said. But they did it. Beer, petrol, milk, it all goes up the same . . . what price competition?

Then we get a lot of talk about the law of supply and demand. Well, this affluent society produces a lot of effluent. So dustmen are in short supply. So they ask for more money. What a howl from the papers, T.V., radio, the lot. No howls about Brooke Bond or the others. Why? If you ask 99 people out of a hundred they can manage all right without stockbrokers. But they don't like being without dustmen. The law of supply and demand is fine for some, but not for others. Why?

I am not a communist or an anarchist. I believe there must be differentials. But the trouble is the differentials are all wrong, and there's too much fiddling at the top. Where I work there are lavatories for bosses . . . you can only get in with a key, hot and cold, air conditioning, nice soap, individual towels. Then there are lavatories for senior staff . . . hot and cold, not so good soap, a few individual towels, but good rollers. Then there is ours . . . no hot and cold, rough towels, cheesecake soap. And no splash plates in the urinals. How do you think we feel about things like that in the twentieth century? Waving Union Jacks doesn't help.

It's no good economists and financial experts preaching. You can use the telly, radio, papers the lot to try to convince us that we have got to be the first to suffer. That's useless. We know the papers and the telly and radio give one side of the story. We know the other. You don't. Or you don't want to. So there will be a fight. We might lose a round or two. But we will win in the end. And if we have to fight to win instead of being sensible on both sides, the losers are going to suffer a lot.

You can call this bloody-minded. Try bringing up three kids on my pay and see how you like it. There's plenty for everybody if it's shared reasonably. And if, as my mate says, we want to try to have the bridge and beaujolais as well as beer and bingo, what's wrong with that?

Letter to newspaper by James Thomson, *c.* 1965

Pigs and sheep are property, and property is well represented in Parliament.

Samuel Plimsoll

'Dockland'

Cranes standing still, no work for them
No movement, a monument to times past.
Silhouette outlined against a London sky.

Their reflection, mirrored in the waters
of a silent dock.
Casting their shadows across the decks
of pleasure yachts.

Like a cancer spreading, with unchecked speed,
Wharves, warehouses closed overnight
Transformed, renovated
Not for people who have no place to live,
But for those who with obscene ease,
Sail their yachts whenever they please . . .

From the poem by Bernie Steer, *c.* 1974; Steer was one of the 'Pentonville Five' – London dockers imprisoned for contempt of court in 1972

'Three Poems for Women'

1

This is a poem for a woman doing dishes.
This is a poem for a woman doing dishes.
It must be repeated.
It must be repeated,
again and again,
again and again,
because the woman doing dishes
because the woman doing dishes
has trouble hearing
has trouble hearing.

2

And this is another poem for a woman
cleaning the floor
who cannot hear at all.
Let us have a moment of silence
for the woman who cleans the floor.

3

And here is one more poem
for the woman at home
with children.
You never see her at night.
Stare at an empty space and imagine her there,
the woman with children
because she cannot be here to speak
for herself,
and listen
to what you think
she might say.

Susan Griffin, *c.* 1980

'Me Aunty Connie'

They made cakes at Carson's.
Enormously sticky ones.
With dollops of cream on top,
Jam tarts and doughnuts
Fancy éclairs,
All made at Carson's,
Me Aunty worked at Carson's,
On the cream button.
She put the dollop on the cake
As it passed along the conveyor belt.
She'd been there fifteen years
Then she was promoted
To Senior Cream Dolloper.
It carried responsibility,
And extra buttons.
She had to ensure
No cakes were eaten.
It was instant dismissal at Carson's
To eat a cake.
Laughing and talking
Was also forbidden.
If she'd stayed another fifteen years,
She'd have been promoted again
To the packing machine
What puts the cakes in boxes,
To take them to the shops.
But she didn't stay.
She was offered a higher paid job.
And on her last day,
She dolloped the wrong cakes.
And the Chelsea buns
Went through with cream on them,
While the gâteaus went without.
And the foreman blew his whistle.
And stopped production.
The emergency light went on
And the manager came down.
Everyone was laughing and talking.
When he asked her why she did it,

She said because she wanted to.
Course she got dismissed instantly.
But she didn't care.
On the way out,
She picked up a cake
And ate it in front of him.
Everyone at Carson's
Knows me Aunty Connie.

Terry Lee, *c.* 1990

Five

OUR FATHER, WHO ART IN HEAVEN, STAY THERE

Man Makes Gods

Homer and Hesiod have attributed to the gods everything that is a shame and reproach among men, stealing and committing adultery and deceiving each other.

But mortals consider that the gods are born, and that they have clothes and speech and bodies like their own.

The Ethiopians say that their gods are snub-nosed and black, the Thracians that theirs have light blue eyes and red hair.

But if cattle and horses or lions had hands, or were able to draw with their hands and do the works that men can do, horses would draw the forms of the gods like horses, and cattle like cattle, and they would make their bodies such as they each had themselves.

Xenophanes, *c.* 560 BCE, as reported by Sextus Empiricus later

There is no Divinity

Now as to celestial phenomena, we must believe that these motions, periods, eclipses, risings, settings, and the like do not take place because there is some divinity in charge of them, who so arranges them in order and will maintain them in that order, and who at the same time enjoys both perfect happiness and immortality; for activity and anxiety, anger and kindness are not in harmony with blessedness, but are found along with weakness, fear, and dependence on one's neighbors. We must also avoid the belief that masses of concentrated fire have attained a state of divine blessedness and undertaken these motions of their own free will . . .

In addition to these general matters, we must observe this also, that there are three things that account for the major disturbances in men's minds. First, they assume that the celestial bodies are blessed and eternal yet have impulses, actions, and purposes quite inconsistent with divinity. Next, they anticipate and foresee eternal suffering as depicted in the myths, or even fear the very lack of consciousness that comes with death as if this could be of concern to them. Finally, they suffer all this, not as a result of reasonable conjecture, but through some sort of unreasoning imagination; and since in imagination they set no limit to suffering, they are beset by turmoil as great as if there were a reasonable basis for their dread, or even greater. But it is peace of mind to have been freed from all this and to have constantly in memory the essential principles of the whole system of belief. We must therefore turn our minds to immediate feelings and sensations – in matters of general concern to the common feelings and sensation of mankind, in personal matters, to our own – and to every immediate evidence from each of the means of judgment. If we heed these, we shall rightly track down the sources of disturbance and fear, and when we have learned the causes of celestial phenomena and of the other occasional happenings, we shall be free from what other men most dread.

Epicurus, *c.* 300 BCE

I Did not Die in Reality

I did not succumb to them as they had planned. But I was not afflicted at all. Those who were there punished me. And I did not die in reality but in appearance, lest I be put to shame by them because these are my kinsfolk. I removed the shame from me and I did not become fainthearted in the face of what happened to me at their hands. I was about to succumb to fear, and I suffered according to their sight and thought, in order that they may never find any word to speak about them. For my death which they think happened, happened to them in their error and blindness, since they nailed their man unto their death. For their Ennoias did not see me, for they were deaf and blind. But in doing these things, they condemn themselves. Yes, they saw me; they punished me. It was another, their father, who drank the gall and the vinegar; it was not I. They struck me with the reed; it was another, Simon, who bore the cross on his shoulder. It was another upon whom they placed the crown of thorns. But I was rejoicing in the height over all the wealth of the archons and the offspring of their error, of their empty glory. And I was laughing at their ignorance.

Heretical manuscript, *c.* 150, in which Jesus speaks about the crucifixion

'Prescriptions Against Heretics'

I must not leave out a description of the heretics' way of life – futile, earthly, all too human, lacking in gravity, in authority, in discipline, as suits their faith. To begin with, one cannot tell who is a catechumen and who is baptized. They come in together, listen together, pray together. Even if any of the heathen arrive, they are quite willing to cast that which is holy to the dogs and their pearls (false ones!) before swine. The destruction of discipline is to them simplicity, and our attention to it they call affectation. They are in communion with everyone everywhere. Differences of theology are of no concern to them as long as they are all agreed in attacking the truth. They are all puffed up, they all promise knowledge. Their catechumens are perfect before they are fully instructed. As for the women of the heretics, how forward they are! They have the impudence to teach, to argue, to perform exorcisms, to promise cures, perhaps even to baptize. Their ordinations are hasty, irresponsible and unstable. Sometimes they appoint novices, sometimes men tied to secular office, sometimes renegades from us, hoping to bind them by ambition as they cannot bind them by the truth. Nowhere can you get quicker promotion than in the camp of the rebels, where your mere presence is a merit. So one man is bishop today, another tomorrow. The deacon of today is tomorrow's reader, the priest of today is tomorrow a layman. For they impose priestly functions even upon laymen.

Tertullian, *c.* 200

Original Sin Denied

Everything good and everything evil, in respect of which we are either worthy of praise or of blame, is *done by us*, not *born with us*. We are not born in our full development, but with a capacity for good and evil; we are begotten as well without virtue as without vice, and before the activity of our own personal will there is nothing in man but what God has stored in him.

From *De peccato originali* by Pelagius, *c.* 400

Heretics Branded, 1166

There were, however, rather more than thirty persons, both men and women, who, dissimulating their errors, came hither as if in peace for the purpose of propagating their noxious teaching, their leader being a certain Gerard, whom they all looked up to as teacher and master; for he alone among them had a smattering of learning, but the others were ignorant folk, unlettered and wholly uncultivated, peasants of German race and tongue. Sojourning for some time in England they only deceived one wretched woman with their lying whispers, and, so it is said, having bewitched her with certain spells they joined her to their coterie. For they could not long lie hidden but were detected by certain men curious to explore to what strange sect they belonged, then seized and held in public custody. The king, however, being unwilling either to discharge them or to punish them without examination, ordered an episcopal synod to meet at Oxford. Here they were solemnly charged concerning their religion; the one among them who seemed literate, under-taking their common defence and speaking for them all, replied that they were Christians and reverenced the apostolic teaching. Interrogated successively concerning the articles of the Holy Faith, they answered rightly concerning the nature of Christ, the heavenly Physician; but concerning the saving remedies whereby he condescends to heal our human infirmity, that is, the Divine Sacraments, they answered perversely. Holy Baptism, the Eucharist, and Holy Matrimony they abhorred, and the Catholic unity sustained by these divine aids they wickedly dared to disparage. When they were pressed by texts taken from Holy Scripture, they answered they believed what they had been taught but were unwilling to dispute about their faith. Admonished that they should do penance and be united to the body of the Church, they spurned all sound advice. They laughed at the threats, with which in all piety they were confronted to induce them to recover their senses through fear; making wrongful use of the Lord's words: 'Blessed are they which are persecuted for righteousness' sake, for theirs is the kingdom of heaven.'

From William of Newburgh's *History of England*, *c.* 1170

Against Gigglings

We have learned from the lips of men worthy of credit, not without grave displeasure, that certain Vicars and other Ministers of our Cathedral Church – to the offence of God and the notable hindrance of divine service and their own damnation and the scandal of our Cathedral Church aforesaid – fear not to exercise irreverently and damnably certain disorders, laughings, gigglings, and other breaches of discipline, during the solemn services of the church; which is shameful to relate and horrible to hear. To specify some out of many cases, those who stand at the upper stalls in the choir, and have lights within their reach at mattins, knowingly and purposely throw drippings or snuffings from the candles upon the heads or the hair of such as stand at the lower stalls, with the purpose of exciting laughter and perhaps of generating discord . . .

From a mandate by Bishop Grandison of Exeter to the Dean and Subdean, 15 October 1330

Lollard Heresies, as Attributed by the Church

5. That it is not laid down in the Gospel that Christ ordained the Mass.
10. That it is contrary to Holy Scripture that ecclesiastics should have possessions.
14. That any deacon or priest may preach the word of God apart from the authority of the Apostolic See or a Catholic bishop.
15. That no one is civil lord, or prelate, or bishop, while he is in mortal sin.
17. That the people can at their own will correct sinful lords.
18. That tithes are mere alms, and that parishioners can withdraw them at their will because of the misdeeds of their curates.
24. That friars are bound to gain their livelihood by the labour of their hands, and not by begging.

John Wycliffe, 1382

A Worldly Abbot

About the second or third hour of the day, when the sun putteth off the cool of dawn and groweth to the strength of a youth, then at last doth the abbot arise from his couch; and, puking still with his supper of yesterday and his potations long-drawn into the night, he doth meditate forthwith how to fill his yet undisburdened maw. For indeed his meditation is more of belly than of God, more of sauce than of sacraments, of salmon than of Solomon; nor need we marvel, seeing that his belly is his god. First, therefore, he putteth on a shirt of finest linen, lest the hard hair vex his soft flesh; yet then, for some show of religion, he layeth a hair shirt over this, not without anxious care lest it wed itself for one moment to his bare body. Then come two fur coats or more, if the weather be cold; upon which he layeth a frock or frocks, adding cowl to cowl if need be. His legs are clad in linen drawers and woollen hosen, with boots not hobnailed but of buckskin, and super-hosen over all. Of over-shoes he hath no certain number; for they vary in accordance with the changes of heat or cold. So this fat and round-bellied abbot, thus stuffed out, goeth into the cloister; and there, seeing the cowled congregation, he throweth back his hood to his ears and thus goeth armed *cap-à-pie*. His manly brow is heavy with menace, his eyes stare forth from bushy eyebrows; his glance wandereth hither and thither like the stars in their courses; his mien is austere; his nostrils gape; and, coughing sharply, he roars and bellows like a tyrant; and thus he goeth ruminating, revolving both in mind and in mouth not the psalms but the sauces of yesternight.

With such kindly embraces doth he raise and foster his flock; with such mercy doth he compassionate their infirmities. For he can cry truly with the apostle [Paul]: 'Who is weak, and I am not strong? who is offended, and I rejoice not thereat?' Then goeth he into the church, and, walking around, he pauseth not beside the altar but by the brothel; for there will be one at least to whom he may say (with Ovid), 'Thou alone art my joy; thou shalt lie with me to-night.' Doth she consent? Yea, truly, nor can we marvel; since there is no wench so poor but she may soon flaunt gold on all her fingers, if a monk itch for her but now and then; the monk pays a pound for that which the clerk gets for a halfpenny or for love. O foul and preposterous thing, that maketh God's temple into a brothel, for hither come the she-wolves daily; and again, as saith the poet, 'Those gaze who come; the women themselves come to be gazed upon.' In short, the abbot goeth back to his fold; there, before the fire, feather-beds are laid for this spouse of Venus, with rugs and quilts so soft and velvety that they seem to swallow him up. After such pastime, my lord abbot's table is laid; but with how many dishes may scarce be told. Yet, innumerable as these are in their abundance, there is naught of four-footed beasts, to taste whereof would be to break the Rule. What then doth he eat? Great fishes, for the small he holdeth in no esteem; fishes boiled and fishes fried, fishes roast and fishes stuffed, fishes gilded with egg-yolk. Doth he then abstain from all flesh-food? Nay, but from the four-footed alone. What, he eateth the winged fowls? Nay: but, once plucked of their wings and cooked, then he may eat them; for they, like fish, are born in the water; and of fish he may lawfully eat. Such men defend their error with the authority of St Ambrose, who wrote, 'Great God! whose mighty power doth raise this kind from the waters, and doth send some of them back to the eddying deep again, whereas Thou raisest others to soar in air.' Thou therefore, my lord abbot, dost send into the depth of thy maw both flying and swimming fowls without distinction, since both are sprung from the deep; to those eddying depths of thine, I say, thou sendest peacocks and swans, cranes and geese, hens and capons. Cocks he eateth not; for their flesh is tough and tasteless; moreover, if both cocks and hens were eaten, their progeny would fail; and my lord would rather be roasted at the fire than that fowls should fail. The raven, again, my lord hath sworn never to eat; for the raven sent forth from Noah's ark found a carcase and returned not; wherefore he is a wicked and unprofitable fowl. Owls he eateth not; for that is a foul and hated bird. Of wolves there are two sorts, the wood-wolf and the water-wolf [pike]. The water-wolf he claimeth for his own, strong in St Ambrose's word; the wood-wolf he loatheth, not only as a quadruped but also as a cruel beast. Of another thing which is raised to hang in the air, of the flitch of bacon, what thinketh he? The flitch itself he eateth not, for that is four-footed; yet, seeing that its flesh is savoury and rich in fat, he doth most diligently comment upon its text, and doth come at last to this conclusion, that if the bacon be so long tormented and tossed in the frying-pan that it be turned altogether to liquor, then (since liquor cannot be eaten), he may lawfully take of that which is now converted into drink. But the twisted osier-rope, whereby the flitch is hung, he eateth not, albeit it be no four-footed beast, and be suspended in the air. Wherefore? First, for that it is of a dry and leathery complexion; and secondly, for that it is not born of water. From the bones also he abstaineth, for these breed gross and indigestible humours; moreover, bones are dogs' food; and our abbot is so religious that he will not unjustly baulk the dogs. Yet, over and above, he eateth many eggs, for these are according to the Rule, and preservative of health; your egg is a comfortable and digestible meat, and (as Ovid testifieth) provocative of lust, which doth the more commend it. But, seeing that the Rule forbiddeth him to exceed the number five, therefore he eateth five hard eggs, five soft, five fried and five boiled, five white eggs in cummin and five black in pepper, five in meat-pasties and five in cheese-pasties, five scrambled and five half-raw, and five blown into ring-cakes; which, albeit they are collectively fifty-five, yet, taken distributively, they are but five of each. Of sauces and condiments what can I tell? he is indignant if each several dish have not his own peculiar sauce. Wines are set before the lord abbot of divers colours, white and red; the white on his right, as being of greater authority, and the red on his left. From each he taketh the first-fruits, drinking nine times, that he may taste and prove the savour of the wine. Then, drinking with intention, he draineth one draught, single but deep, for the peace and stability of the church, secondly for the prelates, thirdly for their subjects, fourthly for all prisoners, fifthly for the sick, sixthly for fair weather, seventhly for a calm sea, ninthly for all travellers and pilgrims, tenthly for those that stay at home, eleventhly that his monks may eat little, twelfthly that he himself may eat much, thirteenthly for all Christian folk, fourteenthly for human affairs, fifteenthly that the Lord God may send His dew upon Mount Gilboa, whereby the harvests may whiten and the vines flourish and the pomegranates may sprout; and thus he concludeth his draught with an uneven number, as saith the poet, 'God loveth odd numbers.' Of the rest, indeed, he drinketh not but sippeth only, that he may temper the inextinguishable heat of his stomach. These are the sufferings which he endureth for Christ. When supper is done, and the tables are set aside, he cannot rise from his seat, unless he be raised by both arms, like a cow stuck in a miry slough; and then, coming to the customary grace, he maketh no long prayers, but pretermitteth the 'Miserere mei Deus,' beginning with a hiccough, 'Laudate Dominum, *puf* omnis gens, laudate, *puf* et omnis spiritus laudet, *puf*.' For, in his psalmody, he joineth not word to word, but with puking interpolations he stealeth one word and halveth another. When, therefore, after supper, this abbot sitteth in his chair, with one to prop him under each arm, and his belly filled to the very gorge, then beginneth he to bring the winds out of his treasures; for else he would burst asunder in the midst; to this purpose he openeth wide his nostrils and gapeth with his mouth; the congregation marvelleth at fumes like the fumes of Enceladus, and blasts as though the prison-house of Aeolus were burst open.

Anon., *c.* 1450

A Heretic

Thomas Wassyngborn is a heretic: he says that the sacrament of the altar is mere bread: he appears 12 September, denies the charge, and is to appear Monday next.

Court proceedings, London, 1482

The Pope's Riches

86. The pope's riches at this day far exceed the wealth of the richest millionaires (*cuius opes sunt opulentissimis Crassis crassiores*), cannot he therefore build one single basilica of S. Peter out of his own money, rather than out of the money of the faithful poor?

Martin Luther, from *The 95 Theses*, 1517

Football in the Cathedral

Against Christopher Dobson and Oswald Atkinson . . . that they have plaied at the foote ball within this Cathedrall Churche of Yorke. To which they awnsweringe confessed that the foote ball was brougte into the Churche by Dobson and thereupon Oswald Atkinson did take the ball from him in the churche and there was but one stroke striken at the same in the Churche. Wherefore the Commissioners did order that Oswald Atkinson shalbe sett in the Stocks at the churche side upon Sonday nexte at nyne of the clocke before nowne and ther to sitt in the stocke by the space of one hole houre and the houre ende be tayken furthe and laid over the stocke and have six yerts with a byrchen rod upon his buttocke and that Chris. Dobson shall have lykewise sex yerts upon his buttocke . . .

Court proceedings, York, 1565

'Christopher Marlowe's Atheist Lecture', Laid Before the Privy Council

A note Containing the opinion of on Christopher Marly Concerning his damnable [opini] Judgment of Religion, and scorn of Gods word.

That the Indians and many Authors of antiquity haue assuredly writen of aboue 16 thousand yeares agone whereas [Moyses] Adam is [said] proued to haue lived within 6 thowsand years.

He affirmeth that Moyses was but a Jugler & that one Heriots being Sir W Raleighs man Can do more then he.

That Moyses made the Jewes to travell xl yeares in the wildernes, (which Jorney might haue bin done in lesse then one yeare) ere they Came to the promised land to thintent that those who were privy to most of his subtilties might perish and so an everlasting superstition Remain in the hartes of the people.

That the first beginning of Religion was only to keep men in awe.

That it was an easy matter for Moyses being brought up in all the artes of the Egyptians to abuse the Jewes being a rude & grosse people.

That Christ was a bastard and his mother dishonest.

That he was the sonne of a Carpenter, and that if the Jewes among whome he was borne did Crucify him theie best knew him and whence he Came.

That Crist deserved better to dy then Barrabas and that the Jewes made a good Choise, though Barrabas was both a thief and a murtherer.

That if there be any god or any good Religion, then it is in the papistes because the service of god is performed with more Cerimonies, as Elevation of the mass, organs, singing men, Shaven Crownes & cta. That all protestantes are Hypocritical asses.

That if he were put to write a new Religion, he would vndertake both a more Exellent and Admirable methode and that all the new testament is filthily written.

That the woman of Samaria & her sister were whores & that Crist knew them dishonestly.

That St John the Evangelist was bedfellow to Christ and leaned alwaies in his bosome, that he vsed him as the sinners of Sodoma.

That all they that loue not Tobacco & Boies were fooles.

That all the apostles were fishermen and base fellowes neyther of wit nor worth, that Paull only had wit but he was a timerous fellow in bidding men to be subiect to magistrates against his Conscience.

That he had as good Right to Coine as the Queen of England, and that he was aquainted with one Poole a prisoner in Newgate who hath greate skill in mixture of mettals and hauing learned some thinges of him he ment through help of a Cunninge stamp maker to Coin ffrench Crownes pistoletes and English shillinges.

That if Christ would haue instituted the sacrament with more Ceremoniall Reverence it would haue bin had in more admiration, that it would haue bin much better being administred in a Tobacco pipe.

That the Angell Gabriell was baud to the holy ghost, because he brought the salutation to Mary.

That on Rich Cholmley [hath Cholmley] hath Confessed that he was perswaded by Marloe's Reasons to become an Atheist.

These thinges, with many other shall by good & honest witnes be aproved to be his opinions and Comon Speeches and that this Marlow doth not only hould them himself, but almost into every Company he Cometh he perswades men to Atheism willing them not to be afeard of bugbeares and hobgoblins, and vtterly scorning both god and his ministers as I Richard Baines will Justify & approue both by mine oth and the testimony of many honest men, and almost al men with whome he hath conversed any time will testify the same, and as i think all men in Christianity ought to indevor that the mouth of / so dangerous a member may be stopped, he saith likewise that he hath quoted a number of Contrarieties oute of the Scripture which he hath giuen to some great men who in Convenient time shalbe named. When these thinges shall be Called in question the witnes shalbe produced.

Richard Baines, 1593; words in brackets scored through in the original

Before the Inquisition

After admitting having said in the past ('but I do not know to whom') that he had been 'born a Christian, and so desired to live as a Christian, but if he had been born a Turk, he would have wanted to remain a Turk,' Menocchio added: 'I beg you, sir, listen to me. There was once a great lord who declared his heir would be the person found to have a certain precious ring of his; and drawing near to his death, he had two other rings similar to the first one made, since he had three sons, and he gave a ring to each son; each one of them thought himself to be the heir and to have the true ring, but because of their similarity it could not be known with certainty. Likewise, God the Father has various children whom he loves, such as Christians, Turks, and Jews and to each of them he has given the will to live by his own law, and we do not know which is the right one. That is why I said that since I was born a Christian I want to remain a Christian, and if I had been born a Turk I would want to live like a Turk.' 'Do you believe then,' the inquisitor retorted, 'that we do not know which is the right law?' To which Menocchio replied: 'Yes sir, I do believe that every person considers his faith to be right, and we do not know which is the right one: but because my grandfather, my father, and my people have been Christians, I want to remain a Christian, and believe that this is the right one.'

'Menocchio' (Domenico Scandella), a miller who had read an uncensored version of Boccaccio's *Decameron* at his trial, 1599, subsequently executed

Excommunication Made Fun Of

Henry Daynes. He hath not repayred to his Church this half yeare. For not receaving the Communion at Easter. He hath stood excommunicate a yeare past, and maketh a jest of it saying he shall save 100 mile going in the yeare, bycawse the church is a mile from his howse. He does not appear and is excommunicated.

Court Proceedings, Redenhall, Norfolk, 1597

Burnt for Blasphemy

On May 20, 1579, Matthew Hamount was burned for having said that 'the New Testament and Gospel of Christ is but mere foolishness, a mere fable; that Christ is not God or the Saviour of the world, but a mere man, a shameful man, and an abominable idol; that he did not rise again from death or ascend unto Heaven; that the Holy Ghost is not God; and that baptism is not necessary, nor the sacrament of the body and blood of Christ.'

From John Stow's *Annals*, 1615

False Printing

Mr. Baker the printer. For false printing of the Bible in diverse places of it, in the Edition of 1631, vizt. in the 20 of Exodus, 'Thou shalt commit adultery'. . . And the Bishop of London shewed that this would undoe the trade, and was a most dishonourable thing . . .

Court proceedings, London, 1632

From 'The Shortest Way with Dissenters'

ANOTHER Argument they use, which is this, That 'tis a time of War, and we have need to unite against the common Enemy.

WE answer, this common Enemy had been no Enemy, if they had not made him so; he was quiet, in peace, and no way disturb'd, or encroach'd upon us, and we know no reason we had to quarrel with him.

But further, We make no question but we are able to deal with this common Enemy without their help; but why must we unite with them because of the Enemy, will they go over to the Enemy, if we do not prevent it by a union with them – We are very well contented they shou'd; and make no question, we shall be ready to deal with them and the common Enemy too, and better without them than with them.

Besides, if we have a common Enemy, there is the more need to be secure against our private Enemies; if there is one common Enemy, we have the less need to have an Enemy in our Bowels.

'Twas a great Argument some People used against suppressing the Old-Money, that 'twas a time of War, and 'twas too great a Risque for the Nation to run, if we shou'd not master it, we shou'd be undone; and yet the Sequel prov'd the Hazard was not so great, but it might be mastered; and the Success was answerable. The suppressing the Dissenters is not a harder Work, nor a Work of less necessity to the Publick; we can never enjoy a settled uninterrupted Union and Tranquility in this Nation, till the Spirit of Whiggisme, Faction, and Schism is melted down like the Old-Money.

To talk of the Difficulty, is to Frighten our selves with Chimæras and Notions of a Powerful Party, which are indeed a Party without Power; Difficulties often appear greater at a distance, than when they are search'd into with Judgment, and distinguish'd from the Vapours and Shadows that attend them.

We are not to be frightened with it; this Age is wiser than that, by all our own Experience, *and their's too*; King *Charles* the First, had early supprest this Party, if he had took more deliberate Measures. In short, 'tis not worth arguing, to talk of their Arms, their *Monmouths*, and *Shaftsburys,* and *Argiles* are gone, their *Dutch-Sanctuary* is at an end, Heaven has made way for their Destruction, and if we do not close with the Divine occasion, we are to blame ourselves and may remember that we had once an opportunity to serve the Church of *England*, by extirpating her implacable Enemies, and having let slip the Minute that Heaven presented, may experimentally Complain, *Post est Occasio Calvo.*

Here are some popular Objections in the way.

As first, THE Queen has promis'd them, to continue them in their tollerated Liberty; and has told us she will be a religious Observer of her Word.

WHAT her Majesty will do we cannot help, but what, as the Head of the Church, she ought to do, is another Case: Her Majesty has promised to Protect and Defend the Church of *England*, and if she cannot effectually do that without the Destruction of the Dissenters, she must of course dispence with one Promise to comply with another. But to answer *this Cavil more effectually*: Her Majesty did never promise to maintain the Tolleration, to the Destruction of the Church; but it is upon supposition that it may be compatible with the well being and safety of the Church, which she had declar'd she would take especial Care of: Now if these two Interests clash, 'tis plain her Majesties Intentions are to Uphold, Protect, Defend, and Establish the Church, and this we conceive is impossible.

Perhaps it may be said, THAT the Church is in no immediate danger from the Dissenters, and therefore 'tis time enough: But this is a weak Answer.

For first, IF a Danger be real, the Distance of it is no Argument against, but rather a Spur to quicken us to prevention, lest it be too late hereafter.

And 2dly, Here is the Opportunity, and the only one perhaps that ever the Church had to secure her self, and destroy her Enemies.

The Representatives of the Nation have now an Opportunity, the Time is come which all good Men ha' wish'd for, that the Gentlemen of *England* may serve the Church of *England*; now they are protected and encouraged by a Church of *England* Queen.

What will ye do for your Sister in the Day that she shall be spoken for.

If ever you will establish the best Christian Church in the World.

If ever you will suppress the Spirit of Enthusiasm.

If ever you will free the Nation from the viperous Brood that have so long suck'd the Blood of their Mother.

If you will leave your Posterity free from Faction and Rebellion, this is the time.

This is the time to pull up this heretical Weed of Sedition, that has so long disturb'd the Peace of our Church, and poisoned the good Corn.

> Daniel Defoe, 1702; a satire on Tory moves to curb the Dissenters, first hailed as a pungent expression of the case, but later used against Defoe when his true intentions were realised and he was arrested and imprisoned

The Crimes of God

Feeble mortals! How long will your imagination, so active and so prompt to seize on the marvellous, continue to seek out of the universe, pretexts to make you injurious to yourselves, and to the beings with whom ye live in society? Wherefore do ye not follow in peace the simple and easy route which your nature has marked out for ye? Wherefore strew with thorns the road of life? Wherefore multiply those sorrows to which your destiny exposes ye? What advantages can ye expect from a Divinity which the united efforts of the whole human species have not been able to make you acquainted with? Be ignorant, then, of that which the human mind is not formed to comprehend; abandon your chimeras; occupy yourselves with truth; learn the art of living happy; perfect your morals, your governments, and your laws; look to education, to agriculture, and to the sciences that are truly useful; labor with ardor; oblige nature by your industry to become propitious to ye, and the Gods will not be able to oppose any thing to your felicity. Leave to idle thinkers, and to useless enthusiasts, the unfruitful labor of fathoming depths from which ye ought to divert your attention: enjoy the benefits attached to your present existence; augment the number of them; never throw yourselves forward beyond your sphere. If you must have chimeras, permit your fellow-creatures to have theirs also; and do not cut the throats of your brethren, when they cannot rave in your own manner. If ye will have Gods, let your imagination give birth to them; but do not suffer these imaginary beings so far to intoxicate ye as to make ye mistake that which ye owe to those real beings with whom ye live. If ye will have unintelligible systems, if ye cannot be contented without marvelous doctrines, if the infirmities of your nature require an invisible crutch, adopt such as may suit with your humor; select those which you may think most calculated to support your tottering frame, do not insist on your neighbors making the same choice with yourself: but do not suffer these imaginary theories to infuriate your mind: always remember that, among the duties you owe to the *real* beings with whom ye are associated, the foremost, the most consequential, the most immediate, is a reasonable indulgence for the foibles of others.

From *The System of Nature* by Baron d'Holbach,
the first modern theorist of atheism, 1770

Against Sceptre and Censer

Frenchmen, I repeat it to you: Europe awaits her deliverance from *sceptre* and *censer* alike. Know well that you cannot possibly liberate her from royal tyranny without at the same time breaking for her the fetters of religious superstition: the shackles of the one are too intimately linked to those of the other; let one of the two survive, and you cannot avoid falling subject to the other you have left intact. It is no longer before the knees of either an imaginary being or a vile impostor a republican must prostrate himself; his only gods must now be *courage* and *liberty*. Rome disappeared immediately Christianity was preached there, and France is doomed if she continues to revere it.

Let the absurd dogmas, the appalling mysteries, the impossible morality of this disgusting religion be examined with attention, and it will be seen whether it befits a republic. Do you honestly believe I would allow myself to be dominated by the opinion of a man I had just seen kneeling before the idiot priest of Jesus? No, certainly not! That eternally base fellow will eternally adhere, by dint of the baseness of his attitudes, to the atrocities of the ancient régime; as of the moment he were able to submit to the stupidities of a religion as abject as the one we are mad enough to acknowledge, he is no longer competent to dictate laws or transmit learning to me; I no longer see him as other than a slave to prejudice and superstition.

To convince ourselves, we have but to cast our eyes upon the handful of individuals who remain attached to our fathers' insensate worship: we will see whether they are not all irreconcilable enemies of the present system, we will see whether it is not amongst their numbers that all of that justly condemned caste of royalists and aristocrats is included. Let the slave of a crowned brigand grovel, if he pleases, at the feet of a plaster image; such an object is ready-made for the soul of mud.

The Marquis de Sade, 1795

'The Little Vagabond'

Dear mother, dear mother, the church is cold;
But the ale-house is healthy, and pleasant and warm.
Besides, I can tell where I am used well;
The poor parson's with wind, like a blown bladder, swell.

But, if at the church they would give us some ale,
And a pleasant fire our souls to regale,
We'd sing and we'd pray all the livelong day,
Nor ever once wish from the church to stray.

Then the parson might preach, and drink, and sing,
And we'd be as happy as birds in the spring;
And modest Dame Lurch, who is always at church,
Would not have bandy children, nor fasting, nor birch.

And God, like a father, rejoicing to see
His children as pleasant and happy as he,
Would have no more quarrel with the devil or the barrel,
But kiss him, and give him both drink and apparel.

William Blake, 1795

The Gospel According to Richard Carlile

Jesus Christ not a real Person.

1. The Christian writings about Jesus Christ, which are here assumed to be so many fables, date his birth about seventy years before the destruction of Jerusalem by Titus, and his death at the age of thirty-three, or thirty-seven years before that period.

2. The objections to such an existence are:

3. That no writer who wrote in the first century, or within one hundred years of the alleged birth, or within seventy years of the alleged death, has made any mention of such a person as Jesus Christ.

4. That such a birth, such a life, and such a death, could not have passed, without the notice of the provincial Roman authorities in Judea, and without the notices of contemporary historians, such as Philo, Josephus, Pliny, sen. and others.

5. That, as no mention was made of the alleged life and death of this Jesus

Christ, by any persons in the first century, what good authority could writers of the second century have to make such mention?

6. That, no responsible historian of the first, second, third, fourth, or any of the eighteen centuries by which we date, has given us a history of the life and death of this Jesus Christ, upon any authority that will bear the least critical examination.

7. That no authority, such as we require for historical facts, is to be found in the Christian story of Jesus Christ.

8. That there is no better authority than is to be found in the story of Jack the Giant Killer, Don Quixote, Valentine and Orson, or any other fabulous and romantic story.

9. That the alleged birth, life, death, and resurrection of Jesus Christ are romantic and not in accordance with probability, or such matters of fact as we find in the present day, or in approved histories.

10. That the fabulousness or defect of the history of Jesus Christ is visible, in the defects of the system of religion founded upon it, throughout the seventeen centuries that it has existed.

11. That, when Gospels of the life and death of Jesus Christ began to appear in the second century, there was no agreement among them, each writer, in some measure, making his story according to his own invention.

12. That the writer of the Epistles called the Epistles of Paul clearly denounces all other Gospels but that which he preached, and what that is we do not now know, as it has not been preserved.

13. That the Gospels and Epistles of the book called the New Testament cannot be consistently received as according testimonies of the life and death of Jesus Christ.

Broadside pamphlet by Richard Carlile, *c.* 1825

My only crime is that I was born a Jew.

Alfred Dreyfus

Are You An Atheist?

Are you really an atheist, Mr. Holyoake?
Really I am.
You deny that there is a God?

No; I deny that there is sufficient reason to believe that there is one.
But if the atheist has so much on his side, why does he not make it known?
Is it generous in you to taunt him with lack of evidence, when you are so prepared to punish its production?
The reason is that your principles are so horrible; as Robert Hall said, 'Atheism is a bloody and ferocious system.'
And, my dear sir, has it never occurred to you that the language of the Christian is shocking to atheistical feeling?
Atheists have a right to their opinions, I allow, but not to publish them.
I shall think you speak reasonably when you permit the same rule to be applied to the Christian.
But you really cannot be an atheist?
And you say this who have been a party to imprisoning me here for being one! If you believe yourself, go and demand my liberation.

From *History of the Last Trial By Jury for Atheism* by George Holyoake, 1844; an account of his conversation with the prison chaplain

'Our Vicar Still Preaches'

Our vicar still preaches that Peter and Paul
Laid a swingeing long curse on the bonny brown bowl;
That there's wrath and despair in the jolly black jack,
And the seven deadly sins in a flagon of sack
Yet, whoop, Barnaby, off with thy liquor;
Drink up; see't out; and a fig for the vicar!

Our vicar he calls it damnation to sip
The ripe ruddy dew of woman's dear lip;
Says that Beelzebub lurks in her 'kerchief so sly,
And Apollion shoots darts from her merry black eye;
Yet whoop, Jack! kiss Gilian the quaker,
Till she bloom like a rose, and a fig for the vicar!

Our vicar thus preaches, and why should he not?
For the dews of his cure are his placket and pot;
And 'tis right of his office poor laymen to lurch,

Who infringe the domains of our good mother-church.
Yet whoop, bully, boys! off with your liquor;
Sweet Margery's the word, and a fig for the vicar!

Sir Walter Scott, 1848

If I were to choose a people to hold in a state of complete subjection, it should be a people divided into religious sects, each condemning the other to perdition.

William Cobbett

Clergymen and Progress

Talk of *social* reform, and they exclaim that poverty is a *divine* ordinance; that God made both *poor* and rich, and the people must, therefore, 'be content in the situation in which Divine Providence has placed them'. Talk of *political* reform, and they remind you that it is our duty, by command of the inspired word of heaven, to submit 'to the powers that be'. Talk of *educational* progress, and they exclaim that all education without religion, which simply means without *them*, 'would be a curse rather than a blessing'. Talk of *moral* reform in the shape of the temperance or any other kindred movement, and they caution us to quote the words of the Rev. Mr Duncan of North Shields, that 'it is an attempt to take the regeneration of man out of God's hands'. Talk of *peace* reform and we behold the mitred priest blessing the fatal emblem of human slaughter. Talk of reform in the blackest, the vilest, the meanest of all mortal abuses, the selling of human flesh, the trading in human slavery, and the man of God points his finger to the infallible page sanctioning the crime!

From *The Immortality of the Soul*, Religiously and Philosophically considered, Robert Cooper, 1852

'Religion, a Delusion and Curse'

(To the tune of 'Battle Cry of Freedom')

We are rousing for free speaking, to censure or applaud,
And claim the sceptic's right to reason.
We must disbelieve all dogmas, the spawn of priest and god,
That curse mankind with crime and folly.

Free speech man's redeemer, arouse sceptics, rouse:
Blot out all bibles – dare speak the truth:
We are humanizing christians, we wean them from their gods,
And give them better sense and morals.

We free thinkers should be honored and pensioned by the church
For having stopped its cruel warfare:
Having snatched the christian's faggot from his fanatic clutch,
And stopped the burning of each other.

Free speech, &c.

Oh, in vain has priestcraft striven to sever mind from brain,
And strove to build a world with spirits.
Mind, no more than life or motion, can never live again,
But dies forever with its organs.

Free speech, &c.

Priests declare mankind are hell-bent, as being born depraved,
Are Satan's convicts till Christ pardoned.
But it is a stupid slander, that they are lost or saved,
Can be *white-washed* with blood of Jesus.

Free speech, &c.

But men's virtues and their vices engender by degrees,
And grow by habits oft repeated;
If well organized and balanced in all their faculties,
Right practice ever gives them virtue.

Free speech, &c.

Lewis Masquerier, *c.* 1875

Against Polygamy

Some things leave an impact deep inside that will not go away. I shall speak of something that touched me profoundly.

Once when I was visiting a friend, I asked her about a woman I had known a long time ago. She sighed and answered me in a sad voice saying that the woman had experienced great sorrow causing her to fall ill. The reason for this was that her husband had contracted to marry another woman and would consummate the marriage soon. I was amazed to hear this. My friend noticed my reaction and asked: 'Isn't this a common occurrence?' I said. 'Yes, I am not surprised because it happened, but because it happened to her. She was among the finest of women in character, beauty, and education. I used to hear from her that she was living in comfort with her husband and I saw her with my own eyes working in her home which was clean and well organised. She had young children. What more does a man need than a wife with education, a good mind, fine character, beauty, and children?'

My friend said that the two children had died within the same month and her husband then started to look for another wife. He became engaged to a woman the same month he lost his children and while his first wife was pregnant. How cruel the man was. Was it her fault that the two children died? Was it not enough that she was grieving over her loss, that he should not shoot another poison arrow into her broken heart? Did he discover a letter from her to the angel of death asking him to come and take her two children away? Were these children only hers and not his? Man is stronger in his will than woman and can endure more misfortune than her. If he endured misfortune would this make him forget kindness and mercy? Oh God, you do not condone this treatment.

If a woman needs kindness and consideration at any time it is in dark days. Is there any day darker than the day she loses two children? In time of great sadness when people far and near extend sympathy is it fitting that her own husband would abandon her to grief? The grieving woman is his wife and those who have departed are his children. If she was grieving for a brother or another relative it would have been his duty to share his grief with her even if only externally. But, if it is their child, who would lessen the pain if he does not? If he, himself, were not saddened and did not console her why then didn't he leave her be? A poet once said, 'I have considered you a strong fortress to protect me from the enemies' arrows but you became their archer. If you cannot protect me, be neither for me nor against me.'

When he married the other woman he broke the heart of his first wife and did something whose outcome he could not control. Is it not possible that his new wife will be barren or that she will give him children who will die like the first children of his first wife? Fate cannot be opposed nor averted. Birth, life, and death are in the hands of God. We do not know when He will grant life or take it. This woman does not have room for both the fetus and sadness. Isn't her husband condemning her and condemning his new child if sadness is its companion and it is born dead? This cruel husband is criminal under the rule of law, decency, humanity, and kindness.

This painful incident reminds me of a similar one. An eminent man began to dislike his wife because all his children were girls. He divorced her and married another woman in the hope of having boys, but his new wife gave him a girl, then another, and still another. God refused to grant except that which He willed. The man got more girls as if he were replacing one set of daughters for another. He lost the love of a good woman and wrought change in the hearts of his first daughters. He thought that he had gained the love of another woman, but he was deluded.

If we think that giving birth to girls is something undesirable as some of us do, is it the decision of the woman to do so? Why isn't the man blamed as the woman is blamed? Why doesn't the woman ask for a divorce and marry another man so that she can bear boys? If one of the spouses clings to this fallacy, it could be that the other would adhere to it as well. They are equally able to do right or wrong in this matter. In our home life there is much to concern us. We have archaic practices that shout for reform. Men should not occupy our time and thoughts complaining about their work. I think they are subject to the injustice of the government on the one hand, and the difficulty of making ends meet on the other. They find no one to take revenge upon except us. I do not believe that there is any opponent who is weaker in weaponry than us, and less vengeful. Oh God, inspire the men of our government to do right because their injustice to the nation has many repercussions on us. It seems that we have not received anything more than men receive except pain. This reverses the Quranic verse that says, 'One man's share shall equal two women's shares.'

'Bahithat al-Badiya' ('Seeker in the Desert'), pen name of Egyptian feminist Malak Hifni Nasif, 1909

'Pie in the Sky'

Long-haired preachers come out ev'ry night,
Try to tell you what's wrong and what's right,
But when asked about something to eat,
They will answer with voices so sweet:

CHORUS:
You will eat (you will eat), bye and bye (bye and bye),
In that glorious land in the sky (way up high).
Work and pray (work and pray), live on hay (live on hay),
You'll get pie in the sky when you die (that's a lie!).

And the starvation army they play,
And they sing and they clap and they pray,
Till they get all your coin on the drum –
Then they tell you when you're on the bum:

If you fight hard for children and wife –
Try to get something good in this life –
You're a sinner and bad man, they tell;
When you die you will sure go to Hell.

Working men of all countries, unite!
Side by side we for freedom will fight.
When the world and its wealth we have gained,
To the grafters we'll sing this refrain:

LAST CHORUS:
You will eat (you will eat), bye and bye, (bye and bye),
When you've learned how to cook and to fry (way up high).
Chop some wood (chop some wood) – 'twill do you good (do you good)
And you'll eat in the sweet bye and bye (that's no lie!).

Song by Joe Hill, *c.* 1910

More pigs, less parsons.

Chartist banner

Sometime in Eternity

Sometime during eternity
some guys show up
and one of them
who shows up real late
is a kind of carpenter
from some square-type place
like Galilee
and he starts wailing
and claiming he is hep
to who made heaven
and earth
and that the cat
who really laid it on us
is his Dad

And moreover
he adds
It's all writ down
on some scroll-type parchments
which some henchmen
leave lying around the Dead Sea somewheres
a long time ago
and which you won't even find
for a coupla thousand years or so
or at least for
nineteen hundred and fortyseven
of them
to be exact
and even then
nobody really believes them
or me
for that matter

You're hot
they tell him

And they cool him
They stretch him on the Tree to cool

And everybody after that
is always making models
of this Tree
with Him hung up
and always crooning His name
and calling Him to come down
and sit in
on their combo
as if he is *the* king cat
who's got to blow
or they can't quite make it

Only he don't come down
from His Tree
Him just hang there
on His Tree
looking real Petered out
and real cool
and also
according to a roundup
of late world news
from the usual unreliable sources
real dead

From *A Coney Island of the Mind* by Laurence Ferlinghetti, 1958

Journey of the Yellow Letters'

For a thousand years, children of my poor village
we have been the yellowed letters
in the Torah
and the Qur'an
And the New Testament,
the encrusted blade of the chisel
carving our frightful shadows in your eyes –
shadows you
worshipped in your hearts,
shadows that became a history void of men.
Each letter swells, and sometimes is
a minaret that stands in prayer;
a church, sometimes, in the dreary mountains;

sometimes black nooses
and ropes.
In sad villages your streets know them,
your sins know them.

For a thousand years
we have been the yellowed letters in the New Testament
and the Torah
and the Qur'an,
the letters of mould
daily manifested
in every shameful pregnancy,
in idols,
in the oppressor's whip
in God, in Satan
but not once in a human being.

For a thousand years, children of my poor village
we have slept the long sleep of history
and worshipped our frightful shadows in your eyes

Buland al-Haydari (a Kurdish poet exiled from Iraq), 1968

Language and the Quran

The Arabic language, like the English language, is very male-oriented. And the language of the Quran is very male. You remember that I wrote in *The Hidden Face of Eve* how the women went to the Prophet Muhammad and told him: 'The Quran is very male-oriented. We fought alongside men like you. Why are we not mentioned in the Quran as women?' And then the verses, the language of the Quran, started to be both feminine and masculine. And, after this event, you will find verses in the Quran that are masculine and feminine. Now, many women in the West are changing language. But, in the Arabic language, I feel that there is a barrier. When Marilyn Booth translated my *Memoirs from the Women's Prison*, she told me she had a problem with the translation because most of the language was male-oriented. For example, we say, '*al-insan wa-ka-annahu . . .*' [man, as though he] and she doesn't know if she should say 'he' or 'she'. Because I use '*al-insan*' [man]. So I told her: 'Yes. You know, in my new novel, I am changing this.' I am really trying to change the language. Because when you change the content, you have to change the form. But it's difficult.

Nawal al-Saadawi, 1986

Jesus Christ Superstar

Jesus Christ, Superstar!
Come down to earth on a Yamaha.
Done a skid,
killed a kid,
and mashed his balls
on a dustbin lid.

Playground rhyme *c.* 1990; tune by Andrew Lloyd Webber

Six

THIS ISLAND'S MINE . . . WHICH THOU TAK'ST FROM ME

'The Wolf and the Watch-dog'

A wolf and a watch-dog met one moonshiny night. The wolf was so lean and hungry that he scarce knew what to do, and the dog was a fat and sleek as possible. 'How is it, friend,' said the wolf, 'that you manage to do so well, and get so much to eat?'

'Why, it is quite easy. You could have as much as I if you cared to do the work that I do.'

'I am quite willing to do anything,' said the wolf, 'so long as I keep from starving. What is your work?'

'To guard my master's house at night, and drive all thieves away.'

'I could do that,' said the wolf. 'I will go along with you and take service at once.'

As they proceeded together the wolf noticed something round his companion's neck, and was full of curiosity. 'What is that you are wearing?'

'Oh! nothing,' said the dog, 'a badge of office.'

'Yes, but,' persisted the wolf, 'what is it and what is it for?'

'It is just my collar to which my chain is fastened.'

'What!' said the wolf, 'a chain! Are you not free?'

'Well, no, not always,' said the dog, 'they do tie me up sometimes in the day. But I am free at night, and just think of all the food I get!'

'No, thank you,' said the wolf, turning to go. 'I had rather be free in the woods and starve, than a slave on a chain and well fed.'

Some men will never accept servitude.

Attributed to Aesop, a slave, possibly Ethiopian, sixth century BCE, ('Aesop' being a variation of 'Ethiope')

View of the Imperial Peace

The Britons, . . . convinced at length that a common danger must be averted by union, had, by embassies and treaties, summoned forth the whole strength of all their states. More than 30,000 armed men were now to be seen, and still there were pressing in all the youth of the country, with all whose old age was yet hale and vigorous, men renowned in war and bearing each decorations of his own. Meanwhile, among the many leaders, one superior to the rest in valour and in birth, Galgacus by name, is said to have thus harangued the multitude gathered around him and clamouring for battle: –

'Whenever I consider the origin of this war and the necessities of our position, I have a sure confidence that this day, and this union of yours, will be the beginning of freedom to the whole of Britain. To all of us slavery is a thing unknown; there are no lands beyond us, and even the sea is not safe, menaced as we are by a Roman fleet. And thus in war and battle, in which the brave find glory, even the coward will find safety. Former contests, in which, with varying fortune, the Romans were resisted, still left in us a last hope of succour, inasmuch as being the most renowned nation of Britain, dwelling in the very heart of the country and out of sight of the shores of the conquered, we could keep even our eyes unpolluted by the contagion of slavery. To us who dwell on the uttermost confines of the earth and of freedom, this remote sanctuary of Britain's glory has up to this time been a defence. Now, however, the furthest limits of Britain are thrown open, and the unknown always passes for the marvellous. But there are no tribes beyond us, nothing indeed but waves and rocks, and the yet more terrible Romans, from whose oppression escape is vainly sought by obedience and submission. Robbers of the world, having by their universal plunder exhausted the land, they rifle the deep. If the enemy be rich, they are rapacious; if he be poor, they lust for dominion; neither the east nor the west has been able to satisfy them. Alone among men they covet with equal eagerness poverty and riches. To robbery, slaughter, plunder, they give the lying name of empire; they make a solitude and call it peace.'

From *Agricola* by Tacitus, *c.* 98

An Arab Opinion of the Crusaders

One day, I entered this mosque, repeated the first formula, 'Allah is great,' and stood up in the act of praying, upon which one of the Franks rushed on me, got hold of me and turned my face eastward saying, 'This is the way thou shouldst pray!' A group of Templars hastened to him, seized him, and repelled him from me. I resumed my prayer. The same man, while the others were otherwise busy, rushed once more on me and turned my face eastward, saying, 'This is the way thou shouldst pray!' The Templars again came in to him and expelled him. They apologized to me, saying, 'This is a stranger who has only recently arrived from the land of the Franks and he has never before seen anyone praying except eastward.' Thereupon I said to myself, 'I have had enough prayer.' So I went out and have ever been surprised at the conduct of this devil of a man, at the change in the colour of his face, his trembling and his sentiment at the sight of one praying towards the *qiblah.*[1]

[1] The direction of Mecca.

Anon., 12th century

A Native People's Complaint

Caliban: This island's mine, by Sycorax my mother,
Which thou tak'st from me. When thou cam'st first,
Thou strok'st me, and made much of me; wouldst give me
Water with berries in 't; and teach me how
To name the bigger light, and how the less,
That burn by day and night: and then I lov'd thee,
And show'd thee all the qualities o' th' isle,
The fresh springs, brine-pits, barren place and fertile:
Curs'd be I that did so! All the charms
Of Sycorax, toads, beetles, bats, light on you!
For I am all the subjects that you have,
Which first was mine own King: and here you sty me
In this hard rock, whiles you do keep from me
The rest o' th' island.

From *The Tempest* by William Shakespeare, 1611

The Spanish Massacres, by an Eye-Witness

OF THE PROVINCE OF NICARAQUA

In the year 1522, the foresaid Governour went to subdue the Province of Nicaraqua. There is no man that can sufficiently express the fertility of this Island, the temperateness of the air, or the multitude of the people that did inhabit it. There was a vast number of people in this Province, for it contained divers cities above four mile in length: and for plenty of fruits (which was the cause that it was so extremely well habited) without compare. This people because their Country was all plain and level, had not the shelter of the Mountains, neither could they be easily persuaded to leave it, so pleasant was their habitation. And therefore they endured far the greater misery, and persecution, and underwent a more unsufferable slavery, being the less able to bear it, by how much they were of a mild and gentle nature. This Tyrant vex'd and tormented these poor creatures with so many continual injuries, slaughters, captivities and cruelties, that no tongue is able to express them. Into this territory he sent above fifty horse, who totally extirpated the people of this Province by the Sword, sparing nor age nor sex, not for any wrong they did them, but sometimes it came not so speedily when they called as they expected, or if they brought not such quantities of corn as they imposed, or if they did not bring a sufficient quantity of Indians to their service: for the Country being in a plain there was no avoiding the fury of the Horsement.

He commanded these Spaniards to go pillage and depopulate other Countries, permitting to these Robbers, and Hangmen, to bring away and enslave what number of these poor people they pleased: whom they laded with chains that weighed above sixty or fifty pounds, that they might not have the opportunity of escaping, so that it seldom happened that above four in four thousand returned home; and if either through the weight of their chains, or for hunger or thirst they did chance to faint by the way, because they would not hinder their journey, they cut off their heads immediately, throwing the head in one place and the body in another. And the poor captive Indians, when they saw the Spaniards preparing for such journeys, at their departure would weep and fall into these kind of sad expression. These are the journeys that we have often gone, to serve the Christians, and then we could return home again to visit our Wives and Children, but now all hope is cut off from us, and we must never see them more.

It happened also, by reason that it came into the Governors mind to change the Indians from one Master to another, pretending to take away force from some that he saw began to envy him, that there was no seed time nor harvest for a whole year; now rather than the Spaniards would want, they took it from the Indians, by which means there perished no less than thirty thousand people; which caused one woman for hunger to eat her own child.

And because these Cities and other places were such pleasant abodes, therefore the Spaniards took up their habitations in these places, dividing the possessions among themselves; and as for the Indians, both old and young they lived in the houses of the Spaniards, drudging day & night in a perpetual captivity, who spared not the smallest children, but impos'd on them burdens as much as they were able to bear, and sometimes more; & by this means allowing them neither houses nor anything else proper to themselves, they destroyed them daily, and do daily destroy them; so that they exceeded the cruelties which they had committed in Hispaniola.

They hastened also the death of many of these poor people, by forcing them to carry timber and planks for shipping to the port that was distant about thirty miles from this place; compelling them also to fetch honey and wax from the Mountains, where they were many times devoured by the Tigers. Neither were they ashamed to lade and burden Women with child, as if they had been only beasts for carriage.

But there was no greater plague that depopulated this Country, than a liberty granted by the Governour to the Spaniards, for the requiring of slaves and captives from the Nobles and potent men of the Kingdom; who as often as the Spaniards obtained leave to demand them, which was every four or five months, and sometimes oftener, gave them constantly fifty servants, whom the Spaniards still threatened, that if they would not be obedient, they would either burn them alive, or throw them to the dogs. Now because the Indians have but few servants, for it is a very great matter to see above three servants in that place waiting upon a Noble man; therefore the Nobility were fain to come to their subjects, from whom first they took all the orphans, then coming to those that had many children, from them that had two they took one, and from those who had three they demanded two; and thus they were fain to make up the Number which the threatening Tyrant required, while the poor people wept and deplor'd the sad misfortune of their Children, over whom they are very tender. Which being done for a daily continuance, in ten or twelve years they made a clean riddance of the inhabitants out of this place. For every foot there came five or six ships which returned full of Indians into the Regions of Panama and Peru, where sold, and ended their days in captivity. For experience hath taught us this, that when ever the Indians are removed from their accustomed habitations into other climates, they quickly die; the Spaniards neither affording them sufficient food, nor in times of sickness diminishing their labour, for which end they were only bought. And thus the number of people hurried from the enjoyment of their freedom into a sad and laborious captivity, amounted to five hundred thousand souls, of which above fifty or sixty thousand are already perished, and more daily perish. All these Massacres were committed within the space of fourteen years. There may be now remaining in the Province of Nicaraqua perhaps some four or five thousand men, though they daily diminish through the immoderate oppressions of the Spaniards. Notwithstanding in former time for number of people, it was the most flourishing place in the whole world.

From *The Tears of the Indians: Being An Historical and true Account Of the Cruel Massacres and Slaughters of above Twenty Millions of innocent People; Committed by the Spaniards In the Islands of Hispaniola, Cuba, Jamaica, &c. As also, in the Continent of Mexico, Peru, & other Places of the West-Indies, To the total destruction of those Countries* by 'Casaus', 1656

A Gaspesian Indian Chief Reproves the French in Nova Scotia

Thou reproachest us very inappropriately, that our country is a little hell on earth in contrast with France, which thou comparest to a terrestrial paradise, inasmuch as it yields thee, so thou sayest, every kind of provision in abundance. Thou sayest of us also that we are the most miserable and most unhappy of all men, living without religion, without manners, without honor, without social order, and in a word, without any rules, like the beasts in our woods and forests, lacking bread, wine, and a thousand other comforts, which thou has in superfluity in Europe. Well, my brother, if thou doest not yet know the real feelings which our Indians have towards thy Country and towards all thy nation, it is proper that I inform thee at once.

I beg thee now to believe that, all miserable as we seem in thy eyes, we consider ourselves nevertheless much happier than thou, in this that we are very content with the little that we have . . . Thou deceivest thyselves greatly if thou thinkest to persuade us that thy country is better than ours. For if France, as thou sayest, is a little terrestrial paradise, art thou sensible to leave it? And why abandon wives, children, relatives, and friends? Why risk thy life and thy property every year? And why venture thyself with such risk in any season whatsoever, to the storms and tempests of the sea in order to come to a strange and barbarous country which thou considerest the poorest and least fortunate of the world. Besides, since we are wholly convinced of the contrary, we scarcely take the trouble to go to France because we fear with good reason, lest we find little satisfaction there, seeing in our own experience that those who are natives thereof leave it every year in order to enrich themselves on our shores. We believe, further, that you are also incomparably poorer than we, and that you are only simple journeymen, valets, servants, and slaves, all masters and Grand Captains though you may appear, seeing that you glory in our old rags, and in our miserable suits of beaver which can no longer be of use to us, and that you find among us in the fishery for cod which you make in these parts, the wherewithall to comfort your misery and the poverty which oppress you. As to us, we find all our riches and all our conveniences among ourselves, without trouble, without exposing our lives to the dangers in which you find yourselves constantly through your long voyages. And whilst feeling compassion for you in the sweetness of our repose, we wonder at the anxieties and cares which you give yourselves, night and day, in order to load your ships. We see also that all your people live, as a rule, only upon cod which you catch among us. It is everlastingly nothing but cod – cod in the morning, cod at midday, cod at evening, and always cod, until things come to such a pass that if you wish some good morsels it is at our expense; and you are obliged to have recourse to the Indians, whom you despise so much, and to beg them to go a-hunting that you may be regaled. Now tell me this one little thing, if thou has any sense, which of these two is the wisest and happiest: he who labors without ceasing and only obtains . . . with great trouble, enough to live on, or he who rests in comfort and finds all that he needs in the pleasure of hunting and fishing.

It is true that we have not always had the use of bread and of wine which your France produces; but, in fact, before the arrival of the French in these parts, did not the Gaspesians live much longer than now? And if we have not any longer among us any of those old men of a hundred and thirty to forty years, it is only because we are gradually adopting your manner of living, for experience is making it very plain that those of us live longest who, despising your bread, your wine, and your brandy, are content with their natural food of beaver, of moose, of waterfowl, and fish, in accord with the custom of our ancestors and of all the Gaspesian nation. Learn now, my brother once for all, because I must open to thee my heart: there is no Indian who does not consider himself infinitely more happy and more powerful than the French.

Anon., 1676

How to Build an Empire

For instance, a crew of pirates are driven by a storm they know not whither; at length a boy discovers land from the top-mast; they go on shore to rob and plunder; they see an harmless people, are entertained with kindness, they give the country a new name, they take formal possession of it for the King, they set up a rotten plank or a stone for a memorial, they murder two or three dozen of the natives, bring away a couple more by force for a sample, return home, and get their pardon. Here commences a new Dominion acquired with a title by *Divine Right*.

Ships are sent with the first opportunity; the natives driven out or destroyed; their princes tortured to discover their gold; a free licence given to all acts of inhumanity and lust, the earth reeking with the blood of its inhabitants: and this execrable crew of butchers, employed in so pious an expedition, is a modern colony sent to convert and civilise an idolatrous and barbarous people.

From *Gulliver's Travels* by Jonathan Swift, 1726

'A Modest Proposal for preventing The Children of Poor People from being a Burden to their Parents, or the Country, and for making them Beneficial to the Public'

It is a melancholy object to those who walk through this great town, [Dublin], or travel in the country, when they see the streets, the roads, and cabin doors, crowded with beggars of the female sex, followed by three, four, or six children, all in rags, and importuning every passenger for an alms. These mothers, instead of being able to work for their honest livelihood, are forced to employ all their time in strolling to beg sustenance for their helpless infants; who, as they grow up, either turn thieves for want of work, or leave their dear native country to fight for the Pretender in Spain, or sell themselves to the Barbadoes.

I think it is agreed by all parties that this prodigious number of children in the arms, or on the backs, or at the heels, of their mothers and frequently of their fathers, is in the present deplorable state of the kingdom a very great additional grievance; and therefore whoever could find out a fair, cheap, and easy method of making these sound useful members of the commonwealth, would deserve so well of the public, as to have his statue set up for a preserver of the nation.

But my intention is very far from being confined to provide only for the children of professed beggars; it is of a much greater extent, and shall take in the whole number of infants at a certain age who are born of parents in effect as little able to support them as those who demand our charity in the streets.

As to my own part, having turned my thoughts for many years upon this important subject, and maturely weighed the several schemes of our projectors, I have always found them grossly mistaken in their computation. It is true, a child just dropped from its dam may be supported by her milk for a solar year, with little other nourishment; at most not above the value of 2s., which the mother may certainly get, or the value in scraps, by her lawful occupation of begging; and it is exactly at one year old that I propose to provide for them in such a manner as, instead of being a charge upon their parents or the parish, or wanting food and raiment for the rest of their lives, they shall on the contrary contribute to the feeding, and partly to the clothing, of many thousands.

There is likewise another great advantage in my scheme; that it will prevent those voluntary abortions, and that horrid practice of women murdering their bastard children, alas, too frequent among us! sacrificing the poor innocent babes, I doubt, more to avoid the expense than the shame; which would move tears and pity in the most savage and inhuman breast.

The number of souls in this kingdom being usually reckoned one million and a half, of these I calculate there may be about 200,000 couple whose wives are breeders; from which number I subtract 30,000 couple who are able to maintain their own children, (although I apprehend there cannot be so many, under the present distresses of the kingdom;) but this being granted, there will remain 170,000 breeders. I again subtract 50,000 for those women who miscarry, or whose children die by accident or disease within the year. There only remain 120,000 children of poor parents annually born. The question therefore is, how this number shall be reared and provided for? which, as I have already said, under the present situation of affairs is utterly impossible by all the methods hitherto proposed. For we can neither employ them in handicraft nor agriculture; we neither build houses (I mean in the country) nor cultivate land; they can very seldom pick up a livelihood by stealing, till they arrive at six years old, except where they are of towardly parts; although I confess they learn the rudiments much earlier; during which time they can, however, be properly looked upon only as probationers; as I have been informed by a principal gentleman in the county of Cavan, who protested to me that he never knew above one or two instances under the age of six, even in a part of the kingdom so renowned for the quickest proficiency in that art.

I am assured by our merchants, that a boy or a girl before twelve years old is no saleable commodity; and even when they come to this age they will not yield above £3, or £3, 2s. 6d. at most, on the Exchange; which cannot turn to account either to the parents or kingdom, the charge of nutriment and rags having been at least four times that value.

I shall now therefore humbly propose my own thoughts, which I hope will not be liable to the least objection.

I have been assured by a very knowing American of my acquaintance in London, that a young healthy child, well nursed, is at a year old a most delicous, nourishing, and wholesome food, whether stewed, roasted, baked, or boiled: and I make no doubt that it will equally serve in a fricasse or a ragout.

I do therefore humbly offer it to public consideration that of the 120,000 children already computed, 20,000 may be reserved for breed, whereof only one-fourth part to be males; which is more than we allow to sheep, black cattle, or swine; and my reason is, that these children are seldom the fruits of marriage, a circumstance not much regarded by our savages, therefore one male will be sufficient to serve four females. That the remaining 100,000 may, at a year old, be offered in sale to the persons of quality and fortune through the kingdom; always advising the mother to let them suck plentifully in the last month, so as to render them plump and fat for a good table. A child will make two dishes at an entertainment for friends; and when the family dines alone, the fore or hind quarter will make a reasonable dish, and, seasoned with a little pepper or salt, will be very good boiled on the fourth day, especially in winter.

I have reckoned upon a medium that a child just born will weigh 12 pounds, and in a solar year, if tolerably nursed, will increase to 28 pounds.

I grant this food will be somewhat dear, and therefore very proper for landlords, who, as they have already devoured most of the parents, seem to have the best title to the children.

Infant's flesh will be in season throughout the year, but more plentifully in March, and a little before and after: for we are told by a grave author, an eminent French physician, that fish being a prolific diet, there are more children born in Roman catholic countries about nine months after Lent than at any other season; therefore, reckoning a year after Lent, the markets will be more glutted than usual, because the number of Popish infants is at least three to one in this kingdom: and therefore it will have one other collateral advantage, by lessening the number of Papists among us.

Jonathan Swift, 1729

An English priest was on a visit to a remote part of the north of Ireland. A local farmer offered to show him the sights.

'That's Devil's Mountain,' said the farmer. 'Over there is Devil's Dyke. Devil's Wood starts on the other side of the river.'

'The devil seems to own a lot of property in these parts,' smiled the priest.

'Aye,' agreed the farmer, 'and like most other landlords he seems to spend most of his time in London.'

The Wife Market at Bath

Every upstart of fortune, harnessed in the trappings of the mode, presents himself at Bath, as in the very focus of observation – clerks and factors from the East Indies, loaded with the spoil of plundered provinces; planters, negro-drivers, and hucksters, from our American plantations, enriched they know not how; agents, commissaries, and contractors, who have fattened, in two successive wars, on the blood of the nation; usurers, brokers, and jobbers of every kind; men of low birth, and no breeding, have found themselves suddenly translated into a state of affluence, unknown to former ages; and no wonder that their brains should be intoxicated with pride, vanity, and presumption.

Knowing no other criterion of greatness but the ostentation of wealth, they discharge their affluence without taste or conduct, through every channel of the most absurd extravagance; and all of them hurry to Bath, because here, without any further qualification they can mingle with the princes and nobles of the land. Even the wives of low tradesmen, who, like shovel-nosed sharks, prey upon the blubber of these uncouth whales of fortune, are infected with the same rage of displaying their importance; and the slightest indisposition serves them for a pretext to insist upon being conveyed to Bath, where they may hobble country-dances and cotillions among lordlings, squires, counsellors, and clergy.

From the *Complete History of England* by Tobias Smollett, 1757–8

'What Happened to them at Surinam, and how Candide became Acquainted with Martin'

The first day's journey of our two travellers was very agreeable, they being elated with the idea of finding themselves masters of more treasure than Asia, Europe or Africa could scrape together. Candide was so transported, that he carved the name of Cunegonde upon almost every tree that he came to. The second day, two of their sheep sank in a morass, and were lost, with all that they carried; two others died of fatigue a few days after; seven or eight died at once of want, in a desert; and some few days after, some others fell down a precipice. In short, after a march of one hundred days, their whole flock amounted to no more than two sheep.

'My friend,' said Candide to Cacambo, 'you see how perishable the riches of this world are; there is nothing durable, nothing to be depended on but virtue, and the happiness of once more seeing Miss Cunegonde.' 'I grant it,' said Cacambo; 'but we have still two sheep left, besides more treasure than ever the King of Spain was master of; and I see a town a good way off, that I take to be Surinam, belonging to the Dutch. We are at the end of our troubles, and at the beginning of our happiness.'

As they drew nigh to the city, they saw a negro stretched on the ground, more than half naked, having only a pair of drawers of blue cloth; the poor fellow had lost his left leg and his right hand. 'Good God!' said Candide to him, in Dutch, 'What do you here, in this terrible condition?' 'I am waiting for my master, Mynheer Vanderdendur, the great merchant,' replied the negro. 'And was it Mynheer Vanderdendur that used you in this manner?' said Candide. 'Yes sir,' said the negro, 'it is the custom of the country. They give us a pair of linen drawers for our whole clothing twice a year. If we should chance to have one of our fingers caught in the mill, as we are working in the sugarhouses, they cut off our hand; if we offer to run away, they cut off one of our legs; and I have had the misfortune to be found guilty of both these offences. Such are the conditions on which you eat sugar in Europe! Yet when my mother sold me for ten crowns at Patagonia on the coast of Guinea, she said to me, My dear boy, bless our fetiches, adore them always, they will make you live happily. You have the honor to be a slave to our lords, the whites, and will by that means be in a way of making the fortunes both of your father and your mother. Alas! I do not know whether I have made their fortunes, but I am sure they have not made mine. The dogs, monkeys, and parrots are a thousand times less wretched than we. The Dutch missionaries who converted me, told me every Sunday, that we all are sons of Adam, both blacks and whites. I am not a genealogist, myself; but if these preachers speak the truth, we are all cousins-german; and you must own that it is a shocking thing to use one's relations in this barbarous manner.'

From *Candide* by 'Voltaire' (François-Marie Arouet), 1759

The American Revolution

AMERICANS
BEAR IN REMEMBRANCE
The HORRID MASSACRE!
Perpertrated in King-Street, BOSTON,
New-England
On the Evening of March the Fifth, 1770.
When FIVE of your fellow countrymen,
GRAY, MAVERICK, CALDWELL, ATTUCKS,
and CAER.
Lay wallowing in their Gore!
Being *basely*, and most *inhumanly*
MURDERED!

And SIX others badly WOUNDED!
By a Party of the XXIXth Regiment,
Under the command of Capt. Tho. Preston
REMEMBER!
That Two of the MURDERERS
Were convicted of MANSLAUGHTER!
By a Jury, of whom I shall say
NOTHING
Branded in the hand!
And *dismissed*
The others were ACQUITTED,
And their Captain PENSIONED!
Also
BEAR IN REMEMBRANCE
That on the 22d Day of February, 1770:
The infamous
EBENEZER RICHARDSON, Informer,
And tool to Ministerial hirelings,
Most *barbarously*
MURDERED
CHRISTOPHER SEIDER,
An innocent youth!
Of which crime he was found guilty
By his Country
On Friday April 20th, 1770;
But remained *Unsentenced*
On Saturday the 22d Day of February, 1772.
When the GRAND INQUEST
For Suffolk county,
Were informed, at request,
By the Judges of the Superior Court,
That EBENEZER RICHARDSON'S *Case*
Then lay before his MAJESTY.
Therefore said *Richardson*
This day, MARCH FIFTH! 1772,
Remains UNHANGED!!!
LET THESE things be told to Posterity!
And handed down
From Generation to Generation,
'Till Time shall be no more!
Forever may AMERICA be preserved,
From weak and wicked monarchs,

Tyrannical Ministers,
Abandoned Governors
Their Underlings and Hirelings!
And may the
Machinations of artful, *designing* wretches,
Who would ENSLAVE THIS People,
Come to an end,
Let their NAMES and MEMORIES
Be buried in eternal oblivion,
And the PRESS,
For a *SCOURGE* to Tyrannical Rulers,
Remain FREE.

Anon., 1770

If Wales be governed by a nation outside our land,
I would prefer to be governed from Dublin

Gwynfor Evans

On Slavery

Natural liberty is the right which nature has given to every one to dispose of himself according to his will . . .

The slave, an instrument in the hands of wickedness, is below the dog which the Spaniard let loose against the American . . .

These are memorable and eternal truths – the foundation of all morality, the basis of all government; will they be contested? Yes! . . .

If self-interest alone prevails with nations and their masters, there is another power. Nature speaks in louder tones than philosophy or self-interest. Already are there established two colonies of fugitive negroes, whom treaties and power protect from assault. Those lightnings announce the thunder. A courageous chief only is wanted. Where is he, that great man whom Nature owes to her vexed, oppressed and tormented children? Where is he? He will appear, doubt it not; he will come forth and raise the sacred standard of liberty. This venerable signal will gather around him the companions of his misfortune. More impetuous than the torrents, they will everywhere leave the indelible traces of their just resentment. Everywhere people will bless the name of the hero who shall have reestablished the rights of the human race; everywhere will they raise trophies in his honour.

Abbé Raynal, 1780

Voodoo Song

Eh! Eh! Bomba Heu! Heu!
Canga, bafio té!
Canga, mouné de lé!
Canga, do ki la!
Canga, li!

[We swear to destroy the whites and all that they possess; let us die rather than fail to keep this vow.]

Haiti, *c.* 1780

Epigram

To purify their wine some people bleed
A lamb into the barrel, and succeed;
No nostrum, planters say, is half so good
To make fine sugar as a negro's blood.
Now lambs and negroes both are harmless things,
And thence perhaps this wondrous virtue springs,
'Tis in the blood of innocence alone –
Good cause why planters never try their own.

William Cowper, *c.* 1780

From 'The File Hewer's Lamentation'

As negroes in Virginia,
In Maryland or Guinea,
Like them I must continue
To be both bought and sold.
While negro-ships are filling
I ne'er can save one shilling,
And must, which is more killing,
A pauper die when old.

At every week's conclusion
New wants bring fresh confusion,
It is but mere delusion
To hope for better days;
While knaves with power invested,
Until by death arrested,
Oppress us unmolested
By their infernal ways.

An hanging day is wanted;
Was it by justice granted,
Poor men distressed and daunted
Would then have cause to sing:
To see in active motion
Rich knaves in full proportion,
For their unjust extortion
And vile offences, swing.

Joseph Mather, 1784

To the French Government

Do they think that men who have been able to enjoy the blessing of liberty will calmly see it snatched away? They supported their chains only so long as they did not know any condition of life more happy than that of slavery. But to-day when they have left it, if they had a thousand lives they would sacrifice them all rather than be forced into slavery again. But no, the same hand which has broken our chains will not enslave us anew. France will not revoke her principles, she will not withdraw from us the greatest of her benefits. She will protect us from all our enemies; she will not permit her sublime morality to be perverted, those principles which do her most honour to be destroyed, her most beautiful achievement to be degraded, her Decree of the 16th Pluviôse which so honours humanity to be revoked. *But if, to re-establish slavery in San Domingo, this was done, then I declare to you it would be to attempt the impossible: we have known how to face dangers to obtain our liberty, we shall know how to brave death to maintain it.*

This, Citizen Directors, is the morale of the people of San Domingo, those are the principles that they transmit to you by me.

My own you know. It is sufficient to renew, my hand in yours, the oath that I have made, to cease to live before gratitude dies in my heart, before I cease to be faithful to France and to my duty, before the god of liberty is profaned and sullied by the liberticides, before they can snatch from my hands that sword, those arms, which France confided to me 'for the defence of its rights and those of humanity, for the triumph of liberty and equality.'

From a letter by Toussaint L'Ouverture 1797,
on the possible restoration of slavery

Wolfe Tone

The favourite object of my life has been the independence of my country, and to that object I have made every sacrifice.

Placed in honourable poverty, the love of liberty was implanted by nature and confirmed by education in my heart. – No seduction, no terror, could banish it from thence; and seduction and terror have not been spared against me. To impart the inestimable blessings of liberty to the land of my birth, I have braved difficulties, bondage, and death.

After an honourable combat, in which I strove to emulate the bravery of my gallant comrades, I was forced to submit, and was dragged in irons through the country, not so much to my disgrace, as that of the person by whom such ungenerous and unmanly orders were issued . . .

Whatever I have written and said on the fate of Ireland, I here reiterate.

The connexion of England I have ever considered as the bane of Ireland, and have done everything in my power to break it, and to raise three millions of my countrymen to the rank of citizens.

Wolfe Tone at his trial, 1798; a Protestant, Tone led the United Irishmen (a league of poor tenant farmers) during their uprising

Whip and Trigger

White man use whip
White man use trigger,
But the Bible and Jesus
Made a slave of the nigger.

Anon. slave, *c.* 1800

What I know is Me

Got one mind for the boss to see,
Got another mind for what I know is me.

Anon. slave, USA, *c.* 1800

Join with me now . . .

Black men if you have now a mind to join with me now is your time for freedom. All clever men who will keep secret these words I give to you is life. I have taken it on myself to let the country be at liberty this lies upon my mind for a long time. Mind men I have told you a great deal I have joined with both black and white which is the common man or poor white people, mulattoes will Join with me to help free the country, although they are free already. I have got 8 or 10 white men to lead me in the fight on the magazine, they will be before me and hand out guns, powder, pistols, shot and other things that will answer the purpose . . . black men I mean to lose my life in this way if they will take it.

Speech made during a slave revolt by Arthur, slave of
William Farrar of Henrico County, 1802

Tek Force wid Force

Oh me good friend Mr Wilberforce mek me free
God Almighty thank ye! God Almighty thank ye!
God Almighty mek me free!

Buckra in dis country no mek we free!
Wa negro fe do? Wa negro fe do?
Tek force wid force
Tek force wid force!

Anon., West Indies, 1816

My old master often got drunk, and then he would get in a fury with his daughter, and beat her till she was not fit to be seen. I remember on one occasion, I had gone to fetch water, and when I was coming up the hill I heard a great screaming; I ran as fast as I could to the house, put down the water, and went into the chamber, where I found my master beating Miss D— dreadfully. I strove with all my strength to get her away from him; for she was all black and blue with bruises. He had beat her with his fist, and almost killed her. The people gave me credit for getting her away. He turned round and began to lick me. Then I said, 'Sir, this is not Turk's Island.' I can't repeat his answer, the words were too wicked – too bad to say. He wanted to treat me the same in Bermuda as he had done in Turk's Island.

He had an ugly fashion of stripping himself quite naked and ordering me then to wash him in a tub of water. This was worse to me than all the licks. Sometimes when he called me to wash him I would not come, my eyes were so full of shame. He would then come to beat me. One time I had plates and knives in my hand, and I dropped both plates and knives, and some of the plates were broken. He struck me so severely for this, that at last I defended myself, for I thought it was high time to do so. I then told him I would not live longer with him, for he was a very indecent man – very spiteful, and too indecent; with no shame for his servants, no shame for his own flesh. So I went away to a neighbouring house and sat down and cried till the next morning, when I went home again, not knowing what else to do . . .

I am often much vexed, and I feel great sorrow when I hear some people in this country say, that the slaves do not need better usage, and do not want to be free. They believe the foreign people, who deceive them, and say slaves are happy. I say, Not so. How can slaves be happy when they have the halter round their neck and the whip upon their back? and are disgraced and thought no more of than beasts? – and are separated from their mothers, and husbands, and children, and sisters, just as cattle are sold and separated? Is it happiness for a driver in the field to take down his wife or sister or child, and strip them, and whip them in such a disgraceful manner? – women that have had children exposed in the open field to shame! There is no modesty or decency shown by the owner to his slaves; men, women, and children are exposed alike. Since I have been here I have often wondered how English people can go out into the West Indies and act in such a beastly manner. But when they go to the West Indies, they forget God and all feeling of shame, I think, since they can see and do such things. They tie up slaves like hogs – moor them up like cattle, and they lick them, so as hogs, or cattle, or horses never were flogged; – and yet they come home and say, and make some good people believe, that slaves don't want to get out of slavery. But they put a cloak about the truth. It is not so. All slaves want to be free – to be free is very sweet. I will say the truth to English people who may read this history that my good friend, Miss S—, is now writing down for me. I have been a slave myself – I know what slaves feel – I can tell by myself what other slaves feel, and by what they have told me. The man that says slaves be quite happy in slavery – that they don't want to be free – that man is either ignorant or a lying person. I never heard a slave say so. I never heard a Buckra man say so, till I heard tell of it in England. Such people ought to be ashamed of themselves. They can't do without slaves as well as in England? No slaves here – no whips – no stocks – no punishment, except for wicked people. They hire servants in England; and if they don't like them, they send them away: they can't lick them. Let them work ever so hard in England, they are far better off than slaves. If they get a bad master, they give warning and go hire to another. They have their liberty. That's just what *we* want. We don't mind hard work, if we had proper treatment, and proper wages like English servants, and proper time given in the week to keep us from breaking the Sabbath. But they won't give it; they will have work – work – work, night and day, sick or well, till we are quite done up; and we must not speak up nor look amiss, however much we be abused. And then when we are quite done up, who cares for us, more than for a lame horse? This is slavery. I tell it to let English people know the truth; and I hope they will never leave off to pray God, and call loud to the great King of England, till all the poor blacks be given free, and slavery done up for evermore.

From *The History of Mary Prince*, 1831, the first black British woman to escape from slavery and publish a record of her experiences

Skinning Eels

There yet remains a class, the general one,
Which has no merit, and pretends to none;
Good easy folk who know that eels are eels,
But never pause to think how skinning feels,
Content to know that eels are made to flay,
And Indians formed by destiny to pay . . .
And hence when they become the great and high,
There is no word they hate so much as – Why?

From '*India': A Poem in Three Cantos*, by 'a Young Civilian of Bengal', 1834

The Slave Trade

What raised Liverpool and Manchester from provincial towns to gigantic cities? What maintains now their ever active industry and their rapid accumulation of wealth?

Their present opulence is as really owing to the toil and suffering of the negro as if his hands had excavated their docks and fabricated their steam engines.

From *Lecture on Colonisation* by H. Merivale, 1840

Those Who Profess Freedom

Those who profess to favour freedom, yet deprecate agitation, are men who want crops without ploughing up the ground. They want rain without thunder and lightning. They want the ocean without the awful wrath of its many waters. Power concedes nothing without demands – it never did and it never will. Find out just what any people will quietly submit to, and you have found out the exact measure of injustice and wrong which will be imposed upon them. And these will continue until they are resisted with either words or blows, or with both. The limits of tyrants are prescribed by the endurance of those whom they oppress.

Frederick Douglass, escaped slave and leading Abolitionist, *c.* 1850

Fourth of July Oration, Rochester, USA

What to the American slave is your Fourth of July? I answer: a day that reveals to him, more than all other days in the year, the gross injustice and cruelty to which he is the constant victim. To him your celebration is a sham; your boasted liberty, an unholy licence; your national greatness, swelling vanity; your sounds of rejoicing are empty and heartless; your denunciation of tyrants, brass-fronted impudence; your shouts of liberty and equality, hollow mockery; your prayers and hymns, your sermons and thanksgivings, with all your religious parade and solemnity, are, to him, more bombast, fraud, deception, impiety and hypocrisy – a thin veil to cover up crimes which would disgrace a nation of savages . . .

You boast of your love of liberty, your superior civilization, and pure Christianity, while the whole political power of the nation (as embodied in the two great political parties) is solemnly pledged to support and perpetuate the enslavement of three millions of your countrymen. You hurl your anathemas at the crown-headed tyrants of Russia and Austria and pride yourselves on your democratic institutions, while you yourselves consent to be the mere *tools* and *bodyguards* of the tyrants of Virginia and Carolina.

You invite to your shores fugitives of oppression from abroad, honor them with banquets, greet them with ovations, cheer them, toast them, salute them, protect them, and pour out your money to them like water; but the fugitive from your own land you advertise, hunt, arrest, shoot, and kill. You glory in your refinement and your universal education; yet you maintain a system as barbarous and dreadful as ever stained the character of a nation – a system begun in avarice, supported in pride, and perpetuated in cruelty.

You shed tears over fallen Hungary, and make the sad story of her wrongs the theme of your poets, statesmen and orators, till your gallant sons are ready to fly to arms to vindicate her cause against the oppressor; but, in regard to the ten thousand wrongs of the American slave, you would enforce the strictest silence, and would hail him as an enemy of the nation who dares to make these wrongs the subject of public discourse!

Frederick Douglass, 1852

'We Raise the Wheat'

We raise the wheat,
They give us the corn
We sift the meal,
They give us the husk,
We peel the meat,
They give us the skin,
And that's the way they take us in.

Slave song, *c.* 1855

Testimony of Chief Seattle

The great chief in Washington sends word that he wishes to buy our land.

The Great Chief also sends us words of friendship and good will. This is kind of him, since we know he has little need of our friendship in return.

But we will consider your offer. For we know that if we do not sell, the white man may come with guns and take our land.

How can you buy or sell the sky, the warmth of the land? The idea is strange to us.

If we do not own the freshness of the air and the sparkle of the water, how can you buy them?

Every part of this earth is sacred to my people. Every shining pine needle, every sandy shore, every mist in the dark woods, every clearing and humming insect is holy in the memory and experience of my people. The sap which courses through the trees carries the memories of the red man.

The white man's dead forget the country of their birth when they go to walk among the stars. Our dead never forget this beautiful earth, for it is the mother of the red man. We are part of the earth and it is part of us.

The perfumed flowers are our sisters; the deer, the horse, the great eagle, these are our brothers. The rocky crests, the juices of the meadows, the body heat of the pony, and man – all belong to the same family. So, when the Great Chief in Washington sends word that he wishes to buy our land, he asks much of us.

The Great Chief sends word he will reserve us a place so that we can live comfortably to ourselves, he will be our father and we will be his children.

So we will consider your offer to buy our land. But it will not be easy. For this land is sacred to us.

This shining water that moves in the streams and rivers is not just water but the blood of our ancestors. If we sell you land, you must remember that it is sacred, and you must teach your children that it is sacred and that each ghostly reflection in the clear water of the lakes tells of events and memories in the life of my people. The water's murmur is the voice of my father's father.

The river are our brothers, they quench our thirst. The rivers carry our canoes, and feed our children. If we sell you our land, you must remember, and teach your children, that the rivers are our brothers, and yours, and you must henceforth give the rivers the kindness you would give any brother.

The red man has always retreated before the advancing white man, as the mist of the mountains runs before the morning sun. But the ashes of our fathers are sacred. Their graves are holy ground, and so these hills, these trees, this portion of the earth is consecrated to us. We know that the white man does not understand our ways. One portion of land is the same to him as the next, for he is a stranger who comes in the night and takes from the land whatever he needs. The earth is not his brother, but his enemy, and when he has conquered it, he moves on. He leaves his fathers' graves behind, and he does not care. He kidnaps the earth from his children. He does not care. His fathers' graves and his children's birthright are forgotten.

He treats his mother, the earth, and his brother, the sky, as things to be bought, plundered, sold like sheep or bright beads. His appetite will devour the earth and leave behind only a desert.

I do not know. Our ways are different from your ways. The sight of your cities pains the eyes of the red man. But perhaps it is because the red man is a savage and does not understand.

There is no quiet place in the white man's cities. No place to hear the unfurling of leaves in spring or the rustle of insect's wings. But perhaps it is because I am a savage and do not understand. The clatter only seems to insult the ears. And what is there to a life if a man cannot hear the lonely cry of the whippoorwill or the arguments of the frogs around a pond at night? I am a red man and do not understand. The Indian prefers the soft sound of the wind darting over the face of a pond, and the smell of the wind itself, cleansed by a midday rain or scented with the piñon pine.

The air is precious to the red man, for all things share the same breath – the beast, the tree, the man, they all share the same breath. The white man does not seem to notice the air he breathes. Like a man dying for many days, he is numb to the stench. But if we sell you our land, you must remember that the air is precious to us, that the air shares its spirit with all the life it supports. The wind that gave our grandfather his first breath also receives his last sigh. And the wind must also give our children the spirit of life. And if we sell you our land, you must keep it apart and sacred, as a place where even the white man can go to taste the wind that is sweetened by the meadow's flowers.

So we will consider your offer to buy our land. If we decide to accept, I will make one condition: The white man must treat the beasts of this land as his brothers.

I am a savage and I do not understand any other way. I have seen a thousand rotting buffalos on the prairie, left by the white man who shot them from a passing train. I am a savage and I do not understand how the smoking iron horse can be more important than the buffalo that we kill only to stay alive.

What is man without the beasts? If all the beasts were gone, men would die from a great loneliness of spirit. For whatever happens to the beasts, soon happens to man. All things are connected.

You must teach your children that the ground beneath their feet is the ashes of our grandfathers. So that they will respect the land, tell your children that the earth is rich with the lives of our kin. Teach your children what we have taught our children, that the earth is our mother. Whatever befalls the earth befalls the sons of the earth. If men spit upon the ground, they spit upon themselves.

This we know. The earth does not belong to man; man belongs to the earth. This we know. All things are connected like the blood which unites one family. All things are connected. Whatever befalls the earth befalls the sons of the earth. Man did not weave the web of life, he is merely a strand in it. Whatever he does to the web, he does to himself.

From a speech by Chief Sealth [Seattle] at a tribal assembly, 1854

When they first came
They had the bible, we had the land.
Now we have the bible and they have our land.

African saying

'The Slave Mother'

Heard you that shriek? It rose
So wildly on the air,
It seem'd as if a burden'd heart
Was breaking in despair.

Saw you those hands so sadly clasped –
The bowed and feeble head –
The shuddering of that fragile form –
That look of grief and dread?

Saw you the sad, imploring eye?
Its every glance was pain,
As if a storm of agony
Were sweeping through the brain.

She is a mother pale with fear,
Her boy clings to her side,
And in her kyrtle vainly tries
His trembling form to hide.

He is not hers, although she bore
For him a mother's pains;
He is not hers, although her blood
Is coursing through his veins!

He is not hers, for cruel hands
May rudely tear apart
The only wreath of household love
That binds her breaking heart.

His love has been a joyous light
That o'er her pathway smiled,
A fountain gushing ever new,
Amid life's desert wild.

His lightest word has been a tone
Of music round her heart,
Their lives a streamlet blent in one –
Oh, Father! must they part?

They tear him from her circling
arms,
Her last and fond embrace: –
Oh! never more may her sad eyes
Gaze on his mournful face.

No marvel, then, those bitter
shrieks
Disturb the listening air;
She is a mother, and her heart
Is breaking in despair.

Frances Ellen Watkins, 1854

The Indian Empire

It is terrible to see our middle-class journals and speakers calling for the destruction of Delhi, and the indiscriminate massacre of prisoners . . .

To read the letters of our officers at the commencement of the outbreak, it seemed as if every subaltern had the power to hang or shoot as many natives as he pleased, and they spoke of the work of blood with as much levity as if they were hunting wild animals . . .

It will be a happy day when England has not an acre of territory in Continental Asia. But . . . where do we find even an individual who is not imbued with the notion that England would sink to ruin if she were deprived of her Indian Empire? Leave me, then, to my pigs and sheep, which are not labouring under any such delusions . . .

From a letter by Richard Cobden to John Bright, 22 September 1857

Revolt in Hindostan

There ought to be but one opinion throughout Europe on the Revolt of Hindostan. It is one of the most just, noble, and necessary ever attempted in the history of the world. We recently analysed and exposed the nature of England's Indian rule. We this week, in another column, give an episode referring to Oude, and illustrating the nefarious, the infamous, the inexpressible infamous conduct, of British domination. How any can hesitate which side to take, is inconceivable to us. England – the people, the English people – sympathise with liberty. On which side were they when Poland struggled for its freedom against Russia? On the side of Poland. On which side were they, when Hungary struggled for its rights with Austria? On the side of Hungary. On which side are they when Italy struggles for its life against the Germans, the French, the Papist, and the despot? On the side of Italy. Was Poland right? Then so is Hindostan. Was Hungary justified? Then so is Hindostan. Was Italy deserving of support? Then so is

Hindostan. For all that Poland, Hungary, or Italy sought to gain, for that the Hindhu strives. Nay! more. The Pole, the Hungarian, the Italian still own their soil. The Hindhu does not. The former have rulers of their own, or a kindred faith, above them. The Hindhu has not. The former are still ruled by something like law, and by servants responsible to their masters. The Hindhu is not. Naples and France, Lombardy and Poland, Hungary and Rome present no tyranny so hideous as that enacted by the miscreants of Leadenhall Street, and Whitehall, in Hindostan. The wonder is, not that one hundred and seventy millions of people should now rise in part; – the wonder is that they should ever have submitted at all. They would not, had they not been betrayed by their own princes, who sold each other to the alien, and the base truckling invader, that with his foul help they might cut each other's throats. Thus kings, princes, and aristocracies have ever proven the enemies and curses of every land that harboured them, in every age.

We bespeak the sympathy of the English people for their Hindhu brethren. Their cause is yours – their success is, indirectly, yours as well. The fearful atrocities committed have nothing to do with the great cause at issue – that cause is just, it is holy, it is glorious. Englishmen, Scotchmen, Irishmen, what would you say if a colony of Dutch Jews came hither and asked permission to build a factory on Woolwich March; if, after having gained the permission on promise of paying a yearly rental for the land, they intrigued with the French or Russians to let them into the country; if after that they promised to help you against the invader, in exchange for half of Kent; if, after having received the land, they betrayed both sides and sold you to the Yankees for a slice of Surrey; if, after eternal peace had been sworn to between all the contending parties, they set them all by the ears, and in the midst of the inextricable confusion they went on invading, conquering on their own account; if, being Protestants, they denounced and punished Protestantism to conciliate the Papists; if, again, they destroy Papists to conciliate Protestants; if, when weak and in danger, they swore to solemn treaties, on the faith in which you spared them when in your power; and if they thus, having gained time for strength and power, rushed upon you, unawares, sacked and burned your cities, outraged your women, and murdered your population, and thus, in the hour of your surprise, dismay, and weakness, subjugated you and your country – what would you say and do? If, still further, having thus enthralled you, they confiscated every acre of your own land; if, having thus confiscated it, they made you pay a rental for what had been your own freehold farms; if they then burdened those farms with such taxation, that the produce could not realise one-half of the amount; if, you being unable to pay, they seized your cattle, your farm implements, your very seed corn; if, having thus stopped your means of production, they next year demanded the same rental and the same tax; if, because you could not pay it, they hung you with your heads downwards in the burning sun, lashed you, tortured you, tied scorpions to the breasts of your women, committed every atrocity and crime – what, we repeat, would you say and do? You would rise – rise in the holy right of insurrection, and cry to Europe and the world, to Heaven and earth, to bear witness to the justice of your cause.

Fellow-countrymen! thus have the Hindhus been treated at the hands of England; this is the cause of their insurrection, and every honest man throughout the world can pass but one judgement on the facts, and breathe but one aspiration for the issue.

From *The People's Paper*, 5 September 1857

Tenants at Will

Whereon the Sheriff, 'We have legal hold.
Return to shelter with the sick and old.
Time shall be given; and there are carts below
If any to the workhouse choose to go.'
A young man makes him answer, grave and clear,
'We're thankful to you! but there's no one here
Goin' back into them houses: do your part.
Nor we won't trouble Pigot's horse and cart.'
At which name, rushing into th' open space,
A woman flings her hood from off her face,
Falls on her knees upon the miry ground,
Lifts hands and eyes, and voice of thrilling sound, –
'Vengeance of God Almighty fall on you,
James Pigot! – may the poor man's curse pursue,
The widow's and the orphan's curse, I pray,
Hang heavy round you at your dying day!'
Breathless and fix'd one moment stands the crowd
To hear this malediction fierce and loud.

But now (our neighbour Neal is busy there)
On steady poles be lifted Oona's chair,
Well-heap'd with borrow'd mantles; gently bear
The sick girl in her litter, bed and all;
Whilst others hug the children weak and small
In careful arms, or hoist them pick-a-back;

And, 'midst the unrelenting clink and thwack
Of iron bar on stone, let creep away
The sad procession from that hill-side gray,
Through the slow-falling rain. In three hours more
You find, where Ballytullagh stood before,
Mere shatter'd walls, and doors with useless latch,
And firesides buried under fallen thatch.

From *Laurence Bloomfield in Ireland* by William Allingham, 1864

Measles in Fiji

Our chiefs consult together,
They consult without being able to decide,
They consult about the ship that is being prepared
For Tui Viti to sail in. It was an evil consultation.

The house of death is opened,
That trouble may come to Viti
And destroy all our people.
One side is already depopulated;
We are very near to the gates of hell.

Anon., 1875

'The Concert'

A concert's what the English like,
Their best clothes they put on;
Never mind if it's day or night,
They're always game to have
some fun.

With wife and child that's where
he'll trot,
For talk and laughing and to
sing;
They like their kind of sport a lot,
It goes on and on without
ending.

So I was very keen to see
What type of show makes them
swarm;
That they can spend such good
money
To hear a Rooinek perform.

With a swallow-tail a big black
coat
I borrowed from Brother Sem,
From Uncle Gert a shilling, a
shirt –
Then I was just like them.

Now in I go with a proud tread,
  I sit on the foremost bench,
Of the local whites I am never
    scared,
  So what do I owe to them?

The house was full. Ah, it was
    grand
  To see such happy settlers here;
Gents and girls sit hand in hand.
  All I lacked was an interpreter.

They played and sang with wild
    applause,
  Each minute something fresh
    and fit;
They improvised with never a
    pause –
  Not that I grasped a word of it!

Then came an item that I confess
  Put me in great apprehension –
Ten black fellows in fancy dress
  Each with a kind of violin

Entered and lolled upon a stool,
  Their hair frizzed out in great
    display,
Rowdy and ugly and each a fool –
  I shivered on the spot, I say.

I thought to myself, what's going
    to be,
  From where are they appearing?
Are they Negro folk from oversea,
  Or are those masks they're
    wearing?

Well, masks they certainly were
    not;
  It was bootblack on their skin;
Where one had wiped his lips all
    hot
  I saw the jaw of Sergeant
    Glynn.

So they dance and play the stupid
    coon,
  Ten creatures on a spree;
When all at once I almost swoon –
  They point and wink at me:

The brown man! Oh, in my own
    hall,
  To be the object of their
    laughter!
In all the noise my bitter gall
  Was going to boil for ever after!

We laboured hard to build this
    school
  Where all our children can
    learn;
Now there seems they've made a
    rule
  To drive us from our home
    again.

Well, blood is thicker than water
    once more,
  For darkies as well as for fair,
If you scratch too much an open
    sore
  The pain is hard to bear.

So 'Christy Minstrels' is what
    they're called;
  Don't they have any shame? –
To give such a really godless act
  Such a very lovely name?

Griqua tribesman (Natal) describing an early 'coon-show', 1876;
the Griquas rose against the Cape garrison in 1878

'The Hanging of Louis Riel'

He died at dawn in the land of snows,
  A priest at the left, a priest at the right;
The doomed man praying for his pitiless foes,
  And each priest holding a low dim light,
To pray for the soul of the dying.
    But Windsor Castle was far away,
    And Windsor Castle was never so gay
    With her gorgeous banners flying!

The hero was hung in the windy dawn –
  'Twas splendidly done, the telegraph said;
A creak of the neck, then the shoulders drawn;
  A heave of the breast – and the man hung dead,

  And, oh! never such valiant dying!
    While Windsor Castle was far away
    With its fops and fools on that windy day,
    And its thousand banners flying!

Some starving babes where a stark stream flows
  Twixt windy banks by an Indian town,
A frenzied mother in the freezing snows,
  While softly the pitying snows came down
To cover the dead and the dying.
    But Windsor Castle was gorgeous and gay
    With lion banners that windy day –
    With lying banners flying.

Joaquin Miller, 1885; Riel was a Franco-Indian schoolmaster hanged after the failed revolt of North-west Canadian Indians in 1885

'A War (?) in the Desert'

Afar in the desert I love to ride,
  While the manacled Bush-boy to my stirrup is tied,
Away from the haunts of civilized men;
  Away from the fear of the journalist's pen;

In places remote, where reporters are not,
  And the captured Bechuana may safely be shot.
With my Burgher contingent I daily patrol,
  And search every cranny, every bush, every hole;
And woe to the 'rebel' whose spoor we can trace,
  For we'll treat and maltreat him and spit in his face;
Then his handcuffs are loosened, he's told to 'voetzak,'
  But he's almost immediately shot in the back.

Afar in the desert I love to ride,
  With the captured Bush-boy no more by my side.
O'er the brown burnt veldt, where his pleading cry
  Went up to his Maker so plaintively;
We were deaf to his cries, nor thought it a sin
  To blow him to bits and his skull to smash in.
To see him lie there, a mere human mess,
  Was to us first-class sport, no more, and no less.
Our thirst for the blood of the nigger is strong,
  And a sharp look-out's kept as we canter along;
Lest by untoward chance we should fail to descry
  The spot where a possible victim may lie.

At night in the desert I love not to ride,
  And think of the Bush-boy no more by my side;
Like the fleet-footed ostrich over the waste,
  I race for the camp, thoughts of spooks make me haste;
I remember the vultures how they wheeled overhead,
  Greedy to scent and to gaze on the dead.
The fiend-like laugh of hyena grim
  Seems to say (*pace* Barham), 'That's *him*! That's *him*!'
I shake with dread as the lines I reach,
  The Bush-boy's cry's in the wild-dogs' screech,
I lie as one dead on the dusty plain,
  And feel on my forehead the brand of Cain.

Anon., signed 'Gibbet', 1897; a parody of Pringle's 'Afar in the Desert', which begins 'Afar in the Desert I love to ride,/With the silent Bush-boy alone by my side'

J'Accuse

It is a crime to accuse of disturbing France those who wish her to be generous, and at the head of free and just nations, whilst hatching oneself an impudent plot to impose error upon the whole world. It is a crime to mislead public opinion, to utilise for a deadly task this opinion which has been perverted until it becomes delirious. It is a crime to poison the minds of the little and the humble, to exasperate the passions of reaction and intolerance, while seeking refuge behind that odious anti-Semitism of which great liberal France, France of the rights of man, will die, unless she is cured of her disease. It is a crime to exploit patriotism for works of hatred, and, finally, it is a crime to make of the sword a modern God when all human science is labouring for the coming work of truth and justice. . . .

I accuse Lieutenant-Colonel du Paty de Clam of having been the diabolical author of the judicial error, unconsciously I am willing to believe, and of having then defended his pernicious work for three years by the most absurd and culpable machinations.

I accuse General Mercier of having rendered himself the accomplice, at least through want of firmness, of one of the greatest iniquities of the century.

I accuse General Billot of having had in his hands certain proofs of the innocence of Dreyfus, and of having suppressed them, of having rendered himself guilty of the crime of treason to humanity and treason to justice with a political object, and in order to screen the compromised Staff.

I accuse General de Boisdeffre and General Gonse of having made themselves accomplices of the same crime, the one doubtless through clerical passion, the other, perhaps, from that *esprit de corps* which makes the War Office the sacred and unassailable ark.

I accuse General de Pellieux and Major Ravary of having made a wicked inquiry, I mean by that an inquiry of the most monstrous partiality, of which we have in the report of the latter an imperishable monument of naïve audacity.

I accuse the three experts in handwriting, Sieurs Belhomme, Varinard, and Couard of having made lying and fraudulent reports, unless a medical inquiry should prove them to be suffering from diseased sight and judgment.

I accuse the War Office of having carried on in the press, particularly in the *Eclair* and the *Echo de Paris* an abominable campaign in order to mislead public opinion and screen their error.

Lastly, I accuse the first Court-Martial of having violated the law by condemning an accused person on one document kept secret, and I accuse the second Court-Martial of having, in obedience to orders, covered this illegality by committing in its turn the judicial crime of knowingly acquitting a guilty person.

In preferring these charges I do not ignore the fact that I am exposing myself to the penalties of Clauses 30 and 31 of the Press Law of July 29, 1881, which punishes libel. And it is voluntarily that I expose myself.

As to the men whom I accuse, I do not know them. I have never seen them. I have no resentment or hatred against them. They are for me merely entities, spirits of social maleficence. And the act which I am accomplishing here is only a revolutionary means of hastening the explosion of truth and justice.

I have but one passion – that of light. This I ask for in the name of humanity, which has suffered so much, and which has a claim to happiness. My passionate protest is but the cry of my soul. Let anyone who dares bring me before an Assize Court, and let the inquiry be held in broad daylight.

I am waiting.

Receive, Monsieur le Président, the assurance of my profound respect.

EMILE ZOLA

From a 'Letter to M. Felix Fauré, President of the Republic', 1898

The French Congo

Who is to blame for the annihilating conditions existing to-day in French Congo? Commerce is dead, towns once prosperous and plentiful are deserted and falling into decay, and whose tribes are being needlessly and ignominiously crushed for the aggrandisement of the few . . . Towns are sacked and plundered; fathers, brothers, husbands, are put in foul-smelling prisons until those at home can get together the taxes necessary to secure their relief. France has granted exclusive rights to *concessionaires* who claim everything upon, above, in or about any *hectare* of land described in their grant . . . To be hurled from active, prosperous freedom into inactive and enforced poverty would demoralise even a civilised country; how farther reaching, then, it is with the savage? . . . As the French say, the entire country is *bouleversé*; i.e., overthrown, in confusion, subverted, agitated, unsettled. And the French are right in so naming the result of their own misdeeds. All is desolation, demoralisation, annihilation. Native customs are violated; native rights ignored . . . Great plains which not long since swarmed with the life and bustle of passing trade caravans are now silent and deserted. Ant-hills and arid grass and wind-swept paths are the only signs of life upon them.

American traveller, 1908

The Nation! So What?

SOCIALISM AND NATIONALISM

Well, you won't get the Irish to help Socialism. Our Irish leaders tell us that all we Irish in this country ought to stand together and use our votes to free Ireland.

Sure, let us free Ireland!

Never mind such base, carnal thoughts as concern work and wages, healthy homes, or lives unclouded by poverty.

Let us free Ireland!

The rackrenting landlord – is he not also an Irishman, and wherefore should we hate him? Nay, let us not speak harshly of our brother – yea, even when he raises our rent.

Let us free Ireland!

The profit-grinding capitalist, who robs us of three-fourths of the fruits of our labour, who sucks the very marrow of our bones when we are young, and then throws us out in the street, like a worn-out tool, when we are grown prematurely old in his service – is he not an Irishman, and mayhap a patriot, and wherefore should we think harshly of him?

Let us free Ireland!

'The land that bred and bore us.' And the landlord who makes us pay for permission to live upon it.

Whoop it up for liberty!

'Let us free Ireland,' says that patriot who won't touch Socialism.

Let us all join together and cr-r-rush the br-r-rutal Saxon. Let us all join together, says he, all classes and creeds.

And, says the town worker, after we have crushed the Saxon and freed Ireland, what will we do?

Oh, then you can go back to your slums, same as before.

Whoop it up for liberty!

And, say the agricultural workers, after we have freed Ireland, what then?

Oh, then you can go scraping around for the landlord's rent or the money-lender's interest, same as before.

Whoop it up for liberty!

After Ireland is free, says the patriot who won't touch Socialism, we will protect all classes, and if you won't pay your rent you will be evicted, same as now. But the evicting party, under command of the sheriff, will wear green uniforms and the Harp without the Crown, and the warrant turning you out on the roadside will be stamped with the arms of the Irish Republic.

Now, isn't that worth fighting for?

And when you cannot find employment, and, giving up the struggle of life in despair, enter the Poorhouse, the band of the nearest regiment of the Irish army will escort you to the Poorhouse door to the tune of 'St. Patrick's Day.'

Oh, it will be nice to live in those days!

'With the green Flag floating o'er us,' and an ever-increasing army of unemployed workers walking about under the Green Flag, wishing they had something to eat. Same as now!

Whoop it up for liberty!

From *Socialism Made Easy* by James Connolly, 1909

'A Proclamation!'

BY GEORGE V., KING OF ENGLAND

To Our Faithful Irish Subjects,

We are at present engaged in war With Our first cousin, the Emperor of Germany. We hate the Germans, because Our father, Our grandfather, Our grandmother, and all our ancestors were Germans, and every sensible man now-a-days hates his ancestors!

YOU, ALSO, OUR BRAVE IRISH, HAD ANCESTORS blood-thirsty rebels, who wanted to own Ireland for themselves, and be separated from Our Glorious Empire; but our predecessors on the Throne of England (who were all Germans by birth or by descent) got rid of these narrow-minded savage ancestors of yours. They flogged, hanged, and burned them in '98. They starved them in '48, and brought the food across to feed our Free-born Britons (for Ireland was England's larder then as now). They shipped a few millions who survived the Famine out in Coffin-ships across the Atlantic, and most of them were thrown overboard, and their bones lie whitening at the bottom of the ocean. A few weeks ago, in Dublin, We managed, with the aid of Our Own Scottish Borderers, to let all who had any recollection of ancestors left, know that We were prepared to clear them out root and branch, and to spare neither women nor children in the clearance.

NOW, OUR BRAVE IRISH, We know you don't want to be reminded that these men were your ancestors, anymore than Our Royal Self do that. We are German by blood.

WE WANT MEN TO FIGHT THESE GERMANS, and We know from history that the Irish are a Fighting Race. A large number of your Countrymen have been sent to the Front to fight the Germans. THE MOST OF THEM HAVE BEEN KILLED, BUT THEY DIED NOBLY FIGHTING FOR US AND OUR EMPIRE. We want more to fill their places, and ONLY IRISHMEN WILL GET THE POST OF HONOR. Come and volunteer for the Army at once and We will arrange that you will be sent to the Front and Killed; if you are not killed, when you are no longer of any use for fighting, Remember the British Laws – the Poor Laws – have provided for your upkeep in the Workhouses of Ireland.

Remember the Empire comes first and the Poorhouse after, if you survive the War. GEORGE R.I.

GOD SAVE THE KING

Poster, Dublin, 1915

The Black Question

The history of the American blacks has prepared them to play a major role in the liberation struggle of the entire African race. 300 years ago the American blacks were torn from their native African soil, transported to America in slave ships and, in indescribably cruel conditions, sold into slavery. For 250 years they were treated like human cattle, under the whip of the American overseer. Their labour cleared the forests, built the roads, picked the cotton, constructed the railroads – on it the Southern aristocracy rested. The reward for their labour was poverty, illiteracy and degradation. The blacks were not docile slaves; their history is full of revolts, uprisings, and an underground struggle for freedom, but all their efforts to free themselves were savagely suppressed. They were tortured into submission, while the bourgeois press and religion justified their slavery. When slavery became an obstacle preventing the full and unhindered development of America towards capitalism, when this slavery came into conflict with the slavery of wage labour, it had to give way. The Civil War, which was not a war for the emancipation of the blacks but a war for the preservation of the industrial hegemony of the North, confronted the blacks with a choice between forced labour in the south and wage slavery in the North. The blood, sweat and tears of the 'emancipated' blacks helped to build American capitalism, and when the country, now become a world power, was inevitably pulled into the World War, black Americans gained equal rights with the whites . . . to kill and to die for 'democracy'. Four hundred thousand coloured proletarians were recruited to the American army and organized into special black regiments. These black soldiers had hardly returned from the bloodbath of the war before they came up against racial persecution, lynchings, murders, the denial of rights, discrimination and general contempt. They fought back, but paid dearly for the attempt to assert their human rights. The persecution of blacks became even more widespread than before the war, and the blacks once again learned to 'know their place'. The spirit of revolt, inflamed by the post-war violence and persecution, was suppressed, but cases of inhuman cruelty, such as the events in Tulsa, still cause it to flare up again. This, plus the post-war industrialization of blacks in the North, places the American blacks, particularly those in the North, in the vanguard of the struggle for black liberation.

The Fourth Congress of the Third International, 1922

'Strange Fruit'

Southern trees bear strange fruit
Blood on the leaves and blood at the root
Black body swinging in the Southern breeze
Strange fruit hanging from the poplar trees

Pastoral scene of the gallant South
The bulging eyes and the twisted mouth
Scent of magnolia sweet and fresh
Then the sudden smell of burning flesh

Here is a fruit for the crows to pluck
For the rain to gather, for the wind to suck
For the sun to rot, for the tree to drop
Here is a strange and bitter crop

Lewis Allen, 1930

Marine Corps Credo

I spent thirty-three years and four months in active service as a member of our country's most agile military force – the Marine Corps. I served in all commissioned ranks from a second lieutenant to major-general. And during that period I spent most of my time being a high-class muscle man for Big Business, for Wall Street, and for the bankers. In short, I was a rackeeter for capitalism . . .

Thus I helped make Mexico and especially Tampico safe for American oil interests in 1914. I helped make Haiti and Cuba a decent place for the National City Bank boys to collect revenues in . . . I helped purify Nicaragua for the international banking house of Brown Brothers in 1909–1912. I brought light to the Dominican Republic for American sugar interests in 1916. I helped make Honduras 'right' for American fruit companies in 1903. In China in 1927 I helped see to it that Standard Oil went its way unmolested.

During those years I had, as the boys in the back room would say, a swell racket. I was rewarded with honors, medals, promotion. Looking back on it, I feel I might have given Al Capone a few hints. The best he could do was to operate his racket in three city districts. We Marines operated on three continents.

Major General Smedley D. Butler; *c.* 1930

To Pétain

I would be obliged if you would tell me what I have to do to withdraw rank from: my brother, a second-lieutenant in the 36th Infantry regiment, killed at Douaumont in April 1916; from my son-in-law, second-lieutenant in the Dragoons, killed in Belgium in May 1940; from my nephew, J-F Masse, lieutenant in the 23rd Colonial Regiment, killed at Rethel in May 1940. Can I leave my brother his Médaille Militaire . . . my son, wounded in June 1940, his rank? Can I be assured that no one will retrospectively take back the Sainte-Hélène medal from my great-grandfather?

From a letter by Pierre Masse to Marshal Pétain, 1940, following the Vichy ordinance stopping Jews becoming army officers

'Black, Brown, and White'

Just listen to the song I'm singin', brother
You'll know it's true.
If you're black and got to work for a livin', boy,
This is what they'll say to you:

Now, if you're white, you're right,
And if you're brown, stick around,
But if you're black, O brother,
'Get back, get back, get back.'

I 'member I was in a place one night,
Everybody was having fun,
They was all drinkin' beer and wine,
But me, I couldn't get none.

I was in an employment office,
I got a number and got in line.
They called everybody's number
But they never did call mine.

Me an' a man was workin' side by side,
And this is what it meant.
He was gettin' a dollar an hour
And I was gettin' fifty cents.

I helped build this country,
I fought for it, too,
Now what I want to know is,
What you gonna do about Jim Crow?

Big Bill Broonzy, 1946

Labour with a white skin cannot emancipate itself where labour with a black skin is branded.

Karl Marx

Hands Up, You Pigswine

BILL: The Affair of the Lone Banana, Chapter Two. With the banana secreted on his person, Neddie Seagoon arrived at the Port of Guatemala where he was accorded the typical Latin welcome to an Englishman.

MORIARTY: Hands up, you pig swine.

SEAGOON: Have a care, Latin devil – I am an Englishman. Remember, this rolled umbrella has more uses than one.

MORIARTY: Oooo!

SEAGOON: Sorry. Now, what's all this about?

MORIARTY: It is the revolution – everywhere there is an armed rising.

SEAGOON: Are you all in it?

MORIARTY: Right in it – you see, the united anti-socialist neo-democratic pro-fascist communist party are fighting to overthrow the unilateral democratic united partisan bellicose pacifist cobelligerent tory labour liberal party.

SEAGOON: Whose side are you on?

MORIARTY: There are no sides – we are all in this together.

From 'The Affair of the Lone Banana' by The Goons, 1954

Walk Through Harlem

Negroes want to be treated like men: a perfectly straightforward statement, containing only seven words. People who have mastered Kant, Hegel, Shakespeare, Marx, Freud, and the Bible find this statement utterly impenetrable. The idea seems to threaten profound, barely conscious assumptions. A kind of panic paralyzes their features, as though they found themselves trapped on the edge of a steep place. I once tried to describe to a very well-known American intellectual the conditions among Negroes in the South. My recital disturbed him and made him indignant; and he asked me in perfect innocence, 'Why don't all the Negroes in the South move North?' I tried to explain what *has* happened, unfailingly, whenever a significant body of Negroes move North. They do not escape Jim Crow: they merely encounter another, not-less-deadly variety. They do not move to Chicago, they move to the South Side; they do not move to New York, they move to Harlem. The pressure within the ghetto causes the ghetto walls to expand, and this expansion is always violent. White people hold the line as long as they can, and in as many ways as they can, from verbal intimidation to physical violence. But inevitably the border which has divided the ghetto from the rest of the world falls into the hands of the ghetto. The white people fall back bitterly before the black horde; the landlords make a tidy profit by raising the rent, chopping up the rooms, and all but dispensing with the upkeep; and what has once been a neighborhood turns into a 'turf.' This is precisely what happened when the Puerto Ricans arrived in their thousands – and the bitterness thus caused is, as I write, being fought out all up and down those streets.

Northerners indulge in an extremely dangerous luxury. They seem to feel that because they fought on the right side during the Civil War, and won, they have earned the right merely to deplore what is going on in the South, without taking any responsibility for it; and that they can ignore what is happening in northern cities because what is happening in Little Rock or Birmingham is worse. Well, in the first place, it is not possible for anyone who has not endured both to know which is 'worse.' I know Negroes who prefer the South and white southerners, because 'At least there, you haven't got to play any guessing games!' The guessing games referred to have driven more than one Negro into the narcotics ward, the madhouse, or the river. I know another Negro, a man very dear to me, who says, with conviction and with truth. 'The spirit of the South is the spirit of America.' He was born in the North and did his military training in the South. He did not, as far as I can gather, find the South 'worse'; he found it, if anything, all too familiar. In the second place, though, even if Birmingham *is* worse, no doubt Johannesburg, South Africa, beats it by several miles, and Buchenwald was one of the worst things that ever happened in the entire history of the world. The world has never lacked for horrifying examples; but I do not believe that these examples are meant to be used as justification for our own crimes. This perpetual justification empties the heart of all human feeling. The emptier our hearts become, the greater will be our crimes. Thirdly, the South is not merely an embarrassingly backward region, but a part of this country, and what happens there concerns every one of us.

As far as the color problem is concerned, there is but one great difference between the southern white and the northerner: the southerner remembers, historically and in his own psyche, a kind of Eden in which he loved black people and they loved him. Historically, the flaming sword laid across this Eden is the Civil War. Personally, it is the southerner's sexual coming of age, when, without any warning, unbreakable taboos are set up between himself and his past. Everything, thereafter, is permitted him except the love he remembers and has never ceased to need. The resulting, indescribable torment affects every southern mind and is the basis of the southern hysteria.

None of this is true for the northerner. Negroes represent nothing to him personally, except, perhaps, the dangers of carnality. He never sees Negroes. Southerners see them all the time. Northerners never think about them whereas southerners are never really thinking of anything else. Negroes are, therefore, ignored in the North and are under surveillance in the South, and suffer hideously in both places. Neither the southerner nor the northerner is able to look on the Negro simply as a man. It seems to be indispensable to the national self-esteem that the Negro be considered either as a kind of ward (in which case we are told how many Negroes, comparatively, bought Cadillacs last year and how few, comparatively, were lynched), or as a victim (in which case we are are promised that he will never vote in our assemblies or go to school with our kids). They are two sides of the same coin and the South will not change – *cannot* change – until the North changes. The country will not change until it reexamines itself and discovers what it really means by freedom. In the meantime, generations keep being born, bitterness is increased by incompetence, pride, and folly, and the world shrinks around us.

It is a terrible, an inexorable, law that one cannot deny the humanity of another without diminishing one's own: in the face of one's victim, one sees oneself. Walk through the streets of Harlem and see what we, this nation, have become.

From the essay 'The Price of the Ticket' by James Baldwin, 1960

'The Wretched of the Earth'

Come, then, comrades; it would be as well to decide at once to change our ways. We must shake off the heavy darkness in which we were plunged, and leave it behind. The new day which is already at hand must find us firm, prudent and resolute.

We must leave our dreams and abandon our old beliefs and friendships of the time before life began. Let us waste no time in sterile litanies and nauseating mimicry. Leave this Europe where they are never done talking of Man, yet murder men everywhere they find them, at the corner of every one of their own streets, in all the corners of the globe. For centuries they have stifled almost the whole of humanity in the name of a so-called spiritual experience. Look at them today swaying between atomic and spiritual disintegration.

And yet it may be said that Europe has been successful in as much as everything that she has attempted has succeeded.

Europe undertook the leadership of the world with ardour, cynicism and violence. Look at how the shadow of her palaces stretches out ever farther! Every one of her movements has burst the bounds of space and thought. Europe has declined all humility and all modesty; but she has also set her face against all solicitude and all tenderness.

She has only shown herself parsimonious and niggardly where men are concerned; it is only men that she has killed and devoured.

So, my brothers, how is it that we do not understand that we have better things to do than to follow that same Europe?

That same Europe where they were never done talking of Man, and where they never stopped proclaiming that they were only anxious for the welfare of Man: today we know with what sufferings humanity has paid for every one of their triumphs of the mind.

Come, then, comrades, the European game has finally ended; we must find something different. We today can do everything, so long as we do not imitate Europe, so long as we are not obsessed by the desire to catch up with Europe.

Europe now lives at such a mad, reckless pace that she has shaken off all guidance and all reason, and she is running headlong into the abyss; we would do well to avoid it with all possible speed.

Yet it is very true that we need a model, and that we want blueprints and examples. For many among us the European model is the most inspiring. We have therefore seen in the preceding pages to what mortifying setbacks such an imitation has led us. European achievements, European techniques and the European style ought no longer to tempt us and to throw us off our balance.

When I search for Man in the technique and the style of Europe, I see only a succession of negations of man, and an avalanche of murders.

The human condition, plans for mankind and collaboration between men in those tasks which increase the sum total of humanity are new problems, which demand true inventions.

Let us decide not to imitate Europe; let us combine our muscles and our brains in a new direction. Let us try to create the whole man, whom Europe has been incapable of bringing to triumphant birth.

From the 'Conclusion' of *The Wretched of the Earth*
by Frantz Fanon, 1961

'The United Fruit Co.'

When the trumpet sounded, it was
all prepared on the earth,
the Jehovah parcelled out the earth
to Coca Cola, Inc., Anaconda,
Ford Motors, and other entities:
The Fruit Company, Inc.
reserved for itself the most succulent,
the central coast of my own land,

the delicate waist of America.
It rechristened its territories
as the 'Banana Republics'
and over the sleeping dead,
over the restless heroes
who brought about the greatness,
the liberty and the flags,
it established the comic opera:
abolished the independencies,
presented crowns of Caesar,
unsheathed envy, attracted
the dictatorship of the flies,
Trujillo* flies, Tacho* flies,
Carias* flies, Martines* flies,
Ubico* flies, damp flies
of modest blood and marmalade,
drunken flies who zoom
over the ordinary graves,
circus flies, wise flies
well trained in tyranny.

Among the blood-thirsty flies
the Fruit Company lands its ships,
taking off the coffee and the fruit;
the treasure of our submerged
territories flow as though
on plates into the ships.

Meanwhile Indians are falling
into the sugared chasms
of the harbours, wrapped
for burial in the mist of the dawn:
a body rolls, a thing
that has no name, a fallen cipher,
a cluster of dead fruit
thrown down on the dump.

*dictators

Pablo Neruda, *c.* 1962

I Am Prepared to Die

Some of the things so far told to the court are true and some are untrue. I do not, however, deny that I planned sabotage. I did not plan it in a spirit of recklessness, nor because I have any love of violence. I planned it as a result of a calm and sober assessment of the political situation that had arisen after many years of tyranny, exploitation and oppression of my people by the whites.

I admit immediately that I was one of the persons who helped to form Umkonto We Sizwe ['Spear of the Nation', the military wing of the ANC], and that I played a prominent role in its affairs until I was arrested in August 1962. I, and the others who started the organization, did so for two reasons. First, we believed that as a result of government policy, violence by the African people had become inevitable, and that unless responsible leadership was given to canalize and control the feelings of our people there would be outbreaks of terrorism which would produce an intensity of bitterness and hostility between the various races of this country which is not produced even by war. Second, we felt that without violence there would be no way open to the African people to succeed in their struggle against the principle of white supremacy. All lawful modes of expressing opposition to this principle had been closed by legislation, and we were placed in a position in which we had either to accept a permanent state of inferiority, or to defy the government. We chose to defy the law. We first broke the law in a way which avoided any recourse to violence; when this form was legislated against, and then the government resorted to a show of force to crush the opposition to its policies, only then did we decide to answer violence with violence.

But the violence which we chose to adopt was not terrorism. We who formed Umkonto were all members of the African National Congress, and had behind us the ANC tradition of non-violence and negotiation as a means of solving political disputes. We believed that South Africa belonged to all the people who lived in it, and not to one group, be it black or white. We did not want an interracial war, and tried to avoid it to the last minute.

The African National Congress was formed in 1912 to defend the right of the African people which had been seriously curtailed by the South Africa Act, and which were then being threatened by the Native Land Act. For thirty-seven years – that is until 1949 – it adhered strictly to a constitutional struggle. It put forward demands and resolutions; it sent delegations to the government in the belief that African grievances could be settled through peaceful discussion and that Africans could advance gradually to full political rights. But white governments remained unmoved, and the rights of Africans became less instead of becoming greater. In the words of my leader, Chief Luthuli, who became President of the ANC in 1952, and who was later awarded the Nobel Peace Prize:

> . . . who will deny that thirty years of my life have been spent knocking in vain, patiently, moderately and modestly at a closed and barred door? What have been the fruits of moderation? The past thirty years have seen the greatest number of laws restricting our rights and progress, until today we have reached a stage where we have almost no rights at all.

Even after 1949, the ANC remained determined to avoid violence. At this time, however, there was a change from the strictly constitutional means of protest which had been employed in the past. The change was embodied in a decision which was taken to protest against apartheid legislation by peaceful, but unlawful, demonstrations against certain laws. Pursuant to this policy the ANC launched the Defiance Campaign, in which I was placed in charge of volunteers. This campaign was based on the principles of passive resistance. More than 8,500 people defied apartheid laws and went to gaol. Yet there was not a single instance of violence in the course of this campaign on the part of any defier. I, and nineteen colleagues were convicted for the role which we played in organizing the campaign, but our sentences were suspended mainly because the Judge found that discipline and non-violence had been stressed throughout.

During the Defiance Campaign, the Public Safety Act and the Criminal Law Amendment Act were passed. These statutes provided harsher penalties for offences committed by way of protests against laws. Despite this, the protests continued and the ANC adhered to its policy of non-violence. In 1956, 156 leading members of the Congress Alliance, including myself, were arrested on a charge of High Treason and charges under the Suppression of Communism Act. The non-violent policy of the ANC was put in issue by the state, but when the court gave judgment some five years later it found that the ANC did not have a policy of violence. We were acquitted on all counts, which included a count that the ANC sought to set up a Communist State in place of the existing regime. The government has always sought to label all its opponents as communists.

In 1960, there was the shooting at Sharpeville, which resulted in the proclamations of a State of Emergency and the declaration of the ANC as an unlawful organization. My colleagues and I, after careful consideration, decided that we would not obey this decree. The African people were not part of the government and did not make the laws by which they were governed. We believed in the words of the Universal Declaration of Human Rights, that 'the will of the people shall be the basis of authority of the government', and for us to accept the banning was equivalent to accepting the silencing of the Africans for all time. The ANC refused to dissolve, but instead went underground. We believed it was our duty to preserve this organization which had been built up with almost fifty years of unremitting toil. I have no doubt that no self-respecting white political organization would disband itself if declared illegal by a government in which it had no say.

In 1960 the government held a referendum which led to the establishment of the Republic. Africans, who constituted approximately seventy per cent of the population of South Africa, were not entitled to vote, and were not even consulted about the proposed constitutional change. All of us were apprehensive of our future under the proposed White Republic, and a resolution was taken to hold an All-In African Conference to call for a National Convention, and to organize mass demonstrations on the eve of the unwanted Republic, if the government failed to call the convention. The conference was attended by Africans of various political persuasions. I was the secretary of the conference and undertook to be responsible for organizing the national stay-at-home which was subsequently called to coincide with the declaration of the Republic. As all strikes by Africans are illegal, the person organizing such a strike must avoid arrest. I was chosen to be this person, and consequently I had to leave my home and family and my practice and go into hiding to avoid arrest.

The stay-at-home, in accordance with ANC policy, was to be a peaceful demonstration. Careful instructions were given to organizers and members to avoid any recourse to violence. The government's answer was to introduce new and harsher laws, to mobilize its armed forces, and to send Saracens, armed vehicles and soldiers into the townships in a massive show of force designed to intimidate the people. This was an indication that the government had decided to rule by force alone, and this decision was a milestone on the road to Umkonto.

It was only when all else had failed, when all channels of peaceful protest had been barred to us, that the decision was made to embark on violent forms of political struggle, and to form Umkonto We Sizwe. We did so not because we desired such a course, but solely because the government had left us with no other choice. In the Manifesto of Umkonto, published on 16 December 1961, which is Exhibit AD, we said: 'The time comes in the life of any nation when there remain only two choices – submit or fight. That time has now come to South Africa. We shall not submit and we have no choice but to hit back by all means in our power in defence of our people, our future and our freedom.' This was our feeling in June of 1961 when we decided to press for a change in the policy of the National Liberation Movement. I can only say that I felt morally obliged to do what I did.

Nelson Mandela, at the Rivona Trial, 1964

What's On That Plate

. . . I'm not a politician, not even a student of politics; in fact, I'm not a student of much of anything. I'm not a Democrat, I'm not a Republican, and I don't even consider myself an American. If you and I were Americans, there'd be no problem. Those Hunkies that just got off the boat, they're already Americans; Polacks are already Americans; the Italian refugees are already Americans. Everything that came out of Europe, every blue-eyed thing, is already an American. And as long as you and I have been over here, we aren't Americans yet.

Well, I am one who doesn't believe in deluding myself. I'm not going to sit at your table and watch you eat, with nothing on my plate, and call myself a diner. Sitting at the table doesn't make you a diner, unless you eat some of what's on that plate. Being here in America doesn't make you an American. Being born here in America doesn't make you an American. Why, if birth made you American, you wouldn't need any legislation, you wouldn't need any amendments to the Constitution, you wouldn't be faced with civil-rights filibustering in Washington, DC, right now. They don't have to pass civil-rights legislation to make a Polack an American.

No, I'm not an American. I'm one of the 22 million black people who are the victims of Americanism. One of the 22 million black people who are the victims of democracy, nothing but disguised hypocrisy. So, I'm not standing here speaking to you as an American, or a patriot, or a flag-saluter, or a flag-waver – no, not I. I'm speaking as a victim of this American system. And I see America through the eyes of the victim. I don't see any American dream; I see an American nightmare.

These 22 million victims are waking up. Their eyes are coming open. They're beginning to see what they used to only look at. They're becoming politically mature. They are realizing that there are new political trends from coast to coast. As they see these new political trends, it's possible for them to see that every time there's an election the races are so close that they have to have a recount. They had to recount in Massachusetts to see who was going to be governor, it was so close. It was the same way in Rhode Island, in Minnesota, and in many other parts of the country. And the same with Kennedy and Nixon when they ran for president. It was so close they had to count all over again. Well, what does this mean? It means that when white people are evenly divided, and black people have a bloc of votes of their own, it is left up to them to determine who's going to sit in the White House and who's going to be in the dog house.

It was the black man's vote that put the present administration in Washington, DC. Your vote, your dumb vote, your ignorant vote, your wasted vote put in an administration in Washington, DC, that has seen fit to pass every kind of legislation imaginable, saving you until last, then filibustering on top of that. And your and my leaders have the audacity to run around clapping their hands and talk about how much progress we're making. And what a good president we have. If he wasn't good in Texas, he sure can't be good in Washington, DC. Because Texas is a lynch state. It is in the same breath as Mississippi, no different; only they lynch you in Texas with a Texas accent and lynch you in Mississippi with a Mississippi accent. And these Negro leaders have the audacity to go and have some coffee in the White House with a Texan, a Southern cracker – that's all he is – and then come out and tell you and me that he's going to be better for us because, since he's from the South, he knows how to deal with the Southerners. What kind of logic is that?

From a speech by Malcolm X, 1964

'Say It Loud – I'm Black and Proud'

Say it loud, I'm black and I'm proud
Say it loud, I'm black and I'm proud
Some people say we got a lot of malice
Some say it's a lot of nerve
But I say we won't quit moving
Until we get what we deserve
We've been 'buked and we've been scorned
We've been treated bad, talked about as sure as you're born
But just as sure as it takes two eyes to make a pair
Brother we can't quit until we get our share.

Whoee – out of sight tomorrow night – it's tough
You're tough enough – whoee – it's hurting me
Say it loud, I'm black and I'm proud
Say it loud, I'm black and I'm proud
Say it loud, I'm black and I'm proud.

I've worked on jobs with my feet and my hands
But all that work I did was for the other man
Now we demand a chance to do things for ourselves
We're tired of beating our head against the wall
And working for someone else

We're people, we're like the birds and the bees
But we'd rather die on our feet than keep living on our knees.

James Brown, 1968

Returning your Immigrants

Should any future Conservative, Powellite or National Front government succeed in repatriating immigrants, we will hope to return your emigrants to take up the vacancies. This would mean that for every West Indian or Indian deported, we could send you, on a fair statistical basis, as replacements, one 'pakeha' New Zealander, four Canadians, half a South African white, part of a white Rhodesian, and no fewer than 50 American WASPS. It would take some time for you to absorb the extra 200 million people involved, but there is no reason why, if phased over a decent period and with sensible birth control measures being taken, England should not be the exclusive home of those who speak English and live in the English manner.

Ngata Te Korov, 1970

'It Dread Inna Inglan'

for George Lindo

dem frame-up George Lindo
up in Bradford Toun
but di Bradford Blacks
dem a rally roun

mi seh dem frame-up George Lindo
up in Bradford Toun
but di Bradford Blacks
dem a rally roun . . .

Maggi Tatcha on di go
wid a racist show
but a she haffi go
kaw,
rite now

African
Asian
West Indian
an' Black British
stan firm inna Inglan
inna disya time yah
far noh matteh wat dey say,
come wat may,
we are here to stay
inna Inglan,
inna disya time yah . . .

George Lindo
him is a working man
George Lindo
him is a family man
George Lindo
him nevah do no wrang
George Lindo
di innocent one
George Lindo
him noh carry no daggah
George Lindo
him is nat no rabbah
George Lindo
dem haffi let him go
George Lindo
dem bettah free him now!

Linton Kwesi Johnson, *c.* 1970; Lindo was wrongly imprisoned for robbery with violence and eventually pardoned and released

Who Shot the Sheriff?

When we read about Eric Clapton's Birmingham concert when he urged support for Enoch Powell, we nearly puked. Come on Eric . . . you've been taking too much of that *Daily Express* stuff and you know you can't handle it. Own up. Half your music is black. You're rock music's biggest colonist. You're a good musician but where would you be without the blues and R & B? You've got to fight the racist poison otherwise you degenerate into the sewer with the rats and all the money men who ripped off rock culture

with their cheque books and plastic crap. We want to organise a rank and file movement against the racist poison in music. We urge support for Rock against Racism.
P.S. Who shot the Sheriff Eric? It sure as hell wasn't you!

Letter to *New Musical Express, Melody Maker* and *Sounds*
by Red Saunders, Roger Huddle and others, 1976

A Unionist candidate in Belfast thought it might be a good idea to stress his connections with England.

'I was born an Englishman, I live like an Englishman, and I shall die an Englishman.'

A voice from the back of the hall:

'Sir, have ye no ambition at all?'

'Equal Opportunity'

in early Canada
when railways were highways

each stop brought new opportunities

there was a rule

    the chinese could only ride
    the last two cars
    of the trains

that is

until a train derailed
killing all those
in front

(the chinese erected an altar and thanked buddha)

a new rule was made

the Chinese must ride
the front two cars
of the trains

that is

until another accident
claimed everyone
in the back

(the chinese erected an altar and thanked buddha)

after much debate
common sense prevailed

the Chinese are now allowed
to sit anywhere
on any train

Jim Wong-Chu, *c.* 1980

'Tourist/Home Movies'

"And here's one of an Indian
Selling Ralph a trinket –
I suppose he'll use the money
To buy some wine and drink it."
Tourist, do you also
tour the Black Man's slums
Photographing winos,
Photographing bums?
Do you really think you're welcome,
Do you really think it's funny
The things that starving people do
For little bits of money?
Do you see the anger?
Do you see the pain?
That says in silence "Go away
And don't come back again."

Bob Bacon, a native American, *c.* 1980

The Hunger Strike of 1980

We, the Republican prisoners of war in H Block, Long Kesh, demand as of right political recognition and that we be accorded the status of political prisoners. We claim this right as captured combatants in the continuing struggle for national liberation and self-determination. We refute most strongly the tag of criminal with which the British have attempted to label us and our struggle . . .

Bearing in mind the serious implications of our final step, not only for us but for our people, we wish to make it clear that every channel has now been exhausted and, not wishing to break faith with those from whom we have inherited our principles, we now commit ourselves to a hunger strike.

We declare that political status is ours of right and we declare that from Monday 27th October 1980 a hunger strike by a number of men representing H Blocks 3, 4 and 5 will commence.

Our widely recognised resistance has carried us through four years of immense suffering and it shall carry us to the bitter climax of death if necessary.

Long Kesh, 1980

From Moss and Merds

The labour that Britain drew from Asia and the Caribbean helped first to bind its wounds of war and then set it on the road to recovery. Black workers swept and cleaned the cities, ran the transport services, manned – and womanned – the Health Service, worked the foundries, factories and mills, sustaining old industries and helping the new to lift off. They were the aid, the Marshall Plan, on which Britain's immediate post-war prosperity was founded. And yet they themselves were kept from the prosperity, from a stake in that society, and by virtue of the work and housing afforded them, the virtue of their colour, condemned to live midst the detritus of inner cities.

But from those very handicaps – from the 'rocks, moss, stonecrop, iron, merds' of the urban ghetto, against the unwavering racism of governments, employers, unions, police and courts – with little more than the traditions and strengths they had brought with them – black people built themselves their communities.

And it is the knowledge and pride of that achievement that binds the communities of Brick Lane, Brixton, Southall, Moss Side, Lumb Lane, Chapeltown, Handsworth . . .

A. Sivanandan, Institute of Race Relations, 1981

Brighton Bombing

The IRA claim responsibility for the detonation of 100 pounds of gelignite in Brighton, against the British cabinet and the Tory warmongers. Thatcher will now realise that Britain cannot occupy our country, torture our prisoners and shoot our people on their own streets and get away with it.

Today we were unlucky, but remember, we have only to be lucky once. You will have to be lucky always. Give Ireland peace and there will be no war.

IRA Communiqué, 1985

Seven

THE OLD LIE

'Lament of the Frontier Guard'

By the North Gate, the wind blows full of sand,
Lonely from the beginning of time until now!
Trees fall, the grass goes yellow with autumn.
I climb the towers and towers
    to watch out the barbarous land:
Desolate castle, the sky, the wide desert.
There is no wall left to this village.
Bones white with a thousand frosts,
High heaps, covered with trees and grass;
Who brought this to pass?
Who has brought the flaming imperial anger?
Who has brought the army with drums and with kettle-drums?
Barbarous kings.
A gracious spring, turned to blood-ravenous autumn,
A turmoil of wars-men, spread over the middle kingdom,
Three hundred and sixty thousand,
And sorrow, sorrow like rain.
Sorrow to go, and sorrow, sorrow returning.
Desolate, desolate fields,
And no children of warfare upon them,
    No longer the men for offence and defence.
Ah, how shall you know the dreary sorrow at the
    North Gate,
With Rihaku's name forgotten,
And we guardsmen fed to the tigers.

Ezra Pound's translation of Rihaku, eighth century

Don't Shoot!

You, our fellow countrymen, the private soldiers of the army, alone being the instrumental authors of your own slavery and ours; therefore, as there is any bowels of men in you, any love for your native country, kindred, friends or relations, any spark of conscience in you, any hopes of glory or immortality in you, or any pity, mercy, or compassion, to an enslaved, undone, perishing, and dying people!

Oh help! help! save and redeem us from total vassalage and slavery, and be no more like brute-beasts, to fight against us or our friends, your loving and dear brethren after the flesh, to your own vassalage as well as ours!

And as an assured pledge of your future cordialness to us (and the true and real liberties of the land of your nativity), we beseech and beg of you (but especially those amongst you that subscribed the Solemn Engagement at Newmarket-heath, the 5th of June, 1647) speedily to choose out amongst yourselves two of the ablest and constantest faithful men amongst you in each troop and company, now at last, by corresponding each with other, and with your honest friends in the nation, to consider of some effectual course, beyond all pretences and cheats, to accomplish the real end of all your engagements and fightings, viz. the settling of the liberties and freedom of the people; which can never be permanently done, but upon the sure foundation of a popular agreement.

An appeal by John Lilburne, a Leveller, to Cromwell's soldiers, *c.* 1650

Against Conscription

SUMMONS . . . for uttering these words against Fr. Comyn, Rob. Bushell, Egidius Wigginer gentlemen and Tho. Skipton esquire, who had received authority from our Sovereign Lord the King to press men for his Majesty's naval service, Viz:

That they had no authority to impress any men for his majesty's naval service, and the persons needed not to obey their authority;

And also did invite and encourage one man to procure a Goadland gentleman to join with him in throwing the said four gentlemen or any of them over the bridge at Whitby into the river, and he would justify them therein and be their warrant for so doing;

Likewise he did say that, if he were in the case of those persons that were pressed he would be hanged before he would serve the King, and that those persons that were impressed needed not to be subject to obey their impression;

Which speeches did cause many of the persons so impressed to run away and abscond themselves.

Court proceedings against a man of Sneaton, 1667

A Satirical Elegy

On the Death of a Late Famous General [The Duke of Marlborough]

His Grace! impossible! what dead!
Of old age too, and in his bed!
And could that Mighty Warrior fall?
And so inglorious, after all!
Well, since he's gone, no matter how,
The last loud trump must wake him now:
And trust me, as the noise grows stronger,
He'd wish to sleep a little longer.
And could he be indeed so old
As by the news-papers we're told?
Threescore, I think, is pretty high;
'Twas time in conscience he should die.
This world he cumber'd long enough;
He burnt his candle to the snuff;
And that's the reason, some folks think,
He left behind *so great a stink*.
Behold his funeral appears,
Nor widow's sighs, nor orphan's tears,
Wont at such times each heart to pierce,
Attend the progress of his herse.
But what of that, his friends may say,
He had those honours in his day.
True to his profit and his pride,
He made them weep before he dy'd.

Come hither, all ye empty things,
Ye bubbles rais'd by breath of Kings;
Who float upon the tide of state,
Come hither, and behold your fate.
Let pride be taught by this rebuke,
How very mean a thing's a Duke;
From all his ill-got honours flung,
Turn'd to that dirt from whence he sprung.

Jonathan Swift, 1722

Mutiny at the Nore

8th May

I beg leave to inform your Lordship that I am just come on shore from H.M.S. *Terrible*, the command of that ship having been perfectly taken from me, and finding that I had no longer any authority over any part of her crew, they have hoisted the Red Flag to call the Delegates on board, and on the arrival of four of them, seized all the arms in the wardroom, and in the officers' cabins, immediately after which they declared it to be their determination that myself and all my officers, except the Master, Surgeon, Purser, three warrant officers, and one Midshipman should quit the ship.

Captain of H.M.S. *Terrible* to the Admiralty, 1797

'The Fate of Those Who Go for Soldiers'

When into the Village or Town,
A Recruiting the Soldiers do come;
With lies and with bullying around,
They rattle away with the Drum;
When large sums of Money they promise,
That they never intend for to pay,
But of this my brave fellows be certain
You'll be shot at for Six-pence a day.
Shot at for Six-pence a day.

With Thieves of all sorts they'll unite you,
From the Gallows that's made their escape;
Your friends and relations will slight you,
Then heart breaking sorrow's your fate;
With such wretches engage not to serve,
Nor join in the Murderous lay;
If you do you'll justly deserve,
To be shot at for Six-pence a day.
Shot at for Six-pence a day.

Then away to the Wars they will drag you,
And victuals you'll get when you call;
But war gives the Soldier in battle,
A Breakfast of Powder and Ball.

Then should you be so foolishly bold,
    And advice you should throw far away;
You ne'er will live to grow old,
    When you're shot at for Six-pence a day.
                        Shot at for Six-pence a day.

Then ne'er mind the sound of the drum,
    Stay at home with your sweethearts and wives;
Free from harms to the Soldier that come,
    That lops off their limbs and their lives;
For the Captains will get all the Gold,
    And the Men lose their lives in the Fray;
Is not he a damned fool young or old,
    That is shot at for Six-pence a day?
                        Shot at for Six-pence a day.

Sixty Thousand Englishmen have been killed this last year in Holland. – Ten Thousand more in the West Indies, and Forty Thousand taken Prisoners. – Soldiers, or Sailors, Death or Misery is your Portion.

Anon., *c.* 1797

United Strength

The Frenchman sailed in freedom's name to smite the Algerine,
The strife was short, the crescent sunk, and then his guile was seen;
For, nestling in the pirate's hold – a fiercer pirate far –
He bade the tribes yield up their flocks, the towns their gates unbar.
Right on he pressed with freeman's hands to subjugate the free,
The Berber in old Atlas glens, the Moor in Titteri; . . .

The Englishman for long, long years, had ravaged Ganges' side;
A dealer first, intriguer next, he conquered far and wide,
Till, hurried on by avarice, and thirst of endless rule,
His sepoys pierced to Candahar, his flag waved in Cabul;
But still within the conquered land was one unconquered man,
The fierce Pushtani lion, the fiery Akhbar Khan –
He slew the sepoys on the snow, till Scindh's full flood they swam it
Right rapidly, content to flee the son of Dost Mohammed,
The son of Dost Mohammed! and brave old Dost Mohammed . . .

But Russia preys on Poland's fields, where Sobieski reigned,
And Austria on Italy – the Roman eagle chained –
Bohemia, Servia, Hungary within her clutches gasp.
And Ireland struggles gallantly in England's loosening grasp.
Oh! would all these their strength unite, or battle on alone,
Like Moor, Pushtani, and Cherkess, they soon would have their own!
Hurrah! hurrah! it can't be far, when from the Scindh to Shannon
Shall gleam a line of freeman's flags begirt by freemen's cannon!
The coming day of freedom – the flashing flags of freedom.

From 'A Ballad of Freedom' by Thomas Davis, *c.* 1830

'The Recruited Collier'

Oh, what's the matter wi' you, my lass,
An' where's your dashin' Jimmy?
The sowdger boys have picked him up
And sent him far, far frae me.

Last pay-day he set off to town,
And them red-coated fellows
Enticed him in and made him drunk,
And he'd better gone to the gallows.

The very sight o' his cockade,
It set us all a-cryin;
And me, I fairly fainted twice,
I thought that I was dyin.

My father would have paid the smart,
And run for the golden guinea,
But the sergeant swore he'd kissed the book,
And now they've got young Jimmy.

When Jimmy talks about the wars
It's worse than death to hear him.
I must go out and hide my tears,
Because I cannot bear him.

For aye he jibes and cracks his jokes,
And bids me not forsake him.

A brigadier or grenadier,
He says they're sure to make him.

As I walked over the stubble field,
Below it runs the seam,
I thought o' Jimmy hewin there,
But it was all a dream.

He hewed the very coals we burn,
And when the fire I'se leetin,
To think the lumps was in his hands,
It sets my heart to beatin.

So break my heart, and then it's ower,
So break my heart, my dearie,
And I'll lie in the cold, cold grave,
For of single life I'm weary.

Anon., *c.* 1850

The Crimea Front

The whole plateau on which stands 'the camp before Sebastopol' . . . is a vast black dreary wilderness of mud, dotted with little lochs of foul water, and seamed by dirty brownish and tawny-coloured streams running down to and along the ravines. On its surface everywhere are strewed the carcasses of horses and miserable animals torn by dogs and smothered in mud. Vultures sweep over the mounds in flocks; carrion crows and 'birds of prey obscene' hover over their prey, menace the hideous dogs who are feasting below, or sit in gloomy dyspepsia, with drooped head and drooping wing, on the remnants of their banquet.

It is over this ground, gained at last by great toil and exhaustion and loss of life on the part of the starving beasts of burden, that man and horse have to struggle from Balaclava for some four or five miles with the hay and corn, the meat, the biscuit, the pork, which form the subsistence of our army. Every day this toil must be undergone . . . Horses drop exhausted on the road, and their loads are removed and added to the burdens of the struggling survivors; then, after a few efforts to get out of their Slough of Despond; the poor brutes succumb and lie down to die in their graves. Men wade and plunge about, and stumble through the mud, with muttered imprecations, or sit down on a projecting stone, exhausted, pictures of dirt and woe unutterable. Sometimes on the route the overworked and sickly soldier is seized with illness, and the sad aspect of a fellow-countryman dying before his eyes shocks every passer-by – the more because aid is all but hopeless and impossible . . . The painful recollection which ever occurs to one is, what necessity is there for all the suffering and privation created by this imperfect state of our communications? Why should not roads have been made when we sat down before the place? Their formation would have saved many lives, and have spared our men much sickness and pain. Had there been the least foresight – nay, had there existed among us the ordinary instincts of self-preservation – we would have set the Turks to work at once while the weather was fine, and have constructed the roads which we are now trying to make under most disadvantageous conditions. The siege operations have been sometimes completely – sometimes partially – suspended, and the attack on Sebastopol has languished and declined. Neither guns nor ammunition could be brought up to the batteries.

The mortality amongst the Turks has now assumed all the dimensions of a plague. Every sense was offended and shocked by the display, day after day, in the streets, of processions of men bearing half-covered corpses on litters at the busiest hour of the day . . .

From *The War* by William Russell, 1855

The truth is that the fall of Napoleon is the hardest blow that our *taxing* system ever felt. It is now impossible to make people believe that immense fleets and armies are necessary.

William Cobbett

The Recruiting Board

PRIEST: I well remember, many years ago
during the War, one day I was at Lundë
when they were holding a recruiting board.
All men were talking of our country's hour
of danger – asking what the future held.
There, seated at the table, in between

the Bailiff and the Sergeant, was the Captain;
each boy in turn he carefully examined
and then enrolled and took him for a soldier.
The room was packed, and from the green, outside,
we heard the laughter of the waiting lads . . .
  A name was called; another lad stepped up,
pale as the snow along the glacier's edge.
They called him nearer. He approached the table.
He had his right hand bandaged with a cloth.
He gasped and swallowed, fumbling after words
but finding none, despite the Captain's orders.
Then, in conclusion, with his cheeks on fire,
his tongue now faltering, now pouring words,
he mumbled something of a scythe that slipped
and sliced his finger off . . . A silence fell,
some exchanged glances, others pursed their lips,
their silent looks pelted the boy like stones;
and though his eyes were shut, he felt the blows.
At last the Captain rose, an old, grey man,
he spat, showed him the door, and said 'Get out!'
  The boy went. Men fell back on either side
so that he ran the gauntlet through their ranks.
He reached the door, and then took to his heels.
Upwards he ran, up through the woods and moorland,
limping and staggering among the rocks
back to his home, high on the mountainside.

From *Peer Gynt* by Henrik Ibsen, 1867

'Evil'

While the red gobs of spit of the grape-shot whistle all day through the infinitude of blue sky; while scarlet or green, close by the King who jeers at them, whole battalions fall crumbling into the fire;

while a terrible madness grinds down and makes of a hundred thousand men a smoking heap; – Poor dead men! – O Nature! in summer, in the grass, in your joy, you who fashioned these men in holiness! . . .

– All this while, there is a God who laughs at damask altar-cloths and incense, and at the great golden chalices; who dozes to the lullaby of Hosannas,

and who wakes up when mothers, drawn together in suffering, and weeping under their old black bonnets, give him the penny which they have tied up in their handkerchiefs!

Arthur Rimbaud, *c.* 1870; poem in prose translation

'The War Prayer'

O Lord our God, help us to tear their soldiers to bloody shreds with our shells; help us to cover their smiling fields with the pale forms of their patriot dead; help us to drown the thunder of the guns with the wounded, writhing in pain; help us to lay waste their humble homes with a hurricane of fire; help us to wring the hearts of their unoffending widows with unavailing grief; help us to turn them out roofless with their little children to wander unfriended through wastes of their desolated land in rags and hunger and thirst, sport of the sun-flames of summer and the icy winds of winter, broken in spirit, worn with travail, imploring Thee for the refuge of the grave and denied it – for our sakes, who adore Thee, Lord, blast their hopes, blight their lives, protract their bitter pilgrimage, make heavy their steps, water their way with their tears, stain the white snow with the blood of their wounded feet! We ask of one who is the Spirit of love and who is the ever-faithful refuge and friend of all that are sore beset, and seek His aid with humble and contrite hearts. Grant our prayer, O Lord, and Thine shall be the praise and honor and glory now and ever, Amen.

Mark Twain, *c.* 1880

'Fight? What For?'

I am 'wanted to go in the army.'
Well, what would they give me to do?
'You'll have to be killing your brothers
If one of them doesn't kill you.'

I am 'wanted to go in the army.'
Say, what is there in it for me?
'You'd help to be saving your country
From brother-men over the sea.'

My country? Who says I've a country?
I live in another man's flat

That hasn't as much as a door yard –
And why should I battle for that?

I haven't a lot nor a building,
No flower, no garden, nor tree.
The landlords have gobbled the country –
Let *them* do the fighting, not me

Celia Whitehead, *c.* 1900

Against Air War

Of all the varying symptoms of madness in the life of modern nations the most dreadful is this prostitution of the conquest of the air to the ends of warfare.

If ever men presented a spectacle of sheer inanity it is now – when, having at long last triumphed in their struggle to subordinate to their welfare the unconquered element, they have straightway commenced to defile that element, so heroically mastered, by filling it with engines of destruction. If ever the gods were justified of their ironic smile – by the gods, it is now! Is there any thinker alive watching this still utterly preventible calamity without horror and despair? Horror at what must come of it, if not promptly stopped; despair that men can be so blind, so hopelessly and childishly the slaves of their own marvellous inventive powers. Was there ever so patent a case for scotching at birth a hideous development of the black arts of warfare; ever such an occasion for the Powers in conference to ban once and for all a new and ghastly menace?

A little reason, a grain of commonsense, a gleam of sanity before it is too late – before vested interests and the chains of a new habit have enslaved us too hopelessly. If this fresh devilry be not quenched within the next few years it will be too late. Water and earth are wide enough for men to kill each other on. For the love of the sun, and stars, and the blue sky, that have given us all our aspirations since the beginning of time, let us leave the air to innocence! Will not those who have eyes to see, good will towards men, and the power to put that good will into practice, bestir themselves while there is yet time, and save mankind from this last and worst of all its follies?

A letter by John Galsworthy to *The Times*, 7 April 1911

Murder is Murder

OPEN LETTER TO BRITISH SOLDIERS

Men! Comrades! Brothers!

You are in the Army

So are We. You in the Army of Destruction. We in the Industrial, or army of Construction.

We work at mine, mill, forge, factory, or dock, producing and transporting all the goods, clothing, stuffs, etc., which make it possible for people to live.

You are Working Men's Sons.

When We go on Strike to better Our lot, which is the lot also of Your Fathers, Mothers, Brothers, and Sisters, YOU are called upon by your officers to MURDER US.

DON'T DO IT!

You know how it happens always has happened.

We stand out as long as we can. Then one of our (and your) irresponsible Brothers, goaded by the sight and thought of his and his loved ones' misery and hunger, commits a crime on property. Immediately You are ordered to Murder Us, as You did at Mitchelstown, at Featherstone, at Belfast.

Don't You know that when You are out of the colours, and become a 'Civy' again, that You, like Us, may be on Strike, and You, like Us, be liable to be Murdered by other soldiers.

Boys, Don't Do It!

'Thou Shalt Not Kill,' says the Book.

Don't Forget That!

It does not say, 'unless you have a uniform on.'

No! MURDER IS MURDER, whether committed in the heat of anger on one who has wronged a loved one, or by pipe-clayed Tommies with a rifle.

Boys, Don't Do It!

Act The Man! Act The Brother Act The Human Being!

Property can be replaced! Human life, never.

The Idle Rich Class, who own and order you about, own and order us about also. They and their friends own the land and means of life of Britain.

You Don't. We Don't.

When We kick, they order You to Murder Us.

When You kick, You get courtmartialled and cells.

Your fight is Our fight. Instead of fighting Against each other, We should be fighting with each other.

Out of Our loins, Our lives, Our homes, You came.

Don't disgrace Your Parents, Your Class, by being the willing tools any longer of the Master Class.

You, like Us, are of the Slave Class. When We rise, You rise; when We fall, even by your bullets, Ye fall also.

England with its fertile valleys and dells, its mineral resources, its sea harvests, is the heritage of ages to us.

You no doubt joined the Army out of poverty.

We work long hours for small wages at hard work, because of Our poverty. And both Your poverty and Ours arises from the fact that Britain with its resources belongs to only a few people. These few, owning Britain, own Our jobs. Owning Our jobs, they own Our very Lives.

Comrades, have We called in vain? Think things out and refuse any longer to Murder Your Kindred. Help Us to win back Britain for the British, and the World for the Workers.

A Leaflet by Tom Mann, first published in *The Syndicalist*, 1912, for which he was imprisoned for six months

Primitive Barbarism

Against the vast majority of my countrymen, even at this moment, in the name of humanity and civilization, I protest against our share in the destruction of Germany.

A month ago Europe was a peaceful comity of nations; if an Englishman killed a German, he was hanged. Now, if an Englishman kills a German, or if a German kills an Englishman, he is a patriot, who has deserved well of his country. We scan the newspapers with greedy eyes for news of slaughter, and rejoice when we read of innocent young men, blindly obedient to the word of command, mown down in thousands by the machine-guns of Liège. Those who saw the London crowds, during the night leading up to the Declaration of War saw a whole population, hitherto peaceable and humane, precipitated in a few days down the steep slope to primitive barbarism, letting loose, in a moment, the instincts of hatred and blood lust against which the whole fabric of society has been raised. 'Patriots' in all countries acclaim this brutal orgy as a noble determination to vindicate the right; reason and mercy are swept away in one great flood of hatred; dim abstractions of unimaginable wickedness – Germany to us and the French, Russia to the Germans – conceal the simple fact that the enemy are men, like ourselves, neither better nor worse – men who love their homes and the sunshine, and all the simple pleasures of common lives; men now mad with terror in the thought of their wives, their sisters, their children, exposed, with our help, to the tender mercies of the conquering Cossack.

And all this madness, all this rage, all this flaming death of our civilization and our hopes, has been brought about because a set of official gentlemen, living luxurious lives mostly stupid, and all without imagination or heart, have chosen that it should occur rather than that any one of them should suffer some infinitesimal rebuff to his country's pride. No literary tragedy can approach the futile horror of the White Paper. The diplomatists, seeing from the first the inevitable end, mostly wishing to avoid it, yet drifted from hour to hour of the swift crisis, restrained by punctilio from making or accepting the small concessions that might have saved the world, hurried on at last by blind fear to loose the armies for the work of mutual butchery.

And behind the diplomats, dimly heard in the official documents, stand vast forces of national greed and national hatred – atavistic instincts, harmful to mankind at its present level, but transmitted from savage and half-animal ancestors, concentrated and directed by Governments and the Press, fostered by the upper class as a distraction from social discontent, artificially nourished by the sinister influence of the makers of armaments, encouraged by a whole foul literature of 'glory', and by every text-book of history with which the minds of children are polluted.

From a letter by Bertrand Russell to the *Nation*, 12 August 1914

Christmas 1914

I was dead beat and snatching a few hours' rest in my dugout when I heard the strains of 'It's a Long Long Way to Tipperary' followed by 'Deutschland Uber Alles'.

I climbed out over the parapet and saw the strangest sight which can ever be seen by any soldier in any war.

All along the line groups of British and German soldiers were laughing and singing together.

Just imagine it: English, Scots, Irish, Prussians, Wurtemburgers in a chorus.

I wrote a report on the whole fantastic episode and ended by saying that if I had seen it on film I would have sworn it was a fake.

From a letter by John Hulse to his mother; both High Commands ordered these units to other parts of the front and most, including Hulse, were killed within three months

'Pursery Rhyme'

Sing a song of Europe,
  Highly civilized.
Four and twenty nations
  Wholly hypnotized.

When the battles open
  The bullets start to sing;
Isn't that a silly way
  To act for any King?

The Kings are in the background
  Issuing commands;
The Queens are in the parlor,
  Per etiquette's demands.

The bankers in the counting house
  Are busy multiplying;
The common people at the front
  Are doing all the dying.

Isaac Sherwood, *c.* 1914

Workers Follow Your Masters

TO ARMS!!

CAPITALISTS PARSONS
POLITICIANS LANDLORDS
NEWSPAPER EDITORS & OTHER
STAY-AT-HOME PATRIOTS
YOUR COUNTRY NEEDS
YOU IN THE TRENCHES.

WORKERS

FOLLOW YOUR MASTERS!

Poster, Sydney, Australia, 1915

Lloyd George in Glasgow

On Saturday morning [December 15, 1915] St Andrew's Hall was fairly well filled . . . the meeting began with a storm of hissing and booing, and the Chairman [Mr Arthur Henderson, M.P.] suffered a running fire of interruptions . . . On rising to speak Mr Lloyd George was received with loud and continued booing and hissing. There was some cheering, certainly, and about a score of hats were waved in the area, but the meeting was violently hostile. Two verses of *The Red Flag* were sung before the Minister could utter a word. Owing to the incessant interruption, and the numerous altercations going on throughout the hall, it was quite impossible to catch every word of Mr Lloyd George's speech.

'. . . Let me put this to you, friends: Whilst we are comfortable at home on a Christmas day – (interruption – 'No sentiment; we're here for business') – there are hundreds of thousands of our fellow-countrymen, some of them our sons, some of them our brothers, in the trenches facing death. ('You're here to talk about the dilution of labour.') It's on their behalf, and at their written request, that I come here to put before the workmen of Glasgow their appeal for help.

'We need a very large number of heavy guns and projectiles, and I am going to put before you a business proposition. ('For the exploiters.') Do you think these men in the trenches are exploiters? ('Don't hedge.') ('The shipowners are doing their bit.') Do let me state the facts. ('We know them.') . . . What steps have we taken? We have started great National Factories, State-owned and State-controlled; every timber and nail in them belonging to the State. My friends, these are great Socialist factories. (Violent interruption.) Believe me, the whole of them owned by the State, erected by the State; no profit made by any Capitalist, because they don't belong to the Capitalist.

'What is the issue? Does anyone deny that these factories we are building are State factories? (A voice: 'Yes.') If you deny that, you would deny anything . . .

'Is it too much to ask the British workman to help his comrades in the field? ('No; what about the Munitions Act?') . . . I want to talk to you in all sincerity as a man brought up in a worker's home. I know as much about the life of the worker as any man here. The responsibility of a Minister of the Crown in a great war is no enviable one. ('The money's good,' and laughter). I can assure you it is no laughing matter.

'There will be unheard-of changes in every country in Europe; changes that go to the root of our social system. You Socialists watch them. It is a convulsion of nature; not merely a cyclone that sweeps away the ornamental plants of modern society and wrecks the flimsy trestle-bridges of modern civilization – it is more. It is an earthquake that upheaves the very rocks of European life.

'And to go on chaffering about a regulation here, and the suspension of a custom there, under these conditions – why, it is just haggling with an earthquake. Workmen, may I make one appeal to you? (Interruption.) Lift up your eyes above the mist of suspicion and distrust. Rise to the heights of the great opportunity now before you. If you do, you will emerge after this War is over into a future which has been the dream of many a great leader.' (Cheers: loud hissing and booing).

From *Forward*, a Glasgow Socialist weekly, 1 January 1916

'To a Nine-Inch Gun'

Whether your shell hits the target or not,
Your cost is Five Hundred Dollars a Shot.
You thing of noise and flame and power,
We feed you a hundred barrels of flour
Each time you roar. Your flame is fed
With twenty thousand loaves of bread.
Silence! A million hungry men
Seek bread to fill their mouths again.

Sent on a crumpled piece of paper to the New York *World* by P. F. McCarthy, *c.* 1915, with the author's address given as Fourth Bench, City Hall Park

'They'

The Bishop tells us: 'When the boys come back
They will not be the same; for they'll have fought
In a just cause: they lead the last attack
On Anti-Christ; their comrades' blood has bought
New right to breed an honourable race,
They have challenged Death and dared him face to face.'

'We're none of us the same!' the boys reply.
'For George lost both his legs; and Bill's stone blind;
Poor Jim's shot through the lungs and like to die;

And Bert's gone syphilitic: you'll not find
A chap who's served that hasn't found *some* change.'
And the Bishop said: The ways of God are strange!'

Siegfried Sassoon, 1916

The Coffin and the Bed

HERE
IS THE C
OFFIN IN
WHICH H
E REST
ED RO
TTING
ANDP
ALE

LONG LIVE FRANCE!
HE SLEEPS IN HIS LI
TTLE SOLDIER'S BED
MY RESUSCITATED
P O
E T

Guillaume Apollinaire, 1918

Shot for Desertion

Shot for desertion: 266 soldiers, 2 officers
Shot for cowardice: 18 soldiers
Shot for disobedience: 5 soldiers
Shot for sleeping on post: 2 soldiers
Shot for quitting post: 7 soldiers
Shot for striking or violence: 6 soldiers

(Some 2,600 other death sentences were passed but the sentences were commuted to various terms of penal servitude).

Official Statistics, 1918

Mutiny in Seletskoi

All have gone on strike – held meetings in IM hut last night and passed resolutions that they must be withdrawn from Russia immediately. Others to the effect that censorship be removed from letters in order that the people in England may get to know the true state of affair out here and that a cable be sent to L. George demanding the immediate withdrawal of all troops in Russia. They all positively decline to go up the line or to obey any orders but are conducting themselves in an orderly manner.

Private Riley Rudd on British soldiers' refusal to be involved in the allied intervention against the Bolsheviks, 1918

'Little Song of the Maimed'

Lend me your arm
to replace my leg
The rats ate it for me
at Verdun
at Verdun
I ate lots of rats
but they didn't give me back my leg
and that's why I was given the *croix de guerre*
and a wooden leg
and a wooden leg

Benjamin Péret, *c.* 1920

Join the Army

When I was young, I used to be
As fine a lad as ever you'd see,
Till the Prince of Wales he said to me
'Come and join the British army'.
Too ra loo ra loo ra loo
They're looking for monkeys up in the zoo –
And if I had a face like you –
I'd join the British army.

Anon., *c.* 1920

Bombing Venice?

A hangar somewhere near the Adriatic Sea.

ALICE SCHALEK [*enters, looking around*]: What fascinates me most in war is individual courage. Even before the war I often speculated about the essence of heroism – I often met men who lived dangerously: American cowboys, pioneers in the jungle, missionaries in desert countries. These men looked the part of heroes, every muscle taut as if forged of steel. How different are the heroes one meets in the Great War! These men are given to telling boyish jokes, quietly craving hot chocolate with whipped cream, and then nonchalantly describing experiences which must be classified among the most amazing stories of world history. And yet . . . (*A lieutenant has entered.*) I don't have much time, so be brief. You are a bombardier – what emotions does dropping bombs arouse in you?

LIEUTENANT: Usually we circle over the enemy coast for half an hour, drop a few bombs on military targets, watch them explode, take a few pictures, and return to base.

SCHALEK: Have you faced death?

LIEUTENANT: Yes.

SCHALEK: What were your emotions?

LIEUTENANT: My emotions?

SCHALEK [*aside*]: He eyes me a bit dubiously, unconsciously wondering how much understanding he can expect for feelings still in ferment. [*Aloud.*] We noncombatants have such stereotyped concepts of courage and cowardice that the man at the front is afraid he won't be able to communicate to us his vast range of changing emotions. Have I guessed right?

LIEUTENANT: You are a noncombatant?

SCHALEK: Do not resent it. You are a combatant, and I'd like to find out how it feels. Most of all: how do you feel afterward?

LIEUTENANT: Well, it is strange. I feel like a king who has suddenly become a beggar. You know, it feels almost like being a king, so high above the enemy city. There they are below – helpless. No one can run away, no one can save himself or hide. You have power over them all. It's majestic – all else becomes insignificant. Nero must have felt that way.

SCHALEK: I can identify with that feeling. Did you ever bomb Venice? . . . What, you have scruples? Well, I'll tell you something. Venice is a problem worth thinking about. We entered the war filled with romantic ideas . . .

LIEUTENANT: Who did?

SCHALEK: We did. We intended to wage it with chivalry. Slowly and after painful lessons we had to change our attitudes. As recently as a year ago, who among us wouldn't have cringed at the thought of dropping bombs on Venice! And now? Everything has changed. If Venice shoots at our soldiers, we have to shoot at Venice – calmly, openly, and without sentimentality.

LIEUTENANT: Don't worry. I've bombed Venice.

SCHALEK: Good for you.

LIEUTENANT: In peacetime I used to spend my vacations in Venice. I loved it. But when I bombed it from the air – no, I didn't feel a spark of false romanticism. We all flew home, happily. It was our day of honor – our day!

SCHALEK: That's what I wanted to hear! Now your buddies from the U-boats expect me. I trust they are as gallant as you! [*Exits.*]

From *The Last Days of Mankind* by Karl Kraus, 1922

The Good Soldier Švejk Celebrates a Drumhead Mass

Preparations for the slaughter of mankind have always been made in the name of God or some supposed higher being which men have devised and created in their own imagination.

Before the ancient Phoenicians cut a prisoner's throat they also performed religious ceremonies just as solemnly as did new generations some thousand years later before marching to war and destroying their enemies with fire and sword.

The cannibals of the Guinea Islands and Polynesia sacrifice to their gods and perform the most diverse religious rites before ceremoniously devouring their captives or unnecessary people like missionaries, travellers, agents of various business firms or persons who are just inquisitive. As the culture of vestments has not yet reached them they decorate the outsides of their thighs with bunches of gaudy feathers of forest birds.

Before the Holy Inquisition burnt its victims, it performed the most solemn religious service – a High Mass with singing.

When criminals are executed, priests always officiate, molesting the delinquents with their presence.

In Prussia the unfortunate victim was led to the block by a pastor, in Austria to the gallows by a Catholic priest, in France to the guillotine, in America to the electric chair by a clergyman and in Spain to a chair where he was strangled by an ingenious appliance. In Russia the revolutionary was taken off by a bearded Orthodox priest etc.

Everywhere on these occasions they used to march about with a crucified Christ figure, as if to say: 'They're only cutting your head off, they're only hanging you, strangling you, putting fifteen thousand volts into you, but think what that chap there had to go through.'

The great shambles of the world war did not take place without the blessing of priests. Chaplains of all armies prayed and celebrated drumhead masses for victory for the side whose bread they ate.

When mutineers were executed a priest appeared. A priest could also be seen at the execution of Czech legionaries.

Nothing has changed from the time when the robber Vojtěch,* whom they nicknamed 'the Saint', operated with a sword in one hand and a cross in the other, murdering and exterminating the Baltic Slavs.

Throughout all Europe people went to the slaughter like cattle, driven there not only by butcher emperors, kings and other potentates and generals, but also by priests of all confessions, who blessed them and made them perjure themselves that they would destroy the enemy on land, in the air, on the sea etc.

Drumhead masses were generally celebrated twice: once when a detachment left for the front and once more at the front on the eve of some bloody massacre and carnage. I remember that once when a drumhead mass was being celebrated an enemy aeroplane dropped a bomb on us and hit the field altar. There was nothing left of the chaplain except some bloodstained rags.

Afterwards they wrote about him as a martyr, while our aeroplanes prepared the same kind of glory for the chaplains on the other side.

We had a great deal of fun out of this, and on the provisional cross, at the stop where they buried the remains of the chaplain, there appeared overnight this epitaph:

What may hit us has now hit you.
You always said we'd join the saints.
Well, now you've caught it at Holy Mass.
And where you stood are only stains.

*St Adalbert – a Czech patron saint

From *The Good Soldier Švejk* by Jaroslav Hašek, 1923

Mother's Song

I never raised my boy
To be a soldier.
I brought him up to be
My pride and joy.

Who dare to lay a gun
  Upon his shoulder,
And teach him how to kill
  Another mother's boy?

I never raised my boy
  To be a soldier.
I brought him up to stay
  At home with me.
There would be no war today,
  If every mother would say,
I never raised my boy
  To be a soldier.

Sung in pubs in the north of England, *c.* 1940

'The Colonel Kicks the Major'

(*To the tune of 'Macnamara's Band'*)

Oh, the colonel kicks the major,
And the major has a go.
He kicks the poor old captain,
Who then kicks the NCO.
And as the kicks get harder,
They are passed on down to me.
And I am kicked to bleeding hell
To save democracy.

Anon., *c.* 1940

'It's a crazy war, guv'nor. I don't see why Jerry doesn't bomb Berlin and let the RAF take care of London. We'd both save petrol and we'd be none the worse.'

Anon., 1941

The Twats in the Ops Room

(*To the tune of 'John Brown's Body'*)

We had been flying all day long at one hundred fucking feet,
The weather fucking awful, fucking rain and fucking sleet,
The compass it was swinging fucking south and fucking north,
But we made a fucking landfall in the Firth of Fucking Forth.

Ain't the Air Force fucking awful?
Ain't the Air Force fucking awful?
Ain't the Air Force fucking awful?
We made a fucking landing in the Firth of Fucking Forth.

We joined the Air Force 'cos we thought it fucking right,
But don't care if we fucking fly or fucking fight,
But what we do object to are those fucking Ops Room twats,
Who sit there sewing stripes on at the rate of fucking knots.

Anon., *c.* 1942

A Bully with an Air Force

. . . Only listen, Lyndon Johnson, you've gone too far this time. you are a bully with an Air Force, and since you will not call off your Air Force, there are young people who will persecute you back. It is a little thing, but it will hound you into nightmares and endless corridors of night without sleep. It will hound you. For listen, this is only one of the thousand things they will do. They will go on marches and they will make demonstrations, and they will begin a war of public protest against you which will never cease. It will go on and on and it will get stronger and stronger. But listen to just one of the thousand things that they could do. Just listen to this little thing, which is one. These young people are, I think, going to print up pictures of you, Lyndon Johnson, the size of post-cards, the size of stamps. And some of them will glue these pictures to walls and posters and telephone booths and bill-boards. I don't advise it. I would tell these students not to do it to you, but they will. They will find places to put these pictures. They will want to paste your picture, Lyndon Johnson, on a postcard and send it to you. Some will send it to your advisers. Some will send these pictures to men and women in other schools. These pictures will be sent everywhere. These pictures will be pasted up everywhere – *upside down!* Without a word, Lyndon Johnson, that photograph of you is going to start appearing everywhere. Your head will speak out, even to the peasant in Asia. It will say that not all Americans are unaware of your monstrous vanity, overweening piety and doubtful motive. It will tell them that we trust our President so little and think so little of him that we send his picture everywhere *upside down.* Vietnam! Hot Damn! You, Lyndon Johnson will see those pictures everywhere – upside down. Four inches high and forty feet high. You, Lyndon Baines Johnson, are going to be coming up for air, everywhere, upside down. Everywhere, upside down! Upside down!

From a speech to a thirty-six hour Vietnam Day rally
in Berkeley, California, by Norman Mailer, 1965

Stopping the War

Since the Revolution, this country had had no experience of foreign occupation and consequently of resistance movements; in that field, it lacks inspiration and inventiveness and is readily discouraged. But the professors and students who lost heart when the teach-ins failed to change US policy might study the example of the Abolitionists – the nearest thing to a resistance movement the Republic has had. Obviously no single plan of action can stop the war in Vietnam, and maybe a hundred plans concerted could not stop it. But if it can be stopped, it will be through initiatives taken by persons or groups of persons (whether they be Johnson or Ho or a Republican president or Big Minh or the readers of this pamphlet) and not through cooked-up 'solutions' handed to somebody else to act on, like inter-office memoranda. The 'hard thinking' about this war needs to begin at home, with the critic asking himself what *he* can do against it, modestly or grandly, with friends or alone. From each according to his abilities, but to be in the town jail, as Thoreau knew, can relieve any sense of imaginary imprisonment.

From *Vietnam* by Mary McCarthy, 1967

'Because I Want Peace'

Because I want peace
and not war
because I don't want to see
hungry children
squalid women
men whose tongues

are silenced
I have to keep on fighting.
Because there are clandestine
cemeteries
and Squadrons of Death
drug-crazed killers
who torture
who maim
who assassinate
I want to keep on fighting.
Because on the peak
of Guazapa
my brothers peer out
from their bunkers
at three battalions
trained in Carolina
and Georgia
I have to keep on fighting.
Because from Huey
helicopters
expert pilots
wipe out villages
with napalm
poison the rivers
and burn the crops
that feed the people
I want to keep on fighting.
Because there are liberated
territories
where people
learn how to read
and the sick are cured
and the fruits of the soil
belong to all
I have to keep on fighting.
Because I want peace
and not war.

Claribel Alegria, El Salvador, *c.* 1980

'Ministry of National Security'

In order to avoid any misunderstanding of the issues at stake in the current war to save democracy it has been felt prudent to supply certain guidelines.
CENSORSHIP – this occurs in Argentina. It has not proved necessary to influence the media in Britain. Any lack of facts, pictures and informed comment from the task force itself is due to technical difficulties only.
FASCISM – this term applies to Argentina. It is not appropriate to describe the Chilean government as a 'fascist junta'. The term 'military administration' may be thought preferable.
CITIZENSHIP – this term should not be bandied about as born and bred Islanders are not British citizens and reports suggest that our nationals in Argentina are supporting the enemy cause.
'WISHES ETC. OF THE ISLANDERS THEMSELVES' – this phrase applies to hypothetical Islanders. It does not necessarily apply to those currently resident in the islands who survive the hostilities.
UNITED NATIONS – this is a namby-pamby organisation of reds, pacifists, and foreigners (and sometimes a combination of all three). Fortunately any criticism of Military policy can be vetoed by Britain.

'ISLAND RACE' – this term applies equally to Britons and Falkland islanders. It is not appropriate to apply it to the former residents of the island of Diego Garcia or to the residents of Hong Kong.
'ARGIES' – desirable as it may be to encourage race hatred towards Latin American people, we must bear in mind the specific history of race-mixing in Argentina itself with large numbers of Germans, Italians, Welsh, etc. breeding with the Spanish. The frequent use of the word 'enemy' may be more suitable.

Postcard circulated during the Falklands war, 1982

Falklands Sound

. . . Of course, what is happening here must feel familiar to you from the Second World War: the bravery and courage of our own pilots, flying an aircraft which was designed simply to intercept Soviet reconnaissance aircraft and which is now being pitted against supersonic fighters and used for bombing with gear little more advanced than the Lancaster. And the bravery and tragic waste of life of the Argentinian pilots, sent against overwhelming anti-aircraft missiles by heartless superiors. The devotion to duty of our frigates in the Falklands Sound, who were sitting ducks for the Argentinian aircraft and which were all hit by bombs. And above all, the tragedy, anguish, and horror of the British lives that have been lost: which have been spent quite willingly by Mrs Thatcher and Mr Nott to make up for the political ineptitude and pigheadedness of the Government. When one considers the total of sorrow, financial loss, loss of ships for Britain (which I doubt will ever be replaced) and destruction to the Falklands – now dotted with war graves – all balanced against a 'principle', a flag, and the ousting of two dozen islanders [those expelled] it does seem to me personally the most pointless of wars ever fought by Britain . . .

I read that Argentina was prepared to accept a deal which involved Argentinian sovereignty and British administration and way of life. Those, to me, sound fair terms to avoid bloodshed. Now that war has started, neither side can give way until the other is exhausted. This is not a war between civilised countries. It is not fought for any good reason (trade, survival, top-nation status etc.) but is fought on a 'principle' by two dictatorships. It is a dangerous state of affairs in Britain when the Prime Minister can tell the forces to go to war without consulting even Parliament. If that is the case, it is time the forces were cut so that it is impossible to use them for anything but the defence of Britain, and [that] they were placed under NATO control. Thinking of wars fought on 'principle' alone

I can only think of religious wars of bigotry, and the Thirty Years War which destroyed Germany. Thinking of enormous expenditure, I can only think of the Spanish Armada, the Dutch Wars of Independence – and Suez! . . .

Do you remember when we were studying Wilfred Owen at Mill Hill? In his poem where he says 'Oh death was never enemy of ours . . . We whistled while he shaved us with his scythe', he ends up (I'm probably misquoting) 'There'll come a day when men make war on death for lives – not men for flags'. This is what it is, a war for a flag . . . I think that Maggie Thatcher sees herself as a Churchill, and as for Nott . . . let him come and lie down on the deck with us while the air raids come in and the missiles go off. He would see what it is really like and soon change his tune.

From letters written on board HMS *Glamorgan* by David Tinker, 1982; Tinker was later killed

The Gulf War

At the time of writing, I have no idea what will happen in the Gulf War. Given that I'm relying on British news for information, I won't have much of an idea what happened when it's all over. But it may be that, by the time of publication, I shall be left looking like a bleating pessimist who underestimates the clean, quick efficacy of modern surgical warfare. I hope so, for the sake of thousands of people. On the other hand, it would mean that Bush had gotten away with it, and I think that if he is not dealt with now we are storing up trouble for the future. The fact that wars are now given names that sound like movies doesn't bode well for the 'stability of the region'. *Deserts Storm II, III, IV* and *V* already seem like sure-fire CNN box-office smashes.

Whatever happens, the involvement or otherwise of Israel shows up one of the shortcomings of Zionism. Instead of ensuring that a mass-slaughter of Jewish people never happens again, the Zionist state makes it extremely likely. I hope that Tel Aviv is not wiped off the map. I feel the same way about Baghdad, for the simple reason that Iraq and Israel are not only aggressive states with brutal armies and foul regimes but also places where a lot of people live.

Of course, Saddam doesn't give a toss about the Palestinians, any more than he gives a toss about the Kurds, whom he has persecuted with a ferocity that only someone supplied by the Western allies can. But the fact that a crime has been committed against the Palestinians is inescapable. Zionists sometimes try to justify it by citing the terrible crimes committed against the Jews. So why shouldn't Saddam use the crimes committed against Palestinians to justify *his* crimes? And why couldn't Bush have used their plight to justify what some might see as the crime of allowing Saddam a way out? There are, after all, UN resolutions about Israel getting out of the Occupied Territories. Indeed, Paddy Ashdown has said, in relation to Palestine, that 'a just peace must follow the just war'. He knows it won't – allied victory will reinforce the determination of the US and Israel to do nothing for the Palestinians.

I accept that there's no point bringing principles into the issue because no party to the Gulf dispute has any. So what's the real reason Britain and America couldn't let Saddam have Kuwait? After all, we gave Lithuania and Latvia to Stalin in 1945, and I can't see us sending a taskforce to the Baltic to liberate them now. Admittedly, there's a difference. We gave Eastern Europe away because it wasn't ours to give. Kuwait is. We thought of it. It wouldn't even exist if it wasn't for us. It would probably just be some tatty old bit of Iraq. You've seen the slogan 'Free Kuwait'. Yes, Kuwait comes free with petrol. Next time you spend more than is reasonable on private transportation, you can get a beautifully Western oil state with its own royal family and a non-democracy guarantee, absolutely free.

I don't wish to make light of Saddam's atrocities against Kuwaitis, but the West was happy enough when he was doing it to Kurds and Iranians, and Iraqis for that matter. So let's have no talk of morality. It looks as though the American public are rather more wise to the hypocrisy of their government than the British are. It is said that they have more reason to be, but I don't think we're in a position to point the finger at them. Every Pentagon and CIA escapade is dutifully cheered or condoned by British governments, Labour or Tory. When it comes to our own record, even if you support the deployment of troops in Northern Ireland, their conduct would seem, at the very least, to tarnish their reputation as international crusaders for peace and justice. I suppose I'm stabbing them in the back as they risk their lives but, to be fair, it's not me who wants them to.

Jeremy Hardy, 1991

Eight

THEN FAREWELL SACRED MAJESTY

How Kings Rule

Doth some one say that there be gods above?
There are not; no, there are not. Let no fool,
Led by the old false fable, thus deceive you.
Look at the facts themselves, yielding my words
No undue credence; for I say that kings
Kill, rob, break oaths, lay cities waste by fraud,
And doing thus are happier than those
Who live calm pious lives day after day.
How many little states that serve the gods
Are subject to the godless but more strong,
Made slaves by might of a superior army!

Euripides (480–406 BCE)

He Killed as Effortlessly as a Dog Squats

[The dead Augustus speaks, opposing the admission of Claudius into Olympus.]

This man, honourable members, who gives you the impression of not being able to startle a fly, used to kill people as effortlessly as a dog squats on its haunches. But why do I mention men of such number and quality? I have no time to bewail national disasters when I contemplate family misfortunes. Therefore I shall pass over the former and deal with the latter. For *I* know that the knee is nearer than the shin, even if my anklebone does not. The specimen you see, lurking under my name for so many years, paid me such thanks as to kill two Julias, my great-granddaughters, one by the sword, the other by starvation, and one great-great-grandson, L. Silanus: you, Jupiter, will judge whether his case was faulty – it was certainly the same as yours, if you are going to be fair. Tell me, deified Claudius, why did you convict any of these men and women, whom you killed, before you could examine the case, before you could hear the evidence? Where is this the customary practice? It is not so in heaven . . .

You killed Messalina, whose great-great-uncle I was just as much as yours. 'I don't know' you say? May the dogs curse you: the fact that you didn't know is far more disgraceful than the fact that you killed. Claudius did not stop making Gaius Caesar his target after his death. Gaius had killed his father-in-law; Claudius killed a son-in-law as well. Gaius forbade

Crassus' son to be called 'the Great'. Claudius gave him back his name but took away his head. In one family he killed Crassus, Magnus, and Scribonia, no blue-blooded clan of Assaracus, but aristocrats all the same, and Crassus truly such a fool that he could even have been king. Is this the man you now wish to make a god? Look at his body, born when the gods were in a rage. In short, let him utter three words in quick succession and he can take me as his slave. Who will worship this man as a god? Who will believe in him? While you create gods of this sort nobody will believe that *you* are gods. This is the heart of the matter, honourable members: if I have behaved myself respectably among you, if I have given no reply to anyone too directly, avenge the wrongs done me. This is the motion I put as my considered opinion (and this is what he read out from his note-pad): 'Whereas the deified Claudius killed his father-in-law Appius Silanus, his two sons-in-law Pompeius Magnus and Lucius Silanus, his daughter's father-in-law Crassus Frugi, a man as like himself as two eggs in a basket, Scribonia his daughter's mother-in-law, his wife Messalina and the others whose number cannot be calculated, my proposal is that he be severely punished and not given exemption from due process of law, and that he be deported as soon as possible and leave heaven within thirty days and Olympus within three.' Members stepped out to support this proposal. There was no delay. Mercury hailed him, with his neck twisted, to the underworld from heaven

from where, they say, no one returns.

From *Apolocyntosis* by Seneca (5 BCE–65 AD), who opposed the deification of Emperor Claudius and wrote this satire of 'Pumpkinification', the fruit referred to being soft and testicular-shaped

---

People with an over-abundance of dignity and an over-supply of power have always in the end been targets for laughter.

Charlie Chaplin

Barbarians?

In what respects can our customs be preferred to those of the Goths and Vandals, or even compared with them? And first, to speak of affection and mutual charity, . . . almost all barbarians, at least those who are of one race and kin, love each other, while the Romans persecute each other . . . The many are oppressed by the few, who regard public exactions as their own peculiar right, who carry on private traffic under the guise of collecting the taxes . . . So the poor are despoiled, the widows sigh, the orphans are oppressed, until many of them, born of families not obscure, and liberally educated, flee to our enemies that they may no longer suffer the oppression of public persecution. They doubtless seek Roman humanity among the barbarians, because they cannot bear barbarian inhumanity among the Romans. And although they differ from the people to whom they flee in manner and in language; although they are unlike as regards the fetid odor of the barbarians' bodies and garments, yet they would rather endure a foreign civilization among the barbarians than cruel injustice among the Romans.

Salvian, *c.* 440

I Too Can Become Like God

Quoth Lucifer, Why then should I slave? There is no shred of need
for me now to serve a master! With these very hands I may
work as many wonders. And power in plenty is mine
for the setting-up a goodlier throne than his,
and a higher, in the heaven! Why should I do him homage,
be bondsman for his favour? I too can become like God.
Stout-hearted comrades stand with me, firm-spirited heroes
who will not falter in the struggle. They have chosen me their chief,
these far-famed fighters. With such staunch companions
good plans can be laid. They are eager friends,
and true to me in all their thoughts.

From *Genesis*, Anon., *c.* 600

'The Charcoal-Seller'

An old charcoal-seller
Cutting wood and burning charcoal in the forests of the Southern Mountain.
His face, stained with dust and ashes, has turned to the colour of smoke.
The hair on his temples is streaked with grey: his ten fingers are black.

The money he gets by selling charcoal, how far does it go?
It is just enough to clothe his limbs and put food in his mouth.
Although, alas, the coat on his back is a coat without lining,
He hopes for the coming of cold weather, to send up the price of coal!
Last night, outside the city, – a whole foot of snow;
At dawn he drives the charcoal wagon along the frozen ruts.
Oxen, – weary; man, – hungry; the sun, already high;
Outside the Gate, to the south of the Market, at last they stop in the mud.
Suddenly, a pair of prancing horsemen. Who can it be coming?
A public official in a yellow coat and a boy in a white shirt.
In their hands they hold a written warrant: on their tongues – the words of an order;
They turn back the wagon and curse the oxen, leading them off to the north.
A whole wagon of charcoal,
More than a thousand catties!
If officials choose to take it away, the woodman may not complain.
Half a piece of red silk and a single yard of damask,
The Courtiers have tied to the oxen's collar, as the price of a wagon of coal!

Po Chü-I, eighth century

Death-Warrant for a King

Whereas Charles Stuart, King of England, is and standeth convicted, attainted and condemned of High Treason and other high Crimes; and Sentence upon Saturday last was pronounced against him by this Court, To be put to death by the severing of his head from his body; of which Sentence execution yet remaineth to be done.

These are therefore to will and require you to see the said Sentence executed, in the open Street before Whitehall, upon the morrow, being the Thirtieth day of this instant month of January, between the hours of Ten in the morning and Five in the afternoon with full effect. And for so doing, this shall be your warrant.

And these are to require all Officers and Soldiers, and others of the good People of this Nation of England, to be assisting unto you in this service.

Given under our hands and seals.

Warrant issued to army officers by fifty-nine members of the High Court of Justice, 1649

The Diggers' Christmas Carol

The DIGGERS

MIRTH,

OR,

Certain Verses composed and fitted to Tunes, for the delight and recreation of all those who Dig, or own that Work, in the Commonwealth of *England.*

Wherein is shewed how the Kingly power doth still Reign in severall sorts of MEN

With a hint of that Freedom which shall come,
When the Father shall reign alone in his Son.

Set forth by those who were the original of that so righteous a Work, and continued still successfull therein at *Cobham* in

SURREY.

(To the Tune of the *Spanish Gypsie*)

1

You people which be wise,
Will Freedom highly prize;
For experience you have
What 'tis to be a slave:
This have you been all your life long,
But chiefly since the Wars begun

2

When great Men disagree
About Supremacy,
Then doe they warn poor men
To aid and assist them
In setting up their self-will power,
And thus they doe the poor devour.

3

Yet they cunningly pretend
They have no other end
But to set the poor Free
From all their slavery:
And thus they do the poor deceive,
In making them such things believe.

4

Their blinde Guides will not spare,
These things for to declare;
Ye they aloud will cry,
Stand for your liberty;
The Gospel that lyes at the stake;
Rise therefore 'tis time to awake.

5

The Priests very sensible be,
If the poor their Liberty see;
Their Tythe-plundring trade will fall,
And then farewell Tythes all.
Then would they not be finely fed,
But they must work for their own bread.

6

The King an Army did gain,
His power for to maintain;
That Army did pretend
For to be *England*'s friend,
In saving of their Libertie
Which lay at stake and like to die.

7

Another Army then
Was raised by mighty Men,
That Army to oppose,
Looking on them as Foes:
Likewise these powers did agree
To make the English Nation free.

8

A Covenant they did take,
And promises they did make
All burthens to remove,
And to unite in love;
Yet we cannot see that good hour,
The taking down of Kingly power.

9

The Nation willingly
Did maintain this Army,
Their Freedom for to gain;
But as yet all in vain:
For still a Kingly power doth stand
In many persons of this Land.

10

A Kingly power I say
Doth in most men bare sway,
But chiefly in Lords of Mannors,
And in the Priests and Lawyers:
This Kingly power is their Self-will,
Which in this manner they do fulfill.

11

The Priests they tyrannize,
By taking of the Tythes;
The poor they much oppresse

By their pride and idlenesse:
No Scripture warrant they can show,
Why any of these things they do.

12

Therefore I pray consider,
And lay your heads together;
For you will never thrive,
Whilst Priests do gain the Tythe.
But let them work as well as you,
For Reason bids them so to do.

13

They neither plow nor sow,
Nor do they reap or mow,
Nor any feed do finde,
But Priests the people grinde:
The tenth of all things they do crave;
And thus each man is made a slave.

14

The Lawyers they are next,
By whom the poor are vext;
Their practice is most base,
For they will pleads mens Case,
According to the length o'th' Purse,
And so the Lawyers prove a Curse.

15

Another trick they have,
The Nation to inslave;
Mens quarrels they'll maintain,
Their Moneys for to gain:
Therefore if Lawyers you uphold,
They'll cheat you of your silver & gold.

16

Therefore my brethren dear,
The Lawyers quite Cashiere;
Go not to them for Law,
For they your sides will claw;
They'l tell you that your case is good,
When they doe mean to suck your blood.

17

Therefore be rul'd by me,
And do not Lawyers Fee,
But end your suits at home,
Lest you be overthrown;
For if Lawyers gain your estate,
You may repent when 'tis too late.

18

Besides the Priests and Lawyers,
There be the Lords of Mannors,
Who lay claim to waste Land,
Which by blood-shed was gain'd;
For Duke *William* the *Norman* King,
By much bloodshed this land did win.

19

When he this Land had gain'd,
He presently Ordain'd,
That his chief Souldiers should
This Land by parcels hold,
Owning him to be the Supream,
In paying tribute unto him.

20

From hence came Lords of
Mannors,
With Fines, quit-Rents and
Heriots,
And all such cursed things,
Which are payed to these Kings:
And thus the people be brought
down
By Lords of Mannors who wear
the Crown.

21

The Lords of Mannors, I say,
Do bear a mighty sway;
The Common Lands they hold,
Herein they are too bold:
They will not suffer men to till
The comon Lands, by their
good wil.

22

But Lords of Mannors must know,
Their title to Commons is low;
For why their title came in
By WILLIAM the Norman King.
But now the *Norman* successor
is dead,
Their Royalty to th'Commons
is fled.

23

Therefore let me advise
All those which Freedom prize,
To Till each Heath and Plain,
For this will Freedom gain:
Heriots and Fines this will
expell,
A bondage great men know full
well.

24

For we do plainly see,
The Sword will not set's free,
But bondage is increased;
Because our wealth is wasted
By paying Taxes and Free-
quarter,
Expecting Freedom would come
after.

25

But Freedom is not wonn,
Neither by Sword nor Gunn:
Though we have eight years
stay'd,
And have our Moneys pay'd:
Then Clubs and Diamonds cast
away,
For Harts & Spades must win
the day.

Probably by Gerald Winstanley, 1650; a complaint, reprinted for the first time here, that the Cromwellians have restored 'Kingly Power' instead of carrying the revolution through

Republican Yeomen

1. Thou had best be quiet for those that thou buildest upon I hope will not last long. I lived as well when there was no King and I hope to do so again when there will be no King.

2. Cromwell and Ireton was as good as the King.
3. Thou and thy father are rogues and traitors, and all is traitors that do fight for the King.
4. I hope ere long to trample in Kings' and Bishops' blood, and I know of six thousand men that will join with me in pulling down the Bishops.

Remarks for which yeomen were brought before Surrey courts, 1661–3

A Parliament of Knaves and Sots

A Parliament of knaves and sots,
  Members by name you must not mention,
He keeps in pay, and buys their votes,
  Here with a place, there with a pension:
When to give money he can't cologue 'em,
He doth with scorn prorogue, prorogue 'em.

New up-starts, pimps, bastards, whores,
  That locust-like devour the land,
By shutting up the Exchequer doors[1]
  (When thither our money was trepanned)
Have rendered Charles his Restoration
But a small blessing to the nation.

Such know no law but their own lust;
  Their subjects' substance and their blood,
They count it tribute true and just,
  Still spent and spilt for subjects' good:
If such are kings by God appointed,
The Devil may be the Lord's anointed.

Such kings (curst be the power and name!)
  Let all the world henceforth abhor' em;
Monsters which knaves sacred proclaim,
  And then like slaves fall down before 'em:
What can there be in kings divine?
The most are wolves, goats, sheep, or swine.

[1] In 1672 Charles despotically stopped the Exchequer, so diverting large sums of public money to his own use.

Then farewell sacred majesty!
Let's pull all brutish tyrants down,
Where men are born and still live free,
Here every head doth wear a crown:
Mankind, like the unhappy Frogs,
Prove wretched, kinged by Storks and Logs.

Attributed to John Wilmot, Earl of Rochester, *c.* 1672

From 'On the Lord Mayor and Court of Aldermen, presenting the late King and Duke of York each with a Copy of their Freedoms, Anno Dom. 1674'

The Londoners Gent to the King do present
In a Box the City Maggot;
'Tis a thing full of weight, that requires the Might
Of whole *Guild-Hall* Team to drag it.

Whilst their Church's unbuilt, and their Houses undwelt,
And their Orphans want Bread to feed 'em;
Themselves they've bereft of the little Wealth they had left,
To make an Offering of their Freedom.

O ye Addle brain'd Cits who henceforth in their Wits
Would intrust their Youth to your heading;
When in Diamonds and Gold you have him thus enroll'd,
You know both his Friends and his Breeding?

Beyond Sea he began, where such a Riot he ran,
That every one there did leave him;
And now he's come o'er ten times worse than before,
When none but such Fools would receive him.

He ne'er knew, not he, how to serve or be free,
Though he has past through so many Adventures;
But e'er since he was bound, (that is he was crown'd)
He has every Day broke his Indentures.

He spends all his Days in running to Plays,
  When he should in the Shop be poring:
And he wasts all his Nights in his constant Delights,
  Of Revelling, Drinking and Whoring.

Andrew Marvell, *c.* 1674

I am sure there was no man born marked of God above another; for none come into the world with a saddle on his back, neither any booted or spurred to ride him.

Colonel Rumbold, 1685

Here Lies Fred

Here lies Fred,
Who was alive and is dead.
Had it been his father,
I had much rather.
Had it been his brother,
Still better than another.
Had it been his sister,
No one would have missed her.
Had it been the whole generation,
Still better for the nation.
But since 'tis only Fred,
Who was alive, and is dead,
There's no more to be said.

Anon., *c.* 1751, on the death of Frederick, Prince of Wales, father of George III

'A Remedy for Unrest'

Ah! Well they know that if the Poor
Were cloathed and fed, they'd work no more;
That nothing makes mankind so good,

So tractable as Want of Food;
And like those frugal Politicians,
Who take their maxims from Physicians,
Thinking Starving is the best foundation
Of popular subordination.

From *Speculation or, A Defence of Mankind* by Christopher Anstey, 1780

The English Parliament

There never did, there never will, and there never can, exist a parliament, or any description of men, or any generation of men, in any country, possessed of the right or the power of binding and controlling posterity to the '*end of time*,' or of commanding for ever how the world shall be governed, or who shall govern it; and therefore all such clauses, acts or declarations by which the makers of them attempt to do what they have neither the right nor the power to do, nor the power to execute, are in themselves null and void. Every age and generation must be as free to act for itself *in all cases* as the ages and generations which preceded it. The vanity and presumption of governing beyond the grave is the most ridiculous and insolent of all tyrannies. Man has no property in man; neither has any generation a property in the generations which are to follow. The parliament of the people of 1688, or of any other period, had no more right to dispose of the people of the present day, or to bind or to control them *in any shape whatever*, than the parliament or the people of the present day have to dispose of, bind or control those who are to live a hundred or a thousand years hence. Every generation is, and must be, competent to all the purposes which its occasions require. It is the living, and not the dead, that are to be accommodated. When man ceases to be, his power and his wants cease with him; and having no longer any participation in the concerns of this world, he has no longer any authority in directing who shall be its governors, or how its government shall be organized, or how administered . . .

The constitution of France says, That every man who pays a tax of sixty sous *per annum* (2s. 6d. English) is an elector. What article will Mr Burke place against this? Can anything be more limited, and at the same time more capricious; than the qualifications of electors are in England? Limited – because not one man in an hundred (I speak much within compass) is admitted to vote. Capricious – because the lowest character that can be supposed to exist, and who has not so much as the visible means of an honest livelihood, is an elector in some places: while in other places, the man who pays very large taxes, and has a known fair character, and the farmer who rents to the amount of three or four hundred pounds a year, with a property on that farm to three or four times that amount, is not admitted to be an elector. Everything is out of nature, as Mr Burke says on another occasion, in this strange chaos, and all sorts of follies are blended with all sorts of crimes. William the Conqueror and his descendants parcelled out the country in this manner, and bribed some parts of it by what they call charters to hold the other parts of it the better subjected to their will. This is the reason why so many of those charters abound in Cornwall; the people were averse to the government established at the conquest, and the towns were garrisoned and bribed to enslave the country. All the old charters are the badges of this conquest, and it is from this source that the capriciousness of elections arises . . .

Everything in the English government appears to me the reverse of what it ought to be, and of what it is said to be. The parliament, imperfectly and capriciously elected as it is, is nevertheless *supposed* to hold the national purse in *trust* for the nation; but in the manner in which an English Parliament is constructed it is like a man being both mortgager and mortgagee, and in the case of misapplication of trust it is the criminal sitting in judgment upon himself. If those who vote the supplies are the same persons who receive the supplies when voted, and are to account for the expenditure of those supplies to those who voted them, it is *themselves accountable to themselves*, and the Comedy of Errors concludes with the Pantomime of Hush . . .

The continual use of the word *Constitution* in the English Parliament shews there is none; and that the whole is merely a form of government without a constitution, and constituting itself with what powers it pleases.

From *The Rights of Man* by Thomas Paine, 1791; written in response to Edmund Burke's *Reflections on the Revolution in France*

'The Deil's[1] awa' wi' the Exciseman'
To the tune of 'The Hempdresser'.

The deil cam fiddling thro' the town,
And danced awa' wi' the Exciseman:
And ilka[2] wife cried 'Auld Mahoun,'
We wish you luck o' your prize, man;

[1]devil [2]every

We'll mak our maut,[3] *and brew our drink,*
We'll dance and sing and rejoice, man;
And monie thanks to the muckle[4] *black deil*
That danced awa' wi' the Exciseman.

There's threesome reels and foursome reels,
There's hornpipes and strathspeys, man;
But the ae best dance e'er came to our lan'
Was 'the deil's awa' wi' the Exciseman.'

We'll mak our maut . . .

[3]malt whisky [4]big

Robert Burns, *c.* 1790

'The Boa Desolator, or Legitimate Vampire'

> It overlays the continent like an ugly Incubus sucking the blood and stopping up the breath of man's life. It claims Mankind as its property, and allows human nature to exist only upon sufferance; it haunts the understanding like a frightful spectre, and oppresses the very air with a weight that is not to be borne.
> *Hazlitt's Political Essays and Characters*, p. 91.

This hideous Beast, not having at any time put forth all his *members*, cannot be accurately described. Every *dark* Century has added to his frightful bulk. More disgusting than the filthiest reptile, his strength exceeds all other *brute force*.

His enormous, bloated, toad-like body is *ferruginous*:* the under surface appears of *polished steel*.† His cavern-like mouth is always open to devour; 'his teeth are as *swords*, and his jaw-teeth as knives' – as millions of *bristling bayonets* intermingled with *black fangs* containing mortal venom. His roar is a voice from the sepulchre. He is marked '*in form of a cross*,'* with a series of *chains*, intersected by the TRIANGLE,† and glittering colours, variegated with *red*.

His aspect is cruel and terrible. He loves the *dark*, but never sleeps. Wherever he makes his lair, nature sickens, and man is brutified. His presence is 'plague, pestilence, and famine, battle, and murder, and sudden death.' His bite rapidly *undermines the strongest* CONSTITUTION, and dissolves the whole into an entire mass of CORRUPTION. He has no *brain*, but the *walls* of the skull emit a *tinkling* sound, that attracts his victims, and lulls them into *passive obedience*. In this state he clutches them in his coils, and *screws* and *squeezes* them to destruction – *slavering* them over, and sucking in their *substance* at leisure. It is difficult to witness the half-stifled cries of his harmless prey, or to behold its anxiety and trepidation, while the monster writhes hideously around it, without imagining *what our own case would be in the same dreadful situation*.‡

His rapacity is increased by *indulgence*. He grinds, cranches, and devours whole multitudes without being satisfied. His blood is cold. His ravening maw does not digest; it is an ever-yawning grave that *engulphs* – a 'bottomless pit' continually crying '*give, give!*' Sometimes he 'rests from his labors,' to admire his loathsome *limbs*, and *slime* them over. He has no affections: yet he appears charmed by the *hum* of the INSECTS that follow him, and pleased by the *tickling crawl* of the MEANEST REPTILES – permitting them to hang upon his lips and partake of his leavings. But his real pleasure is in listening to the cries of his captives, the wail of the broken hearted, and the groans of the dying.

*Shaw's Zoology. Art. Boa, iii. 344. †ibid. 366.
*Linnaeus's Nat. Hist, by Gmelin, 8vo. (Jones) 1816. Art. Boa Consctor, xii. 437. †Shaw's Zoology, iii. 339. ‡Macleod's Wreck of the Alceste, 291, 295.

Broadside pamphlet, *c.* 1820

'The Georges.'

George the First was always reckoned
Vile, but viler George the Second;
And what mortal ever heard
Any good of George the Third?
When from earth the Fourth descended.
(God be praised!) the Georges ended.

Walter Savage Landor, *c.* 1830

'The Fine, Old English Gentleman. New Version'

TO BE SAID OR SUNG AT ALL CONSERVATIVE DINNERS

I'll sing you a new ballad, and I'll warrant its first-rate,
Of the days of that old gentleman who had that old estate;
When they spent the public money at a bountiful old rate
On ev'ry mistress, pimp, and scamp, at ev'ry noble gate,
In the fine old English Tory times;
Soon may they come again!

The good old laws were garnished well with gibbets, whips, and chains,
With fine old English penalties, and fine old English pains,
With rebel heads, and seas of blood once hot in rebel veins;
For all these things were requisite to guard the rich old gains
Of the fine old English Tory times;
Soon may they come again!

This brave old code, like Argus, had a hundred watchful eyes,
And ev'ry English peasant had his good old English spies,
To tempt his starving discontent with fine old English lies,
Then call the good old Yeomanry to stop his peevish cries,
In the fine old English Tory times;
Soon may they come again!

The good old times for cutting throats that cried out in their need,
The good old times for hunting men who held their fathers' creed,
The good old times when William Pitt, as all good men agreed,
Came down direct from Paradise at more than railroad speed . . .
Oh the fine old English Tory times;
When will they come again!

In those rare days, the press was seldom known to snarl or bark,
But sweetly sang of men in pow'r, like any tuneful lark;
Grave judges, too, to all their evil deeds were in the dark;
And not a man in twenty score knew how to make his mark.
Oh the fine old English Tory times;
Soon may they come again!

Those were the days for taxes, and for war's infernal din;
For scarcity of bread, that fine old dowagers might win;
For shutting men of letters up, through iron bars to grin,
Because they didn't think the Prince was altogether thin,
In the fine old English Tory times;
Soon may they come again!

But Tolerance, though slow in flight, is strong-wing'd in the main;
That might must come on these fine days, in course of time was plain;
The pure old spirit struggled, but its struggles were in vain;
A nation's grip was on it, and it died in choking pain,
With the fine old English Tory days,
All of the olden time.

The bright old day now dawns again; the cry runs through the land,
In England there shall be dear bread – in Ireland, sword and brand,
And poverty, and ignorance, shall swell the rich and grand,
So, rally round the rulers with the gentle iron hand,
Of the fine old English Tory days;
Hail to the coming time!

Charles Dickens, 1841

'Resurgemus[1]'

Suddenly, out of its stale and drowsy air, the air of slaves,
Like lightning Europe le'pt forth,
Sombre, superb and terrible,
As Ahimoth, brother of Death.

God, 'twas delicious!
That brief, tight, glorious grip
Upon the throats of kings.

You liars paid to defile the People,
Mark you now:
Not for numberless agonies, murders, lusts,
For court thieving in its manifold mean forms,
Worming from his simplicity the poor man's wages;
For many a promise sworn by royal lips
And broken, and laughed at in the breaking;

Then, in their power, not for all these,
Did a blow fall in personal revenge,
Of a hair draggle in blood:
The People scorned the ferocity of kings.

But the sweetness of mercy brewed bitter destruction,
And frightened rulers come back:
Each comes in state, with his train,
Hangman, priest, and tax-gatherer,
Soldier, lawyer, and sycophant;
An appalling procession of locusts,
And the king struts grandly again.

Yet behind all, lo, a Shape
Vague as the night, draped interminably,
Head, front and form, in scarlet folds;
Whose face and eyes none may see,
Out of its robes only this,
The red robes, lifted by the arm,
One finger pointed high over the top,
Like the head of a snake appears.

Meanwhile, corpses lie in new-made graves,
Bloody corpses of young men;
The rope of the gibbet hangs heavily,
The bullets of tyrants are flying,
The creatures of power laugh aloud:
And all these things bear fruits, and they are good.

Those corpses of young men,
Those martyrs that hang from the gibbets,
Those hearts pierced by the grey lead,
Cold and motionless as they seem,

Live elsewhere with undying vitality;
They live in other young men, O, kings,
They live in brothers, again ready to defy you;
They were purified by death,
They were taught and exalted.

Not a grave of those slaughtered ones
But is growing its seed of freedom,

In its turn to bear seed,
Which the winds shall carry afar and resow,
And the rain nourish.

Not a disembodied spirit
Can the weapon of tyrants let loose,
But it shall stalk invisibly over the earth,
Whispering, counseling, cautioning.

Liberty, let others despair of thee,
But I will never despair of thee:
Is the house shut? Is the master away?
Nevertheless, be ready, be not weary of watching,
He will surely return; his messengers come anon.

[1] 'We shall rise again'

Walt Whitman's first free verse poem, printed in the New York *Daily Tribune*, 1850

Being Ruled

To be governed is to be watched over, inspected, spied upon, directed, legislated at, regulated, docketed, indoctrinated, preached at, controlled, assessed, weighed, censored, ordered about, by men who have neither the right nor the knowledge nor the virtue. To be governed means to be, at each operation, at each transaction, at each movement, noted, registered, controlled, taxed, stamped, measured, valued, assessed, patented, licensed, authorized, endorsed, admonished, hampered, reformed, rebuked, arrested. It is to be, on the pretext of the general interest, taxed, drilled, held to ransom, exploited, monopolized, extorted, squeezed, hoaxed, robbed; then, at the least resistance, at the first word of complaint, to be repressed, fined, abused, annoyed, followed, bullied, beaten, disarmed, garotted, imprisoned, machine-gunned, judged, condemned, deported, flayed, sold, betrayed and finally mocked, ridiculed, insulted, dishonoured. Such is government, such is justice, such is morality.

Pierre-Joseph Proudhon, 1851

I am a Chief

That man came shouting, 'I am a chief.'
Certainly he looks lazy enough for the title;
He also has the appetite of a king's son,
And a very royal waddle.
But he shouts, 'I am a chief':
Therefore I know he is not one.

Anon, Gilbert and Ellice Islands, nineteenth century

Duchess of Portsmouth: Why, woman, you are fine enough to be a queen.
Nell Gwynne: You are entirely right, madam, and I am whore enough to be a duchess!

By Order of the British Public

When the much-anticipated list of Royal Command performers was announced Marie's name was not on it, not even in the finale of one hundred and forty-two 'walk on' artists representing the profession. It was an astonishing snub, and Marie was deeply hurt. She was indisputably at the very top: the only other woman who commanded anything like her drawing power was Vesta Tilley, and the contrast in their fortunes in this instance highlights the prejudice harboured against Marie by the men who held the positions of increasing power at the time . . .

Meanwhile, a short distance from the Palace Theatre where the Command Performance was establishing a long and enduring tradition of dreariness, Marie staged her own show at the London Pavilion. Loyal fans had returned their Command tickets and came to see Marie instead. She was billed as 'The Queen of Comedy' and she introduced new songs. Outside the posters bore strips which announced:

Every Performance by Marie Lloyd
is a Command Performance
By Order of the British Public

From *A Star is Torn* by Robin Morgan, 1986, on Marie Lloyd, *c.* 1908

'The Mayor of Gary'

I asked the Mayor of Gary about the 12-hour day and the 7-day week.
And the Mayor of Gary answered more workmen steal time on the job in Gary than any other place in the United States.
'Go into the plants and you will see men sitting around doing nothing – machinery does everything,' said the Mayor of Gary when I asked him about the 12-hour day and the 7-day week.
And he wore cool cream pants, the Mayor of Gary, and white shoes, and a barber had fixed him up with a shampoo and a shave and he was easy and imperturbable though the government weather bureau thermometer said 96 and children were soaking their heads at bubbling fountains on the street corners.
And I said good-by to the Mayor of Gary and I went out from the city hall and turned the corner into Broadway.
And I saw workmen wearing leather shoes scruffed with fire and cinders, and pitted with little holes from running molten steel.
And some had bunches of specialized muscles around their shoulder blades hard as pig iron, muscles of their forearms were sheet steel and they looked to me like men who had been somewhere.

Carl Sandburg, Indiana, 1915

'Promises'

'Stand by me!' said the Government
Twelve years since, in 'Fourteen.
'The Country's in a fix, lads,
And needs you on the scene.
Stand by the Country's Standard
And see the trouble through –
And when the war is over
Count on US to stand by you!'

'Stand by us!' says the Government,
In Nineteen-Twenty-Six,
'There's trouble in the air, lads,
And the State is in a fix.'
'Stand by us!' says the Government
'And see the trouble through –

And when the Strike is over
Count on us to stand by you!'

Oh hark! the twelve-years' Echo:
'Count on US to stand by You . . .'

Eleanor Farjeon, 1926; in response to the General Strike

The Plague of Dictatorship

The physician or teacher has only *one* obligation, that of practising his profession uncompromisingly, without regard for the powers that attempt to suppress life, and to consider only the welfare of those who are given into his care. He cannot represent ideologies that are in conflict with the true task of the physician or teacher.

He who disputes this right of the scientist, the physician, the teacher, the technician or the writer, and calls himself a democrat, is a hypocrite, or at least a victim of the plague of irrationalism. The struggle against the plague of dictatorship is hopeless without determination and without a serious concern with problems of the life process; for, dictatorship lives – and can only live – in the darkness of *unresolved* problems of the life process. Man is helpless where he lacks knowledge; this helplessness born of ignorance forms the fertile soil for dictatorship. A social order cannot be called democratic if it is afraid of raising decisive questions, of finding unexpected answers, or of the clash of opinions regarding them. If it has such fears, it tumbles under the slightest attack upon its institutions by would-be dictators. This is what happened in Europe.

'Freedom of worship' is dictatorship so long as there is, at the same time, no *freedom of science*, and, consequently, no free competition in the interpretation of the life process. We must once and for all decide whether 'God' is an all-powerful, bearded figure in heaven or the cosmic law of nature governing us. Only when God and natural law are identical, can science and religion be reconciled. There is but one step from the dictatorship of those who represent God on earth to that of those who want to replace him on earth.

Morality is also dictatorship if it results in considering people with a natural feeling for life as on the same level with pornography. Whether it wants to or not, it thus prolongs the existence of smut and brings ruin to natural happiness in love. It is necessary to raise a sharp protest against calling a man immoral who bases his social behavior on inner laws instead of external compulsive forms. People are man and wife not because they have received the sacrament but because they feel themselves man and wife. The inner and not the external law is the yardstick of genuine freedom. Moralistic hypocrisy is the most dangerous enemy of natural morality. Moralistic hypocrisy cannot be fought with another kind of compulsive morality, but only with the knowledge of the natural law of the sexual process. *Natural moral behavior presupposes freedom of the natural sexual process.* Conversely, compulsive morality and pathological sexuality go hand in hand.

The line of compulsion is the line of least resistance. It is easier to demand discipline and to enforce it by authority than it is to bring up children to a joyful initiative in their work and to natural sexual behavior. It is easier to declare oneself an omniscient, god-sent Führer and to decree what millions of people should think and do, than it is to expose oneself to the struggle between the rational and irrational in the clash of opinions. It is easier to insist on legally required performance of respect and love than it is to win friendship through genuinely decent behavior. It is easier to sell one's independence for economic security than it is to lead an independent, responsible existence and to be master of oneself. It is easier to dictate to subordinates what they ought to do than it is to *guide* them while respecting their own individuality. This is why dictatorship is always easier than *true* democracy. This is why the indolent democratic leader envies the dictator, and tries, in his inadequate way, to imitate him. It is easy to represent the commonplace, and difficult to represent the truth.

He who does not have confidence in that which is alive, or has lost it, easily falls prey to the subterranean fear of life which begets dictatorship. *That which is alive is in itself reasonable.* It becomes a caricature when it is not allowed to live. If it is a caricature, life can only create terror. This is why knowledge of that which is alive can alone banish terror.

Whatever the outcome of the bloody struggles of our disjointed world may be for the coming centuries: the science of life is more powerful than all the life-negating forces and tyrannies. It was Galileo and not Nero, Pasteur and not Napoleon, Freud and not Shicklgruber,* who laid the basis for modern technic, who fought epidemics, who explored the mind; who, in other words laid a solid foundation for our existence. The others never did anything but misuse the achievements of the great in order to destroy life. We can take comfort in the fact that the roots of science reach down infinitely deeper than the Fascist turmoil of today.

*Hitler.

From *The Function of the Orgasm* by Wilhelm Reich, 1940

Stalin, Kruschev and Brezhnev are travelling in a train.
The train breaks down.
'Fix it!' orders Stalin.
They repair it but still the train doesn't move.
'Shoot everyone!' orders Stalin.
They shoot everyone but still the train doesn't budge.
Stalin dies.
'Rehabilitate everyone!' orders Kruschev.
They are rehabilitated, but still the train won't go.
Kruschev is removed.
'Close the curtains,' orders Brezhnev, 'and pretend we're moving!'

Kozy Kot in Wembley

Men drawing comfortable salaries were soon tempted to acquire not only their jerry-built villas, but cheap cars, wireless sets, furniture and other amenities, on the 'never-never' system. With each new obligation they became more and more the slaves of their employers. 'Very well, Mr Smith, I'm sorry. But if you are not satisfied, you know your remedy.' This familiar phrase, translated into plain English, meant 'another word from you and you'll find yourself on your backside in the street'. Mr Smith may have been a hero at Mons, but he became a terrified rabbit when he thought of his 'little palace' at Colindale, his Kozy Kot at Wembley, or his overdue instalment on his Austin Seven.

From *The Nineteen Twenties* by D. Goldring, 1945

'Advice to our Children'

Be naughty, that's all right.
Climb up sheer walls,
    up towering trees.
Like an old captain let your hands direct
the course of your bicycle.

And with the pencil which draws the cartoons
    of the master of Religious Knowledge,
    demolish the pages of the Koran.
You must know how to build your own paradise
    on this black soil.
With your geology text-book
you must silence the man who teaches you
that creation began with Adam.
You must recognize
    the importance of the Earth,
you must believe
    that the Earth is eternal
Distinguish not between your mother
and your mother Earth.
You must love it
    as much as you love her.

Nazim Hikmet, *c.* 1950

An Unfit Person

In October 1950, an Oklahoma judge had ruled that a woman called Jean Fields was an 'unfit person' to have custody of her two children whom she alone had brought up and supported for ten years.

In May 1940, Mrs Fields had been deserted by her husband, Vernon Fields, who left a farewell note saying: 'I no longer want the responsibility of a wife and two children, so here it is in your lap. Sorry, but that's the way it is.' The older child was then three years old, the baby three weeks. Mrs Field obtained a divorce and was awarded full custody of her two children. Her husband soon landed in jail on a forgery charge. This was the last she heard of him for the next ten years. Mrs Field and her children moved to California.

In the spring of 1950, the children, now thirteen and ten years of age, went to visit their paternal grand-parents in Oklahoma. It was arranged that they should spend the summer there and return to California in the autumn in time for school opening. In September, Mrs Field received a notification to the effect that her former husband had started legal proceedings for custody of the children on the grounds that she was not a fit mother. Her unfitness was based on a letter which she had addressed to her son Jay, in reply to his question as to what the Korean war was all about. Mrs Field had written that the United States Government was waging a war of intervention, adding 'but do not blame the American soldier. He didn't choose the war – he was sent; he doesn't even know why he is there for sure.'

In the course of tangled legal proceedings, which led back and forth from Oklahoma to California, both Mrs Field and her children were temporarily committed to prison. The children, following the first court hearing, had implored their mother to take them home – they did not even know their father! Contrary to court orders, Mrs Field finally broke down and took her children home.

A hearing in California, a few months later, confirmed the original Oklahoma ruling. Custody was awarded the father, a decree which has since been made permanent. The ruling was given on the basis that Mrs Field was an 'unfit mother' because of her critical attitude to the Korean war, her uncritical attitude to Negroes, her advocacy of peace. The children's grandparents had submitted affidavits one of which stated in part: 'Jay [the thirteen year old boy – author] spoke very critically of the laws of Oklahoma regarding the segregation of white and coloured persons . . . on one occasion he stated that some of his best friends at school were coloured boys.' Elsewhere, one of the affidavits read: 'When a 12-year old boy . . . chooses coloured boys for associates and companions it is not conducive of wholesome living . . .' The father's attorney told the judge: 'I assert to your Honour that what this lady has taught her children is traitorous. I assert that your Honour will not permit such a thing to continue in this country . . . The time has come to consider loyalty oaths as a condition for parenthood.' The Judge agreed.

Mrs Field appealed to the judge for one small favour. 'I've cared for and supported these children,' she said, 'for ten years all by myself. I've gone without food for their sake. Can I have them now alone for ten minutes?'

'I am sorry, Mrs Field,' replied the Judge. 'You had your day in court.'

From *I was American* by Ursula Wassermann 1955

'Yakety Yak'

Take out the papers and the trash,
Or you don't get no spending cash.
If you don't scrub that kitchen floor
You ain't gonna rock and roll no more.
Yakety-yak.
Don't talk back.

Just finish cleaning up your room,
Let's see the dust fly with that broom.
Get all the garbage out of sight.
Or you don't go out Friday night.
Yakety-yak.
Don't talk back.

You just put on your coat and hat,
And walk yourself to the laundromat.
And when you finish doing that,
Bring in the dog and put out the cat.
Yakety-yak.
Don't talk back.

Don't you give me no dirty looks,
Your father's hip, he knows what cooks.
Just tell your hoodlum friend outside,
You ain't got time to take a ride.
Yakety-yak.
Don't talk back.

Yakety-yak.
Yakety-yak.

Leiber and Stoller for 'The Coasters', 1958

'In the days of Ubico the tyrant . . .'

In the days of Ubico the tyrant,
end of '42, as the story goes,
there was a mason in the parish
who dared paint '*Liverty,*
Doun with the blody jenral'
on the city walls.
The mason was caught,
questioned,
– why was he so crazy
as to hate the General
if the General had complete military support
and his power was invincible.

And the mason said: Ubico will fall.
And everyone laughed. This is a crazy man,
they said. The General will rule forever
in Guatemala. Until he dies. Like God,
he is all powerful.
No one will lift a finger against him.
His power is infinite
and the people are cowardly, resigned,
afraid of his granite strength.

But the stubborn mason said: Ubico will fall.
He will not rule forever in Guatemala.
The people will rise against him.

And they shot him, in the morning,
in the barracks,
more for disbeliever than subversive,
the mason of the parish who wrote:
'*Liverty. Doun with th blody jenral*'
on the walls of the city.

Otto René Castillo, *c.* 1965

In England, everything is permitted, except what is expressly forbidden.

In the USSR, everything is forbidden, save what is expressly permitted.

In France, everything is permitted, even what is expressly forbidden.

In China, everything is forbidden, even what is expressly permitted.

'Version of Psalm 22'

My god, my god, why hast thou forsaken me?
I am but the travesty of a man
Despised of the people,

Laughed unto scorn in every daily paper.
Their armoured cars encompass me,
Their machine-gunners have set their sights on me,
Barbed wire besets me round.
From morning till evening I must answer to my name.
They have tattooed me with a number,
They have photographed me hedged about by an electric
fence.
My bones may all be told as on an x-ray screen.
They have taken my identity away from me.
They have led me naked to the gas chamber,
And they have passed my garments among them,
Yea, even down to my shoes.

I call out for morphia, but no-one hears,
I call out in the straightjacket,
Call out all night long.
In lunatic asylums
In the ward for terminal cases
In the isolation wing
In the home for the aged.

Drenched in sweat, I suffer in the psychiatric clinic
Stifle in the oxygen tent,
And weep in the police station,
In the prison yard,
In the torture chamber,
In the orphanage.

I am contaminated by radio activity,
All men shun me, lest it might smite them.
But my word shall be of thee before my brethren,
And I shall exalt thee before the congregation of our people.
My hymn shall rise up in the midst of a multitude.
There will be a banquet set before those that are poor,
And there shall be a great feast among our people,
The new people that is to be born.

Ernesto Cardenal, *c.* 1965

'Subterranean Homesick Blues'

Johnny's in the basement
Mixing up the medicine
I'm on the pavement
Thinking about the government
The man in the trench coat
Badge out, laid off
Says he's got a bad cough
Wants to get it paid off
Look out kid
It's somethin' you did
God knows when
But you're doin' it again
You better duck down the alley
way
Lookin' for a new friend
The man in the coon-skin cap
In the big pen
Wants eleven dollar bills
You only got ten

Maggie comes fleet foot
Face full of black soot
Talkin' that the heat put
Plants in the bed but
The phone's tapped anyway
Maggie says that many say
They must bust in early May
Orders from the D.A.
Look out kid
Don't matter what you did
Walk on your tip toes
Don't try 'No Doz'
Better stay away from those
That carry around a fire hose
Keep a clean nose
Watch the plain clothes
You don't need a weather man
To know which way the wind
blows

Get sick, get well
Hang around a ink well
Ring bell, hard to tell
If anything is goin' to sell
Try hard, get barred
Get back, write braille
Get jailed, jump bail
Join the army, if you fail
Look out kid
You're gonna get hit
But users, cheaters
Six-time losers
Hang around the theaters
Girl by the whirlpool
Lookin' for a new fool
Don't follow leaders
Watch the parkin' meters

Ah get born, keep warm
Short pants, romance, learn to
dance
Get dressed, get blessed
Try to be a success
Please her, please him, buy gifts
Don't steal, don't lift
Twenty years of schoolin'
And they put you on the day shift
Look out kid
They keep it all hid
Better jump down a manhole
Light yourself a candle
Don't wear sandals
Try to avoid the scandals
Don't wanna be a bum
You better chew gum
The pump don't work
'Cause the vandals took the
handles

Bob Dylan, 1965

Same Bastards in Control

What do you think the effect of the Beatles was on the history of Britain?

I don't know about the history. The people who are in control and in power and the class system and the whole bullshit bourgeois scene is exactly the same except that there is a lot of middle-class kids with long hair walking around London in trendy clothes and Kenneth Tynan's making a fortune out of the word 'fuck.' But apart from that, nothing happened except that we all dressed up. The same bastards are in control, the same people are runnin' everything, it's exactly the same. They hyped the kids and the generation.

We've grown up a little, all of us, and there has been a change and we are a bit freer and all that, but it's the same game, nothing's really changed. They're doing exactly the same things, selling arms to South Africa, killing blacks on the street, people are living in fucking poverty with rats crawling over them, it's the same. It just makes you puke. And I woke up to that, too. The dream is over. It's just the same only I'm thirty and a lot of people have got long hair, that's all.

John Lennon, 1970

'A Tourist Guide to England'

£ Welcome to England!
England is a happy country.

£ Here is a happy English businessman.
Hating his money, he spends it all
On bibles for Cambodia
And a charity to preserve
The Indian Cobra from extinction.

£ I'm sorry you can't see our happy coal-miners.
Listen hard and you can hear them
Singing Welsh hymns far underground.
Oh. The singing seems to have stopped.

£ No, that is not Saint Francis of Assisi.
That is a happy English policeman.

£ Here is a happy black man.
No, it is not illegal to be black. Not yet.

£ Here are the slums.
They are preserved as a tourist attraction.
Here is a happy slum-dweller.
Hello, slum-dweller!
No, his answer is impossible to translate.

£ Here are some happy English schoolchildren.
See John. See Susan. See Mike.
They are studying for their examinations.
Study, children, study!
John will get his O-Levels
And an O-Level job and an O-Level house and an O-Level wife.
Susan will get her A-Levels
And an A-Level job and an A-Level house and an A-Level husband.
Mike will fail.

£ Here are some happy English soldiers.
They are going to make the Irish happy.

Adrian Mitchell, *c.* 1970

'Birdbrain!'

Birdbrain runs the World!
Birdbrain is the ultimate product of Capitalism
Birdbrain chief bureaucrat of Russia, yawning
Birdbrain ran FBI 30 years appointed by F. D. Roosevelt and never chased Cosa Nostra!
Birdbrain apportions wheat to be burned, keep prices up on the world market!
Birdbrain lends money to Developing Nation police-states thru the International Monetary Fund!
Birdbrain never gets laid on his own he depends on his office to pimp for him
Birdbrain offers brain transplants in Switzerland
Birdbrain wakes up in middle of night and arranges his sheets
I am Birdbrain!

I rule Russia Yugoslavia England Poland Argentina United States El Salvador
Birdbrain multiplies in China!
Birdbrain inhabits Stalin's corpse inside the Kremlin wall
Birdbrain dictates petrochemical agriculture in Africa desert regions!
Birdbrain lowers North California's water table sucking it up for Orange County Agribusiness Banks
Birdbrain harpoons whales and chews blubber in the tropics
Birdbrain clubs baby harp seals and wears their coats to Paris
Birdbrain runs the Pentagon his brother runs the CIA, Fatass Bucks!
Birdbrain writes and edits *Time Newsweek Wall Street Journal Pravda Izvestia*
Birdbrain is Pope, Premier, President, Commissar, Chairman, Senator!
Birdbrain voted Reagan President of the United States!
Birdbrain prepares Wonder Bread with refined white flour!
Birdbrain sold slaves, sugar, tobacco, alcohol
Birdbrain conquered the New World and murdered mushroom god Xochopili on Popocatepetl!
Birdbrain was President when a thousand mysterious students were machinegunned at Tlatelulco
Birdbrain sent 20,000,000 intellectuals and Jews to Siberia, 15,000,000 never got back to the Stray Dog Café
Birdbrain wore a mustache & ran Germany on Amphetamines the last year of World War II
Birdbrain conceived the Final Solution to the Jewish Problem in Europe
Birdbrain carried it out in Gas Chambers
Birdbrain borrowed Lucky Luciano the Mafia from jail to secure Sicily for U.S. Birdbrain against the Reds
Birdbrain manufactured guns in the Holy Land and sold them to white goyim in South Africa
Birdbrain supplied helicopters to Central America generals, kill a lot of restless Indians, encourage a favorable business climate
Birdbrain began a war of terror against Israeli Jews
Birdbrain sent out Zionist planes to shoot Palestinian huts outside Beirut
Birdbrain outlawed Opiates on the world market
Birdbrain formed the Black Market in Opium
Birdbrain's father shot skag in hallways of the lower East Side
Birdbrain organized Operation Condor to spray poison fumes on the marijuana fields of Sonora

Birdbrain got sick in Harvard Square from smoking Mexican grass
Birdbrain arrived in Europe to Conquer cockroaches with Propaganda
Birdbrain became a great International Poet and went around the
world praising the Glories of Birdbrain
I declare Birdbrain to be victor in the Poetry Contest
He built the World Trade Center on New York Harbor waters
without regard where the toilets emptied –
Birdbrain began chopping down the Amazon Rainforest to build a
woodpulp factory on the river bank
Birdbrain in Iraq attacked Birdbrain in Iran
Birdbrain in Belfast throws bombs at his mother's ass
Birdbrain wrote *Das Kapital*! authored the *Bible*! penned *The Wealth of Nations*!
Birdbrain's humanity, he built the Rainbow Room on top of
Rockefeller Center so we could dance
He invented the Theory of Relativity so Rockwell Corporation could
make Neutron Bombs at Rocky Flats in Colorado
Birdbrain's going to see how long he can go without coming
Birdbrain thinks his dong will grow big that way
Birdbrain sees a new Spy in the Market Platz in Dubrovnik outside
the Eyeglass Hotel –
Birdbrain wants to suck your cock in Europe, he takes life very
seriously, brokenhearted you won't cooperate –
Birdbrain goes to heavy duty Communist Countries so he can get
KGB girlfriends while the sky thunders –
Birdbrain realized he was Buddha by meditating
Birdbrain's afraid he's going to blow up the planet so he wrote this
poem to be immortal –

Hotel Subrovka, Dubrovnik, October 14, 1980, 4:30 A.M.

Allen Ginsberg

Good Intentions

I don't drink
I don't smoke
I don't swear
ah shit, I left my fags at the pub

Oral tradition, collected from Ritchie Shipton, aged 9, 1990

Nine

OPPRESSION IS DISORDER, LIBERTY IS ORDER

Injustice

The suffering of injustice is not the part of a man, but of a slave, who indeed had better die than live; since when he is wronged and trampled upon, he is unable to help himself, or any other about whom he cares. The reason, as I conceive, is that the makers of laws are the majority who are weak; and they make laws and distribute praises and censures with a view to themselves and to their own interests; and they terrify the stronger sort of men, and those who are able to get the better of them, in order that they may not get the better of them; and they say, that dishonesty is shameful and unjust; meaning, by the word injustice, the desire of a man to have more than his neighbours; for knowing their own inferiority, I suspect that they are too glad of equality. And therefore the endeavour to have more than the many, is conventionally said to be shameful and unjust, and is called injustice, whereas nature herself intimates that it is just for the better to have more than the worse, the more powerful than the weaker; and in many ways she shows, among men as well as among animals, and indeed among whole cities and races, that justice consist in the superior ruling over and having more than the inferior.

The young Athenian Callicles' speech, from the *Gorgias* by Plato
(483–376 BCE)

Fuente Ovejuna

[The peasants of the village Fuente Ovejuna have killed Fernando, a tyrannical commander. The 'Judge' is interrogating the peasants]

[Cries within.]

FRONDOSO: I hear cries. They have put a man to the torture unless my ears deceive me. Listen and be still!

The JUDGE *speaks within and Voices are heard in response.*

JUDGE: Old man, I seek only the truth. Speak!

FRONDOSO: An old man tortured?

LAURENCIA: What barbarity!

ESTEBAN: Ease me a little.

JUDGE: Ease him. Who killed Fernando?

ESTEBAN: Fuente Ovejuna.

LAURENCIA: Good, father! Glory and praise!

FRONDOSO: Praise God he had the strength!

JUDGE: Take that boy there. Speak, you pup, for you know. Who was it? He says nothing. Put on the pressure there.
BOY: Judge, Fuente Ovejuna.
JUDGE: Now by the King, carls, I'll hang you to the last name. Who killed the Commander?
FRONDOSO: They torture the child and he replies like this?
LAURENCIA: There is courage in the village.
FRONDOSO: Courage and heart.
JUDGE: Put that woman in the chair. Give her a turn for her good.
LAURENCIA: I can't endure it.
JUDGE: Peasants, be obstinate and this instrument brings death. So prepare! Who killed the Commander?
PASCUALA: Judge, Fuente Ovejuna.
JUDGE: Have no mercy.
FRONDOSO: I cannot think, my mind is blank!
LAURENCIA: Frondoso, Pascuala will not tell them.
FRONDOSO: The very children hold their peace!
JUDGE: They thrive upon it. – More! More!
PASCUALA: Oh, God in heaven!
JUDGE: Again, and answer me! Is she deaf?
PASCUALA: I say Fuente Ovejuna.
JUDGE: Seize that plump lad, half undressed already.
LAURENCIA: It must be Mengo! Poor Mengo!
FRONDOSO: He can never hold out.
MENGO: Oh, oh, oh!
JUDGE: Let him have it.
MENGO: Oh!
JUDGE: Prod his memory.
MENGO: Oh, oh!
JUDGE: Who slew the Commander, slave?
MENGO: Oh, oh! I can't get it out! I'll tell you –
JUDGE: Loosen that hand.
FRONDOSO: We are lost!
JUDGE: Let him have it on the back!
MENGO: No, for I'll give up everything!
JUDGE: Who killed him?
MENGO: Judge, Fuente Ovejuna.
JUDGE: Have these rogues no nerves that they can laugh at pain? The most likely, too, lie by instinct. I will no more today. To the street!
FRONDOSO: Now God bless Mengo! I was afraid, transfixed, but that lad is a cure for fear.

BARRILDO *and the* REGIDOR *enter with* MENGO.

BARRILDO: Good, Mengo, good!
REGIDOR: You have delivered us.
BARRILDO: Mengo, bravo!
FRONDOSO: We cheer you.
MENGO: Oh, oh! Not much.
BARRILDO: Drink, my friend, and eat. Come, come!
MENGO: Oh, oh! What have you got?
BARRILDO: Sweet lemon peel.
MENGO: Oh, oh!
FRONDOSO: Drink, drink. Take this.
BARRILDO: He does, too.
FRONDOSO: He takes it well. Down it goes.
LAURENCIA: Give him another bite.
MENGO: Oh, oh!
BARRILDO: Drink this for me.
LAURENCIA: Swallowed without a smile.
FRONDOSO: A sound answer deserves a round drink.
REGIDOR: Another, son?
MENGO: Oh, oh! Yes, yes!
FRONDOSO: Drink, for you deserve it.
LAURENCIA: He collects for every pang.
FRONDOSO: Throw a coat around him or he will freeze.
BARRILDO: Have you had enough?
MENGO: No, three more. Oh, oh!
FRONDOSO: He is asking for the wine.
BARRILDO: Yes, let him drink as much as he likes for one good turn begets another. What's the matter now?
MENGO: It leaves a taste in my mouth. Oh, I'm catching cold!
FRONDOSO: Another drink will help. Who killed the Commander?
MENGO: Fuente Ovejuna.

Exeunt the REGIDOR MENGO *and* BARRILDO

FRONDOSO: He has earned more than they give him. Ah, love, as you are mine confess to me. Who killed the Commander?
LAURENCIA: Love, Fuente Ovejuna.
FRONDOSO: Who?
LAURENCIA: Don't you think you can torture me. Fuente Ovejuna.
FRONDOSO: It did? How did I get you, then?
LAURENCIA: Love, I got you.

[Exeunt].

From *Fuente Ovejuna* by Lope De Vega, *c.* 1600

Thief Justice

LEAR: What! art mad? A man may see how this world goes with no eyes.
Look with thine ears: see how yond justice rails upon yond simple thief.
Hark, in thine ear: change places, and, handy-dandy, which is the justice,
which is the thief? Thou hast seen a farmer's dog bark at a beggar?
GLOUCESTER: Ay, Sir.
LEAR: And the creature run from the cur? There thou might'st behold
The great image of Authority:
A dog's obey'd in office.
Thou rascal beadle, hold thy bloody hand!
Why dost thou lash that whore? Strip thine own back;
Thou hotly lusts to use her in that kind
For which thou whipp'st her. The usurer hangs the cozener.
Thorough tatter'd clothes small vices do appear;
Robes and furr'd gowns hide all. Plate sin with gold,
And the strong lance of justice hurtless breaks;
Arm it in rags, a pigmy's straw does pierce it.
None does offend, none, I say, none; I'll able 'em:
Take that of me, my friend, who have the power
To seal th' accuser's lips. Get thee glass eyes;
And, like a scurvy politician, seem
To see the things thou dost not. Now, now, now, now;
Pull off my boots; harder, harder; so.
EDGAR [*Aside*]: O! matter and impertinency mix'd; Reason in madness.

From *King Lear* by William Shakespeare, 1604

'How Eulespiegle bit the Tavern-Man at Lubec of his Wine, and how Eulespiegle had like to have been hang'd'

Eulespiegle kept from doing any of his Pranks a good while after he came to *Lubec*, for Justice was very severe in that Place. However it being what he could not live without, there came a Thought into his Head how to cheat the Vintner or *Taverner*, as they call them in that Country.

Now this same *Taverner* was very proud and conceited of his Parts, and used to say, that no Man living could bite him. However *Eulespiegle* had a mind to try, upon which he takes two Pots exactly alike, one full of Water, the other empty; that which was full he carried under his Cloak and went into the Vault for a Pot of Wine, which when it was filled he puts in under his Cloak, and set the other full of Water down upon the Barrel so dextrously that the Taverner could not perceive it.

Well, says he, what does the Wine come to? Ten Pence, said the Taverner. It is too dear then for me, says *Eulespiegle*, for I have no more than Eight Pence. At which the Taverner growing angry, if you will not have it, says he, leave it, I do not sell it under. I did not know it indeed Sir, says *Eulespiegle*, but i'faith I have no more than that Eight pence if it were to save my Soul. At this the Taverner began to curse and swear, and taking up the Pot emptied it into the Barrel. Thou art a senseless Booby and a downright Fool, says he, to make me draw my Wine and have no Money to pay for it. By *Jingo*, says *Eulespiegle* taking up the Pot, and I think you are a Fool, for no one is so wise but may sometimes be cheated by a Fool, as you are now Taverner, and saying this went his Way. The Taverner reflecting upon these Words called a Constable that lived next Door and seized him, where they found the Pot of Wine under his Cloak, for which the Taverner charging him as a Thief the Constable committed him to Prison.

A few Days afterwards he was brought to his Tryal, where some said he deserved to be hang'd, others excused him, and said, it was only an innocent Trick put upon the Taverner, who fancied himself so wise that no one could cheat him; in short, some said one thing, some another, as in like Cases, but it appearing to the Court to be a Robbery, *Eulespiegle* was condemned to be hang'd.

When Execution Day came, all *Lubec* was in an Uproar, Horsemen and Footmen came far and near to see the End of this remarkable Person; some believed he understood *Necromancy*, and would by that means get out of their Clutches; but almost every Body wished he might escape the Gallows. All the while they were carrying him to the Tree, *Eulespiegle* did not speak a Syllable, so that the People said that he was more dead than alive. But when he was upon the Ladder he desired to speak to the Lords of *Lubec*, humbly entreating them that they would grant him one Request, that he would not ask of them his Life, nor Gold nor Silver, but only one little Matter which would be no Detriment to them to grant, and that every one of the Counsellors might do it without costing one Farthing.

The Lords of *Lubec* retired to consult what was to be done, but they came to a speedy Resolution to grant him his Desire. Every Body longed to know what this could be, he having excepted so many things. When the Lords told him they would comply with his Demand with the Exceptions he made. I desire no other, said *Eulespiegle*, only give me your Hands in Token of Sincerity, and your Word and Honour you will do it, which they did accordingly.

Why then, says *Eulespiegle*, I desire all the Lords, Judges, and Counsellors, for three Days after I am dead, to come in the Morning, the Provost first, and the rest of their Order, and kiss my Arse three times before Breakfast. At this they scratched their Heads, (the People laughing all the while) and said it was not a fair Request. No matter for that, says *Eulespiegle*, I hold the Lords and Counsellors of *Lubec* for such honest People that they will keep their Words, which on second Thoughts they did after the old ancient Manner, for they acquitted *Eulespiegle*, who presently went out of their Territories, for he had his Bellyful of *Lubec*.

From *The German Rogue, or the Life and Merry Adventures, Cheats, Strategems and Contrivances of Tiel Eulespiegle*, Anon., 1720 (from the Low German original by Thomas Murner, 1519)

Pray for Me

1. Yesterday the sessions began at the Old Bailey, where several persons were brought to the bar for the highway, etc. Among them were the highwaymen lately taken at Westminster, two of whom, namely, Thomas Green, *alias* Phillips, and Thomas Spigot, refused to plead . . . The former, on sight of the terrible machine, desired to be carried back to the sessions house, where he pleaded not guilty. But the other, who behaved himself very insolently to the ordinary who was ordered to attend him, seemingly resolved to undergo the torture. Accordingly, when they brought cords, as usual, to tie him, he broke them three several times like a twine-thread, and told them if they brought cables he would serve them after the same manner. But, however, they found means to tie him to the ground, having his limbs extended . . .

2. The chaplain found him lying in the vault upon the bare ground, with 350 pounds weight upon his breast, and then prayed with him, and at several times asked him why he should hazard his soul by such obstinate kind of self-murder. But all the answer that he made was, 'Pray for me; pray for me.' He sometimes lay silent under the pressure as if insensible to the pain, and then again would fetch his breath very quick and short. Several times he complained that they had laid a cruel weight upon his face, though it was covered with nothing but a thin cloth, which was afterwards removed and laid more light and hollow; yet he still complained of the prodigious weight upon his face, which might be caused by the blood being forced up thither and pressing the veins so violently as if the force had been externally on his face. When he had remained for half-an-hour under this load, and fifty pounds weight more laid on, being in all four hundred, he told those

who attended him he would plead. The weights were at once taken off, the cords cut asunder; he was raised up by two men, some brandy put into his mouth to revive him, and he was carried to take his trial.

First report: Nottingham Mercury, 19 January 1721; second report: *Annals of Newgate* by the Rev Mr Willette, 1776

A Hymn to the Pillory

After his arrest on 20 May 1703, on the Earl of Nottingham's warrant, for publishing *The Shortest Way with Dissenters* (see p. 233), Defoe was released on bail. He rejected the advice of friends to break bail; he returned to Newgate and was sentenced to a fine of 200 marks, to find sureties of good behaviour for seven years, and to stand three times in the pillory. Nottingham deferred the pillorying in the hope of extracting evidence against leading Whigs, but Defoe refused to 'sell his Friends'; he was put in the pillory on 29, 30 and 31 July. As he stood in the '*State-Trap* of the Law' the *Hymn* was being sold among the onlookers.

Justice is Inverted when
Those Engines of the Law,
Instead of pinching Vicious Men,
Keep Honest ones in awe;
Thy Business is, as all Men know,
To Punish Villains, not to make Men so.

When ever then thou art prepar'd,
To prompt that Vice thou should'st Reward,
And by the Terrors of thy Grisly Face,
Make Men turn Rogues to shun Disgrace;
The End of thy Creation is destroy'd,
Justice expires of Course, and Law's made void . . .

Tell us who 'tis upon thy Ridge stands there,
So full of Fault, and yet so void of Fear;
And from the Paper in his Hat,
Let all Mankind be told for what:
Tell them it was because he was too bold,
And told those Truths, which shou'd not ha' been told.
Extoll the Justice of the Land,

Who Punish what they will not understand.
Tell them he stands Exalted there,
For speaking what we wou'd not hear;
And yet he might ha' been secure,
Had he said less, or woud' he ha' said more.
Tell them that this is his Reward,
And worse is yet for him prepar'd,
Because his Foolish Vertue was so nice
As not to sell his Friends, according to his Friends Advice;

And thus he's an Example made,
To make Men of their Honesty afraid,
That for the time to come they may.
More willingly their Friends betray;
Tell 'em the Men that plac'd him here,
Are Friends unto the Times,
But at a loss to find his Guile,
They can't commit his Crimes.

From *A Hymn to the Pillory* by Daniel Defoe, 1703

Action Against the Death Sentence

About the year 1817 or 1818, there were one-pound Bank of England notes in circulation, and unfortunately there were forged one-pound bank notes in circulation also; and the punishment for passing these forged notes was in some cases transportation for life, and in others DEATH.

At that time, I resided in Dorset Street, Salisbury Square, Fleet Street, and had occasion to go early one morning to a house near the Bank of England; and in returning home between eight or nine o'clock, down Ludgate Hill, and seeing a number of persons looking up the Old Bailey, I looked that way myself, and saw several human beings hanging on the gibbet, opposite Newgate prison, and, to my horror, two of them were women; and upon enquiring what the women had been hung for, was informed that it was for passing forged one-pound notes. The fact that a poor woman could be put to death for such a minor offence had a great effect upon me, and I at once determined, if possible, to put a stop to this shocking destruction of life for merely obtaining a few shillings by fraud; and well knowing the habits of the low class of society in London, I felt quite sure that in very many cases the rascals who had forged the notes induced these poor ignorant women to go into the gin-shops to 'get something to drink,' and thus *pass* the notes, and hand them the change.

My residence was a short distance from Ludgate Hill (Dorset Street); and after witnessing the tragic scene, I went home, and in ten minutes designed and made a sketch of this '*Bank-note not to be imitated.*' About half-an-hour after this was done, William Hone came into my room, and saw the sketch lying on my table; he was much struck with it, and said, 'What are you going to do with this, George?'

'To publish it,' I replied. Then he said. 'Will you let me have it?' To his request I consented, made an etching of it, and it was published. Mr Hone then resided on Ludgate Hill, not many yards from the spot where I had seen the people hanging on the gibbet; and when it appeared in his shop windows, it caused a great sensation, and the people gathered round his house in such numbers that the Lord Mayor had to send the City police (of that day) to disperse the CROWD. The Bank directors held a meeting immediately upon the subject, and AFTER THAT they issued *no more* one-pound notes, and so there was *no more hanging for passing* FORGED *one-pound notes*; not only that, but ultimately no hanging even for forgery. AFTER THIS Sir Robert Peel got a Bill passed in Parliament for the 'Resumption of cash payments.' AFTER THIS he revised the Penal Code, and AFTER THAT *there was not any more hanging or punishment of* DEATH *for minor offences* . . . I consider it the most important design and etching that I ever made in my life; for it has saved the life of thousands of my fellow-creatures; and for having been able to do this Christian act, I am indeed most sincerely thankful.

George Cruikshank, 1818

A Most Worthy Magistrate!

Power in the Hands
of a TYRANT.

Who fined his Tenant renting
£1500. *per Annum*, 13l. 13s.
6d for shooting a Moorhen?

Who was it? why Corfe Castle
BANKS!!
A most worthy Magistrate!!!

Poster at Wareham, 1830

The Trial of the Tolpuddle Martyrs

The greater part of the evidence against us, on our trial, was put into the mouths of the witnesses by the judge; and when he evidently wished them to say any particular thing, and the witness would say 'I cannot remember,' he would say, 'Now think; I will give you another minute to consider;' and he would then repeat over the words, and ask, 'Cannot you remember?' Sometimes, by charging them to be careful what they said, by way of intimidation, they would merely answer, 'yes;' and the judge would set the words down as proceeding from the witness. I shall not soon forget his address to the jury, in summing up the evidence: among other things, he told them, that if such Societies were allowed to exist, it would ruin masters, cause a stagnation in trade, destroy property, – and if *they should not find us guilty, he was certain they would forfeit the opinion of the grand jury*. I thought to myself, there is no danger but we shall be found guilty, as we have a special jury for the purpose, selected from among those who are most unfriendly towards us – the grand jury, landowners, the petty jury, land-renters. Under such a charge, from such a quarter, self-interest alone would induce them to say, 'Guilty.'

George Loveless, 1834

A fool can only think that nations desire disorder.
No, oppression is disorder, liberty is order.
Slaves are turbulent, freemen love peace.

Kossuth

'The Judges Are Going to Jail'

Hurrah for the masses,
The lawyers are asses,
  Their gammon and spinach is stale!
The law is illegal
The Commons are regal,
  And the Judges are going to jail.
    Hurrah for the masses!

The lawyers are asses
The Judges are going to jail.

Lord Dennan's been prigging,
So he'll have a wigging,
And be hung like his wig, on a nail;
What a time to get fogles,
Chains, purses and ogles,
Now the Judges are going to jail.
Hurrah for the masses!
We'll cut off the gasses,
To bother the Judges in jail.

Little Johnny gives orders,
All beaks and recorders,
The stairs without landing to scale,
While we, down at Wapping,
Are drinking hot-stopping,
To the health of the Judges in jail.
Hurrah for the masses!
We'll kiss all the lasses
To the tune of the Judges in jail.

And when soundly rated,
Their goods confiscated,
We'll *jist* keep an eye on the sale;
For the times *are* a mending,
When 'stead of *sending*,
The Judges are *going* to jail.
Hurrah for the masses!
We'll fill our carcasses
With the prog of the Judges in jail.

For old Hatton-garden,
We don't care a farden,
The policemen look seedy and pale:
The chop-and-change Harvey,
Who plated the jarvey,
Shall follow the Judges to jail.
Hurrah for the masses!
We'll rob all that passes,
As a sell for the Judges in jail.

They jaw'd us so cruel,
And fixed us to gruel,
And sent us to grin through the rail;
But, by Goles, now we've broke 'em
They'll sit picking oakum –
Hurrah for the Judges in jail!
Hurrah for the masses!
We'll eat sparrow-grasses,
While the Judges get porridge in jail.

Come feather the nests
Of the Court of Requests,
Which we'll hold in the streets without fail,
And if any besieges,
Our just privileges,
He shall go with the Judges to jail.
Hurrah for the masses!
There are no upper classes.
So reckon the Judges in jail.

We are true British cracksmen,
And know how to tax men,
And we won't be nobody's tail;
But we'll each use a halbert
For the Queen and Prince Albert,
Who have sent them old Judges to jail.

GRAND CHORUS

Hurrah for the masses!
The lawyers are asses,
We'll cut off the gasses,
And shiver the glasses,
And eat sparrow-grasses,
And fill our carcasses,
And kiss all the lasses,
And rob all that passes –
There are no upper classes,
The Judges are going to jail!

Anon., *c.* 1860

A man imprisoned within in a Latin American dictatorship is asked how long is his sentence.
'Twenty years.'
'What did you do?'
'Nothing.'
'That cannot be.'
'Why?'
'Because for nothing you get only ten years.'

My Living Tomb

In 1860 the Reverend Theophilus Packard committed his wife, Elizabeth, to the Illinois State Asylum at Jacksonville. She insisted that she was locked up 'for simply expressing religious opinions in a community who were unprepared to appreciate and understand them,' but according to the Illinois commitment law of 1851, married women could be held in an asylum indefinitely, solely on the authority of their husbands with the concurrence of the asylum superintendent.

Though she was usually denied writing materials Packard kept a journal, hiding the pages behind her mirror, in false liners of her hatbox and satchel, and inside her bonnet. Released in 1863, after three years' confinement, she lobbied to change state commitment laws and in 1867 persuaded the Illinois legislature to pass into law a 'personal liberty bill' requiring trial by jury before a person could be committed.

And now the fatal hour had come that I must be transported into my living tomb. But the better to shield himself in this nefarious work, Mr Packard tried to avail himself of the law for commitment in other cases, which is to secure the certificate of two physicians that the candidate for the Asylum is insane. Therefore at this late hour I passed an examination made by our two doctors, both members of his church and our bible class, and opponents to me in argument, wherein they decided that I was insane, by simply feeling my pulse! . . .

My husband then informed me that the 'forms of law' were now all complied with, and he now wished me to dress for a ride to Jacksonville Insane Asylum. I complied, but at the same time entered my protest against being imprisoned without a trial, or some chance at self-defence. I made no physical resistance however, when he ordered two of his church-members to take me up in their arms, and carry me to the wagon and thence to the cars, in spite of my lady-like protests, and regardless of all my entreaties for some sort of trial before commitment.

My husband replied, 'I am doing as the laws of Illinois allow me to do – you have no protector in law but myself, and I am protecting you now! it is for your good I am doing this, I want to save your soul – you don't believe in total depravity, and I want to make you right.'

'Husband, have I not a right to my opinions?'

'Yes, you have a right to your opinions, if you think right.'

'But does not the constitution defend the right of religious toleration to all American citizens?'

'Yes, to all citizens it does defend this right, but you are not a citizen; while a married woman you are a legal nonentity, without even a soul in law. In short, you are dead as to any legal existence while a married woman, and therefore have no legal protection as a married woman.' Thus I learned my first lesson in that chapter of common law, which denies to married woman a legal right to her own identity or individuality.

From *The Prisoner's Hidden Life, or Insane Asylums Unveiled* by Elizabeth Parsons Ware Packard, 1868

Some English Prisons

Millbank for thick shins and graft at the pump;
Broadmoor for all laggs as go off their chump;
Brixton for good toke and cocoa with fat;
Dartmoor for bad grub but plenty of chat;
Portsmouth a blooming bad place for hard work;
Chatham on Sunday give four ounce of pork;
Portland is worst of the lot for to joke in –
For fetching a lagging there's no place like *Woking*.

Anon., 1885, scratched with a nail on to the bottom of a dinner-can at Millbank prison

GUY FAWKES – THE ONLY MAN TO EVER ENTER PARLIAMENT WITH HONEST INTENTIONS

Graffito

Defiance at the Wicklow Gallows

At Wicklow, in the year 1738, a man named George Manley was hanged for murder, and just before his execution he delivered an address to the crowd, as follows: 'My friends, you assemble to see – what? A man leap into the abyss of death! Look, and you will see me go with as much courage as Curtius, when he leapt into the gulf to save his country from destruction. What will you see of me? You say that no man, without virtue can be courageous! You see what I am – I'm a little fellow. What is the difference between running into a poor man's debt, and by the power of gold, or any other privilege, prevent him from obtaining his right, and clapping a pistol to a man's breast, and taking from him his purse? Yet the one shall thereby obtain a coach, and honours, and titles; the other, what? – a cart and a rope. Don't imagine from all this that I am hardened. I acknowledge the just judgment of God has overtaken me. My Redeemer knows that murder was far from my heart, and what I did was through rage and passion, being provoked by the deceased. Take warning, my comrades; think what would I now give that I had lived another life. Courageous? You'll say I've killed a man. Marlborough killed his thousands, and Alexander his millions. Marlborough and Alexander, and many others, who have done the like, are famous in history for great men. Aye – that's the case – one solitary man. I'm a little murderer, and must be hanged. Marlborough and Alexander plundered countries; they were great men. I ran in debt with the ale-wife. I must be hanged. How many men were lost in Italy, and upon the Rhine, during the last war for settling a king in Poland. Both sides could not be in the right! They are great men; but I killed a solitary man.'

From 'Old Time Punishments' by William Andrews, 1890

Letter from Breslau Prison

. . . Ach, Sonitschka! I have experienced an acute pain here. In the yard where I walk, military wagons often arrive, packed full with sacks, or old uniforms and shirts often spotted with blood . . . They are unloaded here, passed out in the cells, mended, then reloaded, and delivered to the military. The other day, such a wagon came drawn by water buffaloes rather than horses. This was the first time that I saw these animals up close. They are built sturdier and broader than our oxen, with flat heads, their horns bent flat, their skulls rather resembling the skulls of our own sheep; the buffaloes are completely black with large soft eyes. They come from Rumania, they are trophies of war . . . The soldiers who drive the wagon say that it was a very hard job to catch these wild animals and even more difficult to use them, who were so used to freedom, as beasts of burden. They were beaten frightfully to the point where the words apply to them: 'Woe to the defeated.' . . . About a hundred of these animals are said to be in Breslau alone. Moreover, used to the luxuriant pastures of Rumania, they receive miserable and scant fodder. They are mercilessly exploited in dragging all kinds of loads, and so they perish rapidly.

Anyway, a few days ago, a wagon loaded with sacks drove into the prison. The cargo was piled up so high that the buffaloes could not make it over the threshold of the gateway. The attending soldier, a brutal character, began to beat away at the animals with the heavy end of his whip so savagely that the overseer indignantly called him to account 'Don't you have any pity for the animals?' 'No one has any pity for us people either!' he answered with an evil laugh, and fell upon them ever more forcefully . . . Finally, the animals started up and got over the hump, but one of them was bleeding . . . Sonitschka, buffalo hide is proverbial for its thickness and toughness, and it was lacerated. Then, during the unloading, the animal stood completely still, exhausted, and one, the one that was bleeding, all the while looked ahead with an expression on its black face and in its soft black eyes like that of a weeping child. It was exactly the expression of a child who has been severely punished and who does not know why, what for, who does not know how to escape the torment and brutality . . . I stood facing the animal and it looked at me; tears were running from my eyes – they were *his* tears. One cannot quiver any more painfully over one's dearest brother's sorrow than I quivered in my impotence over this silent anguish.

How far, how irretrievably lost, are the free, succulent, green pastures of Rumania! How different it was with the sun shining, the wind blowing; how different were the beautiful sounds of birds, the melodious calls of the shepherds. And here: this strange weird city, the fusty stable, the nauseating mouldy hay mixed with putrid straw, the strange, horrible people – and the blows, the blood running from the fresh wound . . . Oh! My poor buffalo! My poor beloved brother! We both stand here so powerless and spiritless and are united only in pain, in powerlessness and in longing. . . .

Meanwhile, the prisoners bustled busily about the wagon, unloading the heavy sacks and carrying them into the building. The soldier, however stuck both hands into his pockets, strolled across the yard with great strides, smiled and softly whistled a popular song. And the whole glorious war passed in front of my eyes . . . Write quickly. I embrace you, Sonitschka.

Your Rosa

Sonitschka, dearest, in spite of it all, be calm and cheerful. That's life, and that's how one must take it: courageously, intrepidly and smilingly – in spite of it all.

From a letter by Rosa Luxemburg to Sonja Liebknecht, 1917

'The County Jail'

The jail was built by workers for their friends
Who, sickened by the thought of work in shops,
Might take to jobs annoying to the cops.
Brick-layers built the stairway that descends
To dungeons, built the doorway that portends
Of bugs or floggings. Hunkies, Yankees, Wops,
Whose widows someday will be pushing mops,
May see their own sons here before life ends.

So old among us here this jail has grown
That even now there in the cells, in gray,
May be a man whose father built with stone
The high walls; one whose father hauled clay
For those dark bricks that close him in; or one
Whose father wired the gong that marks his day.

Stanley Boone, *c.* 1920

The Bey of Algiers proceeds against his 'disaffected' by chopping off their heads, and our ministers proceed against their 'disaffected' by shutting them up in prison during their pleasure, in any jail in the kingdom, and deprived of light, warmth, and all communication with relations and friends, if they please. That is all the difference.

William Cobbett

Poplar Council

My dear Boys and Girls,

We have received your kind and most welcome letters and thank you all for so kindly thinking of us, we are all as pleased with your remembrance as with the remembrance of our best friends.

We are very glad you all understand why we are here, we have not done anything we are ashamed of, our action was against bad wicked laws and all good men and women should protest and refuse to obey laws which are unjust and bad.

John Hampden who your teachers have told you about refused to pay unjust taxes and commenced a revolution which took off the head of King Charles. George Washington and his friends would not pay taxes which they considered wrong and this resulted in the establishment of the great Republic in America.

Quakers and other Dissenters that is Christians who do not belong to the Church of England refused to pay rates in support of the Church and so the law asking them to do so was abolished.

We are in prison because our people in Poplar are poor and cannot pay the rates and taxes and we shall not do what the Judges told us we must do until Poplar gets money from the rich to help the poor.

We want you to grow up strong active loving men and women we want you never to be contented while there is one single man or woman starving. Do not believe anybody who tells you that God made the rich and also made large numbers of people poor. God and Nature made men and women. It is the selfishness and greed of people that makes poverty.

When you leave school join a Trade Union, do not rush into Army or Navy, none of you need do so unless you like even if you are in the Band, the girls are not obliged to go to domestic service either they can choose other trades and occupations, though often service is best at the moment.

When you have joined your Trade Union go to the branch meetings, learn all you can about the Labour Movement, when you have done this you will soon understand that working people, whether they work in an office, a school, in a mine or on a railway, in a factory or on a ship, that all of them together create all the wealth of the world.

Labour is the only source of all wealth whether it is labour by hand or brain, it is the workers who should enjoy leisure, pleasure, holidays and all the good things of life as you grow up keep steadily in your minds the fact that everybody rich or poor that gets something without themselves working, get it at the expense of those who do work. We hope all you boys and girls will live to see the day when there will be no rich or poor paupers and no millionaires, because you and your fellow men and women will join together to work for each other and by so doing make possible the establishment of Christ's Kingdom on earth which is what you pray for when you say 'Thy Kingdom Come' in your prayers night and morning. We have asked that this letter shall be read in each standard and all of you who are 10 years of age and over shall have a copy.

Here's our love and lots and lots of good wishes from
Yours truly,

S. March, Mayor of Poplar
Henry W. Sloman
W. H. Green
R. J. Hopgood
D. M. Adams
Edgar Lansbury
A. Baker
J. A. Jones
T. E. Kelly
J. J. Heales
Geo. J. Cressall
J. H. Banks
E. E. Williams
B. Fleming
A. Partridge
J. Russell
T. J. Goodway
Wm. Farr
C. Petherick
Minnie Lansbury
C. E. Sumner
J. E. Oakes
George Lansbury
John Scurr
Joseph T. O'Callaghan
J. J. Rugless
Susan Lawrence
Jennie MacKay
Julia Scurr

Poplar Council's letter from Brixton Prison, 25 September 1921; they were imprisoned for refusing to levy the rates

Get Him Out

Scott – will you and Zelda please sit down and write two mild little notes asking clemency. If that kid ought to be in jail we ought all to be there – Yrs Dos

[*what follows is a typed letter Dos sent to numerous friends*]

At the instigation of a certain George L. Darte, professional patriot linked up with various redbaiting organizations, the Daily Worker was prosecuted last summer for publishing a poem supposed to be obscene by David Gordon, a boy of eighteen, at present holding a scholarship of the Zona Gale Foundation at the University of Wisconsin. Gordon and the Daily Worker were found guilty of violating section 1141 of the Penal Law. David Gordon was sentenced to an indeterminate term at the City Reformatory. That means a possible term of three years. By the accident of being subject to the New York City parole law it was made possible to punish this boy to an extent far beyond the provisions of the penal law. Section 1141 sets a maximum penalty of one year but the Parole Law applicable to New York City alone authorizes the Commission to keep Gordon in jail as much as three years. Three years of the company of young criminals of every description, of beating by prison guards, a grim substitute for the college education he had earned by his obvious precocious talent as a writer. He is at present serving his term at the Reformatory. If you read the enclosed excerpts from the remarks of the judges you will understand the atmosphere of meanness and spite that surrounded the trial. The boy's real crime was that he was writing for a communist publication and that he was a Russian Jew. If this is the penalty for obscenity and disgust with America, most of our best writers should be in jail at this moment.

The important thing now is not to complain about fair play or freedom of speech, but to get him out. The length of the sentence is up to the Parole Board. A letter from you to the Parole Board, Municipal Building, New York City, will probably have considerable weight. Please write at once. Naturally a plea on the ground of the boy's youth will carry more with the Parole Board than abstract complaints about the obvious infringement on human rights involved in this case. The courts are always right. Even if you think it is a bad poem you must realize that the penalty is grotesquely disproportionate. Mr. Darte and his friends will do their best to keep Gordon in jail. They must be shown that there are enough men and women in New York with a sense of humanity and fair play to outweigh them.

Please send a copy of any letter you write to Gordon's attorney, Joseph R. Brodsky, 41 Union Square, New York City.

A letter from John Dos Passos to F. Scott Fitzgerald, April 9 1928

'Ballad of the Landlord'

Landlord, landlord,
My roof has sprung a leak
Don't you 'member I told you about it
Way last week?

Landlord, landlord,
These steps is broken down.
When you come up yourself
It's a wonder you don't fall down.

Ten Bucks you say I owe you?
Ten Bucks you say is due?
Well, that's Ten Bucks more'n I'll pay you
Till you fix this house up new.

What? You gonna get eviction orders?
You gonna cut off my heat?
You gonna take my furniture and
Throw it in the street?

Um-huh! You talking high and mighty.
Talk on – till you get through.
You ain't gonna be able to say a word
If I land my fist on you.

Police! Police!
Come and get this man!
He's trying to ruin the government
And overturn the land!

Copper's whistle!
Patrol bell!
Arrest.
Precinct Station.
Iron cell.
Headlines in press:

MAN THREATENS LANDLORD

TENANT HELD NO BAIL

JUDGE GIVES NEGRO 90 DAYS IN COUNTY JAIL

Langston Hughes, *c.* 1940

The law in its majestic equality forbids the rich as well as the poor to sleep under bridges, to beg in the streets and to steal bread.

Anatole France

Obscenity Bust

I want to read this, cause I like it. This is an arrest report. An employee's report, that's what they call it.

Subject: Obscene show.
Sir:
On the above date and time I attended a Lenny Bruce show at the above location, in the company of police-woman Corlene Schnell, 100643 –
in case you ever should see her –
During the half-hour show Bruce used the following words on several occasions:

bullshit
shit
motherfucker
penis
asshole.

These words were clearly understood by both police-woman Schnell and myself. The substance of Bruce's dissertation was primarily based on denouncing religions, God and the police in general, in that order.
Sir:
At the above time and date I attended the entire show of Lenny Bruce with policewoman Schnell. During this show the following words were used repetitively:

> shit
> bullshit
> motherfucker
> fuck
> asshole.

> He had stories regarding unnatural acts with animals, including the Lone Ranger and Tonto, and his horse. The substance of Bruce's shows was a degrading dissertation on the subject of the Jewish religion, God, and the acts of the courts of the United States.

O.K. There's one really great thing in here. Oh yeah.

> Since this time six teams of officers in this division have viewed the Bruce show, and have submitted 15.7 reports. Some of the other obscene words used by Lenny Bruce are as follows:

> bullshit
> ass
> asshole
> tits
> penis
> pricks
> cocks
> cunts.

> He also referred to comic-book characters as dikes and fags.

Now the thing I like about this is that – now this is the last report – and the last report, I can tell that the guy started to listen to me work, cause he says:

> Bruce's show in general made fun of his past experiences with law enforcement and the courts. He also makes fun of all religions and many people that are currently in the news. On October 23, 1962, at approximately 10 P.M., Sgt. Klein and Detectives Frawley and Shire attended location of suspect's act. Suspect's act primarily centered around sexual activities of various sorts. In one anecdote the suspect described an individual as a, uh, c-o-...

Alright.

> a term used to indicate the act of oral copulation

Boy it's weird how he heard just that.

> Various descriptive words such as 'bastard' 'asshole' 'goddamn' were interjected at various times during the performance.

Lenny Bruce, *c.* 1961

'Identity Card'

Write down:
I am an Arab
my I.D. number, 50,000
my children, eight
and the ninth due next summer
– Does that anger you?

Write down:
Arab.
I work with my struggling friends in a quarry
and my children are eight.
I chip a loaf of bread for them,
clothes and notebooks
from the rocks.
I will not beg for a handout at your door
nor humble myself
on your threshold
– Does that anger you?

Write down:
Arab,
a name with no friendly diminutive.
A patient man, in a country
brimming with anger.
My roots have gripped this soil
since time began,
before the opening of ages
before the cypress and the olive,
before the grasses flourished.
My father came from a line of plowmen,
and my grandfather was a peasant
who taught me about the sun's glory
before teaching me to read.
My home is a watchman's shack
made of reeds and sticks
– Does my condition anger you?

There is no gentle name,
write down:
Arab.
The colour of my hair, jet black –
eyes, brown –
trademarks,
a headband over a *keffiyeh*
and a hand whose touch grates
rough as rock.
My address is a weaponless village
with nameless streets.
All its men are in the field and quarry
– Does that anger you?

Write down:
Arab.
You have stolen my ancestors' vineyards
and the land I once ploughed
with my children,
leaving my grandchildren
nothing but rocks.
Will your government
take those too, as the rumour goes?

Write down, then
at the top of Page One:
I do not hate
and do not steal
but starve me, and I will eat
my assailant's flesh.
Beware of my hunger
and of my anger.

Mahmood Darwish, 1964

If Voting Changed Anything, They'd Abolish It

Anon.

'Take a Cop to Dinner'

Take a Cop to Dinner Cop a Dinner to Take a Cop Dinner Cop a Take

Mr. Answer Man
what is
a weapon
worse
ten times
worse,
than the
Hydrogen
Bomb?

Why a cunt
which is
ten times
larger
than the largest
cock
extant,
Mickey.

Degoutante,
said Mickey
kissing cops.
to hedge the bet.

Take a cop to dinner.

Racketeers take cops to dinner with payoffs.

Pimps take cops to dinner with free tricks.

Dealers take cops to dinner with free highs.

Business takes cops to dinner with graft.

Unions and Corporations take cops to dinner with post-retirement jobs.

Schools and Professional Clubs take cops to dinner with free tickets to athletic events and social affairs.

The Catholic Church takes cops to dinner by exempting them from religious duties.

The Justice Department takes cops to dinner with laws giving them the right to do almost anything.

The Defense Department takes cops to dinner by releasing them from all military obligations.

Establishment newspapers take cops to dinner by propagating the image of the friendly, uncorrupt, neighborhood policeman.

Places of entertainment take cops to dinner with free booze and admission to shows.

Merchants take cops to dinner with discounts and gifts.

Neighborhood Committees and Social Organizations take cops to dinner with free discussions offering discriminating insights into hipsterism, black militancy and the drug culture.

Cops take cops to dinner by granting each other immunity to prosecution for misdemeanors and anything else they can get away with.

Cops take themselves to dinner by inciting riots.

And so, if you own anything or you don't take a cop to dinner this week and feed his power to judge, prosecute and brutalize the streets of your city.
n.b. Gourmet George Metesky would remind everyone not to make the same mistake as Arnold Schuster who served the right course at the wrong time.

the diggers.

A Digger Paper, *c.* 1968, responding to hippy merchants in Haight-Ashbury, California, who advised people to share a meal with local police; probably written by Emmett Grogan

Torturer's Eyes

After four hours' torture, Apache and the two other pigs threw a bucket of water over the prisoner to bring him round, and said to him: 'The Colonel has sent word that he's going to give you a chance to save your life. If you can guess which of us has a glass eye, we'll stop torturing you.' After staring at the face of each of his torturers in turn, the prisoner pointed to one of them: 'You. Your right eye is made of glass.'

The astonished pigs replied: 'You've saved your life! But how did you manage to guess? None of your friends could, because the eye was made in the United States, in other words, it's perfect.' 'It's very simple,' the prisoner replied, sensing he was about to pass out again: 'it was the only eyes which didn't look at me with hatred.'

Of course, they carried on torturing him.

Roque Dalton, *c.* 1970

A communist village board meets to consider the following agenda:

1. the construction of a new road
2. the building of a new barn
3. the building of communism

An elder comments:

'Comrades, you know perfectly well that we don't have any funds to build a new road and we don't have wood to build a new barn. Consequently I move that we pass straight to item 3 on our agenda.'

Alexander D. in the Gulag

The cells were all built for two, but prisoners under interrogation were usually kept in them singly. The dimensions were five by six and a half feet. To be absolutely precise, they were 156 centimeters by 209 centimeters. How do we know? Through a triumph of engineering calculation and a strong heart that even Sukhanovka could not break. The measurements were the work of Alexander D., who would not allow them to drive him to madness or despair. He resisted by striving to use his mind to calculate distances. In Lefortovo he counted steps, converted them into kilometers, remembered from a map how many kilometers it was from Moscow to the border, and then how many across all Europe, and how many across the Atlantic Ocean. He was sustained in this by the hope of returning to America. And in one year in Lefortovo solitary he got, so to speak, halfway across the Atlantic. Thereupon they took him to Sukhanovka. Here, realizing how few would survive to tell of it – and all our information about it comes from him – he invented a method of measuring the cell. The numbers 10/22 were stamped on the bottom of his prison bowl, and he guessed that '10' was the diameter of the bottom and '22' the diameter of the outside edge. Then he pulled a thread from a towel, made himself a tape measure, and measured everything with it. Then he began to invent a way of sleeping *standing up*, propping his knees against the small chair, and of deceiving the guard into thinking his eyes were open. He succeeded in this deception, and that was how he managed not to go insane when Ryumin kept him sleepless for a month.

From *The Gulag Archipelago* by Alexander Solzhenitsyn, 1971

On the Run from the CIA

Paris, 6 October

How is it possible? I cannot believe that somewhere in the five or six hundred pages I've written, this editor couldn't see a book. Or if he could, perhaps he thinks I'm a bad risk. What he wants is drama, romance and glorification of what I did. When he left two days ago for Orly he barely showed any interest.

One can force a positive attitude at times, but to hit a new low after three years has its effects. Nevertheless I continue. Yesterday I began to record on tape the essential information that I can remember on what remains of the book in this version. These are descriptions of operations that I knew of or participated in and that will serve as illustrations. This is easily the most important part and will include eighty to ninety episodes that I will reconstruct from press reports in London, adding our role. By the end of next week the tapes will be finished, and I'll store copies in a safe place. The following week I'll go to Brussels for a short visit with my father who will be running through, and from there to London.

The CIA has been active in recent months trying to bring pressure. In September the General Counsel visited my father in Florida, and also Janet, to express Helms's concern over the book and my trips to Cuba. He also left copies of the recent court decision holding former CIA employees to the secrecy agreement and requiring submission of manuscripts for approval prior to publication. Sorry, but the national security for me lies in socialism, not in protection of CIA operations and agents.

Just after the General Counsel's visit to Janet I received a letter from my oldest son – almost eleven now – telling me of the visit:

Hi,

I wanted to tell you that a man from the government came to talk to mom about you, but she did not say anything except your address. What they told her is that they wanted to pay you money to stop and that they would offer another job (the job I'm not certain about).

I went to a telephone at the University of Paris where everyone calls overseas without paying – my son told me he had overheard the conversation while hiding after having been told to go away. The address doesn't matter because it's Sal's – he's been getting my mail since May so that I can keep Catherine's studio secret.

In order to keep money coming from Leslie and Sal during these final weeks I have kept up the fiction of following through with a team effort in London. They have both agreed to accompany me there – Sal will transcribe the tapes and Leslie will help with newspaper research at the British Museum. If I can get support in London I'll break with them completely but meanwhile I need their help. Today at a previously arranged meeting Leslie brought me a used typewriter that she bought only minutes before to replace the one Sal lent me last July. Apparently the owner of the borrowed typewriter called at Sal's and angrily demanded the immediate return of his machine. So I had to rush back to Catherine's studio for the borrowed typewriter which I returned right away to Sal. I don't need the one Leslie bought because I'm making the recordings, so I left it at Therese's apartment there in the Latin Quarter where Leslie gave it to me.

Little things about Sal and Leslie keep me suspicious. Often after preplanned meetings with them I pick up surveillance and they continue to press me about where I'm living. I must hurry to finish the tapes – anyone would be able to use them to finish the research and the book. Things can only get better from now on.

Philip Agee's diary; the borrowed typewriter was bugged by the CIA, 1972

Constantly Threatened

I myself have often wondered why it took so long for anyone to get around to 'taking me in for questioning', considering that I used to waltz along the streets of the West End totally unaware that they were infested with plainclothes coppers. Though they did not arrest me until 1943, they knew that I was in a weak position and constantly threatened me for their own and one another's amusement. Their condescension towards me on these occasions will never fade from my mind. Even now I could never wittingly become acquainted with a policeman; nor would I, except under torture, betray anyone to the authorities. Life is so hard for poor little crooks at the best of times.

I imagine that these opinions which I hold so intensely are, in a milder form, fairly common. As a former police chief has himself said, 'If the police were popular there would be something wrong somewhere.'

Quentin Crisp, from *How to Become a Virgin*, 1981

The Minister of Interior reporting to General Pinochet: 'Robbers have penetrated last night into the Ministry.' 'Have they stolen anything?' 'Yes. The results of the next elections!'

Disorder in the Court

DELLINGER: The first two contempts concerned the Moratorium and Bobby Seale, the two issues that the country refuses to solve, refuses to take seriously.

THE COURT: Get to the subject of punishment and I will be glad to hear you. I don't want you to talk politics.

DELLINGER: You see, that's one of the reasons I have needed to stand up and speak anyway, because you have tried to keep what you call politics, which means the truth, out of this courtroom, just as the prosecution has . . .

THE COURT: I will ask you to sit down . . .

DELLINGER: Therefore it is necessary . . .

THE COURT: I won't let you go any further . . .

DELLINGER: You wanted us to be like good Germans, supporting the evils of our decade, and when we refused to be good Germans, and came to Chicago and demonstrated, despite the threats and intimidation of the Establishment, now you want us to be like good Jews going quietly and politely to the concentration camps while you and this court suppress freedom and the truth. People will not longer be quiet, people are going to speak up. I am an old man, and I am just speaking feebly and not too well, but I reflect the spirit that will echo . . .

THE COURT: Take him out.

DELLINGER: . . . throughout the world.

[Disorder]

From the Chicago Conspiracy Trial, 1972

We are the Poison in the machine
We are the romance behind the screen

The Sex Pistols

The Shrewsbury Trial

Over the past months I have discovered many things about myself and about the laws of this land which I had been led to believe was the finest legal system in the world. But now I can only fear for the working-class people of this country.

If a mighty trade union can be fined a vast amount of money, then building workers arrested, tried and sentenced for picketing, will the day come when it will be a crime in itself to be a member of a trade union? Who can tell?

The sentence passed on me today by this court will not matter. My innocence has been proved time and time again by building workers of

Wrexham whom I led and indeed by building workers from all over the country who have sent messages of support to myself, my family and my colleagues.

Messages have in fact come from many of the very Lumpers whom I picketed during the national stoppage and I thank them all, each and every one for their moral support.

I know my children, when they are old enough, will understand that the struggle we took part in was for their benefit and for the benefit and interests of all building workers and their families because we really do care.

One could complain of the methods used in this trial, of the identification by photograph. Just one bearded man on all the photographs, yet on my coach alone, beards were worn by at least half a dozen chaps.

Statements were thrust on witnesses minutes before they entered the court to give evidence, whether they asked for them or not. Once again is this normal procedure in just an everyday criminal case? I think not.

Police officers prompting and priming witnesses with what to say before entering the witness box.

I would like to ask if the fantastic police enquiries and mammoth statements taken and the thousands of pounds spent on this spectacular are the usual diligent efforts used in an ordinary criminal trial?

I look forward to the day when the real culprits – the McAlpines, Wimpeys, Laings and Bovises and all their political puppets are in the dock facing charges of conspiracy and intimidating workers from doing what is their lawful right – picketing.

Eric Tomlinson, one of the building workers tried in 1973 for conspiracy to cause damage at a building site; he was imprisoned for two years

Masked Violence

30 December 1975

'Masked Violence' is what I am experiencing at the moment. There is no physical bruising for the eye to see. Who can measure the scars on a person's soul? Who can measure the pain? Do I really want to become a part of this? What am I striving for?

I am sick of tiny minded bureaucrats who violate my person with impunity. I realise they have me in a position where they can and are doing what they want. I have to live with myself. Am I going to sit in this cold storage and let them rub my face in the shit? Jimmy, what the fuck are you allowing to happen? When the ultimate coyote rejection was taking place and you lay animalised in your cage you were able to see life in society for what it was. Why pretend it is different now? Why climb the mountain to fall down the other side? Between the past and the future lies the pain of today. The height of impotence – being violent with a typewriter.

Who soothes the heart that beats in agony? Who kisses the soul that writhes in torment? Who mends the shattered self?

From Jimmy Boyle's diary

Soweto Shooting

One morning I decided I also had to participate. I also had a part to play – and I joined the crowd . . . there had been already lots of killings, and the children were playing in the streets when suddenly a police van passed, a . . . seven-year-old child raised his fist and said to the police: 'POWER' – whereupon the policeman got off the van and aimed at the child and shot at him directly . . . When the police started to shoot that is when students picked up stones, hit back, and took dustbin lids to protect themselves.

Sikose Mji, 1976

Carlos Vides Casanova, El Salvador's Minister of Defence, is out fishing with his Joint Chiefs of Staff, but they have had no luck, not a bite all day. Finally Vides Casanova pulls up a fish, but it's very small, only about six inches long.

'That's it,' he announces, unhooking the fish, 'I'll throw this one back and we call it a day.'

'Please, my general, give me the fish,' says the colonel sitting next to him.

'But it's a very small fish,' the Defence Minister replies.

'Please, my general.'

'Well, all right,' said Vides Casanova hands over the fish.

The colonel take its head in one hand and begins slapping it with the open palm of his other hand.

'Where are the big ones?' he shouts. 'Tell us where the big ones are!'

To each according to his needs,
from each according to his faculties.

Louis Blanc

Pogroms in Israel

I am a Jew who survived – 21 members of my family did not . . . What recurs all the time is the holocaust which has not been digested . . . We heard our Palestinian friend and all we can say to him is that we are ashamed – we who had nothing to do with it directly. We have not been able to help the sad people of Israel to come out of the past. We must help them to understand the past and we must find ways and means to be positive about it soon because the dangers are grave . . .

I had much to do with the de-fascistisation of the Italian Army and the treatment of the Nazis when they were Prisoners of War. The sad story is how quickly people can become de-humanised when they are frightened, when they are made to be frightened. This applies to every one of us – this is what is so tragic. The Jews could never take it out on the Germans. The Germans who were representative were not the Germans who put them into concentration camps.

We must accept the fact that we have all failed in being humane enough to really take on board what needs to be done. It is wrong that Palestinians are displaced persons in their own country. It is wrong that there are pogroms against Palestinians in Israel – it is unforgivable, not just wrong. While we, the Jews on the outside, understand that this is a crazy way to compensate for the holocaust and do not help the situation at all . . .

We must learn from history that we, the Jews, are the people who are responsible to see that it does not happen to other people – not just the Palestinians. We are the people who must bring hope, human rights and responsibility to many people. We, the outsiders, cannot allow that there is an attitude in Israel where the great friendships with South Africa shows that they have learned a lot from South Africa on how to treat the Palestinians . . .

We need to find ways and means to come out of this situation. We must meet with our cousins, the Palestinians. We must meet with Israelis who are not entirely obsessed with the holocaust. We must overcome this tremendous difficulty we have which this holocaust has produced – the obsession that it may happen again. We must not allow these people to play these views so well from the point of view of psychological warfare and to influence the young Jews to behave in such a way that they must know in their hearts to be completely wrong – when they hit Palestinians.

Let us also accept the fact that this is not just happening with the Palestinians; it is happening in many parts of the world . . . The situation internationally, from the human point of view, is deteriorating fast. We, who are international people, must be responsible for what is going on anywhere in the world. We can help and we can all learn from each other.

We must do something very quickly, very intelligently, very lovingly and very rudely, if necessary. For this we need new methods, new approaches and a comprehension of what makes kindly, intelligent people commit these horrible acts and how quick the deterioration is when people are surrounded by this. Every one of us is endangered. Do not think it is them – it is every one of us as well.

From a speech by Richard Hauser at a Jewish and Palestinian meeting in London, 1990

When I see an actual flesh and blood worker in conflict with his natural enemy, the policeman, I do not have to say which side I am on.

George Orwell

On the Release of the Birmingham Six

I cannot describe what it feels like to have all that hatred directed at you. To have everybody believe you are a mass murderer, when you aren't. You would think that by this time I would have been used to being an object of hatred and disgust. After all, by the time of the trial, I had already been locked up for nine months. I had been beaten, threatened, and humiliated. But up until the very moment that those verdicts came in, I always had hope . . .

We were always 'the bombers'. Despite the fact that our injuries were obvious and had been photographed, the prison officers were all acquitted. We tried to sue the police and the Home Office for the injuries they had caused us. But Lord Denning stopped us. He said if our story was right and the police were guilty of perjury and violence, this was such an 'appalling vista' that it could not be. That was in January 1980 – 11 years ago. Now he admits he was wrong.

Hugh Callaghan, April 1991

Ten

HE LOOKS FOR HIS SOUL INSPECTS IT PUTS IT TO THE TEST LEARNS IT

Democritus, at any rate, says that either nothing is true, or it is unclear to *us*.

Democritus sometimes does away with what appears to the senses, and says that none of these appears according to truth but only according to opinion: the truth in real things is that there are atoms and void. 'By convention sweet', he says, 'by convention bitter, by convention hot, by convention cold, by convention colour: but in reality atoms and void.'

Leucippus holds that the whole is infinite . . . part of it is full and part void . . . Hence arise innumerable worlds, and are resolved again into these elements. The worlds come into being as follows: many bodies of all sorts of shapes move 'by abscission from the infinite' into a great void; they come together there and produce a single whirl, in which, colliding with one another and revolving in all manner of ways, they begin to separate apart, like to like. But when their multitude prevents them from rotating any longer in equilibrium, those that are fine go out towards the surrounding void as if sifted, while the rest 'abide together' and, becoming entangled, unite their motions and make a first spherical structure. This structure stands apart like a 'membrane' which contains in itself all kinds of bodies; and as they whirl around owing to the resistance of the middle, the surrounding membrane becomes thin, while contiguous atoms keep flowing together owing to contact with the whirl. So the earth came into being, the atoms that had been borne to the middle abiding together there. Again, the containing membrane is itself increased, owing to the attraction of bodies outside; as it moves around in the whirl it takes in anything it touches. Some of these bodies that get entangled form a structure that is at first moist and muddy, but as they revolve with the whirl of the whole they dry out and then ignite to form the substance of the heavenly bodies.

Leucippus and Democritus envelop the world in a circular 'cloak' or 'membrane', which was formed by the hooked atoms becoming entangled.

Democritus holds the same view as Leucippus about the elements, full and void . . . he spoke as if the things that are were in constant motion in the void; and there are innumerable worlds, which differ in size. In some worlds there is no sun and moon, in others they are larger than in our world, and in others more numerous. The intervals between the worlds are unequal; in some parts there are more worlds, in others fewer; some are increasing, some at their height, some decreasing; in some parts they are arising, in others failing. They are destroyed by collision one with another. There are some worlds devoid of living creatures or plants or any moisture.

Aristotle, Sextus Empiricus, Diogenes Laertius, Aetius, Hippolytus concerning philosophy developed *c.* 450 BCE

Experimental Science

He therefore who wishes to rejoice without doubt in regard to the truths underlying phenomena must know how to devote himself to experiment. For authors write many statements, and people believe them through reasoning which they formulate without experience. Their reasoning is wholly false. For it is generally believed that the diamond cannot be broken expect by goat's blood, and philosophers and theologians misuse the idea. But fracture by means of blood of this kind has never been verified, although the effort has been made; and without that blood it can be broken easily. For I have seen this with my own eyes, and this is necessary, because gems cannot be carved except by fragments of this stone. Similarly it is generally believed that the castors employed by physicians are the testicles of the male animal. But this is not true, because the beaver has these under its breast, and both the male and female produce testicles of this kind. Besides these castors the male beaver has its testicles in their natural place; and therefore what is subjoined is a dreadful lie, namely, that when the hunters pursue the beaver, he himself knowing what they are seeking cuts out with his teeth these glands. Moreover, it is generally believed that hot water freezes more quickly than cold water in vessels, and the argument in support of this is advanced that contrary is excited by contrary, just like enemies meeting each other. But it is certain that cold water freezes more quickly for any one who makes the experiment. People attribute this to Aristotle in the second book of the *Meteorologics*; but he certainly does not make this statement, but he does make one like it, by which they have been deceived, namely, that if cold water and hot water are poured on a cold place, as upon ice, the hot water freezes more quickly, and this is true. But if hot water and cold are placed in two vessels, the cold will freeze more quickly. Therefore all things must be verified by experience . . .

Since this experimental science is wholly unknown to the rank and file of students, I am therefore unable to convince people of its utility unless at the same time I disclose its excellence and its proper signification. This science alone, therefore, knows how to test perfectly what can be done by nature, what by the effort of art, what by trickery, what the incantations, conjurations, invocations, deprecations, sacrifices, that belong to magic, mean and dream of, and what is in them, so that all falsity may be removed and the truth alone of art and nature may be retained. This science alone teaches us how to view the mad acts of magicians, that they may not be ratified but shunned, just as logic considers sophistical reasoning . . .

The formation of judgments, as I have said, is a function of this science, in regard to what can happen by nature or be effected in art, and what not. This science, moreover, knows how to separate the illusions of magic and to detect all their errors in incantations, invocations, conjurations, sacrifices, and cults. But unbelievers busy themselves in these mad acts and trust in them, and have believed that the Christians used such means in working their miracles. Wherefore this science is of the greatest advantage in persuading men to accept the faith, since this branch alone of philosophy happens to proceed in this way, because this is the only branch that considers matters of this kind, and is able to overcome all falsehood and superstition and error of unbelievers in regard to magic, such as incantations and the like already mentioned. How far, moreover, it may serve to reprobate obstinate unbelievers is already shown by the violent means that have just been touched upon, and therefore I pass on.

From the *Opus Majus* of Roger Bacon, thirteenth century

Ways of Searching

XIX

There are and can be only two ways of searching into and discovering truth. The one flies from the senses and particulars to the most general axioms, and from these principles, the truth of which it takes for settled and immovable, proceeds to judgment and to the discovery of middle axioms. And this way is now in fashion. The other derives axioms from the senses and particulars, rising by a gradual and unbroken ascent, so that it arrives at the most general axioms last of all. This is the true way, but as yet untried.

XXII

Both ways set out from the senses and particulars, and rest in the highest generalities; but the difference between them is infinite. For the one just glances at experiment and particulars in passing, the other dwells duly and orderly among them. The one, again, begins at once by establishing certain abstract and useless generalities, the other rises by gradual steps to that which is prior and better known in the order of nature.

XXIV

It cannot be that axioms established by argumentation should avail for the discovery of new works; since the subtlety of nature is greater many times over than the subtlety of argument. But axioms duly and orderly formed from particulars easily discover the way to new particulars, and thus render sciences active.

XXV

The axioms now in use, having been suggested by a scanty and manipular experience and a few particulars of most general occurrence, are made for the most part just large enough to fit and take these in: and therefore it is no wonder if they do not lead to new particulars. And if some opposite instance, not observed or not known before, chance to come in the way, the axiom is rescued and preserved by some frivolous distinction; whereas the truer course would be to correct the axiom itself.

XXXI

It is idle to expect any great advancement in science from the superinducing and engrafting of new things upon old. We must begin anew from the very foundations, unless we would revolve for ever in a circle with mean and contemptible progress.

From the *First Book of Aphorisms* by Francis Bacon, *c.* 1620

Galileo's World System

SIMPLICIO

How do you deduce that it is not the earth, but the sun, which is at the centre of the universe?

SALVATO

That is deduced from most obvious and therefore most powerfully convincing observations. The most palpable of these, which excludes the earth from the centre and places the sun there, is that we find all the planets closer to the earth at one time and farther from it at another. The differences are so great that Venus, for example, is six times as distant from us at its furthest or at its closest, and Mars soars nearly eight times as high in one state as in the other. You may then see whether Aristotle was not some trifle deceived in believing that they were always equally distant from us.

SIMPLICIO
But what are the signs that they move around the sun?

SALVATO
This is reasoned out from finding the three other planets – Mars, Jupiter and Saturn – always quite close to the earth when they are in opposition to the sun and very distant when they are in conjunction with it. This approach and recession is of such moment that Mars when close looks sixty times as large as when it is most distant. Next, it is certain that Venus and Mercury must revolve around the sun, because of their never moving far away from it, and because of their being seen now beyond it and now by the side of it, as Venus's changes of shape conclusively prove.

From *Dialogue Concerning the Two Chief World Systems* by Galileo Galilei, 1629; the treatise was banned by the Inquisition and Galileo imprisoned after refusing to recant

---

Roses are red
Violets are blue
Most poems rhyme
This one doesn't.

Pennsylvania Indians Decline to Attend College

We know that you highly esteem the kind of learning taught in those Colleges, and that the Maintenance of our young Men, while with you, would be very expensive to you. We are convinced, that you mean to do us Good by your Proposal; and we thank you heartily. But you, who are wise must know that different Nations have different Conceptions of things and you will therefore not take it amiss, if our Ideas of this kind of Education happen not to be the same as yours. We have had some Experience of it. Several of our young People were formerly brought up at the Colleges of the Northern Provinces: they were instructed in all your Sciences; but, when they came back to us, they were bad Runners, ignorant of every means of living in the woods . . . neither fit for Hunters, Warriors, nor Counsellors, they were totally good for nothing.

We are, however, not the less oblig'd by your kind Offer, tho' we decline accepting it; and, to show our grateful Sense of it, if the Gentlemen of Virginia will send us a Dozen of their Sons, we will take Care of their Education, instruct them in all we know, and make Men of them.

Anon., 1744

Experiments

The majority of the following poems are to be considered as experiments. They were written chiefly with a view to ascertain how far the language of conversation in the middle and lower classes of society is adapted to the purposes of poetic pleasure. Readers accustomed to the gaudiness and inane phraseology of many modern writers, if they persist in reading this book to its conclusion, will perhaps frequently have to struggle with feelings of strangeness and awkwardness: they will look round for poetry, and will be induced to enquire by what species of courtesy these attempts can be permitted to assume that title. It is desirable that such readers, for their own sakes, should not suffer the solitary word Poetry, a word of very disputed meaning, to stand in the way of their gratification; but that, while they are perusing this book, they should ask themselves if it contains a natural delineation of human passions, human characters, and human incidents; and if the answer be favourable to the author's wishes, that they should consent to be pleased in spite of that most dreadful enemy to our pleasures, our own pre-established codes of decision.

Readers of superior judgment may disapprove of the style in which many of these pieces are executed it must be expected that many lines and phrases will not exactly suit their taste. It will perhaps appear to them, that wishing to avoid the prevalent fault of the day, the author has sometimes descended too low, and that many of his expressions are too familiar, and not of sufficient dignity. It is apprehended, that the more conversant the reader is with our elder writers, and with those in modern times who have been the most successful in painting manners and passions, the fewer complaints of this kind will he have to make.

From the 'Advertisement' to *Lyrical Ballads* by William Wordsworth and Samuel Coleridge, 1798

'Monster Science'

A Lord of Steam and Iron am I,
A Monster in the land;
While puny men of bone and blood
Are slaves at my command.

The Monster Science is my name
And I trample on the free,
I laugh at the sight of human tears
And Death is my Victory.

I love the knell of the factory bell
On the long dark winter night,
With hail and storms and shivering forms
Who toil by candlelight.

Of Iron and Steam I reign supreme
But a partial King am I
The few by stealth I heap with wealth
While the masses sicken and die.

From *The Potter's Examiner*, Stoke-on-Trent, *c.* 1850

Not Very Sorry for Wordsworth

WORDSWORTH the POET, *died*, on the 23rd of April in the 80th year of his age. In announcing his death, we must acknowledge that we are not impressed with any very heavy sense of sorrow, for we cannot include him in the list of those who, like BURNS, BYRON, and SHELLEY, have secured the lasting worship of the people by their immortal aspirations for, and soul-inspiring invocations to, Liberty. Unlike those great spirits, WORDSWORTH passes from amongst us unregretted by the great body of his countrymen, who have no tears for the salaried slave of Aristocracy and pensioned parasite of Monarchy.

From *The Democratic Review*, May 1850

Make Oneself A Seer

The first study for a man who wants to be a poet is the knowledge of himself, complete. He looks for his soul, inspects it, puts it to the test, learns it. As soon as he knows it, he must cultivate it! It seems simple: in every brain a natural development takes place; so many *egoists* proclaim themselves authors; there are plenty of others who attribute their intellectual progress to themselves! – But the soul has to be made monstrous, that's the point: after the fashion of the *comprachicos*, if you like! Imagine a man planting and cultivating warts on his face.

I say that one must be a *seer*, make oneself a *seer*.

The poet makes himself a *seer* by a long, prodigious, and rational *disordering* of *all the senses*. Every form of love, of suffering, of madness; he searches himself, he consumes all the poisons in him, and keeps only their quintessences. This is an unspeakable torture during which he needs all his faith and superhuman strength, and during which he becomes the great patient, the great criminal, the great accursed – and the great learned one! – among men. – For he arrives at the *unknown*! Because he has cultivated his own soul – which was rich to begin with – more than any other man! He reaches the unknown; and even if, crazed, he ends up by losing the understanding of his visions, at least he has seen them! Let him die charging through those unutterable, unnameable things: other horrible workers will come; they will begin from the horizons where he has succumbed!

From a letter to Paul Demeny by Arthur Rimbaud, 1871

Nature Has Had Her Day

There, by salting your bath-water and adding sulphate of soda with hydrochlorate of magnesium and lime in the proportions recommended by the Pharmacopoeia; by opening a box with a tight-fitting screw-top and taking out a ball of twine or a twist of rope, bought for the occasion from one of those enormous roperies whose warehouses and cellars reek with the smell of the sea and sea-ports; by breathing in the odours which the twine or the twist of rope is sure to have retained; by consulting a life-like photograph of the casino and zealously reading the *Guide Joanne* describing the beauties of the seaside resort where you would like to be; by letting yourself be lulled by the waves created in your bath by the backwash of the paddle-steamers passing close to the pontoon; by listening to the moaning of the wind as it blows under the arches of the Pont Royal and the dull rumble of the buses crossing the bridge just a few feet over your head; by employing these simple devices, you can produce an illusion of seabathing which will be undeniable, convincing, and complete.

The main thing is to know how to set about it, to be able to concentrate your attention on a single detail, to forget yourself sufficiently to bring about the desired hallucination and so substitute the vision of a reality for the reality itself.

As a matter of fact, artifice was considered by Des Esseintes to be the distinctive mark of human genius.

Nature, he used to say, has had her day; she has finally and utterly exhausted the patience of sensitive observers by the revolting uniformity of her landscape and skyscapes. After all, what platitudinous limitations she imposes, like a tradesman specializing in a single line of business; what petty-minded restrictions, like a shopkeeper stocking one article to the exclusion of all others; what a monotonous store of meadows and trees, what a commonplace display of mountains and seas!

In fact, there is not a single one of her inventions, deemed so subtle and sublime, that human ingenuity cannot manufacture; no moonlit Forest of Fontainebleau that cannot be reproduced by stage scenery under floodlighting; no cascade that cannot be imitated to perfection by hydraulic engineering; no rock that papier-mâché cannot counterfeit; no flower that carefully chosen taffeta and delicately coloured paper cannot match!

There can be no shadow of doubt that with her never-ending platitudes the old crone has by now exhausted the good-humoured admiration of all true artists, and the time has surely come for artifice to take her place whenever possible.

After all, to take what among all her works is considered to be the most exquisite, what among all her creations is deemed to possess the most perfect and original beauty – to wit, woman – has not man for his part, by his own efforts, produced an animate yet artificial creature that is every bit as good from the point of view of plastic beauty? Does there exist, anywhere on this earth, a being conceived in the joys of fornication and born in the throes of motherhood who is more dazzlingly, more outstandingly beautiful than the two locomotives recently put into service on the Northern Railway?

One of these, bearing the name of Crampton, is an adorable blonde with a shrill voice, a long slender body imprisoned in a shiny brass corset, and supple catlike movements; a smart golden blonde whose extraordinary grace can be quite terrifying when she stiffens her muscles of steel, sends the sweat pouring down her steaming flanks, sets her elegant wheels spinning in their wide circles, and hurtles away, full of life, at the head of an express or a boat-train.

The other, Engerth by name, is a strapping saturnine brunette given to uttering raucous, guttural cries, with a thick-set figure encased in armour-plating of cast iron; a monstrous creature with her dishevelled mane of black smoke and her six wheels coupled together low down, she gives an indication of her fantastic strength when, with an effort that shakes the very earth, she slowly and deliberately drags along her heavy train of goods-wagons.

It is beyond question that, among all the fair, delicate beauties and all the dark, majestic charms of the human race, no such superb examples of comely grace and terrifying force are to be found; and it can be stated without fear of contradiction that in his chosen province man has done as well as the God in whom he believes.

From *Against Nature* by 'J-K Huysmans' (Charles Marie Georges), 1884

A drug is that substance which, when injected into a rat,
will produce a scientific report.

Anon.

'People think they have fully understood the theory . . .'

According to the materialist conception of history the determining element in history is *ultimately* the production and reproduction in real life. More than this neither Marx nor I have ever asserted. If therefore somebody twists this into the statement that the economic element is the *only* determining one, he transforms it into a meaningless, abstract and absurd phrase. The economic situation is the basis, but the various elements of the superstructure – political forms of the class struggle and its consequences, constitutions established by the victorious class after a successful battle, etc. – forms of law – and then even the reflexes of all these actual struggles in the brains of the combatants: political, legal, philosophical theories, religious ideas and their further development into systems of dogma – also exercise their influence upon the course of the historical struggles and in many cases preponderate in determining their *form*. There is an interaction of all these elements in which, amid all the endless *host* of accidents (*i.e.*, of things and events, whose inner connection is so remote or so impossible to prove that we regard it as absent and can neglect it) the economic movement finally asserts itself as necessary. Otherwise the application of the theory to any period of history one chose would be easier than the solution of a simple equation of the first degree.

We make our own history, but in the first place under very definite presuppositions and conditions. Among these the economic ones are finally decisive. But the political, etc., ones, and indeed even the traditions which haunt human minds also play a part, although not the decisive one. The Prussian state arose and developed from historical, ultimately from economic causes. But it could scarcely be maintained without pedantry that among the many small states of North Germany, Brandenburg was specifically determined by economic necessity to become the great power embodying the economic, linguistic and, after the Reformation, also the religious difference between north and south and not by other elements as well (above all by its entanglement with Poland, owing to the possession of Prussia, and hence with international, political relations – which were indeed also decisive in the formation of the Austrian dynastic power). Without making oneself ridiculous it would be difficult to succeed in explaining in terms of economics the existence of every small state in Germany, past and present, or the origin of the High German consonant mutations, which the geographical wall of partition formed by the mountains from the Sudetic range to the Taunus extended to a regular division throughout Germany.

In the second place, however, history makes itself in such a way that the final result always arises from conflicts between many individual wills, of which each again has been made what it is by a host of particular conditions of life. Thus there are innumerable intersecting forces, an infinite series of parallelograms of forces which give rise to one resultant – the historical event. This again may itself be viewed as the product of a power which, taken as a whole, works *unconsciously* and without volition. For what each individual wills is obstructed by everyone else, and what emerges is something that no one willed. Thus past history proceeds in the manner of a natural process and is also essentially subject to the same laws of movement. But from the fact that individual wills – of which each desires what he is impelled to by his physical constitution and external, in the last resort economic, circumstances (either his own personal circumstances or those of society in general) – do not attain what they want, but are merged into a collective mean, a common resultant, it must not be concluded that their value=0. On the contrary, each contributes to the resultant and is to this degree involved in it.

I would ask you to study this theory further from its original sources and not at second-hand, it is really much easier. Marx hardly wrote anything in which it did not play a part. But especially *The Eighteenth Brumaire of Louis Bonaparte* is a most excellent example of its application. There are also many allusions in *Capital*. Then I may also direct you to my writings: *Herr Eugen Dühring's Revolution in Science* and *Ludwig Feuerbach and the Outcome of Classical German Philosophy*, in which I have given the most detailed account of historical materialism which, so far as I know, exists.

Marx and I are ourselves partly to blame for the fact that younger writers sometimes lay more stress on the economic side than is due to it. We had to emphasise this main principle in opposition to our adversaries, who denied it, and we had not always the time, the place or the opportunity to allow the other elements involved in the interaction to come into their rights. But when it was a case of presenting a section of history, that is, of a practical application, the thing was different and there no error was possible. Unfortunately, however, it happens only too often that people think they have fully understood a theory and can apply it without more ado from the moment they have mastered its main principles, and those even not always correctly. And I cannot exempt many of the more recent 'Marxists' from this reproach, for the most wonderful rubbish has been produced from this quarter too.

Letter from Friedrich Engels to Joseph Bloch, 21 September 1890

A Warm, Rich Flood

In the very first year of our century, the year 1801, there appeared in Paris a book by Silvain Marechal, entitled 'Shall Woman Learn the Alphabet.' The book proposed a law prohibiting the alphabet to women, and quotes authorities weighty and various, to prove that the woman who knows the alphabet has already lost part of her womanliness. The author declares that women can use the alphabet only as Molière predicted they would, in spelling out the verb *amo*; that they have no occasion to persue Ovid's *Ars Amoris*, since that is already the ground and limit of their intuitive furnishing; that Madame Guion would have been far more adorable had she remained a beautiful ignoramus as nature made her; that Ruth, Naomi, the Spartan woman, the Amazons, Penelope, Andromache, Lucretia, Joan of Arc, Petrarch's Laura, the daughters of Charlemagne, could not spell their names; while Sappho, Aspasia, Madame de Maintenon, and Madame de Staël could read altogether too well for their good; finally, that if women were once permitted to read Sophocles and work with logarithms, or to nibble at any side of the apple of knowledge, there would be an end forever to their sewing on buttons and embroidering slippers.

Please remember this book was published at the *beginning* of the Nineteenth Century. At the end of its first third, (in the year 1833) one solitary college in America decided to admit women within its sacred precincts, and organized what was called a 'Ladies' Course' as well as the regular B. A. or Gentlemen's course.

It was felt to be an experiment – a rather dangerous experiment – and was adopted with fear and trembling by the good fathers, who looked as if they had been caught secretly mixing explosive compounds and were guiltily expecting every moment to see the foundations under them shaken and rent and their fair superstructure shattered into fragments.

But the girls came, and there was no upheaval. They performed their tasks modestly and intelligently. Once in a while one or two were found choosing the gentlemen's course. Still no collapse; and the dear, careful, scrupulous, frightened old professors were just getting their hearts out of their throats and preparing to draw one good free breath, when they found they would have to change the names of those courses; for there were as many ladies in the gentlemen's course as in the ladies', and a distinctively Ladies' Course, inferior in scope and aim to the regular classical course, did not and could not exist.

Other colleges gradually fell into line, and to-day there are one hundred and ninety-eight colleges for women, and two hundred and seven coeducational colleges and universities in the United States alone offering the degree of B. A. to women, and sending out yearly into the arteries of this nation a warm, rich flood of strong, brave, active, energetic, well-equipped, thoughtful women – women quick to see and eager to help the needs of this needy world – women who can think as well as feel, and who feel none the less because they think – women who are none the less tender and true for the parchment scroll they bear in their hands – women who have given a deeper, richer, nobler and grander meaning to the word 'womanly' than any one-sided masculine definition could ever have suggested or inspired – women whom the world has long waited for in pain and anguish till there should be at last added to its forces and allowed to permeate its thought the complement of that masculine influence which has dominated it for fourteen centuries.

From *A Voice from the South: By a Black Woman of the South* by Anna Julia Haywood Cooper, 1892

'Cork and Work and Card and Ward'

I take it you already know
Of tough and bough and cough and dough?
Others may stumble, but not you
On hiccough, thorough, laugh, and through?
I write in case you wish perhaps
To learn of less familiar traps:
Beware of heard, a dreadful word
That looks like beard, and sounds like bird.
And dead: it's said like bed, not bead;
For goodness' sake, don't call it 'deed'!
Watch out for meat and great and threat
(They rhyme with suite and straight and debt).
A moth is not a moth in mother,
Nor both in bother, broth in brother.
And here is not a match for there,
Nor dear for bear, or fear for pear.
There's dose and rose, there's also lose
(Just look them up), and goose, and choose,
And cork and work, and card and ward,
And font and front, and word and sword,
And do and go and thwart and cart –
Come come, I've barely made a start!
A dreadful language? Man alive,
I'd mastered it when I was five!

Anon, *c.* 1900

A Worker's Catechism

What is philosophy?
A seeking of the truth.
Then how can philosophy be the friend of the upper classes?
The upper classes pay the philosopher, in order that he may discover only such truths as are expedient in their eyes.
But suppose uncomfortable truths should be discovered?
They are called lies, and the philosopher gets no pay.
What is history?

The story of the past, presented in a light favourable to the interests of the upper classes.

Suppose the light is unfavorable?

That is scandalous.

What is a scandal?

Anything offending the upper classes.

What is aesthetics?

The art of praising or belittling works of art.

What works of art must be praised?

Those that glorify the upper classes.

Therefore Raphael and Michaelangelo are the most famous artists, for they glorified the religious falsehoods of the upper classes. Shakespeare magnified kings, and Goethe magnified himself, the writer for the upper classes.

But how about other works of art?

There must not be others.

August Strindberg, 1905

I asserted – and I repeat – that a man has no reason
to be ashamed of having an ape for his grandfather.

T. H. Huxley

And so we the Cornyshe men
(wherof certen of vs vnderstade
no Englysh) vtterly refuse thys newe Englysh.

Demands of Rebels, 1647

Dadaist Disgust

Every product of disgust that is capable of becoming a negation of the family is *dada*; protest with the fists of one's whole being in destructive action: DADA; acquaintance with all the means hitherto rejected by the sexual prudishness of easy compromise and good manners: DADA; abolition of logic, dance of those who are incapable of creation: ***DADA***; every hierarchy and social equation established for values by our valets: DADA; every object, all objects, feelings and obscurities, every apparition and the precise shock of parallel lines, are means for the battle of: **DADA**; the abolition of memory: ***DADA***; the abolition of archaeology: **DADA** the abolition of prophets: **DADA**; the abolition of the future: **DADA**; the absolute and indiscutable belief in every god that is an immediate product of spontaneity: **DADA**; the elegant and unprejudiced leap from one harmony to another sphere; the trajectory of a word, a cry, thrown into the air like an acoustic disc; to respect all individualities in their folly of the moment, whether serious, fearful, timid, ardent, vigorous, decided or enthusiastic; to strip one's church of every useless and unwieldy accessory; to spew out like a luminous cascade any offensive or loving thought, or to cherish it – with the lively satisfaction that it's all precisely the same thing – with the same intensity in the bush, which is free of insects for the blue-blooded, and gilded with the bodies of archangels, with one's soul. Liberty: DADA DADA DADA; – the roar of contorted pains, the interweaving of contraries and of all contradictions, freaks and irrelevancies: LIFE.

From *Seven Dada Manifestos* by Tristan Tzara, *c.* 1915

Towards Suprematism

The new life of iron and the machine, the roar of motorcars, the brilliance of electric lights, the growling of propellers, have awakened the soul, which was suffocating in the catacombs of old reason and has emerged at the intersection of the paths of heaven and earth.

If all artists were to see the crossroads of these heavenly paths, if they were to comprehend these monstrous runways and intersections of our bodies with the clouds in the heavens, then they would not paint chrysanthemums.

The dynamics of movement has suggested advocating the dynamics of painterly plasticity.

From *From Cubism to Suprematism: The New Painterly Realism* by Kazimir Malevich, 1915

A distinguished Soviet aesthetician was answering questions on the theory of art.
'What is expressionism?' one questioner asked.
'Expressionism is painting what you feel.'
'What is impressionism?'
'Impressionism is painting what you see.'
'And what is socialist realism?'
'Socialist realism is painting what you hear.'

Write, Persist, Struggle

Literature is one of the products of a civilization like steel or textiles. It is not a child of eternity, but of time. It is always the mirror of its age. It is not any more mystic in its origin than a ham sandwich . . .

We are living in another day. It is dominated by a hard, successful, ignorant jazzy bourgeois of about thirty-five, and his leech-like young wife.

Just as European tours, night clubs, Florida beaches and streamline cars have been invented for this class, just so literature is being produced for them. They have begun to have time, and now read books occasionally to fill in the idle moments between cocktail parties.

They need novels that will take the place of the old fashioned etiquette books to teach them how to spend their money smartly.

Ernest Hemingway is one of the caterers to this demand . . .

The America of the working class is practically undiscovered. It is like a lost continent. Bits of it come above the surface in our literature occasionally and everyone is amazed. But there is no need yet of going to Africa or the Orient for strange new pioneering. The young writer can find all the primitive material he needs working as a wage slave around the cities and prairies of America . . .

Do not be passive. Write. Your life in mine, mill and farm is of deathless significance in the history of the world. Tell us about it in the same language you use in writing a letter. It may be literature – it often is. Write. Persist. Struggle.

From the editorial of *New Masses* by Mike Gold, January 1929

Not Listless Intellectuals

We shall aim at stimulating interest by free discussion, and, in later years, by encouraging argument on every arguable question. At all ages, every question, on no matter what subject, will be answered to the best of our knowledge and ability. We shall, of course, do everything possible to equip older boys and girls to pass necessary examinations, and, where desired, to obtain university scholarships. We shall hope to make definite instruction as thorough as in the most efficient existing schools, but, we believe, with less strain to the pupils. Subject to the limitations set by examinations, we shall aim at a somewhat different outlook towards knowledge from that which is customary in schools. In history, we shall emphasise world history and the history of civilisation rather than national or political history. Although the classics will be taught to older boys and girls to the extent that they may be necessary, the emphasis will be upon science and the modern humanities. Every opportunity will be given for the pupils to discover things for themselves, where possible, by experiment, failing that, by reading rather than by oral teaching. Knowledge will not be viewed as mere knowledge, but as an instrument of progress, the value of which is shown by bringing it into relation with the needs of the world.

We shall aim at producing, not listless intellectuals, but young men and women filled with constructive hopefulness, conscious that there are great things to be done in the world, and possessed of the skill required for taking their part.

Terms etc. Entire charge will be taken if the parents so desire.

From *The Tamarisk Tree* by Dora Russell, 1979, describing 1927

'Manifesto for an Independent Revolutionary Art'

The conception of the writer's function which the young Marx worked out is worth recalling. 'The writer', he said, 'naturally must make money in order to live and write, but he should not under any circumstances live and write in order to make money . . . The writer by no means looks on his work as a means. It is an end in itself and so little a means in the eyes of himself and of others that if necessary he sacrifices his existence to the existence of his work . . . The first condition of freedom of the press is that it is not a business activity.'

It is more than ever fitting to use this statement against those who would regiment intellectual activity in the direction of ends foreign to itself and prescribe, in the guise of so-called reasons of state, the themes of art. The free choice of these themes and the absence of all restrictions on the range of his exploitations – these are possessions which the artist has a right to claim as inalienable. In the realm of artistic creation, the imagination must escape from all constraint and must under no pretext allow itself to be placed under bonds. To those who urge us, whether for today or for tomorrow, to consent that art should submit to a discipline which we hold to be radically incompatible with its nature, we give a flat refusal and we repeat our deliberate intention of standing by the formula *complete freedom for art*.

André Breton and Diego Rivera, in collaboration with Leon Trotsky, July 1938

Epic Theatre

The dramatic theatre's spectator says: Yes, I have felt like that too – Just like me – It's only natural – It'll never change – The sufferings of this man appall me, because they are inescapable – That's great art; it all seems the most obvious thing in the world – I weep when they weep, I laugh when they laugh.

The epic theatre's spectator says: I'd never have thought it – That's not the way – That's extraordinary, hardly believable – It's got to stop – The sufferings of this man appall me, because they are unnecessary – That's great art: nothing obvious in it – I laugh when they weep, I weep when they laugh.

From *Theatre for Pleasure or Theatre for Instruction* by Bertolt Brecht, *c.* 1935

A leader of public thought in Hollywood wouldn't
have sufficient mental acumen anywhere else to hold
down a place in the bread line.

Anita Loos

Bird At Play

Early in April I arranged a party at the Onyx Club for Marshall Stearns and Sidney Finkelstein. Stearns was then associate professor of English at

Cornell University, a Chaucer scholar, authority on English poets Robert Henryson and Dylan Thomas, and America's leading jazz historian. Stearns had founded the first jazz club in America, at Yale, where John Hammond had been a protégé. Finkelstein was the principal Marxist jazz critic, and author of the recently published *Jazz: A People's Music.* The time seemed auspicious to expose these eminences to an intimate hearing of the new music. Both had worldwide prestige and contacts. After months of urging, Stearns had made the trip from Ithaca to hear Charlie live for the first time. Finkelstein, something of a recluse, seldom visited night clubs. Both were eager to meet Charlie.

I found Charlie chastened but hardly crushed. He had pulled a respectable audience to The Street that night. In the house were Georgie Auld, Milt Jackson, Chubby Jackson, Barry Ulanov, Leonard Feather, and Billie Holiday, just released after a six-month sentence for narcotics, looking tragic and lovely in a striking white fur wrap. The Quintet was playing opposite the pleasing Margie Hyams Quartet. After the first set Charlie came to the table 'to meet the wiggy cats' who wrote books about jazz. Charlie very shrewdly and quickly sized up both men. Finkelstein he ignored. The Marxist critic was tough and hardboiled and, as Charlie could see, came from a proletarian background like his own. Charlie figured that Finkelstein, like himself, was a man on the make, but with a new hype. Charlie concentrated on the patrician Stearns, born to wealth, educated at Harvard and Yale. Much to Stearns's discomfort, Charlie insisted on calling him Professor. When Stearns went to the men's room, Charlie followed. As Stearns stood at the urinal, Charlie stood immediately behind, and said: 'Look in the mirror, Professor.'

When Stearns looked up, their eyes met. 'Here we are, Professor,' Charlie said philosophically. 'You and me. Two human beings. You started at the top and I started at the bottom . . . ' Then he explained that he was urgently in need of money and asked for a loan of fifty dollars, a sum that Stearns would never have dreamed of bringing to a night club. As Stearns fumbled to rearrange his clothing, wash his hands, and extricate himself from this strange and embarrassing situation, Charlie began to lower the amount of the requested loan. Down it went – fifty, forty, twenty-five, fifteen, ten dollars. When it reached five dollars, Stearns came across. Later I took Charlie to task for his actions, pointing out that Dr. Stearns was in a position to advance his career, and that his own earnings were probably in excess of an associate English professor's salary at Cornell University. Charlie grinned at me.

'Coming on like Billy Shaw now,' Charlie told me. 'I only hit him for a nickel note, man!' Then he tried me for two hundred dollars. I refused. He fished a five-cent piece from his pocket and held it up. 'That's my hype,' he said. He put the coin back in his pocket and clipped the new saxophone to his neckpiece. Then, with the evening's squares put in their place, he whisked through a brilliant set. After the set he walked past us into Fifty-second Street as if the table were empty.

From *Bird Lives!* by Ross Russell, 1948

'Learning French'

The day they taught us *bonsoir*,
We got a hit on the jaw,
We got our bellyful of prisons and locks.

The day they taught us *bonjour*,
We got a hit on the nose,
All blessings ended for us.

The day they taught us *merci*,
We got a hit on the throat.
A sheep inspires more fear than we do.

The day they taught us *cochon*,
A dog's honor stood higher than ours.
The peasant bought himself a mule.

The day they taught us *le frère*,
We got a hit on the knee;
We walk in shame up to our necks.

The day they taught us *diable*,
We got a beating that drove us mad.
We have become carriers of offal.

Anon., Algeria, *c.* 1950

The Glories of Art

But it is essential to realise that most of the glories of art were produced for a social and not for private consumption. The skill of architect, sculptor, painter and builder-craftsmen were united in the construction of public buildings where the cost counted less than the graciousness they brought to the lives of those who lived around them. At best the rich collector makes us a legacy of his accumulated treasures, in which case they are immured in museums and art galleries, where they look reproachfully down on the long processions of sightseers, who can catch, in such a context, only a small glimpse of their beauty.

Some day, under the impulse of collective action, we shall enfranchise the artists, by giving them our public buildings to work upon; our bridges, our housing estates, our offices, our industrial canteens, our factories and the municipal buildings where we house our civic activities. It is tiresome to listen to the diatribes of some modern art critics who bemoan the passing of the rich patron as though this must mean the decline of art, whereas it could mean its emancipation if the artists were restored to their proper relationship with civic life.

From *In Place of Fear* by Aneurin Bevan, *c.* 1952

Who are the greatest deceivers? The doctors?
And the greatest fools? The patients?

Voltaire

Loamshire

If you seek a tombstone, look about you; survey the peculiar nullity of our drama's prevalent *genre*, the Loamshire play. Its setting is a country house in what used to be called Loamshire but is now, as a heroic tribute to realism, sometimes called Berkshire. Except when someone must sneeze, or be murdered, the sun invariably shines. The inhabitants belong to a social class derived partly from romantic novels and partly from the playwright's vision of the leisured life he will lead after the play is a success – this being the only effort of imagination he is called on to make. Joys and sorrows are giggles and whimpers: the crash of denunciation dwindles into 'Oh, stuff, Mummy!' and 'Oh, really, Daddy!' And so grim is the continuity of these things that the foregoing paragraph might have been written at any time during the last thirty years.

Loamshire is a glibly codified fairy-tale world, of no more use to the student of life than a doll's-house would be to a student of town planning.

Its vice is to have engulfed the theatre, thereby expelling better minds. Never believe that there is a shortage of playwrights; there are more than we have ever known; but they are all writing the same play. Nor is there a dearth of English actors; the land is alive with them; but they are all playing the same part. Should they wish to test themselves beyond Loamshire's simple major thirds, they must find employment in revivals, foreign plays, or films. Perhaps Loamshire's greatest triumph is the crippling of creative talent in English directors and designers. After all, how many ways are there of directing a tea-party? And how may a designer spread his wings in a mews flat or 'The living-room at "Binsgate", Vyvyan Bulstrode's country house near Dymsdyke'? Assume the miracle: assume the advent of a masterpiece. There it crouches, a pink-eyed, many-muscled, salivating monster. Who shall harness it? We have a handful of directors fit to tame something less malleable than a mouse, and a few designers still capable of dressing something less submissive than a clothes-horse. But they are the end, not the beginning, of a tradition.

Some of us need no miracles to keep our faith; we feed it on memories and imaginings. But many more – people of passionate intellectual appetites – are losing heart, falling away, joining the queues outside the Curzon Cinema. To lure them home, the theatre must widen its scope, broaden its horizon so that Loamshire appears merely as the play-pen, not as the whole palace of drama. We need plays about cabmen and demi-gods, plays about warriors, politicians, and grocers – I care not, so Loamshire be invaded and subdued. I counsel aggression because, as a critic, I had rather be a war correspondent than a necrologist.

From 'West-End Apathy' by Kenneth Tynan, 1954

An actor's a guy who, if you ain't talking
about him, ain't listening.

Marlon Brando

'On the Launching of a Sputnik'

What a rotten life this is!
And the whole damn world's like that.
The five o'clock robots mob the newsstands;

in the post office the workers' hands are calloused,
sorting out letters;
and we municipal garbage collectors
puke in the backyards.
There's no free food yet,
and no free clothes.

O universal emptiness
and empty universes,
we are zooming another Sputnik
into another planet,
probably to a hard landing.
So that's man!
For a short hitch he eats and makes love,
but even the young kids
launch from their mother's breast
with a cosmological finger.

Hey, tell me, where the hell
should a garbage collector live?
Should I double my back to gather calluses?
And where are my food and clothes?
Don't I pick up the filth of the whole bloody town,
eh? So that's man?
Free, once in a while, for an hour
in all his sickly fears?

O you magnificent failures,
poking around in your heavy uniforms
in dark and smelly hallways,
why don't you ever repair the goddamn place
and help clean the kitchens
and their filthy cans?

At least I'm a true collector of garbage,
and I, too, have a rage to live.

Dmitry Bobyshev, *c.* 1965; published and circulated as Samizdat

Coursemanship

Grades are your means of getting into graduate or professional school, your means of keeping your parents happy, or your means of avoiding the army. Some such strictly utilitarian purpose should be your reason for working for good grades. Do not imagine that your grade has much to do with what you learned in a course, or anything to do with how your general education is progressing. Your general education must be pursued separately from and sometimes in spite of the formal educational structure of the University.

From *SLATE*, Berkeley College, University of California, Students' Guide to University Courses, 1965

You Won't Remember my Name

Dear Miss
You won't remember me or my name. You have failed so many of us.

On the other hand I have often had thoughts about you, and the other teachers, and about that institution which you call 'school' and about the boys that you fail.

You fail us right out into the fields and factories and there you forget us.

While giving a test you used to walk up and down between the rows of desks and see me in trouble and making mistakes, but you never said a word.

I have the same situation at home. No one to turn to for help for miles around. No books. No telephone.

Now here I am 'in school'. I came from far away to be taught. Here I don't have to deal with my mother, who promised to be quiet and then interrupted me a hundred times. My sister's little boy is not here to ask me for help with his homework. Here I have silence and good light and a desk all to myself.

And over there, a few steps away, you stand. You know all of these things. You are paid to help me.

Instead, you waste your time keeping me under guard as if I were a thief.

You know even less about men than we do. The lift serves as a good machine for ignoring people in your building; the car, for ignoring people who travel in buses; the telephone for avoiding seeing people's faces or entering their homes.

I don't know about you, but your students who know Cicero – how many families of living men do they know intimately? How many of their kitchens have they visited? How many of their sick have they sat with through the night? How many of their dead have they borne on their shoulders? How many can they trust when they are in distress? . . .

A thousand motors roar under your windows every day. You have no idea to whom they belong or where they are going.

But I can read the sounds of my valley for miles around. The sound of the motor in the distance in Nevio going to the station, a little late. If you like, I can tell you everything about hundreds of people, dozens of families and their relatives and personal ties.

Whenever you speak to a worker you manage to get it all wrong: your choice of words, your tone, your jokes. I can tell what a hill farmer is thinking even when he keeps silent, and I know what's on his mind even when he talks about something else.

This is the sort of culture your poets should have given you. It is the culture of nine-tenths of the earth, but no one has yet managed to put it down in words or pictures or films.

Be a bit humble, at least. Your culture has gaps as wide as ours. Perhaps even wider. Certainly more damaging to a teacher in the elementary schools.

At the gymnastics exam the teacher threw us a ball and said, 'Play basketball.' We didn't know how. The teacher looked us over with contempt: 'My poor children.'

He, too, is one of you. The ability to handle a conventional ritual seemed so vital to him. He told the principal that we had not been given any 'physical education' and we should take the exams again in the autumn.

Any one of us could climb an oak tree. Once up there we could let go with our hands and chop off a two-hundred pound branch with a hatchet. Then we could drag it through the snow to our mother's doorstep.

I heard of a gentleman in Florence who rides upstairs in his house in a lift. But then he has bought himself an expensive gadget and pretends to row in it. You would give him an A in physical education.

From *A Letter to a Teacher* by the School of Barbiana, Italy, 1969

Correct English is the slang of prigs.

George Eliot

Free John Sinclair

Finally, seven hours after the concert began, John and Yoko came on: his first concert appearance in the United States since the Beatles waved goodbye at San Francisco's Candlestick Park five years earlier. 'The room was so high you felt like laughing or crying with happiness or pinching yourself to see if it was really happening,' Jerry Rubin recalled. 'John was terrified going onstage,' Stu Werbin said. 'He was following Stevie Wonder, with a makeshift band, trying out new material. He worried that people might start yelling for "Hey Jude."'

John opened with 'John Sinclair,' followed by Yoko's 'Sisters, O Sisters' and John's 'Attica State.' None had ever been heard before. The basic tracks for these songs on the album *Some Time in New York City* were recorded that night. The song 'John Sinclair' is stronger and more intriguing than critics have realized, especially when one sees John singing it in the (unreleased) film *Ten for Two*. John ended each verse with the phrase 'gotta set him free,' repeating 'gotta' no less than fifteen times over a dissonant guitar chord. The lyrics referred to recent revelations that the CIA was involved in heroin trafficking in Southeast Asia on a massive scale while Sinclair rotted in jail for selling two joints.

From *Come Together – John Lennon in his Time*, 1984

Nudity on stage? I think it's disgusting. But if I were 22 with a great body, it would be artistic, tasteful, patriotic and a progressive religious experience.

Shelley Winters

The Automotive Nightmare

Each year, one group of people rob the country of twice as much as all other criminals combined. They seriously wound five times as many people, and kill at least twenty times as many. Yet these destroyers, maimers and killers are uniquely privileged. When they wound, they are given a small fine, though others usually go to jail for at least a year. Even if they kill, they are less likely to be sent to prison than convicted prostitutes. When they merely wreck and damage, they almost always get off scot-free.

The reason for this leniency is simple. These are the criminal drivers, who in the UK are found guilty of a million crimes a year.

In practice, this means that any driver, over a period, is more likely to be convicted than to remain guiltless. The convicted include those who make laws, those who administer them, those who talk about them and form opinion about them, those who lead and govern . . . The probability of conviction hangs over most electors. When the convicted criminals outnumber the innocent, is it surprising that the guilty are exceptionally favoured? Or that eminently respectable theorists sometimes almost manage to explain away the bloody havoc wrought by motorists as an accident of nature?

One favourite theory at the moment is that motorists who crash or hit people are the victims of uncertain risks and hazards which simply can't be avoided. Once motorists enter their car – so the theory goes – they surrender control over their movements to an imperfect machine. They become part of a compelling mechanical mythology, as 'bio-robots' – curious mechanical centaurs whose behaviour is such an elevated mystery that it needs the canons of an entirely new science to interpret.

Blandly, the high priests of the car cult go to amazing lengths to absolve criminal motorists from all blame, by pinning their guilt on the most unlikely scapegoat. One distinguished road engineer, understandably very popular with the motoring magazines, has even managed to argue that 'the law is probably the largest single factor in accident causation. It even teaches bad driving; obviously, if the driver is always at fault no one else need take any care and the young who start their road career on foot or on bicycles are then taught by the full majesty of the law that their safety depends on others. If they then carry that idea with them to the wheel when they start driving who can blame them?'

The law's failing is not that it pins too *much* guilt on the driver, but that it treats with reckless leniency people who wound and kill on the roads.

From *The Automotive Nightmare* by Alisdair Aird, 1972

You are now a Contagious Disease

1 Walk into record companies and pretend that nobody knows you despite the fact that they asked you there in the first place.

2 Always announce your name in the most theatrical manner possible.

3 Show no interest in the music you are about to play them and even less interest in what they have to offer you in return, but display a genuine desire to obstruct every other group's progress in order to advance your own group's career.

4 If little interest is shown, demonstrate that this group alone can create profit in their jaded industry and revive their flagging record sales. This is what every record company wants to hear.

5 Titillate them – play on their deviances and neuroses.

6 Understand their attraction for young, untamed boys.

7 Use this basic insecurity to play off one record company against another.

8 You are moving into the realm of politics, which with close advice from your lawyer, means even more money.

9 Forget the future and get as much money as possible on the dotted line.

10 Create a lot of different faces to provide intrigue.

11 Remember the man who sold the Eiffel Tower, twice.

12 Demand a formal signing to create credibility.

13 The next stage is to get the band off the record company as soon as possible, ensuring that you obtain as much money as possible in the process.

14 Intensify the group's misbehaviour in public.

15 Make the company think that *you* are an anarchist.

16 Remove any members of the group who show signs of developing musical ability. Replace them with gimmicks designed purely to upset people.

17 Shove drugs, incest, necrophilia and any other stories to the papers.

18 When your first record company eventually terminates your contract and pays you off, demand that they find an alternative to which you can sign for even more money.

19 Sign outside Buckingham Palace, and insult your queen.

20 Make the group threaten a TV disc jockey with his life in some famous late-night rock club.

21 Intimidate pillars of the pop establishment. They love being shat on, and great press-coverage can be achieved by this.

22 Create a drunken rampage at the signing session.

23 Tell the group that sex is for the asking with all these record-company employees, and you can get off your second record company in as little as seven days.

24 You are now a contagious disease and are being given cheques simply for going in and out of doors.

Malcolm McLaren, 1976

In the present state of society,
happiness is only possible to artists and thieves.

Oscar Wilde

'You Did Do It'

I was walking down the stairs behind a teacher,
when I got to the bottom she came over to me and said,
'You done it.'
and I said, 'What?'
she said, 'You know what. Go on. Admit it. You did do it.'
Then she just walked off.
So I stood there trying to think what
I was meant to have done.

Sunny Carvana, a pupil at a London secondary school, 1979

ART IS STORED IN THE SAME VAULTS
AS THE MONEY THAT BUYS IT

'White Poetess'

She saw Africa as a continent
with festering sores
bleeding and clotting
in defiance of western therapy.

Something ghoulish from the north
of the Zambezi river offended
those who, like her, were civilised
although there was no end to the prospect
of titillating tattle about Africans.

So, she stepped into the sun
and into the smell of tangible haze
which you could peel with your fingernails
to see the virgin Zimbabwe spring
courting the rains of the summer
and embracing the mountains.

Close to tears,
she clutched them close to her heart
and surrendered to the intoxication
of endless safari dreaming.

But she couldn't see that beneath
the mountain, a shadow with living eyes
and witching black lips, beard, body and legs,
her own servant, was thrusting roots around her.

She had no dreams that night,
merely sat on the typewriter
and composed a romantic piece
about the Rhodesian veld in which
the shadow of the servant had no place,
save for a grudging vernacular word, wrongly spelt,
making wild reference.

Musaemura Zimunya, *c.* 1980

Uranium

We been fight for Yeelirrie. The sacred ground is each side of Yeelirrie. 'Yeelirrie' is white man's way of saying, right way is 'Youlirrie'. Youlirrie mean by Aboriginal word means 'death', dead. Wongi way. Anything been shifted from there means death. People been finished from there, early days, all dead, but white fella can't see it. How the Wongi's know it? But it's there.

Uranium, they say uranium they make anything from it, invent anything, yet during the War when Americans flew over, what happened to Hiroshima? And that'll happen here too if they're messing about with that thing. They never learn.

We just hope that they stand their grounds at Noonkanbah and don't let the Government take 'em. We the Aboriginal people of Leonora support them.

Roley Hill whose tribal name is Nulli, Peter Hogarth whose tribal name is Yambilli, and Croydon Beaman; Western Australia, 1980

Castrated Shelley

I still have a slim navy blue volume, entitled *Shelley*, which I was forced to buy at school. Its editor is one A.M.D. Hughes. In his 'selected works', there is no *Queen Mab*, no *Revolt of Islam*, no *Mask of Anarchy*, no *Peter Bell*, no *Swellfoot the Tyrant* – no *ideas* of any description. In the Penguin edition of Shelley, published in my last year at school (1956), the editor, a celebrated lady of letters called Isabel Quigly, writes: 'No poet better repays cutting; no great poet was ever less worth reading in his entirety.' She sets to her scissors with a will, extracting with devoted thoroughness every trace of political or social thought from Shelley's work.

In the beautiful Nonesuch edition of *Shelley: Selected Poetry, Prose and Letters*, published in 1951, the editor, a well-read gentleman called A.S.B. Glover, rejoices as he leaves out two of Shelley's greatest longer poems, both political from start to finish. '*Peter Bell* and *Oedipus* [*Swellfoot the Tyrant*]' writes Mr Glover, 'are mainly of interest as proof that a great lyric poet may fail lamentably outside his own proper field.'

Similarly, Kathleen Raine in her selection of Shelley in the Penguin 'Poet to Poet' series, writes: 'Without regret, I have omitted *Laon and Cythna* (later revised and renamed *The Revolt of Islam*), and a great deal of occasional political verse by Shelley the student activist in which the inspirers had no hand.'

These are just a few examples from my own literary upbringing and education. They are repeated over and over again in perhaps a hundred castrated editions of Shelley over the last 150 years.

The castration is horrible. The treatment of Shelley's 'Philosophical View of Reform', for instance, is almost incredible. It was written at the height of Shelley's literary powers. It ranks in style and in content with the most famous radical pamphlets of our history – with Tom Paine's *Rights of Man*, with Mary Wollstonecraft's *Vindication of the Rights of Women*, with the pamphlets of Bentham or Robert Owen or Marx and Engels. It was available and known to all the people who had access to Shelley's notebooks after his death. Yet it stayed there, not even transcribed, for *one hundred years* after it was written. And even then – in 1920 – it was published only as a collector's item for members of the Shelley Society.

Shelley's most explicit work on sex and love, *A Discourse on the Manners of the Ancient Greeks, Relative to the Subject of Love*, was held back even longer. It first appeared in an edition edited by Roger Ingpen in 1931, 113 years after it was written, and even then it was privately printed.

By this process of censorship and omission, Shelley has been sheltered from young people at school and university even more carefully than have most other radical or revolutionary writers.

From *Words as Weapons* by Paul Foot, 1981

Anthros, Go Home

Dear Sir, – This is to advise that the Government of Province do not want to accept any more anthropologists entering the country to come to Milne Bay Province to carry out research on my people. The reason for this is that since the days of Dr Malinowski, that famous anthropologist, hundreds of these creatures have carried out so many researches on the lives of my ancestors and even now they are still carrying out research on my people. Voluminous amount of books, theses and academic publications have been published on the private and intimate lives of my people.

Much of these academic publications benefited the anthropologists themselves and other big time academics. My people who were used as guinea pigs got nothing out of these researchers.

Please kindly advise all foreign anthropology researchers that we do not want them carrying out any more research on my people.

Anon., Papua New Guinea, 1986

One day we shall strangle the last publisher with the entrails of the last literary agent.

David Mercer

Not Mere Cattle

In 1983, when Sakharov and I were on hunger strike, I asked our personal KGB officer, 'Why do you write such nonsense about Sakharov saying that he sold jeans and pens?'

The officer answered, 'It's not for us. It's for the cattle.'

Mr Yanayev [leader of the coup] regards the Soviet population as cattle. We'll show them we are not mere cattle.

Yelena Bonner, widow of Andrei Sakharov, to 200,000 Moskovites outside Russian Parliament building, 20th August, 1991

Acknowledgements

The editors and publishers gratefully acknowledge permission to reprint copyright material from the following sources:

1. RISE LIKE LIONS AFTER SLUMBER
'The Spartacus Uprising' reprinted by permission of Harvard University Press and the Loeb Classical Library from *Appian: Roman History*, volumes I–IV, translated by Horace White, Cambridge, Mass., Harvard University Press, 1912–13. 'Get Drunk' by Charles Baudelaire from *Unrespectable Verse* by Geoffrey Grigson, reproduced by permission of Penguin Books Ltd. Excerpt from *The Years of The Week* by Patricia Cockburn (Macdonald). Excerpt from *Blather* by Flann O'Brien, quoted in *No Laughing Matter: The Life and Times of Flann O'Brien* by Antony Cronin, HarperCollins Publishers. Excerpt from *Good Morning Brothers* by Jack Dash, Lawrence and Wishart, London 1969. 'The Swing Movement' and 'Franz Otto Colliery' from *Inside Nazi Germany* by Detlev J. K. Peukert, translated by Richard Deveson, Batsford Publishers. Extract from the obituary of Ted Bramley by Margot Heinemann from the *Guardian*, February 1991. Excerpt from *Inquisition in Eden* by Alvah Bessie, Seven Seas Publishers, 1967. Excerpt from *Rabelais and his World* by Mikhail Bakhtin, London, 1968. Excerpt from 'Secret Report to the 20th Party Congress of the CPSU' by Nikita S Krushchev, reproduced by permission of Penguin Books Ltd. 'In Place of a Foreword' by Anna Akhmatova, from *Poets from the Russian Underground*, translated by Joseph Layland, Thomas Aczel and Laszlo Tikos, Harper & Row Publishers. Excerpt from *Last Exit to Brooklyn* by Hubert Selby Jr, reprinted by permission of Marion Boyars Publishers. Excerpt from *The Electric Kool-Acid Test* by Tom Wolfe, permission granted by the Peters Fraser & Dunlop Group Ltd. Excerpt from *Solzhenitsyn: A Documentary Record*, edited by Leopold Labetz (Penguin Books, 2nd Ed, 1974) copyright © Leopold Labetz 1970, 1974. 'Chile Stadium' by Victor Jara, copyright © Joan Jara 1973, reprinted in *I See a Voice*, edited by Michael Rosen, Thames TV Publications. 'If I had a Gun' by Gig Ryan from the *Penguin Book of Australian Women's Poetry*, edited by Susan Hampton and Kate Llewellyn. Excerpt from *Grunwick* by Joe Rogaly, by permission of Rogers Coleridge and White. 'Apres Nous le Deluge' translated by Nurit Galron, first published in RETURN magazine, 1984. 'Tramp the Dirt Down' by D. P. A. MacManus, copyright © Plangent Visions Music. 'Deng, where are you hiding?' by Shi Xiang published in the *Guardian*, 31 May 1990.

2. WORDS MUST BE GIVEN THEIR TRUE MEANING

Excerpt from *The Unknown Revolution: Kronstadt 1921, Ukraine 1918–21*; Voline (Freedom Press) excerpt from *Vladimir Ilyich Lenin* by Vladimir Mayakovsky, by permission of Carcanet Press Ltd. Untitled poem by Osip Mandelstam, from *The Eyesight of Wasps*, translated by James Greene, Angel Books. Excerpt from *The Lion and The Unicorn* by George Orwell, Secker & Warburg 1941. Excerpt from *Let Us Now Praise Famous Men* by James Agee, 1941, reprinted by permission of Peter Owen Ltd. Copyright © James Agee, renewed Mia Fritsch Agee 1969. Excerpt from *7000 Days in Siberia* by Karlo Stajner, Canongate Publishers. 'The Solution' from *Poems 1913–1956* by Bertolt Brecht, translated by Derek Bowman, reprinted by permission of Methuen London. 'Little Boxes' by Malvina Reynolds copyright © 1962, reprinted by permission of Tro Essex Music Ltd. An excerpt from *Catch-22* by Joseph Heller, Jonathan Cape 1962, reprinted by permission of A. M. Heath Ltd. Excerpt from *Words* by Jean-Paul Sartre, translated by Irene Clephane (Hamish Hamilton). 'Emperor', translated by Czeslaw Milosz, from *Zbigniew Herbert: Selected Poems* (Penguin Books, 1968), translation copyright © Czeslaw Milosz and Peter Dale Scott, 1968. An excerpt from *The Memorandum* by Vaclav Havel, translated by Vera Blackwell (Jonathan Cape). 'Footnotes to the Book of the Setback' by Nizar Qabbani, translated by Abdullah al-Udhari from *Modern Poetry of the Arab World*, Penguin Books 1986. Excerpt from *Revolution for the Hell of It* by Abbie Hoffmann, Bantam Doubleday Dell Publishing. 'How to Blame the Victim' from *Blaming the Victim* by William Ryan, by permission of Mary Yost Associates. 'Awful Australia' by Anna Walwicz, from the *Penguin Book of Australian Women's Poetry*, edited by Susan Humphries and Kate Llewellyn.

3. FIE ON THE FALSEHOODE OF MEN

Excerpt from *The Marriage of Figaro* by Beaumarchais, translated by John Wood (Penguin Classics, 1964) copyright © John Wood 1964. 'We Do Not Want Condescension' by Bahithat al-Badia, translated by Margot Badran and Ali Badran, reprinted in *Opening the Gates: a Century of Arab Feminist Writing* (Virago Publishers). Excerpt from *A Room of One's Own* by Virginia Woolf, reprinted by permission of the Estate of Virginia Woolf and The Hogarth Press. Excerpt from *Nightwood* by Djuna Barnes, Faber and Faber Ltd, 1936. 'Unfortunate Coincidence' by Dorothy Parker, reprinted by permission of Duckworth. Letter in Isis magazine by Sylvia Plath, 1956, reprinted by permission of Olwyn Hughes. Excerpt from *The Prime of Life* (La Force de l'Age) by Simone de Beauvoir, translated by Peter O'Brien, by permission of André Deutsch Ltd. 'A Terminal Note' from *Maurice* by E. M. Forster, by permission of King's College, Cambridge, and the Society of Authors as the literary representatives of the E. M. Forster estate. Excerpt from *Thinking About Women* by Mary Ellmann, Harcourt Brace Jovanovich, 1968. Excerpt from *Dreams and Dilemmas* by Sheila Rowbotham reprinted by permission of Virago Publishers. 'I am a Dangerous Woman' by Joan Cavanagh first published by the War Resisters League. 'What I'm Not Song' from *True Confessions and New Clichés* by Liz Lochhead, by permission of Polygon. 'Medallion Man' by Andrea Solomons broadcast on television in *Three of a Kind* and first published in *The Joke's On Us* (Pandora), reprinted by permission of Curtis Brown Ltd. 'Blow Jobs' by Fiona Pitt-Kethley, reprinted by permission of the *London Review of Books*.

4. OPULENCE IS ALWAYS THE RESULT OF THEFT
Excerpt from *Ancient Egyptian Literature* by Miriam Lichtheim (University of California Press). ''Ilda' by Marie Makino from *Best Music Hall and Vanity Songs*, EMI Music Publishing Ltd. 'Song of the Deportees' by Woody Guthrie copyright © 1962, reprinted by permission of Tro Essex Music Ltd. 'Measure for Measure' from *The Soweto I Love* by Sipho Sepamla, reprinted by permission of Rex Collings Ltd. 'Three Poems for Women' by Susan Griffin, published in *In The Pink*, Harper & Row Publishers. 'Me Aunty Connie' by Terry Lee from *Down to Earth and On Its Feet* (Bristol Broadsides).

5. OUR FATHER WHO ART IN HEAVEN, STAY THERE
Quotation from Menocchio (Domenico Scandella) from *The Cheese and The Worms* by Carlo Ginzburg, Johns Hopkins University Press. Excerpt by Bahithat al-Badia, translated by Margot Badran and Ali Badran, reprinted in *Opening the Gates: A Century of Arab Feminist Writing* (Virago Publishers). 'Sometime in Eternity' from *A Coney Island of the Mind* copyright © Laurence Ferlinghetti 1958, reprinted by permission of New Directions Publishing Corporation. 'Journey of the Yellow Letters' by Buland al-Haydari, from *When the Words Burn: An Anthology of Modern Arabic Poetry, 1945–1987*, permission of editor and translator, John Asfour, and the publishers, Cormorant Books.

6. THIS ISLAND'S MINE . . . WHICH THOU TAK'ST FROM ME
Excerpt from *Touch The Earth* by T. C. McLuhan (Outer Bridge and Lazard publishers). Letter from Toussaint L'Ouverture, reprinted in *A History of Pan-African Revolt* by C. L. R. James. Excerpt from *The History of Mary Prince*, ed. Moira Ferguson (Pandora 1987). 'Strange Fruit' by Lewis Allen copyright © 1939 Edward B. Marks Music, reprinted by permission of Warner Chappell Music Ltd. 'Black, Brown and White' by Big Bill

Broonzy, reprinted in *North American Folksongs*, ed. Alan Lomax (Macmillan Publishers). 'The Affair of the Lone Banana', Goon Show 104, 1954, by The Goons. Excerpt from 'The Price of the Ticket' from *Collected Essays* by James Baldwin, Michael Joseph Ltd. 'The United Fruit Co.' by Pablo Neruda, from *Twenty Poems of Pablo Neruda*, translated by James Wright and Robert Bly, The Sixties Press, 1967. Excerpt from a speech by Malcolm X at Cleveland Corey Methodist Church, 1964. 'Say It Loud, I'm Black and I'm Proud' by James Brown, 1968, copyright © Warner Chappell Music Ltd. 'It Dread Inna Inglan' by Linton Kwesi Johnson copyright © 1978, Virgin Music (Publishers) Ltd. 'Equal Opportunity' reprinted with permission from *Chinatown Ghosts* by Jim Wong-Chu (Arsenal Pulp Press; Vancouver, Canada, 1986). 'Tourist/Home Movies' from *Akwesasne Notes* by Bob Bacon, reprinted in *Indigenous Voices*, ed. Roger Moody (CIMRA). Excerpt by A. Sivanandan first published as a preface to *Southall: The Birth of a Black Community*, (London, The Institute of Race Relations, 1981).

7. THE OLD LIE
'Lament of the Frontier Guard' from *Collected Shorter Poems* by Ezra Pound, reprinted by permission of Faber & Faber Ltd. 'They' by Siegfried Sassoon by permission of George Sassoon. 'Little Song of the Maimed' by Benjamin Peret from *Remove Your Hat and Other Works*, translated by David Gascoyne (Atlas Press). A scene from *In the Last Days of Mankind* by Karl Kraus, reprinted in *In These Great Times* and reproduced by permission of Carcanet Press. Excerpt from *The good Soldier Svejk* by Jaroslav Hasek, translated by Cecil Parrott, reprinted by permission of William Heinemann Ltd. Excerpt from a speech by Norman Mailer first published in *We Accuse* and reproduced by permission of Diablo Press. Excerpt from *Vietnam* by Mary McCarthy, 1967, by permission of Penguin Books. 'Because I Want Peace' by Claribel Alegria (El Salvador Solidarity Campaign). Excerpt from a letter by David Tinker reprinted in *Letter from the Falklands*, edited by Hugh Tinker, Junction Books. Excerpt from an editorial by Jeremy Hardy in *City Limits* magazine, Jan 31st–Feb 7, 1991.

8. THEN FAREWELL SACRED MAJESTY
'The Charcoal-Seller' by Po Chu-I, from *170 Chinese Poems* translated by Arthur Waley, by permission of Constable Publishers. Excerpt from *A Star is Torn* by Robin Archer and Diana Simmonds (Virago 1986). 'Promises' by Eleanor Farjeon from *More Tomfooleries* (Unwin Hyman). Excerpt from *the Function of the Orgasm* by Wilhelm Reich, translated by Theodor P. Wolfe, Panther Books. 'Advice to Our Children' by Nazim Hikmet, by permission of Sheil Land Associates Ltd. Excerpt from *I Was an American* by Ursula Wassermann, by permission of The Bodley Head. 'Yakety Yak' by Jerry

Leiber and Mike Stoller, reprinted by permission of Carlin Music Corporation, Ironbridge House, 3 Bridge Approach, London, NW1 8BD. 'In the days of Ubico the tyrant . . .' from *Let's Go! Vamonos Patria a Caminar* by Otto Rene Castillo, translated by Margaret Randall (Jonathan Cape Publishers). 'Subterranean Homesick Blues' by Bob Dylan, 1965, reprinted by permission of Bob Dylan/Dwarf Music. Excerpt from Jann Wenner's interview with John Lennon, *Rolling Stone Magazine*, 1970. 'A Tourist Guide to England' from *For Beauty Douglas* by Adrian Mitchell, with permission of the Peters Fraser and Dunlop Group Ltd. Neither this nor any other of Adrian Mitchell's poems is to be used in connection with any examination whatsoever. 'Birdbrain!' by Allen Ginsberg from *Allen Ginsberg Collected Poems 1947–1980* (Viking 1985), copyright © Allen Ginsberg 1984.

9. OPPRESSION IS DISORDER, LIBERTY IS ORDER.
Excerpt from *Fuente Ovejuna* by Lope de Vega, translated by John Garrett Underhill (Charles Scribners and Sons). Excerpt from *The Fourteenth Chronicle* by John Dos Passos, copyright © Elizabeth H. Dos Passos and Townsend Ludington, reprinted with permission from the Harvard Common Press. 'Ballad of the Landlord' from *Selected Poems of Langston Hughes*, reprinted by permission of David Higham Associates. Excerpt from *The Essential Lenny Bruce* (Open Gate Books in conjunction with Macmillan 1973), reprinted by permission of the Estate of Lenny Bruce. 'Identity Card' by Mahmood Darwish from *When the Words Burn: An Anthology of Modern Arabic Poetry, 1945–1987*, permission of editor and translator, John Asfour, and the publisher, Cormorant Books. 'Torturer's Eyes' by Roque Dalton from *Poesia Militante* (El Salvador Solidarity Campaign). Excerpt from *The Gulag Archipelago* by Alexander Solzhenitsyn, copyright © 1974 Aleksandr Solzhenitsyn, English translation copyright © Harper & Row Publishers Inc., reprinted by permission of Harper Collins Publishers. Excerpt from *Inside the Company: CIA Diary* by Philip Agee (Penguin books, 1975), copyright © Philip Agee 1975. Excerpt from *How to Become a Virgin* by Quentin Crisp, copyright © Quentin Crisp 1981 (HarperCollins Publishers). Excerpt from *A Sense of Freedom* by Jimmy Boyle (Canongate Publishing). Excerpt from a speech by Richard Hauser, first printed in Jewish Socialist Magazine, no. 12.

10. HE LOOKS FOR HIS SOUL, INSPECTS IT, PUTS IT TO THE TEST
Excerpts from *Presocratic Philosophers* by Kirk, Raven and Schofield, reprinted by permission from Cambridge University Press. Excerpt from *Seven Dada Manifestos and Lampisteries* by Tristan Tzara, reproduced here by permission of John Calder (Publishers) Ltd, London; copyright this trans-

lation John Calder (Publishers) Ltd 1977, 1981. Excerpt from *From Cubism to Suprematism: The New Painterly Realism* by Kazimir Malevich, quoted in *Russian Art of the Avant-Garde* by John Rewald, by permission of Thames and Hudson Ltd. Excerpt from *In Place of Fear* by Aneurin Bevan (William Heinemann 1952), with permission of David Higham Associates. 'White Poetess' by Musaemura Zimunya from *Thought Tracks*, by permission of Longman Group UK.

Index